THE URANTIA BOOK WORKBOOKS

URANTIA®

URANTIA FOUNDATION
533 WEST DIVERSEY PARKWAY
CHICAGO, ILLINOIS 60614
U.S.A.

URANTIA®

THE URANTIA BOOK WORKBOOKS

VOLUME III

Topical
and
Doctrinal Studies

This series of workbooks originally was published in the 1950s and 1960s to assist those early students who wanted to pursue an in-depth study of *The Urantia Book*. The workbook creators recognized that the materials were imperfect and were far from being definitive works on these subjects. Current students may be able to make more exhaustive analyses due to advances in knowledge and computerization of the text that are available today. Nevertheless, we recognize the enormous effort that went into this attempt to enhance understanding of *The Urantia Book* by some of its earliest students. We think these materials will be of interest to many and are therefore republishing them for their historic and educational value.

FIRST PRINTING 2003

THE URANTIA BOOK WORKBOOKS
VOLUME III
TOPICAL AND DOCTRINAL STUDIES

The *Urantia Book* Workbooks

Volume I: Transcripts of Lecture and Discussion of the Foreword
and An Analytic Study of Part One of *The Urantia Book*

Volume II: Science in *The Urantia Book*

Volume III: Topical Studies in *The Urantia Book* and A Short Course in
Doctrine

Volume IV: The Teachings of Jesus in *The Urantia Book*, The Life of
Jesus Compared to the four Gospels

ISBN:
0-942430-97-2

PUBLISHED BY URANTIA FOUNDATION
Original Publisher since 1955
533 Diversey Parkway
Chicago, Illinois 60614 U.S.A.
Telephone: +1 (773) 525-3319
Fax: +1 (773) 525-7739
Website: http://www.urantia.org
E-mail: urantia@urantia.org

Information

URANTIA Foundation has Representatives in Argentina, Belgium, Brazil, Bulgaria, Colombia, Ecuador, Estonia, Greece, Indonesia, Korea, Lithuania, México, Norway, Perú, Senegal, Spain, Uruguay, and Venezuela. If you require information on study groups, where you can obtain *The URANTIA Book*, or a Representative's telephone number, please contact the office nearest you or the head office in Chicago, Illinois.

International Offices:

Head Office

533 West Diversey Parkway
Chicago, Illinois 60614 U.S.A.
Tel.: +(773) 525-3319
Fax: +(773) 525-7739
Website: www.urantia.org
E-mail: urantia@urantia.org

Canada—English

PO Box 92006
West Vancouver, BC Canada V7V 4X4
Tel: +(604) 926-5836
Fax: +(604) 926-5899
E-mail: urantia@telus.net

Finland/Estonia/Sweden

PL 18,
15101 Lahti Finland
Tel./Fax: +(358) 3 777 8191
E-mail: urantia-saatio@urantia.fi

Great Britain/Ireland

Tel./Fax: +(44) 1491 641-922
E-Mail: urantia@easynet.co.uk

Australia/New Zealand/Asia

Tel./Fax: +(61) 2 9970-6200
E-mail: urantia@urantia.org.au

Canada—French

C. P. 233
Cap-Santé (Québec) Canada G0A 1L0
Tel.: +(418) 285-3333
Fax: +(418) 285-0226
E-mail: fondation@urantia-quebec.org

St. Petersburg, Russia

Tel./Fax: +(7) 812-580-3018
E-mail: vitgen@peterlink.ru

Other books available from URANTIA Foundation:

The URANTIA Book	hard cover		ISBN 0-911560-02-5
The URANTIA Book	leather collector ($7^5/8$" x $5^3/4$")		ISBN 0-911560-75-0
The URANTIA Book	small hard cover ($8^7/16$" x $5^1/2$")		ISBN 0-911560-07-6
The URANTIA Book	paperback	($8^7/16$" x $5^1/2$")	ISBN 0-911560-51-3
The URANTIA Book	gift-box leather ($8^7/16$" x $5^1/2$")		ISBN 0-911560-08-4
The URANTIA Book	softcover*	($8^7/16$" x $5^1/2$")	ISBN 0-911560-50-5
Le Livre d'URANTIA	hard cover	French	ISBN 0-911560-05-X
Le Livre d'URANTIA	soft cover	French	ISBN 0-911560-53-X
El libro de URANTIA	paperback	Spanish ($8^7/16$" x $5^1/2$")	ISBN 1-883395-02-X
El libro de URANTIA	hard cover	Spanish ($8^7/16$" x $5^1/2$")	ISBN 1-883395-03-8
URANTIA-kirja	hard cover	Finnish	ISBN 0-911560-03-3
URANTIA-kirja	soft cover	Finnish	ISBN 0-911560-52-1
Книга Урантии	hard cover	Russian* ($8^7/16$" x $5^1/2$")	ISBN 0-911560-80-7
Het URANTIA Boek	hard cover	Dutch	ISBN 0-911560-54-6
유란시아서	hard cover	Korean	ISBN 0-911560-40-8
The URANTIA Book Concordance		English Index	ISBN 0-911560-00-9
URANTIA-kirja Hakemisto		Finnish Index	ISBN 0-911560-04-1
The URANTIA Book	Audio	English*	ISBN 0-911560-30-0
The URANTIA Book	CD ROM	English, Finnish, French	ISBN 0-911560-63-7

The URANTIA Book Workbooks

Forward and Part I	Paperback	English	ISBN 0-942430-99-9
Science	Paperback	English	ISBN 0-942430-98-0
Topical and Doctrinal Study	Paperback	English	ISBN 0-942430-97-2
Jesus	Paperback	English	ISBN 0-942430-96-4

INTRODUCTION

Much has already been written regarding the study groups called "The Forum" and "The Seventy". Therefore I will try to confine my remarks more closely to the compiling and printing of several workbooks by Dr. William Sadler to be used in conjunction with *The Urantia Book*.

"The Forum" was the larger of the two groups and met on Sunday afternoons. The Wednesday night group was much smaller, studied in more depth, and was called "The Seventy" as that was the number of its members. Both met at the home of Dr. Sadler at 533 Diversey Parkway in Chicago. Doctor and some others in the group felt that something concrete was needed to train teachers for the future. Workbooks would help the teachers to form classes in the state or country in which they lived and use them to understand and present the concepts and new ideas from the Book in a uniform manner.

For several years members of the Wednesday night group were asked to prepare topical papers and teach the contents to the others in the group thus giving them experience in teaching. Dr. Sadler and his son, Bill, also taught the members of the group the information contained in the Papers of *The Urantia Book*. From the information Dr. Sadler taught at these classes the workbooks were developed for use by the group and for future teachers of the revelation.

The titles of the workbooks were:
Urantia Doctrine;
The Theology of *The Urantia Book*, Part I, Part II, and Part III;
Worship and Wisdom;
The Short Course in Doctrine,
 Summary Of The Theology Of *The Urantia Book*;
Science in *The Urantia Book* Volume I (with the collaboration of Alvin Kulieke);
    and
The Teachings Of Jesus.

Dr. Sadler possessed a great intellect, which may be one of the reasons he was selected by the Contact Commission to be the recipient of the *Urantia Papers*. He was able to understand and present, in a form that is understandable for others, many of the more difficult concepts and information in *The Urantia Book*. This is a great advantage for students who may be teaching these concepts in the future. The reprinting of these study aids will help many students of *The Urantia Book* gain a more comfortable understanding of the more difficult teachings in the book and an insight into Dr. Sadler's plan for instructing the future teachers of the revelation.

What a legacy has been left to us!

Katharine

Katharine Lea Jones Harries

TOPICAL STUDIES IN
THE URANTIA BOOK

THE SHORT COURSE IN DOCTRINE
SUMMARY OF THE
THEOLOGY OF *THE URANTIA BOOK*

TABLE OF CONTENTS

TOPICAL STUDIES IN
THE URANTIA BOOK

BIBLICAL ABBREVIATIONS USED IN THIS SECTION

The Old Testament

Gen .... The Book of Genesis

Ex .... The Book of Exodus

Lev .... The Book of Leviticus

Num ...... The Book of Numbers

Deut ...... The Book of
Deuteronomy

Josh .... The Book of Joshua

Judges .... The Book of Judges

Ruth ...... The Book of Ruth

1 Sam ..... The First Book of Samuel

2 Sam ..... The Second Book
of Samuel

1 Kings ... The First Book of Kings

2 Kings ... The Second Book of Kings

1 Chron .. The First Book
of Chronicles

2 Chron .. The Second Book
of Chronicles

Ezra .... The Book of Ezra

Neh .... The Book of Nehemiah

Esther .... The Book of Esther

Job .... The Book of Job

Ps .... The Book of Psalms

Prov ...... The Book of Proverbs

Eccl .... Ecclesiastes

Song ...... The Song of Songs

Isa .... The Book of Isaiah

Jer .... The Book of Jeremiah

Lam .... Lamentations

Eze .... The Book of Ezekiel

Dan .... The Book of Daniel

Hos .... The Book of Hosea

Joel .... The Book of Joel

Amos ..... The Book of Amos

Obad ..... The Book of Obadiah

Jon .... The Book of Jonah

Nah .... The Book of Nahum

Hab .... The Book of Habakkuk

Zeph ...... The Book of Zephaniah

Hag .... The Book of Haggai

Zec .... The Book of Zechariah

Mal .... The Book of Malachi

The New Testament

Matt ...... The Gospel According
to Matthew

Mark ...... The Gospel According
to Mark

Luke ...... The Gospel According
to Luke

John ...... The Gospel According
to John

Acts .... The Acts of the Apostles

Rom ...... The Epistle to the Romans

1 Cor ..... The First Epistle to
the Corinthians

2 Cor ..... The Second Epistle to
the Corinthians

Gal .... The Epistle to
the Galatians

Eph .... The Epistle to
the Ephesians

Phil .... The Epistle to
the Philippians

Col .... The Epistle to
the Colossians

1 Thess ... The First Epistle to
the Thessalonians

2 Thess ... The Second Epistle to
the Thessalonians

1 Tim ..... The First Epistle to Timothy

2 Tim ..... The Second Epistle to Timothy

Tit .... The Epistle to Titus

Phmon ... The Epistle to Philemon

Heb .... The Epistle to
the Hebrews

Jas .... The Epistle of James

1 Peter ... The First Epistle of Peter

2 Peter ... The Second Epistle
of Peter

1 John .... The First Epistle of John

2 John .... The Second Epistle
of John

3 John .... The Third Epistle of John

Jude ...... Jude

Rev .... Revelation

1. LOVE

I.   GOD IS LOVE.

II.   LOVE IS AN ATTRIBUTE OF PERSONALITY.

III.   JESUS REVEALS GOD'S LOVE.

IV.   GOD'S LOVE FOR US AND OUR WORLD.

V.   FATHERLY AND BROTHERLY LOVE.

VI.   THE GROWTH OF LOVE.

VII.   LOVING OUR FELLOW MEN.

VIII.   HOW WE EXPERIENCE GOD'S LOVE.

IX.   HOW JESUS LOVED MEN.

X.   ERRONEOUS IDEAS ABOUT GOD'S LOVE.

XI.   CHARACTERISTIC MANIFESTATIONS OF LOVE.

LOVE AS PRESENTED IN THE BIBLE

I.   DIVINE LOVE.

II.   HUMAN LOVE.

LOVE

I. GOD IS LOVE

1. God's reactions are always those of divine affection.

"'God is love'; therefore his only personal attitude towards the affairs of the universe is always a reaction of divine affection. The Father loves us sufficiently to bestow his life upon us. 'He makes his sun to rise on the evil and on the good and sends rain on the just and on the unjust.'" P. 38-9. 1 John 4:8.

2. True and dynamic love comes from God.

"All true love is from God, and man receives the divine affection as he himself bestows this love upon his fellows. Love is dynamic. It can never be captured; it is alive, free, thrilling, and always moving. Man can never take the love of the Father and imprison it within his heart. The Father's love can become real to mortal man only by passing through that man's personality as he in turn bestows this love upon his fellows." P. 1289.

3. How the divine love is revealed.

"The great circuit of love is from the Father, through sons to brothers, and hence to the Supreme. The love of the Father appears in the mortal personality by the ministry of the indwelling Adjuster. Such a God-knowing son reveals this love to his universe brethren, and this fraternal affection is the essence of the love of the Supreme." P. 1289.

4. Restrained justice proves the love of God.

"Supreme justice can act instantly when not restrained by divine mercy. But the ministry of mercy to the children of time and space always provides for this time lag, this saving interval between seedtime and harvest. If the seed sowing is good, this interval provides for the testing and upbuilding of character; if the seed sowing is evil, this merciful delay provides time for repentance and rectification. This time delay in the adjudication and execution of evildoers is inherent in the mercy ministry of the seven superuniverses. This restraint of justice by mercy proves that God is love, and that such a God of love dominates the universes and in mercy controls the fate and judgment of all his creatures." P. 616.

5. **A divine lover lives in man.**

"Unless a divine lover lived in man, he could not unselfishly and spiritually love. Unless an interpreter lived in the mind, man could not truly realize the unity of the universe. Unless an evaluator dwelt with man, he could not possibly appraise moral values and recognize spiritual meanings.

And this lover hails from the very source of infinite love; this interpreter is a part of Universal Unity; this evaluator is the child of the Center and Source of all absolute values of divine and eternal reality." P. 2094.

II. LOVE IS AN ATTRIBUTE OF PERSONALITY

1. **Love is the secret of personal associations.**

"Love is the secret of beneficial association between personalities. You cannot really know a person as the result of a single contact. You cannot appreciatingly know music through mathematical deduction, even though music is a form of mathematical rhythm. The number assigned to a telephone subscriber does not in any manner identify the personality of that subscriber or signify anything concerning his character." P. 141.

2. **We may admire beauty. We love only persons.**

"The concept of truth might possibly be entertained apart from personality, the concept of beauty may exist without personality, but the concept of divine goodness is understandable only in relation to personality. Only a *person* can love and be loved. Even beauty and truth would be divorced from survival hope if they were not attributes of a personal God, a loving Father." P. 31.

3. **Combined wisdom and love control God's actions.**

"Nevertheless, the Father as a person may at any time interpose a fatherly hand in the stream of cosmic events all in accordance with the will of God and in consonance with the wisdom of God and as motivated by the love of God." P. 1305.

III. JESUS REVEALS GOD'S LOVE

1. **Jesus revealed a God of love.**

"The Hebrews based their religion on goodness; the Greeks on beauty; both religions sought truth. Jesus revealed a God of love, and love is all-embracing of truth, beauty, and goodness." P. 67.

2. **Divine love related to God, man, and the Supreme.**

"Michael, a creator, revealed the divine love of the Creator Father for his terrestrial children. And having discovered and received this divine affection, men can aspire to reveal this love to their brethren in the flesh. Such creature affection is a true reflection of the love of the Supreme." P. 1279.

3. **Jesus' concept of God's love.**

"Though many of the temple rituals very touchingly impressed his sense of the beautiful and the symbolic, he was always disappointed by the explanation of the real meanings of these ceremonies which his parents would offer in answer to his many searching inquiries. Jesus simply would not accept explanations of worship and religious devotion which involved belief in the wrath of God or the anger of the Almighty. In further discussion of these questions, after the conclusion of the temple visit, when his father became mildly insistent that he acknowledge acceptance of the orthodox Jewish beliefs, Jesus turned suddenly upon his parents and, looking appealingly into the eyes of his father, said: 'My father, it cannot be true—the Father in heaven cannot so regard his erring children on earth. The heavenly Father cannot love his children less than you love me. And I well know, no matter what unwise thing I might do, you would never pour out wrath upon me nor vent anger against me. If you, my earthly father, possess such human reflections of the Divine, how much more must the heavenly Father be filled with goodness and overflowing with mercy. I refuse to believe that my Father in heaven loves me less than my father on earth.'" P. 1378.

IV. GOD'S LOVE FOR US AND OUR WORLD

1. **Our world is lovingly fostered.**

"Your planet is a member of an enormous cosmos; you belong to a well-nigh infinite family of worlds, but your sphere is just as precisely administered and just as lovingly fostered as if it were the only inhabited world in all existence." P. 183.

2. **Planetary isolation does not lessen God's love.**

"Your isolated world is not forgotten in the counsels of the universe. Urantia is not a cosmic orphan stigmatized by sin and shut away from divine watchcare by rebellion. From Uversa to Salvington and on down to Jerusem, even in Havona and on Paradise, they all know we are here; and you mortals now dwelling on Urantia are just as lovingly cherished and just as faithfully watched over as if the sphere had never been betrayed by a faithless Planetary Prince, even more so. It is eternally true, 'the Father himself loves you.'" P. 1259. John 16:27.

3. God's love is individualized for each creature.

"The love of the Father absolutely individualizes each personality as a unique child of the Universal Father, a child without duplicate in infinity, a will creature irreplaceable in all eternity. The Father's love glorifies each child of God, illuminating each member of the celestial family, sharply silhouetting the unique nature of each personal being against the impersonal levels that lie outside the fraternal circuit of the Father of all. The love of God strikingly portrays the transcendent value of each will creature, unmistakably reveals the high value which the Universal Father has placed upon each and every one of his children from the highest creator personality of Paradise status to the lowest personality of will dignity among the savage tribes of men in the dawn of the human species on some evolutionary world of time and space." P. 138.

4. God as a father transcends God as a judge.

"The affectionate heavenly Father, whose spirit indwells his children on earth, is not a divided personality—one of justice and one of mercy—neither does it require a mediator to secure the Father's favor or forgiveness. Divine righteousness is not dominated by strict retributive justice; God as a father transcends God as a judge." P. 41.

5. God's love follows us through the eternal ages.

"The Father's love follows us now and throughout the endless circle of the eternal ages. As you ponder the loving nature of God, there is only one reasonable and natural personality reaction thereto: You will increasingly love your Maker; you will yield to God an affection analogous to that given by a child to an earthly parent; for, as a father, a real father, a true father, loves his children, so the Universal Father loves and forever seeks the welfare of his created sons and daughters." P. 40.

6. Magnitude of the Father's love.

"'Because my Father is a God of love and delights in the practice of mercy, do not imbibe the idea that the service of the kingdom is to be one of monotonous ease. The Paradise ascent is the supreme adventure of all time, the rugged achievement of eternity. The service of the kingdom on earth will call for all the courageous manhood that you and your coworkers can muster. Many of you will be put to death for your loyalty to the gospel of this kingdom.

It is easy to die in the line of physical battle when your courage is strengthened by the presence of your fighting comrades, but it requires a higher and more profound form of human courage and devotion calmly and all alone to lay down your life for the love of a truth enshrined in your mortal heart.

"'Today, the unbelievers may taunt you with preaching a gospel of nonresistance and with living lives of nonviolence, but you are the first volunteers of a long line of sincere believers in the gospel of this kingdom who will astonish all mankind by their heroic devotion to these teachings. No armies of the world have ever displayed more courage and bravery than will be portrayed by you and your loyal successors who shall go forth to all the world proclaiming the good news—the fatherhood of God and the brotherhood of men. The courage of the flesh is the lowest form of bravery. Mind bravery is a higher type of human courage, but the highest and supreme is uncompromising loyalty to the enlightened convictions of profound spiritual realities. And such courage constitutes the heroism of the God-knowing man. And you are all God-knowing men; you are in very truth the personal associates of the Son of Man.'" P. 1608.

V. FATHERLY AND BROTHERLY LOVE

1. **Fatherly and brotherly affection.**

"From the Sermon on the Mount to the discourse of the Last Supper, Jesus taught his followers to manifest *fatherly* love rather than *brotherly* love. Brotherly love would love your neighbor as you love yourself, and that would be adequate fulfillment of the 'golden rule.' But fatherly affection would require that you should love your fellow mortals as Jesus loves you." P. 1573.

2. **Jesus loves both as father and brother.**

"Jesus loves mankind with a dual affection. He lived on earth as a twofold personality—human and divine. As the Son of God he loves man with a fatherly love—he is man's Creator, his universe Father. As the Son of Man, Jesus loves mortals as a brother—he was truly a man among men." P. 1573.

3. **The nature of fatherly love.**

"'When a wise man understands the inner impulses of his fellows, he will love them. And when you love your brother, you have already forgiven him. This capacity to understand man's nature and forgive his apparent wrong-doing is Godlike. If you are wise parents, this is the way you will love and understand your children, even forgive them when transient misunderstanding has apparently separated you. The child, being immature and lacking in the fuller understanding of the depth of the child-father relationship, must frequently feel a sense of guilty separation from a father's full approval, but the true father is never conscious of any such separation. Sin is an experience of creature consciousness; it is not a part of God's consciousness.'" P. 1898.

4. **God deals with us as a father.**

"God the Father deals with man his child on the basis, not of actual virtue or worthiness, but in recognition of the child's motivation— the creature purpose and intent. The relationship is one of parent-child association and is actuated by divine love." P. 1133.

VI. THE GROWTH OF LOVE

1. **Love of God displaces the fear of God.**

"'The "fear of the Lord" has had different meanings in the successive ages, coming up from fear, through anguish and dread, to awe and reverence. And now from reverence I would lead you up, through recognition, realization, and appreciation, to *love*. When man recognizes only the works of God, he is led to fear the Supreme; but when man begins to understand and experience the personality and character of the living God, he is led increasingly to love such a good and perfect, universal and eternal Father. And it is just this changing of the relation of man to God that constitutes the mission of the Son of Man on earth.'" P. 1675. Prov. 1:7; 9:10. Ps. 111:10. Job 28:28.

2. **How love overcomes fear.**

"'Your forebears feared God because he was mighty and mysterious. You shall adore him because he is magnificent in love, plenteous in mercy, and glorious in truth. The power of God engenders fear in the heart of man, but the nobility and righteousness of his personality beget reverence, love, and willing worship. A dutiful and affectionate son does not fear or dread even a mighty and noble father.'" P. 1675.

3. **Jesus comes to put love in place of fear.**

"'I have come into the world to put love in the place of fear, joy in the place of sorrow, confidence in the place of dread, loving service and appreciative worship in the place of slavish bondage and meaningless ceremonies. But it is still true of those who sit in darkness that "the fear of the Lord is the beginning of wisdom." But when the light has more fully come, the sons of God are led to praise the Infinite for what he *is* rather than to fear him for what he *does*.'" P. 1675. Ps. 111:10.

4.   Command to love instead of fear.

"'You have been taught that you should "fear God and keep his commandments, for that is the whole duty of man." But I have come to give you a new and higher commandment. I would teach you to "love God and learn to do his will, for that is the highest privilege of the liberated sons of God." Your fathers were taught to "fear God—the Almighty King." I teach you, "Love God—the all-merciful Father."'" P. 1676. Eccl. 12:13.

5.   Love must grow to meet new conditions.

"Love, unselfishness, must undergo a constant and living readaptative interpretation of relationships in accordance with the leading of the Spirit of Truth. Love must thereby grasp the ever-changing and enlarging concepts of the highest cosmic good of the individual who is loved. And then love goes on to strike this same attitude concerning all other individuals who could possibly be influenced by the growing and living relationship of one spirit-led mortal's love for other citizens of the universe. And this entire living adaptation of love must be effected in the light of both the environment of present evil and the eternal goal of the perfection of divine destiny." P. 1950.

6.   Loving God makes man real in the universe.

"God's gifts—his bestowal of reality—are not divorcements from himself; he does not alienate creation from himself, but he has set up tensions in the creations circling Paradise. God first loves man and confers upon him the potential of immortality—eternal reality. And as man loves God, so does man become eternal in actuality. And here is mystery: The more closely man approaches God through love, the greater the reality—actuality—of that man. The more man withdraws from God, the more nearly he approaches nonreality—cessation of existence. When man consecrates his will to the doing of the Father's will, when man gives God all that he *has*, then does God make that man more than he is." P. 1285.

7.   Growth of love is unconscious.

"Man cannot cause growth, but he can supply favorable conditions. Growth is always unconscious, be it physical, intellectual, or spiritual. Love thus grows; it cannot be created, manufactured, or purchased; it must grow. Evolution is a cosmic technique of growth. Social growth cannot be secured by legislation, and moral growth is not had by improved administration. Man may manufacture a machine, but its real value must be derived from human culture and personal appreciation. Man's sole contribution to growth is the mobilization of the total powers of his personality—living faith." P. 1097.

8. **Ceaseless expansion of divine love.**

"The ceaseless and expanding march of the Paradise creative forces through space seems to presage the ever-extending domain of the gravity grasp of the Universal Father and the never-ending multiplication of varied types of intelligent creatures who are able to love God and be loved by him, and who, by thus becoming God-knowing, may choose to be like him, may elect to attain Paradise and find God." P. 645.

VII. LOVING OUR FELLOW MEN

1. **Only God-knowers can love others as themselves.**

"Unselfish social consciousness must be, at bottom, a religious consciousness; that is, if it is objective; otherwise it is a purely subjective philosophic abstraction and therefore devoid of love. Only a God-knowing individual can love another person as he loves himself." P. 196.

2. **Jesus asks us to love even our enemies.**

"'I say to you: Love your enemies, do good to those who hate you, bless those who curse you, and pray for those who despitefully use you. And whatsoever you believe that I would do to men, do you also to them.'" P. 1571. Matt. 5:44. Luke 6:27,28,35.

3. **Loving others as a way of life.**

"Throughout the vicissitudes of life, remember always to love one another. Do not strive with men, even with unbelievers. Show mercy even to those who despitefully abuse you. Show yourselves to be loyal citizens, upright artisans, praiseworthy neighbors, devoted kinsmen, understanding parents, and sincere believers in the brotherhood of the Father's kingdom. And my spirit shall be upon you, now and even to the end of the world." P. 1932.

4. **Each day learn to love one more person.**

"You cannot truly love your fellows by a mere act of will. Love is only born of thoroughgoing understanding of your neighbor's motives and sentiments. It is not so important to love all men today as it is that each day you learn to love one more human being. If each day or each week you achieve an understanding of one more of your fellows, and if this is the limit of your ability, then you are certainly socializing and truly spiritualizing your personality. Love is infectious, and when human devotion is intelligent and wise, love is more catching than hate. But only genuine and unselfish love is truly contagious. If each mortal could only become a focus of dynamic affection, this benign virus of love would soon pervade the sentimental emotion-stream of humanity to such an extent that all civilization would be encompassed by love, and that would be the realization of the brotherhood of man." P. 1098.

5. **Love is never self-seeking.**

"You are destined to live a narrow and mean life if you learn to love only those who love you. Human love may indeed be reciprocal, but divine love is outgoing in all its satisfaction-seeking. The less of love in any creature's nature, the greater the love need, and the more does divine love seek to satisfy such need. Love is never self-seeking, and it cannot be self-bestowed. Divine love cannot be self-contained; it must be unselfishly bestowed." P. 1739.

VIII. HOW WE EXPERIENCE GOD'S LOVE

1. **The religionist knows a God of love.**

"The fact-seeking scientist conceives of God as the First Cause, a God of force. The emotional artist sees God as the ideal of beauty, a God of aesthetics. The reasoning philosopher is sometimes inclined to posit a God of universal unity, even a pantheistic Deity. The religionist of faith believes in a God who fosters survival, the Father in heaven, the God of love." P. 68.

2. **Our faith trusts a God of love.**

"The religionist of philosophic attainment has faith in a personal God of personal salvation, something more than a reality, a value, a level of achievement, an exalted process, a transmutation, ultimate of timespace, an idealization, the personalization of energy, the entity of gravity, a human projection, the idealization of self, nature's upthrust, the inclination to goodness, the forward impulse of evolution, or a sublime hypothesis. The religionist has faith in a God of love. Love is the essence of religion and the wellspring of superior civilization." P. 1124.

3. The experience of feeling God's love.

"Mortal man cannot possibly know the infinitude of the heavenly Father. Finite mind cannot think through such an absolute truth or fact. But this same finite human being can actually *feel*—literally experience—the full and undiminished impact of such an infinite Father's LOVE. Such a love can be truly experienced, albeit while quality of experience is unlimited, quantity of such an experience is strictly limited by the human capacity for spiritual receptivity and by the associated capacity to love the Father in return." P. 50.

4. Love is man's dearest approach to God.

"Finite appreciation of infinite qualities far transcends the logically limited capacities of the creature because of the fact that mortal man is made in the image of God—there lives within him a fragment of infinity. Therefore man's nearest and dearest approach to God is by and through love, for God is love. And all of such a unique relationship is an actual experience in cosmic sociology, the Creator-creature relationship—the Father-child affection." P. 50.

5. Enjoy love regardless of your deserts.

"Avoid dishonesty and unfairness in all your efforts to preach truth and proclaim the gospel. Seek no unearned recognition and crave no undeserved sympathy. Love, freely receive from both divine and human sources regardless of your deserts, and love freely in return. But in all other things related to honor and adulation seek only that which honestly belongs to you." P. 1740.

IX. HOW JESUS LOVED MEN

1. Jesus' love for men was sincere.

"Jesus could help men so much because he loved them so sincerely. He truly loved each man, each woman, and each child. He could be such a true friend because of his remarkable insight—he knew so fully what was in the heart and in the mind of man. He was an interested and keen observer. He was an expert in the comprehension of human need, clever in detecting human longings." P. 1874.

2. How Jesus loved men.

"Jesus was never in a hurry. He had time to comfort his fellow men 'as he passed by.' And he always made his friends feel at ease. He was a charming listener. He never engaged in the meddlesome probing of the souls of his associates. As he comforted hungry minds and ministered to thirsty souls, the recipients of his mercy did not so much feel that they were confessing *to* him as that they were conferring *with* him. They had unbounded confidence in him because they saw he had so much faith in them.

"He never seemed to be curious about people, and he never manifested a desire to direct, manage, or follow them up. He inspired profound self-confidence and robust courage in all who enjoyed his association. When he smiled on a man, that mortal experienced increased capacity for solving his manifold problems." P. 1874-5. Mark 2:14. John 9:1.

3. Jesus' love was so real he could discipline men.

"Jesus loved men so much and so wisely that he never hesitated to be severe with them when the occasion demanded such discipline. He frequently set out to help a person by asking for help. In this way he elicited interest, appealed to the better things in human nature." P. 1875.

4. Living in Jesus' love.

"'As the Father has loved me, so have I loved you. Live in my love even as I live in the Father's love. If you do as I have taught you, you shall abide in my love even as I have kept the Father's word and evermore abide in his love.'" P. 1945. John 15:9,10.

5. We are to love as Jesus loved.

"In fact, the branch exists only for, and can do nothing except, fruit bearing, yielding grapes. So does the true believer exist only for the purpose of bearing the fruits of the spirit: to love man as he himself has been loved by God—that we should love one another, even as Jesus has loved us." P. 1946. John 13:34.

6. Why we should love one another.

"'But remember my promise: When I am raised up, I will tarry with you for a season before I go to the Father. And even this night will I make supplication to the Father that he strengthen each of you for that which you must now so soon pass through. I love you all with the love wherewith the Father loves me, and therefore should you henceforth love one another, even as I have loved you.'" P. 1962. John 15:12.

7. The power of Jesus' personal love.

"Jesus, by the power of his personal love for men, could break the hold of sin and evil. He thereby set men free to choose better ways of living. Jesus portrayed a deliverance from the past which in itself promised a triumph for the future. Forgiveness thus provided salvation. The beauty of divine love, once fully admitted to the human heart, forever destroys the charm of sin and the power of evil." P. 2018.

8. **God's love as related to the cross.**

"The cross forever shows that the attitude of Jesus toward sinners was neither condemnation nor condonation, but rather eternal and loving salvation. Jesus is truly a savior in the sense that his life and death do win men over to goodness and righteous survival. Jesus loves men so much that his love awakens the response of love in the human heart. Love is truly contagious and eternally creative. Jesus' death on the cross exemplifies a love which is sufficiently strong and divine to forgive sin and swallow up all evil-doing. Jesus disclosed to this world a higher quality of righteousness than justice—mere technical right and wrong. Divine love does not merely forgive wrongs; it absorbs and actually destroys them. The forgiveness of love utterly transcends the forgiveness of mercy. Mercy sets the guilt of evil-doing to one side; but love destroys forever the sin and all weakness resulting therefrom. Jesus brought a new method of living to Urantia. He taught us not to resist evil but to find through him a goodness which effectually destroys evil. The forgiveness of Jesus is not condonation; it is salvation from condemnation. Salvation does not slight wrongs; it *makes them right*. True love does not compromise nor condone hate; it destroys it. The love of Jesus is never satisfied with mere forgiveness. The Master's love implies rehabilitation, eternal survival. It is altogether proper to speak of salvation as redemption if you mean this eternal rehabilitation." P. 2018.

X. ERRONEOUS IDEAS ABOUT GOD'S LOVE

1. **The Sons of God not mediators for man.**

"The ministry of the Eternal Son is devoted to the revelation of the God of love to the universe of universes. This divine Son is not engaged in the ignoble task of trying to persuade his gracious Father to love his lowly creatures and to show mercy to the wrongdoers of time. How wrong to envisage the Eternal Son as appealing to the Universal Father to show mercy to his lowly creatures on the material worlds of space! Such concepts of God are crude and grotesque. Rather should you realize that all the merciful ministrations of the Sons of God are a direct revelation of the Father's heart of universal love and infinite compassion. The Father's love is the real and eternal source of the Son's mercy." P. 75.

2. **Sacrifice not required to enlist God's love.**

"It is wrong to think of God as being coaxed into loving his children because of the sacrifices of his Sons or the intercession of his subordinate creatures, 'for the Father himself loves you.' It is in response to this paternal affection that God sends the marvelous Adjusters to indwell the minds of men. God's love is universal; 'whosoever will may come.' He would 'have all men be saved by coming into the knowledge of the truth.' He is 'not willing that any should perish.'

"The Creators are the very first to attempt to save man from the disastrous results of his foolish transgression of the divine laws. God's love is by nature a fatherly affection; therefore does he sometimes 'chasten us for our own profit, that we may be partakers of his holiness.' Even during your fiery trials remember that 'in all our afflictions he is afflicted with us.'" P. 39. John 16:27. Acts 2:21. 1 Tim. 2:4. 2 Peter 3:9. Heb. 12:6,10. Isa. 63:9.

3. **Origin of the atonement doctrine.**

"Righteousness implies that God is the source of the moral law of the universe. Truth exhibits God as a revealer, as a teacher. But love gives and craves affection, seeks understanding fellowship such as exists between parent and child. Righteousness may be the divine thought, but love is a father's attitude. The erroneous supposition that the righteousness of God was irreconcilable with the selfless love of the heavenly Father, presupposed absence of unity in the nature of Deity and led directly to the elaboration of the atonement doctrine, which is a philosophic assault upon both the unity and the free-willness of God." P. 41.

4. **Atonement idea an insult to God.**

"The bestowal of a Paradise Son on your world was inherent in the situation of closing a planetary age; it was inescapable, and it was not made necessary for the purpose of winning the favor of God. This bestowal also happened to be the final personal act of a Creator Son in the long adventure of earning the experiential sovereignty of his universe. What a travesty upon the infinite character of God! this teaching that his fatherly heart in all its austere coldness and hardness was so untouched by the misfortunes and sorrows of his creatures that his tender mercies were not forthcoming until he saw his blameless Son bleeding and dying upon the cross of Calvary!" P. 60.

5. **Anger and wrath in relation to love.**

   "'Anger is a material manifestation which represents, in a general way, the measure of the failure of the spiritual nature to gain control of the combined intellectual and physical natures. Anger indicates your lack of tolerant brotherly love plus your lack of self-respect and self-control. Anger depletes the health, debases the mind, and handicaps the spirit teacher of man's soul. Have you not read in the Scriptures that "wrath kills the foolish man," and that man "tears himself in his anger"? That "he who is slow of wrath is of great understanding," while "he who is hasty of temper exalts folly"? You all know that "a soft answer turns away wrath," and how "grievous words stir up anger." "Discretion defers anger," while "he who has no control over his own self is like a defenseless city without walls." "Wrath is cruel and anger is outrageous." "Angry men stir up strife, while the furious multiply their transgressions." "Be not hasty in spirit, for anger rests in the bosom of fools.'" Before Jesus ceased speaking, he said further: 'Let your hearts be so dominated by love that your spirit guide will have little trouble in delivering you from the tendency to give vent to those outbursts of animal anger which are inconsistent with the status of divine sonship.'" P. 1673. Job 5:2; 18:4. Prov. 14:29; 15:1; 19:11; 25:28; 27:4; 29:22. Eccl. 7:9.

6. **Losing sight of God's love.**

   "When man loses sight of the love of a personal God, the kingdom of God becomes merely the kingdom of good. Notwithstanding the infinite unity of the divine nature, love is the dominant characteristic of all God's personal dealings with his creatures." P. 40.

7. **We must not presume on God's love.**

   "But Jesus earnestly warned his apostles against the foolishness of the child of God who presumes upon the Father's love. He declared that the heavenly Father is not a lax, loose, or foolishly indulgent parent who is ever ready to condone sin and forgive recklessness. He cautioned his hearers not mistakenly to apply his illustrations of father and son so as to make it appear that God is like some overindulgent and unwise parents who conspire with the foolish of earth to encompass the moral undoing of their thoughtless children, and who are thereby certainly and directly contributing to the delinquency and early demoralization of their own offspring. Said Jesus: 'My Father does not indulgently condone those acts and practices of his children which are self-destructive and suicidal to all moral growth and spiritual progress. Such sinful practices are an abomination in the sight of God.'" P. 1653.

8. **Job comprehends God's love.**

"'Job was altogether right when he challenged the doctrine that God afflicts children in order to punish their parents. Job was ever ready to admit that God is righteous, but he longed for some soul-satisfying revelation of the personal character of the Eternal. And that is our mission on earth. No more shall suffering mortals be denied the comfort of knowing the love of God and understanding the mercy of the Father in heaven. While the speech of God spoken from the whirlwind was a majestic concept for the day of its utterance, you have already learned that the Father does not thus reveal himself, but rather that he speaks within the human heart as a still, small voice, saying, "This is the way; walk therein." Do you not comprehend that God dwells within you, that he has become what you are that he may make you what he is!'" P. 1664.

XI. CHARACTERISTIC MANIFESTATIONS OF LOVE

1. **Love is man's supreme motivation.**

"Religious insight possesses the power of turning defeat into higher desires and new determinations. Love is the highest motivation which man may utilize in his universe ascent. But love, divested of truth, beauty, and goodness, is only a sentiment, a philosophic distortion, a psychic illusion, a spiritual deception. Love must always be redefined on successive levels of morontia and spirit progression." P. 2096.

2. **True religion is a living love.**

"But true religion is a living love, a life of service. The religionist's detachment from much that is purely temporal and trivial never leads to social isolation, and it should not destroy the sense of humor. Genuine religion takes nothing away from human existence, but it does add new meanings to all of life; it generates new types of enthusiasm, zeal, and courage. It may even engender the spirit of the crusader, which is more than dangerous if not controlled by spiritual insight and loyal devotion to the commonplace social obligations of human loyalties." P. 1100-1.

3. **Love is doing good to others.**

"To finite man truth, beauty, and goodness embrace the full revelation of divinity reality. As this love-comprehension of Deity finds spiritual expression in the lives of God-knowing mortals, there are yielded the fruits of divinity: intellectual peace, social progress, moral satisfaction, spiritual joy, and cosmic wisdom. The advanced mortals on a world in the seventh stage of light and life have learned that love is the greatest thing in the universe—and they know that God is love.

"Love is the desire to do good to others." P. 648.

4. **Reality of Spirit affection.**

"'The love of the Spirit' is real, as also are his sorrows; therefore 'Grieve not the Spirit of God.' Whether we observe the Infinite Spirit as Paradise Deity or as a local universe Creative Spirit, we find that the Conjoint Creator is not only the Third Source and Center but also a divine person. This divine personality also reacts to the universe as a person. The Spirit speaks to you, 'He who has an ear, let him hear what the Spirit says.' 'The Spirit himself makes intercession for you.' The Spirit exerts a direct and personal influence upon created beings, 'For as many as are led by the Spirit of God, they are the sons of God.'" P. 96. Eph. 4:30. Rev. 13:9. Rom. 8:26; 8:14.

5. **God the Father loves men.**

"God the Father loves men; God the Son serves men; God the Spirit inspires the children of the universe to the ever-ascending adventure of finding God the Father by the ways ordained by God the Sons through the ministry of the grace of God the Spirit." P. 53.

LOVE AS PRESENTED IN THE BIBLE
I. DIVINE LOVE

1. **God is love.**

"God is love, and he who abides in love abides in God." **1 John 4:16.**

2. **God's love is personal.**

"The Father himself loves you." **John 16:27.**

3. **God's love is everlasting—eternal.**

"I have loved you with an everlasting love." **Jer. 31:3.**

4. **God protects and prospers those who love him.**

"The Lord preserves all who love him; but all the wicked he will destroy." **Ps. 145:20.**

"Endowing with wealth those who love me, and filling their treasuries." **Prov. 8:21.**

"May they prosper who love you." Ps. 122:6.

5. The Lord loves us as children.

"See what love the Father has given us, that we should be called the children of God." **1 John 3:1.**

6. God loves us first.

"We love, because he first loved us." **1 John 4:19.**

7. God loves those who hate evil.

"Hate evil, and love good...the Lord...will be gracious." **Amos 5:15.**

"The Lord loves those who hate evil." **Ps. 97:10.**

8. God disciplines those whom he loves.

"Those whom I love, I reprove and chasten." **Rev. 3:19. (Prov. 3:12.)**

"For the Lord disciplines him whom he loves." **Heb. 12:6.**

9. God's love ministered by the Holy Spirit.

"Hope does not disappoint us, because God's love has been poured into our hearts through the Holy Spirit which has been given to us." **Rom. 5:5.**

10. God gives love—not timidity and fear.

"For God did not give us a spirit of timidity but a spirit of power and love and self-control." **2 Tim. 1:7.**

11. There is no fear in love.

"There is no fear in love, but perfect love casts out fear." **1 John 4:18.**

12. God loves a cheerful giver.

"For God loves a cheerful giver." **2 Cor. 9:7.**

13. Love of Christ controls us.

"The love of Christ controls us." **2 Cor. 5:14.**

14. God so loved us that he gave his Son.

"For God so loved the world that he gave his only Son, that whoever believes in him should not perish but have eternal life." **John 3:16.**

II. HUMAN LOVE

A. LOVING GOD

1. Our duty to love God wholeheartedly.

"And you shall love the Lord your God with all your heart, and with all your soul, and with all your might." **Deut. 6:5.**

"And to love him with all the heart, and with all the understanding, and with all the strength." **Mark 12:33.**

2. If we love God, we keep his commandments.

"If you love me, you will keep my commandments." **John 14:15.**

"And this is love, that we follow his commandments; this is the commandment, as you have heard from the beginning, that you follow love." **2 John 6.**

3. Love magnifies God.

"May those who love thy salvation say evermore, 'God is great!'" **Ps. 70:4.**

4. Love is the fulfilling of the law.

"Love is the fulfilling of the law." **Rom. 13:10.**

"That Christ may dwell in your hearts through faith; that you, being rooted and grounded in love, may have power to comprehend with all the saints what is the breadth and length and height and depth, and to know the love of Christ which surpasses knowledge, that you may be filled with all the fulness of God." **Eph. 3:17,18.**

"Speaking the truth in love." **Eph. 4:15.**

5. We love God even though we cannot see him.

"Without having seen him you love him." **1 Peter 1:8.**

6. Obedience perfects love.

"But whoever keeps his word, in him truly love for God is perfected." **1 John 2:5.**

B. LOVE FOR MAN

1. Love your neighbor as yourself.

"You shall love your neighbor as yourself." **Matt. 22:39.**

2. Love the Brotherhood.

"Love the Brotherhood. Fear God." **1 Peter 2:17.**

"Let brotherly love continue." **Heb. 13:1**.

"Beloved, let us love one another; for love is of God, and he who loves is born of God and knows God." **1 John 4:7**.

"By this all men will know that you are my disciples, if you have love for one another." **John 13:35**.

3. **Said Jesus: Love one another as I have loved you.**

    "This is my commandment, that you love one another as I have loved you." **John 15:12. (John 13:34.)**

4. **Love your enemies.**

    "Love your enemies and pray for those who persecute you." **Matt. 5:44**.

5. **Love covers our offenses.**

    "Hatred stirs up strife, but love covers all offenses." **Prov. 10:12**.

6. **Love is the prime fruit of the spirit.**

    "But the fruit of the spirit is love, joy, peace, patience, kindness, goodness, faithfulness, gentleness, self-control." **Gal. 5:22**.

    "So faith, hope, love abide, these three; but the greatest of these is love." **1 Cor. 13:13**.

7. **The penalty of not loving.**

    "He who does not love does not know God; for God is love." **1 John 4:8**.

8. **Supreme love.**

    "Greater love has no man than this, that a man lay down his life for his friends." **John 15:13**.

C. PERVERTED LOVE

"For the love of money is the root of all evils." **1 Tim. 6:10**.

"Do not love the world or the things in the world. If any one loves the world, love for the Father is not in him." **1 John 2:15**.

NOTE: In many passages in the King James version love is translated as "charity." Practically all of these "charity" passages are changed to "love" in the Revised Version.

On the whole, the Bible presents the Greek concept of love, and in so doing recognizes five types:

1. **Sexual love.**

2. **Family affection.**

3. **Social love—friendship.**

4. **Racial love—ethical kindness.**

5. **Religious love:**

    a.   *Love for God.*

    b.   *Love of one's fellows.*

2. MERCY

MERCY AS PRESENTED IN THE BIBLE.

MERCY

I. WHAT IS MERCY?

1. Mercy is justice tempered by wisdom.

"Mercy is simply justice tempered by that wisdom which grows out of perfection of knowledge and the full recognition of the natural weaknesses and environmental handicaps of finite creatures. 'Our God is full of compassion, gracious, long-suffering, and plenteous in mercy.' Therefore 'whosoever calls upon the Lord shall be saved,' 'for he will abundantly pardon.' 'The mercy of the Lord is from everlasting to everlasting'; yes, 'his mercy endures forever.' 'I am the Lord who executes loving-kindness, judgment, and righteousness in the earth, for in these things I delight.' 'I do not afflict willingly nor grieve the children of men,' for I am 'the Father of mercies and the God of all comfort.'" P. 38. Ps. 103:8. Joel 2:32. Isa. 55:7. Ps. 103:17; 106:1. Jer. 9:24. Lam. 3:33. 2 Cor. 1:3.

2. Mercy represents the technique of fairness.

"Divine mercy represents a fairness technique of adjustment between the universe levels of perfection and imperfection. Mercy is the justice of Supremacy adapted to the situations of the evolving finite, the righteousness of eternity modified to meet the highest interests and universe welfare of the children of time. Mercy is not a contravention of justice but rather an understanding interpretation of the demands of supreme justice as it is fairly applied to the subordinate spiritual beings and to the material creatures of the evolving universes. Mercy is the justice of the Paradise Trinity wisely and lovingly visited upon the manifold intelligences of the creations of time and space as it is formulated by divine wisdom and determined by the all-knowing mind and the sovereign free will of the Universal Father and all his associated Creators." P. 38.

3. Mercy delays are not interminable.

"But these mercy delays are not interminable. Notwithstanding the long delay (as time is reckoned on Urantia) in adjudicating the Lucifer rebellion, we may record that, during the time of effecting this revelation, the first hearing in the pending case of Gabriel *vs.* Lucifer was held on Uversa, and soon thereafter there issued the mandate of the Ancients of Days directing that Satan be henceforth confined to the prison world with Lucifer. This ends the ability of Satan to pay further visits to any of the fallen worlds of Satania. Justice in a mercy-dominated universe may be slow, but it is certain." P. 616.

4. Mercy is not a contravention of justice.

"Mercy is the natural and inevitable offspring of goodness and love. The good nature of a loving Father could not possibly withhold the wise ministry of mercy to each member of every group of his universe children. Eternal justice and divine mercy together constitute what in human experience would be called *fairness*." P. 38.

II. GOD'S MERCY IS REPLETE

1. The richness of the divine mercy.

"The 'richness of the goodness of God leads erring man to repentance.' 'Every good gift and every perfect gift comes down from the Father of lights.' 'God is good; he is the eternal refuge of the souls of men.' 'The Lord God is merciful and gracious. He is long-suffering and abundant in goodness and truth.' 'Taste and see that the Lord is good! Blessed is the man who trusts him.' 'The Lord is gracious and full of compassion. He is the God of salvation.' 'He heals the brokenhearted and binds up the wounds of the soul. He is man's all-powerful benefactor.'" P. 41. Rom. 2:4. Jas. 1:17. Deut. 33:27. Ex. 34:6. Ps. 34:8; 111:4. Isa. 61:1.

2. God's mercy is all-knowing.

"The Universal Father is the only personality in all the universe who does actually know the number of the stars and planets of space. All the worlds of every universe are constantly within the consciousness of God. He also says: 'I have surely seen the affliction of my people, I have heard their cry, and I know their sorrows.' For 'the Lord looks from heaven; he beholds all the sons of men; from the place of his habitation he looks upon all the inhabitants of the earth.' Every creature child may truly say: 'He knows the way I take, and when he has tried me, I shall come forth as gold.' 'God knows our downsittings and our uprisings; he understands our thoughts afar off and is acquainted with all our ways.' 'All things are naked and open to the eyes of him with whom we have to do.' And it should be a real comfort to every human being to understand that 'he knows your frame; he remembers that you are dust.' Jesus, speaking of the living God, said, 'Your Father knows what you have need of even before you ask him.'" P. 49. Ex. 3:7. Ps. 33:14. Job 23:10. Ps. 139:2. Heb. 4:13. Ps. 103:14. Matt. 6:8.

3. **God is naturally and everlastingly merciful.**

"God is inherently kind, naturally compassionate, and everlastingly merciful. And never is it necessary that any influence be brought to bear upon the Father to call forth his loving-kindness. The creature's need is wholly sufficient to insure the full flow of the Father's tender mercies and his saving grace. Since God knows all about his children, it is easy for him to forgive. The better man understands his neighbor, the easier it will be to forgive him, even to love him." P. 38.

III. THE MERCY MINISTERS

1. **The Eternal Son is mercy—applied love.**

"God is love, the Son is mercy. Mercy is applied love, the Father's love in action in the person of his Eternal Son. The love of this universal Son is likewise universal. As love is comprehended on a sex planet, the love of God is more comparable to the love of a father, while the love of the Eternal Son is more like the affection of a mother. Crude, indeed, are such illustrations, but I employ them in the hope of conveying to the human mind the thought that there is a difference, not in divine content but in quality and technique of expression, between the love of the Father and the love of the Son." P. 75-6.

2. **The Eternal Son is the great mercy minister.**

"The Son shares the justice and righteousness of the Trinity but overshadows these divinity traits by the infinite personalization of the Father's love and mercy; the Son is the revelation of divine love to the universes. As God is love, so the Son is mercy. The Son cannot love more than the Father, but he can show mercy to creatures in one additional way, for he not only is a primal creator like the Father, but he is also the Eternal Son of that same Father, thereby sharing in the sonship experience of all other sons of the Universal Father.

"The Eternal Son is the great mercy minister to all creation. Mercy is the essence of the Son's spiritual character. The mandates of the Eternal Son, as they go forth over the spirit circuits of the Second Source and Center, are keyed in tones of mercy." P. 75.

3. **The Infinite Spirit is also a mercy minister.**

"Though in every way sharing the perfection, the righteousness, and the love of the Universal Father, the Infinite Spirit inclines towards the mercy attributes of the Eternal Son, thus becoming the mercy minister of the Paradise Deities to the grand universe. Ever and always—universally and eternally—the Spirit is a mercy minister, for, as the divine Sons reveal the love of God, so the divine Spirit depicts the mercy of God." P. 92.

4. Mercy ministry is the purpose of the bestowals.

"The purpose of these creature incarnations is to enable such Creators to become wise, sympathetic, just, and understanding sovereigns. These divine Sons are innately just, but they become understandingly merciful as a result of these successive bestowal experiences; they are naturally merciful, but these experiences make them merciful in new and additional ways. These bestowals are the last steps in their education and training for the sublime tasks of ruling the local universes in divine righteousness and by just judgment." P. 1308.

5. Jesus is a merciful friend.

"Jesus knows about the thoughts and feelings, the urges and impulses, of the evolutionary and ascendant mortals of the realms, from birth to death. He has lived the human life from the beginnings of physical, intellectual, and spiritual selfhood up through infancy, childhood, youth, and adulthood—even to the human experience of death. He not only passed through these usual and familiar human periods of intellectual and spiritual advancement, but he *also* fully experienced those higher and more advanced phases of human and Adjuster reconciliation which so few Urantia mortals ever attain. And thus he experienced the full life of mortal man, not only as it is lived on your world, but also as it is lived on all other evolutionary worlds of time and space, even on the highest and most advanced of all the worlds settled in light and life." P. 1425.

6. To obtain mercy you must show mercy.

"They who would receive mercy must show mercy; judge not that you be not judged. With the spirit with which you judge others you also shall be judged. Mercy does not wholly abrogate universe fairness. In the end it will prove true: 'Whoso stops his ears to the cry of the poor, he also shall some day cry for help, and no one will hear him.' The sincerity of any prayer is the assurance of its being heard; the spiritual wisdom and universe consistency of any petition is the determiner of the time, manner, and degree of the answer. A wise father does not *literally* answer the foolish prayers of his ignorant and inexperienced children, albeit the children may derive much pleasure and real soul satisfaction from the making of such absurd petitions." P. 1639. Matt. 5:7; 7:1,2. Prov. 21:13.

MERCY AS PRESENTED IN THE BIBLE

1. **The divine compassion is over all.**

   "The Lord is good to all, and his compassion is over all that he has made." **Ps. 145:9.**

2. **God is the Father of mercies.**

   "The Father of mercies and the God of all comfort." 2 Cor. 1:3.

3. **God is rich in mercy.**

   "But God, who is rich in mercy, out of the great love with which he loved us—." **Eph. 2:4.**

4. **We are betrothed to God in mercy.**

   "I will betroth you to me in righteousness and in justice, in steadfast love, and in mercy." **Hosea 2:19.**

5. **Mercy seat on top of the ark of the law.**

   "And you shall put the mercy seat on top of the ark." **Ex. 25:21.**

6. **God is merciful and gracious.**

   "But thou, O Lord, art a God merciful and gracious, slow to anger and abounding in steadfast love and faithfulness." **Ps. 86:15.**

7. **Goodness and mercy follow us.**

   "Surely goodness and mercy shall follow me all the days of my life." **Ps. 23:6.**

8. **The Mercy Psalm.**

   In the King James version, every one of the twenty-five verses of the **136th Psalm** ends with "For his steadfast mercy endures forever." In the Revised Version, this reads: "For his steadfast love endures forever."

   Among many other passages when mercy is translated "love," are **Ps. 25:10; 57:10; 85:10; 130:7. Hosea 6:6; 10:12.**

9. **The merciful shall receive mercy.**

   "Blessed are the merciful, for they shall obtain mercy." **Matt. 5:7.**

10. We should show mercy with cheerfulness.

"He who gives aid, with zeal; he who does acts of mercy, with cheerfulness."
Rom. 12:8.

Note: Words used in place of mercy in Old Testament and New Testament are: compassion, pity, goodness, kindness, and loving kindness.

3. JUSTICE

JUSTICE AS PRESENTED IN THE BIBLE.

JUSTICE

I. THE NATURE OF DIVINE JUSTICE

1. Impartiality of divine justice.

"God is righteous; therefore is he just. 'The Lord is righteous in all his ways.' '"I have not done without cause all that I have done," says the Lord.' 'The judgments of the Lord are true and righteous altogether.' The justice of the Universal Father cannot be influenced by the acts and performances of his creatures, 'for there is no iniquity with the Lord our God, no respect of persons, no taking of gifts.'" P. 36. Ps. 145:17; 19:9. 2 Chron. 19:7.

2. Justice associated with mercy and wisdom.

"Only the discernment of infinite wisdom enables a righteous God to minister justice and mercy at the same time and in any given universe situation. The heavenly Father is never torn by conflicting attitudes towards his universe children; God is never a victim of attitudinal antagonisms. God's all-knowingness unfailingly directs his free will in the choosing of that universe conduct which perfectly, simultaneously, and equally satisfies the demands of all his divine attributes and the infinite qualities of his eternal nature." P. 38.

3. Divine justice is eternally fair.

"'A part of every father lives in the child. The father enjoys priority and superiority of understanding in all matters connected with the child-parent relationship. The parent is able to view the immaturity of the child in the light of the more advanced parental maturity, the riper experience of the older partner. With the earthly child and the heavenly Father, the divine parent possesses infinity and divinity of sympathy and capacity for loving understanding. Divine forgiveness is inevitable; it is inherent and inalienable in God's infinite understanding, in his perfect knowledge of all that concerns the mistaken judgment and erroneous choosing of the child. Divine justice is so eternally fair that it unfailingly embodies understanding mercy.'" P. 1898.

II. JUSTICE A TRINITY ATTITUDE

1. Justice is inherent in the Paradise Trinity.

"*Justice* is inherent in the universal sovereignty of the Paradise Trinity, but goodness, mercy, and truth are the universe ministry of the divine personalities, whose Deity union constitutes the Trinity. Justice is not the attitude of the Father, the Son, or the Spirit. Justice is the Trinity attitude of these personalities of love, mercy, and ministry. No one of the Paradise Deities fosters the administration of justice. Justice is never a personal attitude; it is always a plural function." P. 114.

2. Ancients of Days administer Trinity justice.

"The Ancients of Days and their Trinity-origin associates mete out the just judgment of supreme fairness to the seven superuniverses. In the central universe such functions exist in theory only; there fairness is self-evident in perfection, and Havona perfection precludes all possibility of disharmony." P. 115.

3. Justice is always a collective action.

"Justice is the collective thought of righteousness; mercy is its personal expression. Mercy is the attitude of love; precision characterizes the operation of law; divine judgment is the soul of fairness, ever conforming to the justice of the Trinity, ever fulfilling the divine love of God. When fully perceived and completely understood, the righteous justice of the Trinity and the merciful love of the Universal Father are coincident. But man has no such full understanding of divine justice. Thus in the Trinity, as man would view it, the personalities of Father, Son, and Spirit are adjusted to co-ordinate ministry of love and law in the experiential universes of time." P. 115.

III. THE MERCY INTERVAL OF JUSTICE

1. The justice delay of mercy.

"The very fact that an evil-doing creature can actually choose to do wrong—commit sin—establishes the fact of free-willness and fully justifies any length delay in the execution of justice provided the extended mercy might conduce to repentance and rehabilitation." P. 616.

2. Mercy extended in the Lucifer rebellion.

"There are many reasons known to us why the Supreme Rulers did not immediately destroy or intern the leaders of the Lucifer rebellion. There are no doubt still other and possibly better reasons unknown to us. The mercy features of this delay in the execution of justice were extended personally by Michael of Nebadon. Except for the affection of this Creator-father for his erring Sons, the supreme justice of the superuniverse would have acted. If such an episode as the Lucifer rebellion had occurred in Nebadon while Michael was incarnated on Urantia, the instigators of such evil might have been instantly and absolutely annihilated." P. 616.

3. **Love always provides the time lag of mercy.**

"Supreme justice can act instantly when not restrained by divine mercy. But the ministry of mercy to the children of time and space always provides for this time lag, this saving interval between seedtime and harvest. If the seed sowing is good, this interval provides for the testing and upbuilding of character; if the seed sowing is evil, this merciful delay provides time for repentance and rectification. This time delay in the adjudication and execution of evildoers is inherent in the mercy ministry of the seven superuniverses. This restraint of justice by mercy proves that God is love, and that such a God of love dominates the universes and in mercy controls the fate and judgment of all his creatures." P. 616.

4. **Exhaustion of mercy brings justice action.**

"The elevation of a sevenfold bestowal Son to the unquestioned sovereignty of his universe means the beginning of the end of agelong uncertainty and relative confusion. Subsequent to this event, that which cannot be sometime spiritualized will eventually be disorganized; that which cannot be sometime co-ordinated with cosmic reality will eventually be destroyed. When the provisions of endless mercy and nameless patience have been exhausted in an effort to win the loyalty and devotion of the will creatures of the realms, justice and righteousness will prevail. That which mercy cannot rehabilitate justice will eventually annihilate." P. 241.

5. **Justice conditions rejected mercy.**

"God is never wrathful, vengeful, or angry. It is true that wisdom does often restrain his love, while justice conditions his rejected mercy. His love of righteousness cannot help being exhibited as equal hatred for sin. The Father is not an inconsistent personality; the divine unity is perfect. In the Paradise Trinity there is absolute unity despite the eternal identities of the co-ordinates of God." P. 41.

IV. JESUS DISCUSSES JUSTICE

1. **Jesus talks with Ganid about mercy and justice.**

"'Ganid, it is true, you do not understand. Mercy ministry is always the work of the individual, but justice punishment is the function of the social, governmental, or universe administrative groups. As an individual I am beholden to show mercy; I must go to the rescue of the assaulted lad, and in all consistency I may employ sufficient force to restrain the aggressor. And that is just what I did. I achieved the deliverance of the assaulted lad; that was the end of mercy ministry. Then I forcibly detained the aggressor a sufficient length of time to enable the weaker party to the dispute to make his escape, after which I withdraw from the affair. I did not proceed to sit in judgment on the aggressor, thus to pass upon his motive—to adjudicate all that entered into his attack upon his fellow—and then undertake to execute the punishment which my mind might dictate as just recompense for his wrongdoing. Ganid, mercy may be lavish, but justice is precise. Cannot you discern that no two persons are likely to agree as to the punishment which would satisfy the demands of justice? One would impose forty lashes, another twenty, while still another would advise solitary confinement as a just punishment. Can you not see that on this world such responsibilities had better rest upon the group or be administered by chosen representatives of the group? In the universe, judgment is vested in those who fully know the antecedents of all wrongdoing as well as its motivation. In civilized society and in an organized universe the administration of justice presupposes the passing of just sentence consequent upon fair judgment, and such prerogatives are vested in the juridical groups of the worlds and in the all-knowing administrators of the higher universes of all creation.'" P. 1469.

2. **Angels as related to justice.**

"The technique of justice demands that personal or group guardians shall respond to the dispensational roll call in behalf of all nonsurviving personalities. The Adjusters of such nonsurvivors do not return, and when the rolls are called, the seraphim respond, but the Adjusters make no answer. This constitutes the 'resurrection of the unjust,' in reality the formal recognition of the cessation of creature existence. This roll call of justice always immediately follows the roll call of mercy, the resurrection of the sleeping survivors. But these are matters which are of concern to none but the supreme and all-knowing Judges of survival values. Such problems of adjudication do not really concern us." P. 1247.

V. EVOLUTION OF HUMAN JUSTICE

1. **There is no justice in nature.**

"Natural justice is a man-made theory; it is not a reality. In nature, justice is purely theoretic, wholly a fiction. Nature provides but one kind of justice—inevitable conformity of results to causes." P. 794.

2. **Justice among primitive men.**

"Justice, as conceived by man, means getting one's rights and has, therefore, been a matter of progressive evolution. The concept of justice may well be constitutive in a spirit-endowed mind, but it does not spring fullfledgedly into existence on the worlds of space.

"Primitive man assigned all phenomena to a person. In case of death the savage asked, not *what* killed him, but *who?* Accidental murder was not therefore recognized, and in the punishment of crime the motive of the criminal was wholly disregarded; judgment was rendered in accordance with the injury done." P. 794-5.

3. **Vengeance and retaliation in evolving justice.**

"Society early adopted the paying-back attitude of retaliation: an eye for an eye, a life for a life. The evolving tribes all recognized this right of blood vengeance. Vengeance became the aim of primitive life, but religion has since greatly modified these early tribal practices. The teachers of revealed religion have always proclaimed.' "Vengeance is mine, "says the Lord.' Vengeance killing in early times was not altogether unlike presentday murders under the pretense of the unwritten law." P. 795. Deut. 19:21. Rom. 12:19.

4. **Evolution of justice administration.**

"Justice was thus first meted out by the family, then by the clan, and later on by the tribe. The administration of true justice dates from the taking of revenge from private and kin groups and lodging it in the hands of the social group, the state." P. 796.

JUSTICE AS PRESENTED IN THE BIBLE

1. **Justice the foundation of God's throne.**

"Righteousness and justice are the foundation of thy throne." **Ps. 89:14.**

2. **His judgments are true and just.**

"Salvation and glory and power belong to our God, for his judgments are true and just." **Rev. 19:1,2; (Rev. 16:7.)**

"I know, O Lord, that thy judgments are right." **Ps. 119:75.**

3. **The judgments of God are righteous.**

"The ordinances of the Lord are true, and righteous altogether." **Ps. 19:9.**

4. **God's judgments are universal.**

   "He is the Lord our God; his judgments are in all the earth." **1 Chron. 16:14.**

5. **His judgments are unsearchable.**

   "How unsearchable are his judgments and how inscrutable his ways!" **Rom. 11:33.**

6. **Justice supersedes sacrifice.**

   "To do righteousness and justice is more acceptable to the Lord than sacrifice." **Prov. 21:3.**

   Old Testament justice was very literal and primitive—*"Eye for eye and tooth for tooth."* **Ex. 21:24.**

4. FAITH

A. THE BIBLE

INTRODUCTION

    I.   FAITH AS A GLORIFIED BELIEF.
    II.   HEALING FAITH.
    III.   FAITH AS THEOLOGIC BELIEF.
    IV.   THE FAITH OF JESUS.
    V.   FAITH AS PERSONAL DEDICATION.

B. *THE URANTIA BOOK*

    I.   FAITH DEFINED.
    II.   THE CERTITUDE OF FAITH.
    III.   FAITH—THE METHOD OF RELIGION.
    IV.   FAITH AND BELIEF.
    V.   FAITH AND FEAR—DOUBTS.
    VI.   FAITH AND FEELING.
    VII.   FAITH AND EDUCATION—SCIENCE AND RELIGION.
    VIII.   ABRAHAM'S FAITH.
    IX.   SAVING FAITH—ASSURANCE.
    X.   SCOPE AND POTENTIALS OF FAITH.
    XI.   HEALING FAITH.
    XII.   SPIRIT CONSCIOUSNESS—FRUITS OF FAITH.
    XIII.   DYNAMIC FAITH.
    XIV.   FAITH AND VICTORY.

TOPIC FOUR

FAITH

A. THE BIBLE

INTRODUCTION

The Bible makes use of the term "faith" with five differing meanings.

1. *Faith as a sort of glorified belief*—as one might, in a nominal manner, say "I'm a Protestant" or "I'm a Catholic."

2. *Healing Faith*—Faith as associated with the cure of disease or other natural phenomena.

3. *Theologic Faith*—Faith as designating one's religious beliefs—the same meaning as creed, the gospel, your theology.

4. *The Faith of Jesus.*

5. *Faith as one's wholehearted convictions—saving faith* just as presented in *The Urantia Book.*

I. FAITH AS A GLORIFIED BELIEF

1. Faith as a general belief in a mode of life.

"And without faith it is impossible to please him. For whoever would draw near to God must believe that he exists and that he rewards those who seek him.

"By faith Noah, being warned by God concerning events as yet unseen, took heed and constructed an ark...

"By faith Abraham obeyed when he was called to go out to a place which he was to receive as an inheritance.

"Gideon, Barak, Samson, Jephthah, of David and Samuel...who through faith conquered kingdoms, enforced justice." **Heb. 11:6-8, 32,33.**

2. As pertaining to wisdom and the intellectual life.

"If any of you lacks wisdom, let him ask God who gives to all men...But let him ask in faith, with no doubting." **Jas. 1:5,6.**

3. Faith as the dynamics of works.

"What does it profit, my brethren, if a man says he has faith but has not works? Can his faith save him?" **Jas. 2:14.**

4. An all-over attitude of believing.

"The father of the child cried out and said 'I believe, help my unbelief!'" **Mark 9:24.**

5. Referring to the belief of large groups of people.

*"And more than ever believers were added to the Lord, multitudes both of men and women."***Acts 5:14.**

II. HEALING FAITH

1. **The miracle-minded early Christians believed in prayer for the sick.**

   *"And the prayer of faith will save the sick man, and the Lord will raise him up."***Jas. 5:15.**

2. **Even Jesus associated faith with his healing episodes.**

   *"Then he touched their eyes, saying, 'According to your faith be it done to you.'"***Matt. 9:29.**

3. **Faith was symbolically related to even the material world.**

   *"And the Lord said, 'If you had faith as a grain of mustard seed, you could say to this sycamine tree "Be rooted up, and be planted in the sea,"and it would obey you.'"***Luke 17:6.**

III. FAITH AS THEOLOGIC BELIEF
The Gospel, your Creed, the Doctrines of the Church.

1. **Faith as the teachings of the church.**

   *"Strengthening the souls of the disciples, exhorting them to continue in the faith, and saying that through many tribulations we must enter the kingdom of God."***Acts 14:22.**

2. **The church—the household of faith.**

   *"Let us do good to all men, and especially to those who are of the household of faith."***Gal. 6:10.**

3. **The sum total of religious belief.**

   *"One Lord, one faith, one baptism, one God and Father of us all."***Eph. 4:5,6.**

   "Until we all attain to the unity of the faith and of the knowledge of the Son of God." Eph. 4:13.

4. **The gospel.**

   *"Stand firm in one spirit...side by side for the faith of the gospel."***Phil. 1:27.**

5. **Doctrinal teachings.**

   "Nourished on the words of the faith and the good doctrine which you have followed." **1 Tim. 4:6.**

6. Covering the whole religious life.

*"Fight the good fight of the faith; take hold of the eternal life to which you were called."***1 Tim. 6:12.**

"I have fought the good fight, I have finished the race, I have kept the faith." **2 Tim. 4:7.**

7. All of truth and doctrine.

*"Appealing to you to contend for the faith which was once for all delivered to the saints."***Jude 3.**

IV. THE FAITH OF JESUS

"Here is a call for the endurance of the saints, those who keep the commandments of God and the faith of Jesus." **14:12.**

*"My brethren, show no partiality as you hold the faith of our Lord Jesus Christ."***Jas. 2:1.**

V. FAITH AS PERSONAL DEDICATION

Faith as used in *The Urantia Book.*

1. Faith defined.

*"Now faith is the assurance of things hoped for, the conviction of things not seen."***Heb. 11:1.**

(The more familiar King James version reads: "Now faith is the substance of things hoped for, the evidence of things not seen.")

"Looking to Jesus the pioneer and perfector of our faith." **Heb. 12:2.**

(King James version: *"Looking unto Jesus the author and finisher of our faith."*)

2. Faith enhanced by learning.

*"So faith comes from what is heard, and what is heard comes by the preaching of Christ."***Rom. 10:17.**

3. Faith as a personal experience.

"The faith that you have keep between yourself and God." **Rom. 14:22.**

(King James version: "Hast thou faith? have it to thyself before God.")

4. Saving faith.

*"For by grace you have been saved through faith, and this is not your own doing, it is the gift of God."***Eph. 2:8.**

5. **Final victory through faith.**

   "For whatever is born of God overcomes the world, and this is the victory that overcomes the world, our faith." **1 John 5:4.**

Christian Faith. There is a special type of faith associated with the Christian's belief in Christ.

1. *"We believe that Jesus died and rose again."* **1 Thess. 4:14.**

2. *"While we were yet sinners, Christ died for us."* **Rom. 5:8.**

3. *"All this is from God, who through Christ reconciled us to him."* **2 Cor. 5:18.**

4. *"Christ also died for sins once for all...that he might bring us to God."* **1 Pet. 3:18.**

5. *"Believe in God, believe also in me."* **John 14:1.**

6. *"Simon Peter replied, 'You are the Christ, the Son of the Living God.'"* **Matt. 16:16.**

B. *THE URANTIA BOOK*

I. FAITH DEFINED

1. **Faith defined.**

   "That faith is concerned only with the grasp of ideal values is shown by the New Testament definition which declares that faith is the substance of things hoped for and the evidence of things not seen." P. 1091. Heb. 11:1.

2. **Faith has an eternal basis.**

   "The reason of science is based on the observable facts of time; the faith of religion argues from the spirit program of eternity. What knowledge and reason cannot do for us, true wisdom admonishes us to allow faith to accomplish through religious insight and spiritual transformation." P. 1119.

3. **The dual meanings of faith.**

   "Just as certainly as men share their religious beliefs, they create a religious group of some sort which eventually creates common goals. Someday religionists will get together and actually effect co-operation on the basis of unity of ideals and purposes rather than attempting to do so on the basis of psychological opinions and theological beliefs. Goals rather than creeds should unify religionists. Since true religion is a matter of personal spiritual experience, it is inevitable that each individual religionist must have his own and personal interpretation of the realization of that spiritual experience.

Let the term 'faith' stand for the individual's relation to God rather than for the creedal formulation of what some group of mortals have been able to agree upon as a common religious attitude. 'Have you faith? Then have it to yourself.'" P. 1091. Rom. 14:22.

II. THE CERTITUDE OF FAITH

1. **We are justified by faith.**

"The full summation of human life is the knowledge that man is educated by fact, ennobled by wisdom, and saved—justified—by religious faith." P. 2094. Rom. 5:1.

2. **Faith, trust, and assurance.**

"Religion is designed to find those values in the universe which call forth faith, trust, and assurance; religion culminates in worship. Religion discovers for the soul those supreme values which are in contrast with the relative values discovered by the mind. Such superhuman insight can be had only through genuine religious experience." P. 2075.

3. **Faith is man's only sustenance.**

"It is only natural that mortal man should be harassed by feelings of insecurity as he views himself inextricably bound to nature while he possesses spiritual powers wholly transcendent to all things temporal and finite. Only religious confidence—living faith—can sustain man amid such difficult and perplexing problems." P. 1222.

4. **Faith perceives the personal love of God.**

"Even though material mortals cannot see the person of God, they should rejoice in the assurance that he is a person; by faith accept the truth which portrays that the Universal Father so loved the world as to provide for the eternal spiritual progression of its lowly inhabitants; that he 'delights in his children.' God is lacking in none of those superhuman and divine attributes which constitute a perfect, eternal, loving, and infinite Creator personality." P. 28. Prov. 8:31.

5. **Faith knows and never really doubts.**

"If science, philosophy, or sociology dares to become dogmatic in contending with the prophets of true religion, then should God-knowing men reply to such unwarranted dogmatism with that more farseeing dogmatism of the certainty of personal spiritual experience, 'I know what I have experienced because I am a son of I AM.' If the personal experience of a father is to be challenged by dogma, then this faith-born son of the experiencible Father may reply with that unchallengeable dogma, the statement of his actual sonship with the Universal Father.

"Only an unqualified reality, an absolute, could dare consistently to be dogmatic. Those who assume to be dogmatic must, if consistent, sooner or later be driven into the arms of the Absolute of energy, the Universal of truth, and the Infinite of love.

"If the nonreligious approaches to cosmic reality presume to challenge the certainty of faith on the grounds of its unproved status, then the spirit experiencer can likewise resort to the dogmatic challenge of the facts of science and the beliefs of philosophy on the grounds that they are likewise unproved; they are likewise experiences in the consciousness of the scientist or the philosopher." P. 1127.

III. FAITH—THE METHOD OF RELIGION

1. **Faith is the method of religion.**

    "Reason is the method of science; faith is the method of religion; logic is the attempted technique of philosophy. Revelation compensates for the absence of the morontia viewpoint by providing a technique for achieving unity in the comprehension of the reality and relationships of matter and spirit by the mediation of mind. And true revelation never renders science unnatural, religion unreasonable, or philosophy illogical." P. 1106.

2. **Faith alone can validate a God of salvation.**

    "Reason, through the study of science, may lead back through nature to a First Cause, but it requires religious faith to transform the First Cause of science into a God of salvation; and revelation is further required for the validation of such a faith, such spiritual insight." P. 1106.

3. **Faith is the proof of religion.**

    "Reason is the proof of science, faith the proof of religion, logic the proof of philosophy, but revelation is validated only by human *experience*. Science yields knowledge; religion yields happiness; philosophy yields unity; revelation confirms the experiential harmony of this triune approach to universal reality." P. 1106.

4. **Faith affirms religious experience.**

    "And it is just such a vital and vigorous performance of faith in the domain of religion that entitles mortal man to affirm the personal possession and spiritual reality of that crowning endowment of human nature, religious experience." P. 1109.

5. **Faith unites insight and values.**

"Faith unites moral insight with conscientious discriminations of values, and the pre-existent evolutionary sense of duty completes the ancestry of true religion. The experience of religion eventually results in the certain consciousness of God and in the undoubted assurance of the survival of the believing personality." P. 1105.

6. **Faith validates true values.**

"That religionists have believed so much that was false does not invalidate religion because religion is founded on the recognition of values and is validated by the faith of personal religious experience. Religion, then, is based on experience and religious thought; theology, the philosophy of religion, is an honest attempt to interpret that experience. Such interpretative beliefs may be right or wrong, or a mixture of truth and error." P. 1130.

IV. FAITH AND BELIEF

1. **Faith transcends all beliefs and convictions.**

"Belief has attained the level of faith when it motivates life and shapes the mode of living. The acceptance of a teaching as true is not faith; that is mere belief. Neither is certainty nor conviction faith. A state of mind attains to faith levels only when it actually dominates the mode of living. Faith is a living attribute of genuine personal religious experience. One believes truth, admires beauty, and reverences goodness, but does not worship them; such an attitude of saving faith is centered on God alone, who is all of these personified and infinitely more." P. 1114.

2. **Faith is living and personal—God-knowing and man-serving.**

"Belief is always limiting and binding; faith is expanding and releasing. Belief fixates, faith liberates. But living religious faith is more than the association of noble beliefs; it is more than an exalted system of philosophy; it is a living experience concerned with spiritual meanings, divine ideals, and supreme values; it is God-knowing and man-serving. Beliefs may become group possessions, but faith must be personal. Theologic beliefs can be suggested to a group, but faith can rise up only in the heart of the individual religionist." P. 1114.

3. **What faith does not do.**

"Faith has falsified its trust when it presumes to deny realities and to confer upon its devotees assumed knowledge. Faith is a traitor when it fosters betrayal of intellectual integrity and belittles loyalty to supreme values and divine ideals. Faith never shuns the problem-solving duty of mortal living. Living faith does not foster bigotry, persecution, or intolerance.

"Faith does not shackle the creative imagination, neither does it maintain an unreasoning prejudice toward the discoveries of scientific investigation. Faith vitalizes religion and constrains the religionist heroically to live the golden rule. The zeal of faith is according to knowledge, and its strivings are the preludes to sublime peace." P. 1114-5.

4.   Faith transforms belief into saving experience.

"Faith transforms the philosophic God of probability into the saving God of certainty in the personal religious experience. Skepticism may challenge the theories of theology, but confidence in the dependability of personal experience affirms the truth of that belief which has grown into faith." P. 1124.

5.   Faith is the will that believes.

"In science, the idea precedes the expression of its realization; in religion, the experience of realization precedes the expression of the idea. There is a vast difference between the evolutionary will-to-believe and the product of enlightened reason, religious insight, and revelation—the *will that believes*." P. 1122.

6.   Faith progresses in eternal realities.

"Your religion shall change from the mere intellectual belief in traditional authority to the actual experience of that living faith which is able to grasp the reality of God and all that relates to the divine spirit of the Father. The religion of the mind ties you hope-lessly to the past; the religion of the spirit consists in progressive revelation and ever beckons you on toward higher and holier achievements in spiritual ideals and eternal realities." P. 1731.

V. FAITH AND FEAR—DOUBTS

1.   Spiritual progress changes fear to faith.

"This same purposive supremacy is shown in the evolution of mind ideation when primitive animal fear is transmuted into the constantly deepening reverence for God and into increasing awe of the universe. Primitive man had more religious fear than faith, and the supremacy of spirit potentials over mind actuals is demonstrated when this craven fear is translated into living faith in spiritual realities." P. 1124.

2. The faith struggles of progress.

"The religion of the spirit means effort, struggle, conflict, faith, determination, love, loyalty, and progress. The religion of the mind—the theology of authority—requires little or none of these exertions from its formal believers. Tradition is a safe refuge and an easy path for those fearful and halfhearted souls who instinctively shun the spirit struggles and mental uncertainties associated with those faith voyages of daring adventure out upon the high seas of unexplored truth in search for the farther shores of spiritual realities as they may be discovered by the progressive human mind and experienced by the evolving human soul." P. 1729.

3. Faith surmounts all obstacles.

"The God-knowing individual is not one who is blind to the difficulties or unmindful of the obstacles which stand in the way of finding God in the maze of superstition, tradition, and materialistic tendencies of modern times. He has encountered all these deterrents and triumphed over them, surmounted them by living faith, and attained the highlands of spiritual experience in spite of them. But it is true that many who are inwardly sure about God fear to assert such feelings of certainty because of the multiplicity and cleverness of those who assemble objections and magnify difficulties about believing in God. It requires no great depth of intellect to pick flaws, ask questions, or raise objections. But it does require brilliance of mind to answer these questions and solve these difficulties; faith certainty is the greatest technique for dealing with all such superficial contentions." P. 1126.

4. Faith functions in spite of doubts.

"When Jesus had listened to this recital, he touched the kneeling father and bade him rise while he gave the near-by apostles a searching survey. Then said Jesus to all those who stood before him: 'O faithless and perverse generation, how long shall I bear with you? How long shall I be with you? How long ere you learn that the works of faith come not forth at the bidding of doubting unbelief?' And then, pointing to the bewildered father, Jesus said, 'Bring hither your son.' And when James had brought the lad before Jesus, he asked, 'How long has the boy been afflicted in this way?' The father answered, 'Since he was a very young child.' And as they talked, the youth was seized with a violent attack and fell in their midst, gnashing his teeth and foaming at the mouth. After a succession of violent convulsions he lay there before them as one dead. Now did the father again kneel at Jesus' feet while he implored the Master, saying: 'If you can cure him, I beseech you to have compassion on us and deliver us from this affliction.' And when Jesus heard these words, he looked down into the father's anxious face, saying: 'Question not my Father's power of love, only the sincerity and reach of your faith. All things are possible to him who really believes.' And then James of Safed spoke those long-to-be-remembered words of commingled faith and doubt, 'Lord, I believe. I pray you help my unbelief.'" P. 1757. Mark 9:14-24.

VI. FAITH AND FEELING

1. Must have faith as well as feeling.

"But emotion alone is a false conversion; one must have faith as well as feeling. To the extent that such psychic mobilization is partial, and in so far as such human-loyalty motivation is incomplete, to that extent will the experience of conversion be a blended intellectual, emotional, and spiritual reality." P. 1099.

2. Faith leads to knowing God.

"Faith leads to knowing God, not merely to a mystical feeling of the divine presence. Faith must not be overmuch influenced by its emotional consequences. True religion is an experience of believing and knowing as well as a satisfaction of feeling." P. 1142.

3. Faith and insight vs. sight and feeling.

"Religion lives and prospers, then, not by sight and feeling, but rather by faith and insight. It consists not in the discovery of new facts or in the finding of a unique experience, but rather in the discovery of new and spiritual *meanings* in facts already well known to mankind. The highest religious experience is not dependent on prior acts of belief, tradition, and authority; neither is religion the offspring of sublime feelings and purely mystical emotions. It is, rather, a profoundly deep and actual experience of spiritual communion with the spirit influences resident within the human mind, and as far as such an experience is definable in terms of psychology, it is simply the experience of experiencing the reality of believing in God as the reality of such a purely personal experience." P. 1105.

4. **Faith and spiritual insight.**

"Scientists assemble facts, philosophers co-ordinate ideas, while prophets exalt ideals. Feeling and emotion are invariable concomitants of religion, but they are not religion. Religion may be the feeling of experience, but it is hardly the experience of feeling. Neither logic (rationalization) nor emotion (feeling) is essentially a part of religious experience, although both may variously be associated with the exercise of faith in the furtherance of spiritual insight into reality, all according to the status and temperamental tendency of the individual mind." P. 1110.

VII. FAITH AND EDUCATION—SCIENCE AND RELIGION

1. **Faith not dependent on learning.**

"The realization of religion never has been, and never will be, dependent on great learning or clever logic. It is spiritual insight, and that is just the reason why some of the world's greatest religious teachers, even the prophets, have sometimes possessed so little of the wisdom of the world. Religious faith is available alike to the learned and the unlearned." P. 1107.

2. **Faith independent of worldly wisdom.**

"Regarding the status of any religion in the evolutionary scale, it may best be judged by its moral judgments and its ethical standards. The higher the type of any religion, the more it encourages and is encouraged by a constantly improving social morality and ethical culture. We cannot judge religion by the status of its accompanying civilization; we had better estimate the real nature of a civilization by the purity and nobility of its religion. Many of the world's most notable religious teachers have been virtually unlettered. The wisdom of the world is not necessary to an exercise of saving faith in eternal realities." P. 1127.

3. **Faith certainty of God-knowing mortal.**

"If you truly believe in God—by faith know him and love him—do not permit the reality of such an experience to be in any way lessened or detracted from by the doubting insinuations of science, the caviling of logic, the postulates of philosophy, or the clever suggestions of well-meaning souls who would create a religion without God." P. 1140.

4. **Faith surmounts materialistic doubting.**

"The certainty of the God-knowing religionist should not be disturbed by the uncertainty of the doubting materialist; rather should the uncertainty of the unbeliever be mightily challenged by the profound faith and unshakable certainty of the experiential believer." P. 1140.

5. **Faith, reason, and wisdom.**

"When theology masters religion, religion dies; it becomes a doctrine instead of a life. The mission of theology is merely to facilitate the self-consciousness of personal spiritual experience. Theology constitutes the religious effort to define, clarify, expound, and justify the experiential claims of religion, which, in the last analysis, can be validated only by living faith. In the higher philosophy of the universe, wisdom, like reason, becomes allied to faith. Reason, wisdom, and faith are man's highest human attainments. Reason introduces man to the world of facts, to things; wisdom introduces him to a world of truth, to relationships; faith initiates him into a world of divinity, spiritual experience." P. 1141.

6. **Faith dares to adventure with truth.**

"Faith most willingly carries reason along as far as reason can go and then goes on with wisdom to the full philosophic limit; and then it dares to launch out upon the limitless and never-ending universe journey in the sole company of TRUTH." P. 1141.

7. **Faith as related to fundamental assumptions.**

"Science (knowledge) is founded on the inherent (adjutant spirit) assumption that reason is valid, that the universe can be comprehended. Philosophy (co-ordinate comprehension) is founded on the inherent (spirit of wisdom) assumption that wisdom is valid, that the material universe can be co-ordinated with the spiritual. Religion (the truth of personal spiritual experience) is founded on the inherent (Thought Adjuster) assumption that faith is valid, that God can be known and attained." P. 1141.

8. **Faith in relation to science and philosophy.**

"The highest attainable philosophy of mortal man must be logically based on the reason of science, the faith of religion, and the truth insight afforded by revelation. By this union man can compensate somewhat for his failure to develop an adequate metaphysics and for his inability to comprehend the mota of the morontia." P. 1137.

9. **Faith transcends science and philosophy.**

"Science is sustained by reason, religion by faith. Faith, though not predicated on reason, is reasonable; though independent of logic, it is nonetheless encouraged by sound logic. Faith cannot be nourished even by an ideal philosophy; indeed, it is, with science, the very source of such a philosophy. Faith, human religious insight, can be surely instructed only by revelation, can be surely elevated only by personal mortal experience with the spiritual Adjuster presence of the God who is spirit." P. 1137.

VIII. ABRAHAM'S FAITH

1. **Abraham's faith was counted for righteousness.**

"And Melchizedek made a formal covenant with Abraham at Salem. Said he to Abraham: 'Look now up to the heavens and number the stars if you are able; so numerous shall your seed be.' And Abraham believed Melchizedek, 'and it was counted to him for righteousness.' And then Melchizedek told Abraham the story of the future occupation of Canaan by his offspring after their sojourn in Egypt." P. 1020. Gen. 15:1-6.

2. **Terms of the Melchizedek covenant.**

"This covenant of Melchizedek with Abraham represents the great Urantian agreement between divinity and humanity whereby God agrees to do *everything*; man only agrees to *believe* God's promises and follow his instructions. Heretofore it had been believed that salvation could be secured only by works—sacrifices and offerings; now, Melchizedek again brought to Urantia the good news that salvation, favor with God, is to be had by *faith*. But this gospel of simple faith in God was too advanced; the Semitic tribesmen subsequently preferred to go back to the older sacrifices and atonement for sin by the shedding of blood." P. 1020-1. Gen. 15.

3. **Melchizedek teaches justification by faith.**

"And thus did Melchizedek prepare the way and set the monotheistic stage of world tendency for the bestowal of an actual Paradise Son of the one God, whom he so vividly portrayed as the Father of all, and whom he represented to Abraham as a God who would accept man on the simple terms of personal faith. And Michael, when he appeared on earth, confirmed all that Melchizedek had taught concerning the Paradise Father." P. 1017.

IX. SAVING FAITH—ASSURANCE

1. **"Your faith has saved you."**

"When Simon and his friends who sat at meat with him heard these words, they were the more astonished, and they began to whisper among themselves, 'Who is this man that he even dares to forgive sins?' And when Jesus heard them thus murmuring, he turned to dismiss the woman, saying, 'Woman, go in peace; your faith has saved you.'" P. 1652. Luke 7:50.

2. **Saving faith the gift of God.**

"Your sonship is grounded in faith, and you are to remain unmoved by fear. Your joy is born of trust in the divine word, and you shall not therefore be led to doubt the reality of the Father's love and mercy. It is the very goodness of God that leads men into true and genuine repentance. Your secret of the mastery of self is bound up with your faith in the indwelling spirit, which ever works by love. Even this saving faith you have not of yourselves; it also is the gift of God. And if you are the children of this living faith, you are no longer the bondslaves of self but rather the triumphant masters of yourselves, the liberated sons of God.'" P. 1610. Eph. 2:8.3.

3. **Salvation by faith.**

"One evening at Shunem, after John's apostles had returned to Hebron, and after Jesus' apostles had been sent out two and two, when the Master was engaged in teaching a group of twelve of the younger evangelists who were laboring under the direction of Jacob, together with the twelve women, Rachel asked Jesus this question: 'Master, what shall we answer when women ask us, What shall I do to be saved?' When Jesus heard this question, he answered:...

"'Salvation is the gift of the Father and is revealed by his Sons. Acceptance by faith on your part makes you a partaker of the divine nature, a son or a daughter of God. By faith you are justified; by faith are you saved; and by this same faith are you eternally advanced in the way of progressive and divine perfection. By faith was Abraham justified and made aware of salvation by the teachings of Melchizedek. All down through the ages has this same faith saved the sons of men, but now has a Son come forth from the Father to make salvation more real and acceptable.'" P. 1682-3.

4. **Despair dispelled by one brave stretch of faith.**

"To the unbelieving materialist, man is simply an evolutionary accident. His hopes of survival are strung on a figment of mortal imagination; his fears, loves, longings, and beliefs are but the reaction of the incidental juxtaposition of certain lifeless atoms of matter. No display of energy nor expression of trust can carry him beyond the grave. The devotional labors and inspirational genius of the best of men are doomed to be extinguished by death, the long and lonely night of eternal oblivion and soul extinction. Nameless despair is man's only reward for living and toiling under the temporal sun of mortal existence. Each day of life slowly and surely tightens the grasp of a pitiless doom which a hostile and relentless universe of matter has decreed shall be the crowning insult to everything in human desire which is beautiful, noble, lofty, and good.

"But such is not man's end and eternal destiny; such a vision is but the cry of despair uttered by some wandering soul who has become lost in spiritual darkness, and who bravely struggles on in the face of the mechanistic sophistries of a material philosophy, blinded by the confusion and distortion of a complex learning. And all this doom of darkness and all this destiny of despair are forever dispelled by one brave stretch of faith on the part of the most humble and unlearned of God's children on earth." P. 1118.

5. **The birth of saving faith.**

"This saving faith has its birth in the human heart when the moral consciousness of man realizes that human values may be translated in mortal experience from the material to the spiritual, from the human to the divine, from time to eternity." P. 1118.

6. **The evolution of faith.**

"The work of the Thought Adjuster constitutes the explanation of the translation of man's primitive and evolutionary sense of duty into that higher and more certain faith in the eternal realities of revelation. There must be perfection hunger in man's heart to insure capacity for comprehending the faith paths to supreme attainment. If any man chooses to do the divine will, he shall know the way of truth. It is literally true, 'Human things must be known in order to be loved, but divine things must be loved in order to be known.' But honest doubts and sincere questionings are not sin; such attitudes merely spell delay in the progressive journey toward perfection attainment. Childlike trust secures man's entrance into the kingdom of heavenly ascent, but progress is wholly dependent on the vigorous exercise of the robust and confident faith of the full-grown man." P. 1118.

7. Faith and reason in philosophy.

"Though reason can always question faith, faith can always supplement both reason and logic. Reason creates the probability which faith can transform into a moral certainty, even a spiritual experience. God is the first truth and the last fact; therefore does all truth take origin in him, while all facts exist relative to him. God is absolute truth. As truth one may know God, but to understand—to explain—God, one must explore the fact of the universe of universes. The vast gulf between the experience of the truth of God and ignorance as to the fact of God can be bridged only by living faith. Reason alone cannot achieve harmony between infinite truth and universal fact." P. 1125.

8. The thief on the cross.

"One of the brigands railed at Jesus, saying, 'If you are the Son of God, why do you not save yourself and us?' But when he had reproached Jesus, the other thief, who had many times heard the Master teach, said: 'Do you have no fear even of God? Do you not see that we are suffering justly for our deeds, but that this man suffers unjustly? Better that we should seek forgiveness for our sins and salvation for our souls.' When Jesus heard the thief say this, he turned his face toward him and smiled approvingly. When the malefactor saw the face of Jesus turned toward him, he mustered up his courage, fanned the flickering flame of his faith, and said, 'Lord, remember me when you come into your kingdom.' And then Jesus said, 'Verily, verily, I say to you today, you shall sometime be with me in Paradise.'" P. 2008-9. Luke 23:39-43.

X. SCOPE AND POTENTIALS OF FAITH

1. Faith makes secure in the kingdom.

"And then long into the night Jesus propounded to his apostles the truth that it was their faith that made them secure in the kingdom of the present and the future, and not their affliction of soul nor fasting of body. He exhorted the apostles at least to live up to the ideas of the prophet of old and expressed the hope that they would progress far beyond even the ideals of Isaiah and the older prophets. His last words that night were: 'Grow in grace by means of that living faith which grasps the fact that you are the sons of God while at the same time it recognizes every man as a brother.'" P. 1656.

2. **Dynamic religious faith.**

"The relation between the creature and the Creator is a living experience, a dynamic religious faith, which is not subject to precise definition. To isolate part of life and call it religion is to disintegrate life and to distort religion. And this is just why the God of worship claims all allegiance or none." P. 1124.

3. **Faith in a personal God of love.**

"The religionist of philosophic attainment has faith in a personal God of personal salvation, something more than a reality, a value, a level of achievement, an exalted process, a transmutation, the ultimate of time-space, an idealization, the personalization of energy, the entity of gravity, a human projection, the idealization of self, nature's upthrust, the inclination to goodness, the forward impulse of evolution, or a sublime hypothesis. The religionist has faith in a God of love. Love is the essence of religion and the wellspring of superior civilization." P. 1124.

4. **Faith creates a God of salvation.**

"Faith transforms the philosophic God of probability into the saving God of certainty in the personal religious experience. Skepticism may challenge the theories of theology, but confidence in the dependability of personal experience affirms the truth of that belief which has grown into faith." P. 1124.

5. **Faith dares to say "I know."**

"Convictions about God may be arrived at through wise reasoning, but the individual becomes God-knowing only by faith, through personal experience. In much that pertains to life, probability must be reckoned with, but when contacting with cosmic reality, certainty may be experienced when such meanings and values are approached by living faith. The God-knowing soul dares to say, 'I know,' even when this knowledge of God is questioned by the unbeliever who denies such certitude because it is not wholly supported by intellectual logic. To every such doubter the believer only replies, 'How do you know that I do not know?'" P. 1124-5.

6. **Faith discovers the God of certitude.**

"To science God is a possibility, to psychology a desirability, to philosophy a probability, to religion a certainty, an actuality of religious experience. Reason demands that a philosophy which cannot find the God of probability should be very respectful of that religious faith which can and does find the God of certitude.

Neither should science discount religious experience on grounds of credulity, not so long as it persists in the assumption that man's intellectual and philosophic endowments emerged from increasingly lesser intelligences the further back they go, finally taking origin in primitive life which was utterly devoid of all thinking and feeling." P. 1125.

7. Religious faith identifies man with the Infinite.

"Religion effectually cures man's sense of idealistic isolation or spiritual loneliness; it enfranchises the believer as a son of God, a citizen of a new and meaningful universe. Religion assures man that, in following the gleam of righteousness discernible in his soul, he is thereby identifying himself with the plan of the Infinite and the purpose of the Eternal. Such a liberated soul immediately begins to feel at home in this new universe, his universe." P. 1117.

8. Faith triumphs over all.

"When you experience such a transformation of faith, you are no longer a slavish part of the mathematical cosmos but rather a liberated volitional son of the Universal Father. No longer is such a liberated son fighting alone against the inexorable doom of the termination of temporal existence; no longer does he combat all nature, with the odds hopelessly against him; no longer is he staggered by the paralyzing fear that, perchance, he has put his trust in a hopeless phantasm or pinned his faith to a fanciful error.

"Now, rather, are the sons of God enlisted together in fighting the battle of reality's triumph over the partial shadows of existence. At last all creatures become conscious of the fact that God and all the divine hosts of a well-nigh limitless universe are on their side in the supernal struggle to attain eternity of life and divinity of status. Such faith-liberated sons have certainly enlisted in the struggles of time on the side of the supreme forces and divine personalities of eternity; even the stars in their courses are now doing battle for them; at last they gaze upon the universe from within, from God's viewpoint, and all is transformed from the uncertainties of material isolation to the sureties of eternal spiritual progression. Even time itself becomes but the shadow of eternity cast by Paradise realities upon the moving panoply of space." P. 1117.

9. Creative potential of faith.

"When my children once become self-conscious of the assurance of the divine presence, such a faith will expand the mind, ennoble the soul, reinforce the personality, augment the happiness, deepen the spirit perception, and enhance the power to love and be loved." P. 1766.

10. Faith releases the potentials of the "divine spark."

"Faith acts to release the superhuman activities of the divine spark, the immortal germ, that lives within the mind of man, and which is the potential of eternal survival. Plants and animals survive in time by the technique of passing on from one generation to another identical particles of themselves. The human soul (personality) of man survives mortal death by identity association with this indwelling spark of divinity, which is immortal, and which functions to perpetuate the human personality upon a continuing and higher level of progressive universe existence. The concealed seed of the human soul is an immortal spirit. The second generation of the soul is the first of a succession of personality manifestations of spiritual and progressing existences, terminating only when this divine entity attains the source of its existence, the personal source of all existence, God, the Universal Father." P. 1459.

XI. HEALING FAITH

1. Saving and healing faith.

"Then came forward Simon Zelotes to remonstrate with Norana. Said Simon: 'Woman, you are a Greek-speaking gentile. It is not right that you should expect the Master to take the bread intended for the children of the favored household and cast it to the dogs.' But Norana refused to take offense at Simon's thrust. She replied only: 'Yes, teacher, I understand your words. I am only a dog in the eyes of the Jews, but as concerns your Master, I am a believing dog. I am determined that he shall see my daughter, for I am persuaded that, if he shall but look upon her, he will heal her. And even you, my good man, would not dare to deprive the dogs of the privilege of obtaining the crumbs which chance to fall from the children's table.'

"At just this time the little girl was seized with a violent convulsion before them all, and the mother cried out: 'There, you can see that my child is possessed by an evil spirit. If our need does not impress you, it would appeal to your Master, who I have been told loves all men and dares even to heal the gentiles when they believe. You are not worthy to be his disciples. I will not go until my child has been cured.'

"Jesus, who had heard all of this conversation through an open window, now came outside, much to their surprise, and said: 'O woman, great is your faith, so great that I cannot withhold that which you desire; go your way in peace. Your daughter already has been made whole.' And the little girl was well from that hour. As Norana and the child took leave, Jesus entreated them to tell no one of this occurrence; and while his associates did comply with this request, the mother and the child ceased not to proclaim the fact of the little girl's healing throughout all the countryside and even in Sidon, so much so that Jesus found it advisable to change his lodgings within a few days." P. 1735. Mark 7:24-30.

2. Faith cures spirit of infirmity.

"Abner had arranged for the Master to teach in the synagogue on this Sabbath day, the first time Jesus had appeared in a synagogue since they had all been closed to his teachings by order of the Sanhedrin. At the conclusion of the service Jesus looked down before him upon an elderly woman who wore a downcast expression, and who was much bent in form. This woman had long been fear-ridden, and all joy had passed out of her life. As Jesus stepped down from the pulpit, he went over to her and, touching her bowed-over form on the shoulder, said: 'Woman, if you would only believe, you could be wholly loosed from your spirit of infirmity.' And this woman, who had been bowed down and bound up by the depressions of fear for more than eighteen years, believed the words of the Master and by faith straightened up immediately. When this woman saw that she had been made straight, she lifted up her voice and glorified God." P. 1835-6. Luke 13:10-19.

XII. SPIRIT CONSCIOUSNESS—FRUITS OF FAITH

1. Faith the validity of spirit consciousness.

"*Reason* is the act of recognizing the conclusions of consciousness with regard to the experience in and with the physical world of energy and matter. *Faith* is the act of recognizing the validity of spiritual consciousness—something which is incapable of other mortal proof. *Logic* is the synthetic truth-seeking progression of the unity of faith and reason and is founded on the constitutive mind endowments of mortal beings, the innate recognition of things, meanings, and values." P. 1139.

2. Faith consciousness of sonship.

"The gospel of the good news that mortal man may, by faith, become spirit conscious that he is a son of God, is not dependent on the death of Jesus. True, indeed, all this gospel of the kingdom has been tremendously illuminated by the Master's death, but even more so by his life." P. 2002.

3. The social faith fruits of the spirit.

"Belief may not be able to resist doubt and withstand fear, but faith is always triumphant over doubting, for faith is both positive and living. The positive always has the advantage over the negative, truth over error, experience over theory, spiritual realities over the isolated facts of time and space. The convincing evidence of this spiritual certainty consists in the social fruits of the spirit which such believers, faithers, yield as a result of this genuine spiritual experience. Said Jesus: 'If you love your fellows as I have loved you, then shall all men know that you are my disciples.'" P. 1125. John 13:35.

4. The amazing performances of faith.

"Through religious faith the soul of man reveals itself and demonstrates the potential divinity of its emerging nature by the characteristic manner in which it induces the mortal personality to react to certain trying intellectual and testing social situations. Genuine spiritual faith (true moral consciousness) is revealed in that it:

"1. Causes ethics and morals to progress despite inherent and adverse animalistic tendencies.

"2. Produces a sublime trust in the goodness of God even in the face of bitter disappointment and crushing defeat.

"3. Generates profound courage and confidence despite natural adversity and physical calamity.

"4. Exhibits inexplicable poise and sustaining tranquillity notwithstanding baffling diseases and even acute physical suffering.

"5. Maintains a mysterious poise and composure of personality in the face of maltreatment and the rankest injustice.

"6. Maintains a divine trust in ultimate victory in spite of the cruelties of seemingly blind fate and the apparent utter indifference of natural forces to human welfare.

"7. Persists in the unswerving belief in God despite all contrary demonstrations of logic and successfully withstands all other intellectual sophistries.

"8. Continues to exhibit undaunted faith in the soul's survival regardless of the deceptive teachings of false science and the persuasive delusions of unsound philosophy.

"9. Lives and triumphs irrespective of the crushing overload of the complex and partial civilizations of modern times.

"10. Contributes to the continued survival of altruism in spite of human selfishness, social antagonisms, industrial greeds, and political mal-adjustments.

"11. Steadfastly adheres to a sublime belief in universe unity and divine guidance regardless of the perplexing presence of evil and sin.

"12. Goes right on worshiping God in spite of anything and everything. Dares to declare, 'Even though he slay me, yet will I serve him.'" P. 1108. Job. 13:15.

XIII. DYNAMIC FAITH

1. Dynamic power of living faith.

"'But fear not; every one who sincerely desires to find eternal life by entrance into the kingdom of God shall certainly find such everlasting salvation. But you who refuse this salvation will some day see the prophets of the seed of Abraham sit down with the believers of the gentile nations in this glorified kingdom to partake of the bread of life and to refresh themselves with the water thereof. And they who shall thus take the kingdom in spiritual power and by the persistent assaults of living faith will come from the north and the south and from the east and the west. And, behold, many who are first will be last, and those who are last will many times be first.'" P. 1829. Luke 13:30.

2. Faith is the open door to God's love.

"Jesus made plain to his apostles the difference between the repentance of so-called good works as taught by the Jews and the change of mind by faith—the new birth—which he required as the price of admission to the kingdom. He taught his apostles that *faith* was the only requisite to entering the Father's kingdom. John had taught them 'repentance—to flee from the wrath to come.' Jesus taught, 'Faith is the open door for entering into the present, perfect, and eternal love of God.' Jesus did not speak like a prophet, one who comes to declare the word of God. He seemed to speak of himself as one having authority. Jesus sought to divert their minds from miracle seeking to the finding of a real and personal experience in the satisfaction and assurance of the indwelling of God's spirit of love and saving grace." P. 1545.

3. **By faith we become God-conscious.**

"'And now you should give ear to my words lest you again make the mistake of hearing my teaching with the mind while in your hearts you fail to comprehend the meaning. From the beginning of my sojourn as one of you, I taught you that my one purpose was to reveal my Father in heaven to his children on earth. I have lived the God-revealing bestowal that you might experience the God-knowing career. I have revealed God as your Father in heaven; I have revealed you as the sons of God on earth. It is a fact that God loves you, his sons. By faith in my word this fact becomes an eternal and living truth in your hearts. When, by living faith, you become divinely God-conscious, you are then born of the spirit as children of light and life, even the eternal life wherewith you shall ascend the universe of universes and attain the experience of finding God the Father on paradise.'" P. 2052

4. **Faith and the remembrance supper.**

"When Jesus had thus established the supper of the remembrance, he said to the twelve: 'And as often as you do this, do it in remembrance of me. And when you do remember me, first look back upon my life in the flesh, recall that I was once with you, and then, by faith, discern that you shall all some time sup with me in the Father's eternal kingdom. This is the new Passover which I leave with you, even the memory of my bestowal life, the word of eternal truth; and of my love for you, the outpouring of my Spirit of Truth upon all flesh.'" P. 1943. Luke 22:19,20.

5. **The perversions of faith.**

"And then Jesus discoursed on the dangers of courage and faith, how they sometimes lead unthinking souls on to recklessness and presumption. He also showed how prudence and discretion, when carried too far, lead to cowardice and failure. He exhorted his hearers to strive for originality while they shunned all tendency toward eccentricity. He pleaded for sympathy without sentimentality, piety without sanctimoniousness. He taught reverence free from fear and superstition." P. 1673.

XIV. FAITH AND VICTORY

1. **Faith—the victory over the world.**

"The consciousness of a victorious human life on earth is born of that creature faith which dares to challenge each recurring episode

of existence when confronted with the awful spectacle of human
limitations, by the unfailing declaration: Even if I cannot do this,
there lives in me one can and will do it, a part of the Father-
Absolute of the universe of universes. And that is 'the victory which
overcomes the world, even your faith.'" P. 59. 1 John 5:4.

2. The working of victorious faith.

"'The Supreme Spirit shall bear witness with your spirits that you
are truly the children of God. And if you are the sons of God, then
have you been born of the spirit of God; and whosoever has been
born of the spirit has in himself the power to overcome all doubt,
and this is the victory that overcomes all uncertainty, even your
faith.'" P. 1601. Rom. 8:16.

3. The assurance of everlasting life.

"'Said the Prophet Isaiah, speaking of these times: "When the spirit
is poured upon us from on high, then shall the work of righteous
ness become peace, quietness, and assurance forever." And for all
who truly believe this gospel, I will become surety for their
reception into the eternal mercies and the everlasting life of my
Father's kingdom. You, then, who hear this message and believe this
gospel of the kingdom are the sons of God, and you have life
everlasting; and the evidence to all the world that you have been
born of the spirit is that you sincerely love one another.'" P. 1601.
Isa. 32:15-17.

4. The transformations of faith.

"'This transformed woman whom some of you saw at Simon's
house today is, at this moment, living on a level which is vastly
below that of Simon and his well-meaning associates; but while
these Pharisees are occupied with the false progress of the illusion
of traversing deceptive circles of meaningless ceremonial services,
this woman has, in dead earnest, started out on the long and
eventful search for God, and her path toward heaven is not blocked
by spiritual pride and moral self-satisfaction. The woman is,
humanly speaking, much farther away from God than Simon, but
her soul is in progressive motion; she is on the way toward an
eternal goal. There are present in this woman tremendous spiritual
possibilities for the future. Some of you may not stand high in actual
levels of soul and spirit, but you are making daily progress on the
living way opened up, through faith, to God. There are tremendous
possibilities in each of you for the future. Better by far to have a

small but living and growing faith than to be possessed of a great intellect with its dead stores of worldly wisdom and spiritual unbelief.'" P. 1653. Luke 7:36-50.

5. **Faith wins perfection of purpose for ascenders.**

"Faith has won for the ascendant pilgrim a perfection of purpose which admits the children of time to the portals of eternity. Now must the pilgrim helpers begin the work of developing that perfection of understanding and that technique of comprehension which are so indispensable to Paradise perfection of personality." P. 290.

XV. THE FAITH OF JESUS

1. **Jesus' courage was born of faith.**

"His courage was magnificent, but he was never foolhardy. His watchword was, 'Fear not.' His bravery was lofty and his courage often heroic. But his courage was linked with discretion and controlled by reason. It was courage born of faith, not the recklessness of blind presumption. He was truly brave but never audacious." P. 1103.

2. **Jesus' faith was wholehearted.**

"Jesus enjoyed a sublime and wholehearted faith in God. He experienced the ordinary ups and downs of mortal existence, but he never religiously doubted the certainty of God's watchcare and guidance. His faith was the outgrowth of the insight born of the activity of the divine presence, his indwelling Adjuster. His faith was neither traditional nor merely intellectual; it was wholly personal and purely spiritual." P. 2087.

3. **Jesus' faith made God a living reality.**

"Jesus did not cling to faith in God as would a struggling soul at war with the universe and at death grips with a hostile and sinful world; he did not resort to faith merely as a consolation in the midst of difficulties or as a comfort in threatened despair; faith was not just an illusory compensation for the unpleasant realities and the sorrows of living. In the very face of all the natural difficulties and the temporal contradictions of mortal existence, he experienced the tranquillity of supreme and unquestioned trust in God and felt the tremendous thrill of living, by faith, in the very presence of the heavenly Father. And this triumphant faith was a living experience of actual spirit attainment. Jesus' great contribution to the values of human experience was not that he revealed so many new ideas about the Father in heaven, but rather that he so magnificently and humanly demonstrated a new and higher type of *living faith in God*. Never on all the worlds of this universe, in the life of any one mortal, did God ever become such a *living reality* as in the human experience of Jesus of Nazareth." P. 2087.

4. **The unique faith of Jesus.**

"Theology may fix, formulate, define, and dogmatize faith, but in the human life of Jesus faith was personal, living, original, spontaneous, and purely spiritual. This faith was not reverence for tradition nor a mere intellectual belief which he held as a sacred creed, but rather a sublime experience and a profound conviction which *securely held him*. His faith was so real and all-encompassing that it absolutely swept away any spiritual doubts and effectively destroyed every conflicting desire. Nothing was able to tear him away from the spiritual anchorage of this fervent, sublime, and undaunted faith. Even in the face of apparent defeat or in the throes of disappointment and threatening despair, he calmly stood in the divine presence free from fear and fully conscious of spiritual invincibility. Jesus enjoyed the invigorating assurance of the possession of unflinching faith, and in each of life's trying situations he unfailingly exhibited an unquestioning loyalty to the Father's will. And this superb faith was undaunted even by the cruel and crushing threat of an ignominious death." P. 2087-8.

5. **No fanaticism in Jesus' faith.**

"In a religious genius, strong spiritual faith so many times leads directly to disastrous fanaticism, to exaggeration of the religious ego, but it was not so with Jesus. He was not unfavorably affected in his practical life by his extraordinary faith and spirit attainment because this spiritual exaltation was a wholly unconscious and spontaneous soul expression of his personal experience with God." P. 2088.

6. **The faith of a unified personality.**

"The all-consuming and indomitable spiritual faith of Jesus never became fanatical, for it never attempted to run away with his well-balanced intellectual judgments concerning the proportional values of practical and commonplace social, economic, and moral life situations. The Son of Man was a splendidly unified human personality; he was a perfectly endowed divine being; he was also magnificently co-ordinated as a combined human and divine being functioning on earth as a single personality. Always did the Master co-ordinate the faith of the soul with the wisdom-appraisals of seasoned experience. Personal faith, spiritual hope, and moral devotion were always correlated in a matchless religious unity of harmonious association with the keen realization of the reality and sacredness of all human loyalties—personal honor, family love, religious obligation, social duty, and economic necessity." P. 2088.

7. **Jesus had a well balanced faith.**

"The faith of Jesus visualized all spirit values as being found in the kingdom of God; therefore he said, 'Seek first the kingdom of heaven.' Jesus saw in the advanced and ideal fellowship of the kingdom the achievement and fulfillment of the 'will of God.' The very heart of the prayer which he taught his disciples was, 'Your kingdom come; your will be done.' Having thus conceived of the kingdom as comprising the will of God, he devoted himself to the cause of its realization with amazing self-forgetfulness and un-bounded enthusiasm. But in all his intense mission and throughout his extraordinary life there never appeared the fury of the fanatic nor the superficial frothiness of the religious egotist." P. 2088.

8. **Jesus lived a faith-conditioned life.**

"The Master's entire life was consistently conditioned by this living faith, this sublime religious experience. This spiritual attitude wholly dominated his thinking and feeling, his believing and praying, his teaching and preaching. This personal faith of a son in the certainty and security of the guidance and protection of the heavenly Father imparted to his unique life a profound endowment of spiritual reality. And yet, despite this very deep consciousness of close relationship with divinity, this Galilean, God's Galilean, when addressed as Good Teacher, instantly replied, 'Why do you call me good?' When we stand confronted by such splendid self-forgetful-ness, we begin to understand how the Universal Father found it possible so fully to manifest himself to him and reveal himself through him to the mortals of the realms." P. 2088. Matt. 19:17.

9. **Jesus' faith was truly child-like.**

"The faith of Jesus attained the purity of a child's trust. His faith was so absolute and undoubting that it responded to the charm of the contact of fellow beings and to the wonders of the universe. His sense of dependence on the divine was so complete and so confident that it yielded the joy and the assurance of absolute personal security. There was no hesitating pretense in his religious experience. In this giant intellect of the full-grown man the faith of the child reigned supreme in all matters relating to the religious consciousness. It is not strange that he once said, 'Except you become as a little child, you shall not enter the kingdom.' Notwithstanding that Jesus' faith was *childlike*, it was in no sense *childish*." P. 2089.

10. **Jesus wants us to believe as he believed.**

"Jesus does not require his disciples to believe in him but rather to believe *with* him, believe in the reality of the love of God and in full confidence accept the security of the assurance of sonship with the heavenly Father. The Master desires that all his followers should fully share his transcendent faith. Jesus most touchingly challenged his followers, not only to believe *what* he believed, but also to believe *as* he believed. This is the full significance of his one supreme requirement, 'Follow me.'" P. 2089.

5. HOPE

Hope as Presented in the Bible.

Hope Among the Philosophers.

HOPE

I. THE SURE FOUNDATIONS OF OUR HOPE

1. Hope is the triumph of faith.

"Religion, the conviction-faith of the personality, can always triumph over the superficially contradictory logic of despair born in the unbelieving material mind. There really is a true and genuine inner voice, that 'true light which lights every man who comes into the world.' And this spirit leading is distinct from the ethical prompting of human conscience. The feeling of religious assurance is more than an emotional feeling. The assurance of religion transcends the reason of the mind, even the logic of philosophy. Religion *is* faith, trust, and assurance." P. 1104. John 1:9.

2. Hope is the fruit of personal experience.

"We cannot fully understand how God can be primal, changeless, all-powerful, and perfect, and at the same time be surrounded by an ever-changing and apparently law-limited universe, an evolving universe of relative imperfections. But we can *know* such a truth in our own personal experience since we all maintain identity of personality and unity of will in spite of the constant changing of both ourselves and our environment." P. 31.

3. The sure foundations of hope.

"It is because of this God fragment that indwells you that you can hope, as you progress in harmonizing with the Adjuster's spiritual leadings, more fully to discern the presence and transforming power of those other spiritual influences that surround you and impinge upon you but do not function as an integral part of you. The fact that you are not intellectually conscious of close and intimate contact with the indwelling Adjuster does not in the least disprove such an exalted experience. The proof of fraternity with the divine Adjuster consists wholly in the nature and extent of the fruits of the spirit which are yielded in the life experience of the individual believer. 'By their fruits you shall know them.'" P. 64-5. Matt. 7:20.

4. The basis of our hope.

"There is no limitation of the forces and personalities which the Father may use to uphold his purpose and sustain his creatures. 'The eternal God is our refuge, and underneath are the everlasting arms.'

'He who dwells in the secret place of the Most High shall abide under the shadow of the Almighty.' 'Behold, he who keeps us shall neither slumber nor sleep.' 'We know that all things work together for good to those who love God,' 'for the eyes of the Lord are over the righteous, and his ears are open to their prayers.'" P. 55. Deut. 33:27. Ps. 91:1; 121:3. Rom. 8:28. Ps. 34:15.

5. Faith grasps supermaterial realities.

"Although religious experience is a purely spiritual subjective phenomenon, such an experience embraces a positive and living faith attitude toward the highest realms of universe objective reality. The ideal of religious philosophy is such a faith-trust as would lead man unqualifiedly to depend upon the absolute love of the infinite Father of the universe of universes. Such a genuine religious experience far transcends the philosophic objectification of idealistic desire; it actually takes salvation for granted and concerns itself only with learning and doing the will of the Father in Paradise. The earmarks of such a religion are: faith in a supreme Deity, hope of eternal survival, and love, especially of one's fellows." P. 1141.

II. THE CERTAINTY OF OUR HOPE

1. The certainty of religious hope.

"The intellectual earmark of religion is certainty; the philosophical characteristic is consistency; the social fruits are love and service." P. 1126.

2. God-conscious mortal is sure of salvation.

"The God-conscious mortal is certain of salvation; he is unafraid of life; he is honest and consistent. He knows how bravely to endure unavoidable suffering; he is uncomplaining when faced by inescapable hardship.

"The true believer does not grow weary in well-doing just because he is thwarted. Difficulty whets the ardor of the truth lover, while obstacles only challenge the exertions of the undaunted kingdom builder." P. 1740.

3. The religious soul knows—and knows now.

"Time is an invariable element in the attainment of knowledge; religion makes its endowments immediately available, albeit there is the important factor of growth in grace, definite advancement in all phases of religious experience. Knowledge is an eternal quest; always are you learning, but never are you able to arrive at the full knowledge of absolute truth. In knowledge alone there can never be absolute certainty, only increasing probability of approximation; but the religious soul of spiritual illumination *knows*, and knows *now*. And yet this profound and positive certitude does not lead such a sound-minded religionist to take any less interest in the ups and downs of the progress of human wisdom, which is bound up on its material end with the developments of slow-moving science." P. 1120.

4.   Sublimity of the soul's trust.

"True religion is an insight into reality, the faith-child of the moral consciousness, and not a mere intellectual assent to any body of dogmatic doctrines. True religion consists in the experience that 'the Spirit itself bears witness with our spirit that we are the children of God.' Religion consists not in theologic propositions but in spiritual insight and the sublimity of the soul's trust." P. 1107. Rom. 8:16.

III. JESUS TAUGHT A GLORIOUS HOPE

1.   The sublime hope of Jesus' gospel.

"The teachings of Jesus constituted the first Urantian religion which so fully embraced a harmonious co-ordination of knowledge, wisdom, faith, truth, and love as completely and simultaneously to provide temporal tranquillity, intellectual certainty, moral enlightenment, philosophic stability, ethical sensitivity, God-consciousness, and the positive assurance of personal survival. The faith of Jesus pointed the way to finality of human salvation, to the ultimate of mortal universe attainment, since it provided for:

"1.   Salvation from material fetters in the personal realization of sonship with God, who is spirit.

"2.   Salvation from intellectual bondage: man shall know the truth, and the truth shall set him free.

"3.   Salvation from spiritual blindness, the human realization of the fraternity of mortal beings and the morontian awareness of the brotherhood of all universe creatures; the service-discovery of spiritual reality and the ministry-revelation of the goodness of spirit values.

"4.   Salvation from incompleteness of self through the attainment of the spirit levels of the universe and through the eventual realization of the harmony of Havona and the perfection of Paradise.

"5.   Salvation from self, deliverance from the limitations of self-consciousness through the attainment of the cosmic levels of the Supreme mind and by co-ordination with the attainments of all other self-conscious beings.

"6.   Salvation from time, the achievement of an eternal life of unending progression in God-recognition and God-service.

"7.   Salvation from the finite, the perfected oneness with Deity in and through the Supreme by which the creature attempts the transcendental discovery of the Ultimate on the postfinaliter levels of the absonite." P. 1112-13.

2.   Hope in the teachings of Jesus.

"It is just because the gospel of Jesus was so many-sided that within a few centuries students of the records of his teachings became divided up into so many cults and sects. This pitiful subdivision of Christian believers results from failure to discern in the Master's manifold teachings the divine oneness of his matchless life. But someday the true believers in Jesus will not be thus spiritually divided in their attitude before unbelievers. Always we may have diversity of intellectual comprehension and interpretation, even varying degrees of socialization, but lack of spiritual brotherhood is both inexcusable and reprehensible.

"Mistake not! there is in the teachings of Jesus an eternal nature which will not permit them forever to remain unfruitful in the hearts of thinking men. The kingdom as Jesus conceived it has to a large extent failed on earth; for the time being, an outward church has taken its place; but you should comprehend that this church is only the larval stage of the thwarted spiritual kingdom, which will carry it through this material age and over into a more spiritual dispensation where the Master's teachings may enjoy a fuller opportunity for development. Thus does the so-called Christian church become the cocoon in which the kingdom of Jesus' concept now slumbers. The kingdom of the divine brotherhood is still alive and will eventually and certainly come forth from this long submergence, just as surely as the butterfly eventually emerges as the beautiful unfolding of its less attractive creature of metamorphic development." P. 1866.

IV. HAPPINESS—THE FATHER'S OVERCARE

1.   Fundamentals of genuine hope.

"'Simon, some persons are naturally more happy than others. Much, very much, depends upon the willingness of man to be led and directed by the Father's spirit which lives within him. Have you not read in the Scriptures the words of the wise man, "The spirit of man is the candle of the Lord, searching all the inward parts"? And also that such spirit-led mortals say: "The lines are fallen to me in pleasant places; yes, I have a goodly heritage." "A little that a righteous man has is better than the riches of many wicked," for "a good man shall be satisfied from within himself." "A merry heart makes a cheerful countenance and is a continual feast. Better is a little with the reverence of the Lord than great treasure and trouble therewith. Better is a dinner of herbs where love is than a fatted ox and hatred therewith. Better is a little with righteousness than great revenues without rectitude." "A merry heart does good like a medicine." "Better is a handful with composure than a superabundance with sorrow and vexation of spirit."'" P. 1674. Prov. 20:27. Ps. 16:6; 37:16. Prov. 14:14; 15:13-17; 16:8; 17:22. Eccl. 4:6.

2. Seek true consolation.

"'Much of man's sorrow is born of the disappointment of his ambitions and the wounding of his pride. Although men owe a duty to themselves to make the best of their lives on earth, having thus sincerely exerted themselves, they should cheerfully accept their lot and exercise ingenuity in making the most of that which has fallen to their hands. All too many of man's troubles take origin in the fear soil of his own natural heart. "The wicked flee when no man pursues." "The wicked are like the troubled sea, for it cannot rest, but its waters cast up mire and dirt; there is no peace, says God, for the wicked."

"'Seek not, then, for false peace and transient joy but rather for the assurance of faith and the sureties of divine sonship which yield composure, contentment, and supreme joy in the spirit.'" P. 1674. Prov. 28:1. Isa. 57:20,21.

3. Hope based on the Father's overcare.

"'Consider the lilies, how they grow; they toil not, neither do they spin; yet I say to you, even Solomon in all his glory was not arrayed like one of these. If God so clothes the grass of the field, which is alive today and tomorrow is cut down and cast into the fire, how much more shall he clothe you, the ambassadors of the heavenly kingdom. O you of little faith! When you wholeheartedly devote yourselves to the proclamation of the gospel of the kingdom, you should not be of doubtful minds concerning the support of yourselves or the families you have forsaken. If you give your lives truly to the gospel, you shall live by the gospel. If you are only believing disciples, you must earn your own bread and contribute to the sustenance of all who teach and preach and heal. If you are anxious about your bread and water, wherein are you different from the nations of the world who so diligently seek such necessities? Devote yourselves to your work, believing that both the Father and I know that you have need of all these things. Let me assure you, once and for all, that, if you dedicate your lives to the work of the kingdom, all your real needs shall be supplied. Seek the greater thing, and the lesser will be found therein; ask for the heavenly, and the earthly shall be included. The shadow is certain to follow the substance.'" P. 1823. Luke 12:27,28.

HOPE AS PRESENTED IN THE BIBLE

1. **Our hope is in God.**

    "My hope is in thee." **Ps. 39:7**.

    "The eye of the Lord is on.... those who hope in his steadfast love." **Ps. 33:18**.

2. **We hope continually.**

    "But I will hope continually." **Ps. 71:14**.

3. **Hope in the word of God.**

    "I hope in thy word." **Ps. 119:81**.

4. **God is pleased by our hope.**

    "The Lord takes pleasure in ... those who hope in his steadfast love." **Ps. 147:11**.

5. **Hope brings joy and gladness.**

    "The hope of the righteous ends in gladness." **Prov. 10:28**.

    "May the God of hope fill you with all joy and peace." **Rom. 15:13**.

    "Rejoice in your hope, be patient in tribulation." **Rom. 12:12**.

6. **We are called to hope.**

    "That you may know what is the hope to which he has called you." **Eph. 1:18**.

7. **The strength of trust.**

    "In quietness and in trust shall be your strength." **Isa. 30:15**.

    "He who trusts in the Lord is safe." **Prov. 29:25**.

8. **We hope for eternal life.**

    "In hope of eternal life which God...promised ages ago." **Titus 1:2**.

"*And become heirs in hope of eternal life.*"**Titus 3:7**.

9. **Faith the assurance of things hoped for.**

    "*Now faith is the assurance of things hoped for.*" **Heb. 11:1**.

    "*So faith, hope, love abide.*" **1 Cor. 13:13**. (This is Paul's TRIAD - variously arranged.)

10. **Hope and supreme trust.**

    "*I will trust, and will not be afraid.*" **Isa. 12:2**.

    "*Commit your way to the Lord; trust in him, and he will act.*" **Ps. 37:5**.

11. **Hope is the ancestor of confidence.**

    "*And you will have confidence, because there is hope.*" **Job 11:18**.

12. **Hope in Christ.**

    "*This mystery, which is Christ in you, the hope of glory.*" **Col. 1:27**.

    "For in this hope we are saved." Rom. 8:24.

13. **Love hopes all things.**

    "*Love bears all things, believes all things, hopes all things, endures all things.*" **1 Cor. 13:7**.

14. **Hope and endurance.**

    "*Endurance produces character, and character produces hope.*" **Rom. 5:4**.

15. **Deferred hope.**

    "*Hope deferred makes the heart sick.*"**Prov. 13:12**.

Note: The rainbow was an Old Testament symbol of hope. In the Old Testament faith and hope are not well differentiated. Trust and confidence are used in place of hope.

HOPE AMONG THE PHILOSOPHERS

1. Zeus, mad at mankind, ordered Pandora to open up her box to pour all sorts of evil upon mortals. Among these evils were insect pests, but the last was hope.

2. These fatalistic philosophers looked upon hope as an illusion—an evil fiction.

3. Look at some Greek opinions:

    Aeschylus— "*The food of exiles.*"
    Euripides— "*Man's curse.*"
    Sophocles— "*We hate your filthy hope.*"

4. The Hebrews dared to entertain some small hopes for mankind. **See Ps. 4:2 and Isa. 40.**

5. Paul heroically rescued hope from these pessimistic fatalists when he declared—*"so faith, hope, love abide."* **(1 Cor. 13:13.)**

6. Later, Luther said: "Everything that is done in the world is done by hope."

7. Said Tennyson: "The mighty hopes that make us men."

8. But not all later philosophers caught Paul's inspiration. Note these sayings:

   a. **Cowley** (1647)— *"Hope—fortune's cheating lottery, where for one prize a hundred blanks there be."*

   b. **Shelley** (1819)— *"Worse than despair, worse than bitterness of death, is hope."*

   c. **Nietzsche** (1819)— *"Hope is the worst of evils, for it prolongs the torment of man."*

9. Hope is based on FAITH—it is more than optimism.

10. I have seen hope cure the incurable and keep the dying alive—even for days and weeks.

11. The Greeks were wrong. I would put Paul's Triad in this order— love, faith, and hope.

6. MINISTRY

Bible Teaching about Ministry

MINISTRY

I. INFINITE SPIRIT THE GOD OF MINISTRY

1. Minister of the Father's love and the Son's mercy.

"The Infinite Spirit, the Conjoint Creator, is a universal and divine minister. The Spirit unceasingly ministers the Son's mercy and the Father's love, even in harmony with the stable, unvarying, and righteous justice of the Paradise Trinity. His influence and personalities are ever near you; they really know and truly understand you." P. 98.

2. Infinite Spirit is the God of ministry.

"God is love, the Son is mercy, the Spirit is ministry—the ministry of divine love and endless mercy to all intelligent creation. The Spirit is the personification of the Father's love and the Son's mercy; in him are they eternally united for universal service. The Spirit is *love applied* to the creature creation, the combined love of the Father and the Son." P. 94.

3. Conjoint Creator is the universal mercy minister.

"The Conjoint Creator is truly and forever the great ministering personality, the universal mercy minister. To comprehend the ministry of the Spirit, ponder the truth that he is the combined portrayal of the Father's unending love and of the Son's eternal mercy. The Spirit's ministry is not, however, restricted solely to the representation of the Eternal Son and the Universal Father. The Infinite Spirit also possesses the power to minister to the creatures of the realm in his own name and right; the Third Person is of divine dignity and also bestows the universal ministry of mercy in his own behalf." P. 95.

4. Infinite Spirit is the universal mind minister.

"The unique feature of mind is that it can be bestowed upon such a wide range of life. Through his creative and creature associates the Third Source and Center ministers to all minds on all spheres. He ministers to human and subhuman intellect through the adjutants of the local universes and, through the agency of the physical controllers, ministers even to the lowest nonexperiencing entities of the most primitive types of living things. And always is the direction of mind a ministry of mind-spirit or mind-energy personalities." P. 103.

Note: Ministry is the measure of socialization—brotherhood attainment. God the Father is infinitely socialized.

II. MINISTRY OF THE PARADISE SONS

1. **The Paradise Sons are ministers of salvation.**

   "The Paradise Sons are the divine presentation of the acting natures of the three persons of Deity to the domains of time and space. The Creator, Magisterial, and Teacher Sons are the gifts of the eternal Deities to the children of men and to all other universe creatures of ascension potential. These Sons of God are the divine ministers who are unceasingly devoted to the work of helping the creatures of time attain the high spiritual goal of eternity." P. 232.

2. **The Paradise Sons are a revelation of Deity.**

   "In the local universes these orders of sonship collaborate to effect the revelation of the Deities of Paradise to the creatures of space: As the Father of a local universe, a Creator Son portrays the infinite character of the Universal Father. As the bestowal Sons of mercy, the Avonals reveal the matchless nature of the Eternal Son of infinite compassion. As the true teachers of ascending personalities, the Trinity Daynal Sons disclose the teacher personality of the Infinite Spirit. In their divinely perfect cooperation, Michaels, Avonals, and Daynals are contributing to the actualization and revelation of the personality and sovereignty of God the Supreme in and to the time-space universes. In the harmony of their triune activities these Paradise Sons of God ever function in the vanguard of the personalities of Deity as they follow the never-ending expansion of the divinity of the First Great Source and Center from the everlasting Isle of Paradise into the unknown depths of space." P. 233.

III. JESUS' LIFE OF MINISTRY

1. **Jesus came to minister.**

   "'And mark well my words: I have not come to call the righteous, but sinners. The Son of Man came not to be ministered to, but to minister and to bestow his life as the gift for all. I declare to you that I have come to seek and to save those who are lost.'" P. 1750. Matt. 9:13. Mark 10:45.

2. **Jesus went about doing good.**

   "He loved men as brothers, at the same time recognizing how they differed in innate endowments and acquired qualities. 'He went about doing good.'" P. 1102. Acts 10:38.

3. **Jesus' life was one of ministry.**

"But the Master was so reasonable, so approachable. He was so practical in all his ministry, while all his plans were characterized by such sanctified common sense. He was so free from all freakish, erratic, and eccentric tendencies. He was never capricious, whimsical, or hysterical. In all his teaching and in everything he did there was always an exquisite discrimination associated with an extraordinary sense of propriety." P. 1101.

4. **Jesus acts a parable of ministry.**

"'Do you really understand what I have done to you? You call me Master, and you say well, for so I am. If, then, the Master has washed your feet, why was it that you were unwilling to wash one another's feet? What lesson should you learn from this parable in which the Master so willingly does that service which his brethren were unwilling to do for one another? Verily, verily, I say to you: A servant is not greater than his master; neither is one who is sent greater than he who sends him. You have seen the way of service in my life among you, and blessed are you who will have the gracious courage so to serve. But why are you so slow to learn that the secret of greatness in the spiritual kingdom is not like the methods of power in the material world?'" P. 1939-40. John 13:5-17.

IV. MINISTRY OF THE LOCAL UNIVERSE MOTHER SPIRIT

1. **Ministry of Local Universe Mother Spirit.**

"Mortal man first experiences the ministry of the Spirit in conjunction with mind when the purely animal mind of evolutionary creatures develops reception capacity for the adjutants of worship and of wisdom. This ministry of the sixth and seventh adjutants indicates mind evolution crossing the threshold of spiritual ministry. And immediately are such minds of worship- and wisdom-function included in the spiritual circuits of the Divine Minister." P. 379.

2. **How the Universe Mother ministers.**

"As individuals you do not personally possess a segregated portion or entity of the spirit of the Creator Father-Son or the Creative Mother Spirit; these ministries do not contact with, nor indwell, the thinking centers of the individual's mind as do the Mystery Monitors. Thought Adjusters are definite individualizations of the prepersonal reality of the Universal Father, actually indwelling the mortal mind as a very part of that mind, and they ever work in perfect harmony with the combined spirits of the Creator Son and Creative Spirit." P. 379-80.

3. **The far-flung Spirit ministry.**

"From the heights of eternal glory the divine Spirit descends, by a long series of steps, to meet you as you are and where you are and then, in the partnership of faith, lovingly to embrace the soul of mortal origin and to embark on the sure and certain retracement of those steps of condescension, never stopping until the evolutionary soul is safely exalted to the very heights of bliss from which the divine Spirit originally sallied forth on this mission of mercy and ministry." P. 380.

4. **The adjutant mind-spirits.**

"The seven adjutant mind-spirits are called by names which are the equivalents of the following designations: intuition, understanding, courage, knowledge, counsel, worship, and wisdom. These mind-spirits send forth their influence into all the inhabited worlds as a differential urge, each seeking receptivity capacity for manifestation quite apart from the degree to which its fellows may find reception and opportunity for function." P. 401. Isa. 11:2,3. Rev. 1:4.

V. THE HOST OF MINISTERING SPIRITS

1. **Spirit beings the living ladder to glory.**

"The spirit personalities of the vast family of the Divine and Infinite Spirit are forever dedicated to the service of the ministry of the love of God and the mercy of the Son to all the intelligent creatures of the evolutionary worlds of time and space. These spirit beings constitute the living ladder whereby mortal man climbs from chaos to glory." P. 107. Gen. 28:12. Heb. 1:14.

2. **Tireless celestial ministers.**

"As man learns more of the loving and tireless ministry of the lower orders of the creature family of this Infinite Spirit, he will all the more admire and adore the transcendent nature and matchless character of this combined Action of the Universal Father and the Eternal Son. Indeed is this Spirit the eyes of the Lord which are ever over the righteous' and 'the divine ears which are ever open to their prayers.'" P. 95. Ps. 34:15.

3. **Hammers of suffering wielded by children of mercy.**

"In addition to this supercontrol of energy and things physical, the Infinite Spirit is superbly endowed with those attributes of patience, mercy, and love which are so exquisitely revealed in his spiritual ministry. The Spirit is supremely competent to minister love and to overshadow justice with mercy. God the Spirit possesses all the supernal kindness and merciful affection of the Original and Eternal Son. The universe of your origin is being forged out between the anvil of justice and the hammer of suffering; but those who wield the hammer are the children of mercy, the spirit offspring of the Infinite Spirit." P. 100.

VI. HUMAN MINISTERS

1. **True religion leads to social service.**

"But true religion is a living love, a life of service. The religionist's detachment from much that is purely temporal and trivial never leads to social isolation, and it should not destroy the sense of humor. Genuine religion takes nothing away from human existence, but it does add new meanings to all of life; it generates new types of enthusiasm, zeal, and courage. It may even engender the spirit of the crusader, which is more than dangerous if not controlled by spiritual insight and loyal devotion to the commonplace social obligations of human loyalties." P. 1100-1.

2. **To be great you must minister.**

"'Whosoever would become great in my Father's kingdom shall become a minister to all; and whosoever would be first among you, let him become the server of his brethren. But when you are once truly received as citizens in the heavenly kingdom, you are no longer servants but sons, sons of the living God. And so shall this kingdom progress in the world until it shall break down every barrier and bring all men to know my Father and believe in the saving truth which I have come to declare. Even now is the kingdom at hand, and some of you will not die until you have seen the reign of God come in great power.'" P. 1569. Matt. 20:25,26.

3. **Jesus gives the new commandment.**

"After a few moments of informal conversation, Jesus stood up and said: "When I enacted for you a parable indicating how you should be willing to serve one another, I said that I desired to give you a new commandment; and I would do this now as I am about to leave you. You well know the commandment which directs that you love one another; that you love your neighbor even as yourself. But I am not wholly satisfied with even that sincere devotion on the part of my children. I would have you perform still greater acts of love in the kingdom of the believing brotherhood. And so I give you this new commandment: That you love one another even as I have loved you. And by this will all men know that you are my disciples if you thus love one another.'" P. 1944. John 13:34,35.

4. The supreme measure of affection.

"'When I give you this new commandment, I do not place any new burden upon your souls; rather do I bring you new joy and make it possible for you to experience new pleasure in knowing the delights of the bestowal of your heart's affection upon your fellow men. I am about to experience the supreme joy, even though enduring outward sorrow, in the bestowal of my affection upon you and your fellow mortals.

"'When I invite you to love one another, even as I have loved you, I hold up before you the supreme measure of true affection, for greater love can no man have than this: that he will lay down his life for his friends. And you are my friends; you will continue to be my friends if you are but willing to do what I have taught you. You have called me Master, but I do not call you servants. If you will only love one another as I am loving you, you shall be my friends, and I will ever speak to you of that which the Father reveals to me.'" P. 1944-5.

5. Sharing the master's service.

"'You have not merely chosen me, but I have also chosen you, and I have ordained you to go forth into the world to yield the fruit of loving service to your fellows even as I have lived among you and revealed the Father to you. The Father and I will both work with you, and you shall experience the divine fullness of joy if you will only obey my command to love one another, even as I have loved you.'

"If you would share the Master's joy, you must share his love. And to share his love means that you have shared his service. Such an experience of love does not deliver you from the difficulties of this world; it does not create a new world, but it most certainly does make the old world new." P. 1945.

BIBLE TEACHING ABOUT MINISTRY
I. MINISTRY IN THE OLD TESTAMENT

The Old Testament recognized as ministers only priests and prophets. The priesthood was divided into *priests*—the sons of Aaron—and *Levites*—the other members of the tribe of Levi.

1. **PRIESTS** (*Sons of Aaron.*)

   "And put upon Aaron the holy garments, and you shall anoint him and consecrate him that he may serve me as a priest." **Ex. 40:13**.

2. **LEVITES** (*Servants of the priests.*)

   "But appoint the Levites over the tabernacle of the testimony, and over all its furnishings, ...they are to carry the tabernacle....and they shall tend it." **Num. 1:50**.

   "And the priest....shall be with the Levites when the Levites receive the tithes." **Neh. 10:38**.

II.   MINISTRY IN THE NEW TESTAMENT

In the New Testament all believers are reckoned as priests.

"But you are a chosen race, a royal priesthood, a holy nation, God's own people." 1 **Pet. 2:9**.

"And made us a kingdom, priests to his God and Father." **Rev. 1:6**.

The New Testament recognizes many groups of ministers.

1. **APOSTLES**

   "And his gifts were that some should be apostles, some prophets, some evangelists, some pastors and teachers....for the work of the ministry." **Eph. 4:11,12**.

   "I, Paul,..... called to be an apostle." **Rom. 1:1**.

   Referring to Barnabas, "But the people of the city were divided, some sided with the Jews, and some with the apostles." **Acts 14:4**.

   Referring to James, the Lord's brother, "But I saw none of the other apostles except James the Lord's brother." **Gal. 1:19**.

   Referring to Andronicus and Junias, "Greet Andronicus and Junias, my kinsmen and my fellow prisoners; they are men of note among the apostles." **Rom. 16:7**.

2. **PROPHETS**

   "Now in these days prophets came down from Jerusalem to Antioch." **Acts 11:27**.

   "And Judas and Silas, who were themselves prophets, exhorted the brethren with many words." **Acts 15:32**.

   "And there was a prophetess Anna, the daughter of Phanuel." **Luke 2:36**.

Speaking of John the Baptist, *"And through he wanted to put him to death, he feared the people, because they held him to be a prophet."* **Matt. 14:5.**

3. *EVANGELISTS (The Seventy.)*

    "On the morrow we departed and came to Caesarea; and we entered the house of Philip the evangelist." **Acts 21:8.**

    "As for you....do the work of an evangelist, fulfil your ministry." **2 Tim. 4:5.**

    (**Note:** Timothy was first a traveling evangelist—afterward he became a settled pastor.)

4. *TEACHERS*

    "Now in the church at Antioch there were prophets and teachers." **Acts 13:1.**

5. *PASTORS* (**Eph. 4:11.**)

    (Bear in mind that pastor, bishop, elder, presbyter, and overseer are many times used interchangeably. They were all administrators.)

    a. *Bishops*
        "To all the saints in Christ Jesus who are at Philipi, with the bishops and deacons." **Phil. 1:1.** (Marginal reading for bishops is over-seers.)
        "Now a bishop must be above reproach, married only once, temperate, sensible, dignified, hospitable, an apt teacher, no drunkard, not violent but gentle, not quarrelsome, and no lover of money. He must manage his own household well, keeping his children submissive and respectful in every way." **1 Tim. 3:2-4.**
        On ordaining Titus a bishop: *"For a bishop, as God's steward, must be blameless; he must not be arrogant or quick-tempered or a drunkard or violent or greedy for gain, but hospitable, a lover of goodness, master of himself, upright, holy, and self-controlled."* **Titus 1:7,8.**

    b. *Elders*
        "That you might....appoint elders in every town as I directed you, men who are blameless, married only once, whose children are believers and not open to the charge of being profligate or insubordinate." **Titus 1:5,6.**
        "On the following day Paul went in with us to James; and all the elders were present." **Acts 21:18.**
        Speaking to Timothy, *"Do not neglect the gift you have, which was given you by prophetic utterance when the elders laid their hands upon you."* **1 Tim. 4:14.**

"Let the elders who rule well be considered worthy of double honor, especially those who labor in preaching and teaching." **1 Tim. 5:17.**

"Is any among you sick? Let him call for the elders of the church, and let them pray over him, anointing him with oil in the name of the Lord." **Jas. 5:14.**

c. **Presbyters**

1 **Tim. 4:14** uses the term presbytery in place of elders in the King James Version.

d. **Overseers**

"Take heed to yourselves and to all the flock, in which the Holy Spirit has made you guardians, to feed the church of the Lord." **Acts 20:28.**

(**Note**: Guardians is rendered overseers in the King James Version.)

6. **DEACONS AND DEACONESSES Supervisors of finances and all types of social service.**

"Deacons likewise must be serious, not double-tongued, nor addicted to much wine, nor greedy for gain; they must hold the mystery of the faith with a clear conscience." **1 Tim. 3:8.**

"For those who serve well as deacons gain a good standing for themselves and also great confidence in the faith." **1 Tim. 3:13.**

"I commend you to our sister Phoebe, a deaconess of the church at Cenchreae." **Rom. 16:1.**

"The women likewise must be serious, no slanderers, but temperate, faithful in all things." **1 Tim. 3:11.**

III. JESUS' EARTHLY MINISTRY

1. **To preach the gospel—to establish the new and living way—to proclaim the kingdom of heaven, the Fatherhood of God and the brotherhood of men—to heal sick minds and bodies.**

"And he went about all Galilee.... preaching the gospel of the kingdom and healing every disease and every infirmity among the people." **Matt. 4:23.**

"From that time Jesus began to preach, saying, 'Repent, for the kingdom of heaven is at hand.'" **Matt. 4:17.**

(**Note**: Called kingdom of God in other gospels.)

"The new and living way which he opened up for us." **Heb. 10:20.**

2. **To proclaim man's sonship with God.**

"So that you may be sons of your Father who is in heaven." **Matt. 5:45**.

"Your reward will be great, and you will be the sons of the Most High." **Luke 6:35**.

"But to all who received him....he gave power to become children of God." **John 1:12**.

3. **To save sinners.**

"Jesus said to them, 'Those who are well have no need of a physician, but those who are sick; I come not to call the righteous, but sinners.'" **Mark 2:17**.

4. **He came to serve mankind.**

He went about doing good.

"I am among you as one who serves." **Luke 22:27**.

"The Son of man came not to be served but to serve." **Matt. 20:28**.

"Whoever would be great among you must be your servant." **Matt. 20:26**.

"How he went about doing good and healing all that were oppressed." **Acts 10:38**.

5. **To reveal the Father and do his will.**

"And no one knows the Father except the Son and any one to whom the Son chooses to reveal him." **Matt. 11:27**.

"I can do nothing on my own authority....because I seek not my own will but the will of him who sent me." **John 5:30**.

"For I have come down from heaven, not to do my own will, but the will of him who sent me." **John 6:38**.

IV. ANGELIC MINISTRY

"For he will give his angels charge of you to guard you in all your ways." **Ps.91:11**.

"Are they not all ministering spirits sent forth to serve, for the sake of those who are to obtain salvation?" **Heb. 1:14**.

"Who makest the winds thy messengers, fire and flame thy ministers." **Ps. 104:4**.

See Heb. 1:7. *"Of the angels he says, 'who makes his angels winds, and his servants flames of fire.'"*

"And behold, angels came and ministered to him." **Matt. 4:11**.

"And there appeared to him an angel from heaven, strengthening him." **Luke 22:43**.

"The poor man died and was carried by the angels to Abraham's bosom." **Luke 16:22**.

> **Note**: Speaking of the work of the guardian angel after death, *The Urantia Book* says: Page 1246. Par. 6. "Upon your death, your records, identity specifications, and the morontia entity of the human soul—conjointly evolved by the ministry of mortal mind and the divine Adjuster—are faithfully conserved by the destiny guardian together with all other values related to your future existence, everything that constitutes you, the real you...."

V. HUMAN MINISTRY

"Of this gospel I was made a minister according to the gift of God's grace which was given me by the working of his power." **Eph. 3:7**.

"For I have appeared to you for this purpose, to appoint you to serve and bear witness to the things in which you have seen me." **Acts 26:16**.

"We will devote ourselves to prayer and to the ministry of the word." **Acts 6:4**.

"To be a minister of Christ Jesus to the Gentiles in the priestly service of the gospel of God." **Rom. 15:16**.

"I say to you, whoever gives you a cup of water to drink because you bear the name of Christ, will by no means lose his reward." **Mark 9:41**.

"And whoever would be first among you must be slave of all." **Mark 10:44**.

"If any one would be first, he must be last of all and servant of all." **Mark 9:35**.

"I was sick and you visited me, I was in prison and you came to me....as you did it to one of the least of these my brethren, you did it to me." **Matt. 25:36,40**.

"Go into all the world, and preach the gospel to the whole creation." **Mark 16:15**.

THE GOLDEN RULE

7. PRAYER

BIBLE TEACHING ABOUT PRAYER

PRAYER

I. THE EVOLUTION OF PRAYER

1. The evolution of prayer.

"Prayer, as an agency of religion, evolved from previous nonreligious monologue and dialogue expressions. With the attainment of self-consciousness by primitive man there occurred the inevitable corollary of other-consciousness, the dual potential of social response and God recognition.

"The earliest prayer forms were not addressed to Deity. These expressions were much like what you would say to a friend as you entered upon some important undertaking. "Wish me luck.' Primitive man was enslaved to magic; luck, good and bad, entered into all the affairs of life. At first, these luck petitions were monologues—just a kind of thinking out loud by the magic server. Next, these believers in luck would enlist the support of their friends, and families, and presently some form of ceremony would be performed which included the whole clan or tribe.

"When the concepts of ghosts and spirits evolved, these petitions became superhuman in address, and with the consciousness of gods, such expressions attained to the levels of genuine prayer. As an illustration of this, among certain Australian tribes primitive religious prayers antedated their belief in spirits and superhuman personalities." P. 994.

2. First prayers were verbalized wishes.

"The first prayers were merely verbalized wishes, the expression of sincere desires. Prayer next became a technique of achieving spirit co-operation. And then it attained to the higher function of assisting religion in the conservation of all worth-while values." P. 995.

3. Bargaining with God.

"Primitive forms of prayer were nothing more nor less than bargaining with the spirits, an argument with the gods. It was a kind of bartering in which pleading and persuasion were substituted for something more tangible and costly. The developing commerce of the races had inculcated the spirit of trade and had developed the shrewdness of barter; and now these traits began to appear in man's worship methods. And as some men were better traders than others, so some were regarded as better prayers than others. The prayer of a just man was held in high esteem. A just man was one who had paid all accounts to the spirits, had fully discharged every ritual obligation to the gods." P. 983.

4. Primitive concepts of prayer.

"Religion and its agencies, the chief of which is prayer, are allied only with those values which have general social recognition, group approval. Therefore, when primitive man attempted to gratify his baser emotions or to achieve unmitigated selfish ambitions, he was deprived of the consolation of religion and the assistance of prayer. If the individual sought to accomplish anything antisocial, he was obliged to seek the aid of non-religious magic, resort to sorcerers, and thus be deprived of the assistance of prayer. Prayer, therefore, very early became a mighty promoter of social evolution, moral progress, and spiritual attainment." P. 995.

5. Prayer a part of evolving religion.

"During the earlier times of racial evolution and even at the present time, in the day-by-day experience of the average mortal, prayer is very much a phenomenon of man's intercourse with his own subconscious. But there is also a domain of prayer wherein the intellectually alert and spiritually progressing individual attains more or less contact with the superconscious levels of the human mind, the domain of the indwelling Thought Adjuster. In addition, there is a definite spiritual phase of true prayer which concerns its reception and recognition by the spiritual forces of the universe, and which is entirely distinct from all human and intellectual association." P. 996.

6. Prayer in relation to the ego.

"As it is conceived by successive generations of praying mortals, the alter ego evolves up through ghosts, fetishes, and spirits to polytheistic gods, and eventually to the One God, a divine being embodying the highest ideals and the loftiest aspirations of the praying ego. And thus does prayer function as the most potent agency of religion in the conservation of the highest values and ideals of those who pray. From the moment of the conceiving of an alter ego to the appearance of the concept of a divine and heavenly Father, prayer is always a socializing, moralizing, and spiritualizing practice.

"The simple prayer of faith evidences a mighty evolution in human experience whereby the ancient conversations with the fictitious symbol of the alter ego of primitive religion have become exalted to the level of communion with the spirit of the Infinite and to that of a bona fide consciousness of the reality of the eternal God and Paradise Father of all intelligent creation." P. 997.

7. **Sundry aspects of prayer.**

    "When man learned that prayer could not coerce the gods, then it became more of a petition, favor seeking. But the truest prayer is in reality a communion between man and his Maker.

    "The appearance of the sacrifice idea in any religion unfailingly detracts from the higher efficacy of true prayer in that men seek to substitute the offerings of material possessions for the offering of their own consecrated wills in the doing of the will of God.

    "When religion is divested of a personal God, its prayers translate to the levels of theology and philosophy. When the highest God concept of a religion is that of an impersonal Deity, such as in pantheistic idealism, although affording the basis for certain forms of mystic communion, it proves fatal to the potency of true prayer, which always stands for man's communion with a personal and superior being." P. 996.

II. THE FUNCTION OF PRAYER

1. **Prayer factor in spiritual progress.**

    "Prayer has been an indispensable factor in the progress and preservation of religious civilization, and it still has mighty contributions to make to the further enhancement and spiritualization of society if those who pray will only do so in the light of scientific facts, philosophic wisdom, intellectual sincerity, and spiritual faith. Pray as Jesus taught his disciples—honestly, unselfishly, with fairness, and without doubting." P. 999.

2. **The province of prayer.**

    "Prayer, unless in liaison with the will and actions of the personal spiritual forces and material supervisors of a realm, can have no direct effect upon one's physical environment. While there is a very definite limit to the province of the petitions of prayer, such limits do not equally apply to the *faith* of those who pray.

    "Prayer is not a technique for curing real and organic diseases, but it has contributed enormously to the enjoyment of abundant health and to the cure of numerous mental, emotional, and nervous ailments. And even in actual bacterial disease, prayer has many times added to the efficacy of other remedial procedures. Prayer has turned many an irritable and complaining invalid into a paragon of patience and made him an inspiration to all other human sufferers." P. 999.

3. The mission of prayer.

"Prayer is an antidote for harmful introspection. At least, prayer as the Master taught it is such a beneficent ministry to the soul. Jesus consistly employed the beneficial influence of praying for one's fellows. The Master usually prayed in the plural, not in the singular. Only in the great crises of his earth life did Jesus ever pray for himself.

"Prayer is the breath of the spirit life in the midst of the material civilization of the races of mankind. Worship is salvation for the pleasure-seeking generations of mortals.

"As prayer may be likened to recharging the spiritual batteries of the soul, so worship may be compared to the act of tuning in the soul to catch the universe broadcasts of the infinite spirit of the Universal Father. "Prayer is the sincere and longing look of the child to its spirit Father; it is a psychologic process of exchanging the human will for the divine will. Prayer is a part of the divine plan for making over that which is into that which ought to be." P. 1621.

4. Even futile prayers expand the soul.

"The earnest and longing repetition of any petition, when such a prayer is the sincere expression of a child of God and is uttered in faith, no matter how ill-advised or impossible of direct answer, never fails to expand the soul's capacity for spiritual receptivity." P. 1621.

5. Prayer prevents isolation of personality.

"Prayer contributes greatly to the development of the religious sentiment of an evolving human mind. It is a mighty influence working to prevent isolation of personality.

"Prayer represents one technique associated with the natural religions of racial evolution which also forms a part of the experiential values of the higher religions of ethical excellence, the religions of revelation." P. 996.

6. Twofold functional aspects of prayer.

"Prayer ever has been and ever will be a twofold human experience: a psychologic procedure interassociated with a spiritual technique. And these two functions of prayer can never be fully seperated.

"Enlightened prayer must recognize not only an external and personal God but also an internal and impersonal Divinity, the indwelling Adjuster. It is altogether fitting that man, when he prays, should strive to grasp the concept of the Universal Father on Paradise; but the more effective technique for most practical purposes will be to revert to the concept of a near-by alter ego, just as the primitive mind was wont to do, and then to recognize that the idea of this alter ego has evolved from a mere fiction to the truth of God's indwelling mortal man in the factual presence of the Adjuster so that man can talk face to face, as it were, with a real and genuine and divine alter ego that indwells him and is the very presence and essence of the living God, the Universal Father." P. 997.

III. ETHICAL PRAYING

1. **Unselfish and non-materialistic praying.**

   "No prayer can be ethical when the petitioner seeks for selfish advantage over his fellows. Selfish and materialistic praying is incompatible with the ethical religions which are predicated on unselfish and divine love. All such unethical praying reverts to the primitive levels of pseudo magic and is unworthy of advancing civilizations and enlightened religions. Selfish praying transgresses the spirit of all ethics founded on loving justice." P. 997.

2. **Praying in all fairness.**

   "In all your praying be *fair*; do not expect God to show partiality, to love you more than his other children, your friends, neighbors, even enemies. But the prayer of the natural or evolved religions is not at first ethical, as it is in the later revealed religions. All praying, whether individual or communal, may be either egoistic or altruistic. That is, the prayer may be centered upon the self or upon others. When the prayer seeks nothing for the one who prays nor anything for his fellows, then such attitudes of the soul tend to the levels of true worship. Egoistic prayers involve confessions and petitions and often consist in requests for material favors. Prayer is somewhat more ethical when it deals with forgiveness and seeks wisdom for enhanced self-control." P. 998.

3. **Ethical prayers elevate the ego.**

   "Aside from all that is superself in the experience of praying, it should be remembered that ethical prayer is a splendid way to elevate one's ego and reinforce the self for better living and higher attainment. Prayer induces the human ego to look both ways for help: for material aid to the subconscious reservoir of mortal experience, for inspiration and guidance to the superconscious borders of the contact of the material with the spiritual, with the Mystery Monitor." P. 997.

IV. CONDITIONS OF EFFECTIVE PRAYER

"If you would engage in effective praying, you should bear in mind the laws of prevailing petitions:

"1. You must qualify as a potent prayer by sincerely and couragiously facing the problems of universe reality. You must possess cosmic stamina.

"2. You must have honestly exhausted the human capacity for human adjustment. You must have been industrious.

"3. You must surrender every wish of mind and every craving of soul to the transforming embrace of spiritual growth. You must have experienced an enhancement of meanings and an elevation of values.

"4. You must make a wholehearted choice of the divine will. You must obliterate the dead center of indecision.

"5. You not only recognize the Father's will and choose to do it, but you have effected an unqualified consecration, and a dynamic dedication, to the actual doing of the Father's will.

"6. Your prayer will be directed exclusively for divine wisdom to solve the specific human problems encountered in the Paradise ascension—the attainment of divine perfection.

"7. And you must have faith—living faith." P. 1002.

V. ANSWERS TO PRAYER

1. **Prayer transmission to the Father.**

    "The spirit-gravity circuit is the basic channel for transmitting the genuine prayers of the believing human heart from the level of human consciousness to the actual consciousness of the Deity. That which represents true spiritual value in your petitions will be seized by the universal circuit of spirit gravity and will pass immediately and simultaneously to all divine personalities concerned. Each will occupy himself with that which belongs to his personal province. Therefore, in your practical religious experience, it is immaterial whether, in addressing your supplications, you visualize the Creator

Son of your local universe or the Eternal Son at the center of all things.

"The discriminative operation of the spirit-gravity circuit might possibly be compared to the functions of the neural circuits in the material human body: Sensations travel inward over the neural paths; some are detained and responded to by the lower automatic spinal centers; others pass on to the less automatic but habit-trained centers of the lower brain, while the most important and vital incoming messages flash by these subordinate centers and are immediately registered in the highest levels of human consciousness.

"But how much more perfect is the superb technique of the spiritual world! If anything originates in your consciousness that is fraught with supreme spiritual value, when once you give it expression, no power in the universe can prevent its flashing directly to the Absolute Spirit Personality of all creation." P. 84.

2. Persist in seeking the answer.

"'Prayer is the breath of the soul and should lead you to be persistent in your attempt to ascertain the Father's will. If any one of you has a neighbour, and you go to him at midnight and say: "Friend, lend me three leaves, for a friend of mine on a journey has come to see me, and I have nothing to set before him"; and if your neighbour answers, "Trouble me not, for the door is now shut and the children and I are in bed; therefore I cannot rise and give you bread," you will persist, explaining that your friend hungers, and that you have no food to offer him. I say to you, though your neighbour will not rise and give you bread because he is your friend, yet because of your importunity he will get up and give you as many loaves as you need. If, then, persistence will win favors even from mortal man, how much more will your persistence in the spirit win the bread of life for you from the willing hands of the Father in heaven. Again I say to you: Ask and it shall be given you; seek and you shall find; knock and it shall be opened to you. For every one who asks receives; he who seeks finds; and to him who knocks the door of salvation will be opened.

"'Which of you who is a father, if his son asks unwisely, would hesitate to give in accordance with parental wisdom rather than in the terms of the son's faulty petition? If the child needs a loaf, will you give him a stone just because he unwisely asks for it? If your son needs a fish, will you give him a watersnake just because it may chance to come up in the net with the fish and the child foolishly asks for the serpent? If you, then, being mortal and finite, know how to answer prayer and give good and appropriate gifts to your children, how much more shall your heavenly Father give the spirit and many additional blessings to those who ask him? Men ought always to pray and not become discouraged.'" P. 1619. Luke 11:5-13.

3. **The wicked judge and prayer answer.**

"'Let me tell you the story of a certain judge who lived in a wicked city. This judge feared not God nor had respect for man. Now there was a needy widow in that city who came repeatedly to this unjust judge, saying, "Protect me from my adversary." For some time he would not give ear to her, but presently he said to himself: "Though I fear not God nor have regard for man, yet because this widow ceases not to trouble me, I will vindicate her lest she wear me out by her continual coming." These stories I tell you to encourage you to persist in praying and not to intimate that your petitions will change the just and righteous Father above. Your persistence, however, is not to win favor with God but to change your earth attitude and to enlarge your soul's capacity for spirit receptivity.

"'But when you pray, you exercise so little faith. Genuine faith will remove mountains of material difficulty which may chance to lie in the path of soul expansion and spiritual progress.'" P. 1619. Luke 18:2-8.

4. **Right answers to wrong prayers.**

"When there exists this living connection between divinity and humanity, if humanity should thoughtlessly and ignorantly pray for selfish ease and vainglorious accomplishments, there could be only one divine answer: more and increased bearing of the fruits of the spirit on the stems of the living branches. When the branch of the vine is alive, there can be only one answer to all its petitions: increased grape bearing. In fact, the branch exists only for, and can do, nothing except, fruit bearing, yielding grapes. So does the true believer exist only for the purpose of bearing the fruits of the spirit: to love man as he himself has been loved by God—that we should love one another, even as Jesus has loved us." P. 1946.

5. **Jesus discourses on the answer to prayer.**

"The apostles were much stirred up in their minds and spent

considerable time discussing their recent experiences as they were related to prayer and its answering. They all recalled Jesus' statement to the Bethany messenger at Philadelphia, when he said plainly, 'This sickness is not really to the death.' And yet, in spite of this promise, Lazarus actually died. All that day, again and again, they reverted to the discussion of this question of the answer to prayer.

"Jesus' answers to their many questions may be summarized as follows:

"1. Prayer is an expression of the finite mind in an effort to approach the Infinite. The making of a prayer must, therefore, be limited by the knowledge, wisdom, and attributes of the finite; likewise must the answer be conditioned by the vision, aims, ideals, and prerogatives of the Infinite. There never can be observed an unbroken continuity of material phenomena between the making of a prayer and the reception of the full spiritual answer thereto.

"2. When a prayer is apparently unanswered, the delay often betokens a better answer, although one which is for some good reason greatly delayed. When Jesus said that Lazarus's sickness was really not to the death, he had already been dead eleven hours. No sincere prayer is denied an answer except when the superior viewpoint of the spiritual world has devised a better answer, an answer which meets the petition of the spirit of man as contrasted with the prayer of the mere mind of man.

"3. The prayers of time, when indited by the spirit and expressed in faith, are often so vast and all-encompassing that they can be answered only in eternity; the finite petition is sometimes so fraught with the grasp of the Infinite that the answer must long be postponed to await the creation of adequate capacity for receptivity; the prayer of faith may be so all-embracing that the answer can be received only on Paradise.

"4. The answers to the prayer of the mortal mind are often of such a nature that they can be received and recognized only after that same praying mind has attained the immortal state. The prayer of material being can many times be answered only when such an individual has progressed to the spirit level.

"5. The prayer of a God-knowing person may be so distorted by ignorance and so deformed by superstition that the answer thereto would be highly undesirable. Then must the intervening spirit beings so translate such a prayer that, when the answer arrives, the petitioner wholly fails to recognize it as the answer to his prayer.

"6. All true prayers are addressed to spiritual beings, and all such petitions must be answered in spiritual terms, and all such answers must consist in spiritual realities. Spirit beings cannot bestow material answers to the spirit petitions of even material beings. Material beings can pray effectively only when they 'pray in the spirit.'

"7. No prayer can hope for an answer unless it is born of the spirit and nurtured by faith. Your sincere faith implies that you have in advance virtually granted your prayer hearers the full right to answer your petitions in accordance with that supreme wisdom and that divine love which your faith depicts as always actuating those beings to whom you pray.

"8. The child is always within his rights when he presumes to petition the parent; and the parent is always within his parental obligations to the immature child when his superior wisdom dictates that the answer to the child's prayer be delayed, modified, segregated, transcended, or postponed to another stage of spiritual ascension.

"9. Do not hesitate to pray the prayers of spirit longing; doubt not that you shall receive the answer to your petitions. These answers will be on deposit, awaiting your achievement of those future spiritual levels of actual cosmic attainment, on this world or on others, whereon it will become possible for you to recognize and appropriate the long-waiting answers to your earlier but ill-timed petitions.

"10. All genuine spirit-born petitions are certain of an answer. Ask and you shall receive. But you should remember that you are progressive creatures of time and space; therefore must you constantly reckon with the time-space factor in the experience of your personal reception of the full answers to your manifold prayers and petitions." P. 1848-9.

VI. PRAYER AS RELATED TO WORSHIP

1. Primitive praying hardly worship.

"Early prayer was hardly worship; it was a bargaining petition for health, wealth, and life. And in many respects prayers have not much changed with the passing of the ages. They are still read out of books, recited formally, and written out for emplacement on wheels and for hanging on trees, where the blowing of the winds will save man the trouble of expending his own breath." P. 983.

2. Prayer must not displace worship.

"Prayer is indeed a part of religious experience, but it has been wrongly emphasized by modern religions, much to the neglect of the more essential communion of worship. The reflective powers of the mind are deepened and broadened by worship. Prayer may enrich the life, but worship illuminates destiny." P. 1123.

3. Prayer as related to worship.

"Supplications of all kinds belong to the realm of the Eternal Son and the Son's spiritual organization. Prayers, all formal communications, everything except adoration and worship of the Universal Father, are matters that concern a local universe; they do not ordinarily proceed out of the realm of the jurisdiction of a Creator Son. But worship is undoubtedly encircuited and dispatched to the person of the Creator by the function of the Father's personality circuit. We further believe that such registry of the homage of an Adjuster-indwelt creature is facilitated by the Father's spirit presence. There exists a tremendous amount of evidence to substantiate such a belief, and I know that all orders of Father fragments are empowered to register the bona fide adoration of their subjects acceptably in the presence of the Universal Father. The Adjusters undoubtedly also utilize direct prepersonal channels of communication with God, and they are likewise able to utilize the spirit-gravity circuits of the Eternal Son." P. 65.

4. Prayer may lead to worship.

"Prayer led Jesus up to the supercommunion of his soul with the Supreme Rulers of the universe of universes. Prayer will lead the mortals of earth up to the communion of true worship. The soul's spiritual capacity for receptivity determines the quantity of heavenly blessings which can be personally appropriated and consciously realized as an answer to prayer.

"Prayer and its associated worship is a technique of detachment from the daily routine of life, from the monotonous grind of material existence. It is an avenue of approach to spiritualized self-realization and individuality of intellectual and religious attainment." P. 1621.

VII. THE PERSONAL PRAYER LIFE

1. Remember sonship is a gift.

"In all praying, remember that sonship is a *gift*. No child has aught to do with *earning* the status of son or daughter. The earth child comes into being by the will of its parents. Even so, the child of God comes into grace and the new life of the spirit by the will of the Father in heaven. Therefore must the kingdom of heaven—divine sonship—be *received* as by a little child. You earn righteousness—progressive character development—but you receive sonship by grace and through faith." P. 1621.

2. Personal repercussions of prayer.

"No matter how difficult it may be to reconcile the scientific doublings regarding the efficiency of prayer with the ever-present urge to seek help and guidance from divine sources, never forget that the sincere prayer of faith is a mighty force for the promotion of personal happiness, individual self-control, social harmony, moral progress, and spiritual attainment.

"Prayer, even as a purely human practice, a dialogue with one's alter ego, constitutes a technique of the most efficient approach to the realization of those reserve powers of human nature which are stored and conserved in the unconscious realms of the human mind. Prayer is a sound psychologic practice, aside from its religious implications and its spiritual significance. It is a fact of human experience that most persons, if sufficiently hard pressed, will pray in some way to some source of help." P. 999.

3. Transcending prayers.

"But the efficacy of prayer in the personal spiritual experience of the one who prays is in no way dependent on such a worshiper's intellectual understanding, philosophic acumen, social level, cultural status, or other mortal acquirements. The psychic and spiritual concomitants of the prayer of faith are immediate, personal, and experiential. There is no other technique whereby every man, regardless of all other mortal accomplishments, can so effectively and immediately approach the threshold of that realm wherein he can communicate with his maker, where the creature contacts with the reality of the Creator, with the indwelling Thought Adjuster." P. 1000.

4. Tolerance for ignorant praying.

"While the nonselfish type of prayer is strengthening and comforting, materialistic praying is destined to bring disappointment and disillusionment as advancing scientific discoveries demonstrate that man lives in a physical universe of law and order. The childhood of an individual or a race is characterized by primitive, selfish, and materialistic praying. And, to a certain extent, all such petitions are efficacious in that they unvaryingly lead to those efforts and exertions which are contributory to achieving the answers to such prayers. The real prayer of faith always contributes to the augmentation of the technique of living, even if such petitions are not worthy of spiritual recognition. But the spiritually advanced, person should exercise great caution in attempting to discourage the primitive or immature mind regarding such prayers.

"Remember, even if prayer does not change God, it very often effects great and lasting changes in the one who prays in faith and confident expectation. Prayer has been the ancestor of much peace of mind, cheerfulness, calmness, courage, self-mastery, and fair-mindedness in the men and women of the evolving races." P. 998.

VIII. PRAYING AS A PERSONAL EXPERIENCE

"There is a truly spontaneous aspect to prayer, for primitive man found himself praying long before he had any clear concept of a God. Early man was wont to pray in two diverse situations: When in dire need, he experienced the impulse to reach out for help; and when jubilant, he indulged the impulsive expression of joy.

"Prayer is not an evolution of magic; they each arose independently. Magic was an attempt to adjust Deity to conditions; prayer is the effort to adjust the personality to the will of Deity. True prayer is both moral and religious; magic is neither.

"Prayer may become an established custom; many pray because others do. Still others pray because they fear something direful may happen if they do not offer their regular supplications.

"To some individuals prayer is the calm expression of gratitude; to others, a group expression of praise, social devotions; sometimes it is the imitation of another's religion, while in true praying it is the sincere and trusting communication of the spiritual nature of the creature with the anywhere presence of the spirit of the Creator.

"Prayer may be a spontaneous expression of God-consciousness or a meaningless recitation of theologic formulas. It may be the ecstatic praise of a Godknowing soul or the slavish obeisance of a fear-ridden mortal. It is sometimes the pathetic expression of spiritual craving and sometimes the blatant shouting of pious phrases. Prayer may be joyous praise or a humble plea for forgiveness.

"Prayer may be the childlike plea for the impossible or the mature entreaty for mortal growth and spiritual power. A petition may be for daily bread or may embody a wholehearted yearning to find God and to do his will. It may be a wholly selfish request or a true and magnificent gesture toward the realization of unselfish brotherhood.

"Prayer may be an angry cry for vengeance or a merciful intercession for one's enemies. It may be the expression of a hope of changing God or the powerful technique of changing one's self. It may be the cringing plea of a lost sinner before a supposedly stern Judge or the joyful expression of a liberated son of the living and merciful heavenly Father.

"Modern man is perplexed by the thought of talking things over with God in a purely personal way. Many have abandoned regular praying; they only pray when under unusual pressure—in emergencies. Man should be unafraid to talk to God, but only a spiritual child would undertake to persuade, or presume to change, God.

"But real praying does attain reality. Even when the air currents are ascending, no bird can soar except by outstretched wings. Prayer elevates man because it is a technique of progressing by the utilization of the ascending spiritual currents of the universe.

"Genuine prayer adds to spiritual growth, modifies attitudes, and yields that satisfaction which comes from communion with divinity. It is a spontaneous outburst of God-consciousness.

"God answers man's prayer by giving him an increased revelation of truth, an enhanced appreciation of beauty, and an augmented concept of goodness. Prayer is a subjective gesture, but it contacts with mighty objective realities on the spiritual levels of human experience; it is a meaningful reach by the human for superhuman values. It is the most potent spiritual-growth stimulus.

"Words are irrelevant to prayer; they are merely the intellectual channel in which the river of spiritual supplication may chance to flow. The word value of a prayer is purely autosuggestive in private devotions and sociosuggestive in group devotions. God answers the soul's attitude, not the words.

"Prayer is not a technique of escape from conflict but rather a stimulus to growth in the very face of conflict. Pray only for values, not things; for growth, not for gratification." P. 1001-2.

IX. SOCIAL REPERCUSSIONS OF PRAYER

1. **Social repercussions of praying.**

"If you truly desire to overcome the habit of critizing some friend, the quickest and surest way of achieving such a change of attitude is to establish the habit of praying for that person every day of your life. But the social repercussions of such prayers are dependent largely on two conditions:

"1. The person who is prayed for should know that he is being prayed for.

"2. The person who prays should come into intimate social contact with the person for whom he is praying." P. 998-9.

2. The efficacy of group prayer.

"But prayer need not always be individual. Group or congregational praying is very effective in that it is highly socializing in its repercussions. When a group engages in community prayer for mortal enhancement and spiritual uplift, such devotions are reactive upon the individuals composing the group; they are all made better because of participation. Even a whole city or an entire nation can be helped by such prayer devotions. Confession, repentance, and prayer have led individuals, cities, nations, and whole races to mighty efforts of reform and courageous deeds of valorous achievement." P. 998.

3. Tolerance for another's prayers.

"But the minds of greater spiritual illumination should be patient with, and tolerant of, those less endowed intellects that crave symbolism for the mobilization of their feeble spiritual insight. The strong must not look with disdain upon the weak. Those who are God-conscious without symbolism must not deny the grace-ministry of the symbol to those who find it difficult to worship Deity and to revere truth, beauty, and goodness without form and ritual. In prayerful worship, most mortals envision some symbol of the object-goal of their devotions." P. 999.

4. Formalization of prayer.

"Prayer is the technique whereby, sooner or later, every religion becomes institutionalized. And in time prayer becomes associated with numerous secondary agencies, some helpful, others decidedly deletreious, such as priests, holy books, worship rituals, and ceremonials." P. 999.

X. THE LORD'S PRAYER

1. Evolution of the Lord's Prayer.

"During this year Jesus first formulated the prayer which he subsequently taught to his apostles, and which to many has become known as "The Lord's Prayer." In a way it was an evolution of the family altar; they had many forms of praise and several formal prayers. After his father's death Jesus tried to teach the older children to express themselves individually in prayer—much as he so enjoyed doing—but they could not grasp his thought and would invariably fall back upon their memorized prayer forms. It was in this effort to stimulate his older brothers and sisters to say individual prayers that Jesus would endeavor to lead them along by suggestive phrases, and presently, without intention on his part, it developed that they were all using a form of prayer which was largely built up from these suggestive lines which Jesus had taught them." P. 1389.

2. The Believer's Prayer.

"But the apostles were not yet satisfied; they desired Jesus to give them a model prayer which they could teach the new disciples. After listening to this discourse on prayer, James Zebedee said: "Very good, Master, but we do not desire a form of prayer for ourselves so much as for the newer believers who so frequently beseech us, 'Teach us how acceptably to pray to the Father in heaven.'"

"When James had finished speaking, Jesus said: "If, then, you still desire such a prayer, I would present the one which I taught my brothers and sisters in Nazareth":

Our Father who is in heaven,
    Hallowed be your name.
Your kingdom come; your will be done
    On earth as it is in heaven.
Give us this day our bread for tomorrow;
    Refresh our souls with the water of life.
And forgive us every one our debts
    As we also have forgiven our debtors.
Save us in temptation, deliver us from evil,
    And increasingly make us perfect like yourself.

"It is not strange that the apostles desired Jesus to teach them a model prayer for believers. John the Baptist had taught his followers several prayers; all great teachers had formulated prayers for their pupils. The religious teachers of the Jews had some twenty-five or thirty set prayers which they recited in the synagogues and even on the street corners. Jesus was particularly averse to praying in public. Up to this time the twelve had heard him pray only a few times. They observed him spending entire nights at prayer or worship, and they were very curious to know the manner or form of his petitions. They were really hard pressed to know what to answer the multitudes when they asked to be taught how to pray as John had taught his disciples." P. 1619-20. Luke 11:1-4.

3.   **Jesus' Teaching regarding the prayer.**

"Jesus taught the twelve always to pray in secret; to go off by themselves amidst the quiet surroundings of nature or to go in their rooms and shut the doors when they engaged in prayer.

"After Jesus' death and ascension to the Father it became the practice of many believers to finish this so-called Lord's prayer by the addition of—'In the name of the Lord Jesus Christ.' Still later on, two lines were lost in copying, and there was added to this prayer an extra clause, reading: 'For yours is the kingdom and the power and the glory, forever more.'

"Jesus gave the apostles the prayer in collective form as they had prayed it in the Nazareth home. He never taught a formal personal prayer, only group, family, or social petitions. And he never volunteered to do that.

"Jesus taught that effective prayer must be:

"1.   Unselfish—not alone for oneself.
"2.   Believing—according to faith.
"3.   Sincere—honest of heart.
"4.   Intelligent—according to light.
"5.   Trustful—in submission to the Father's all-wise will." P. 1620.

XI. EXAMPLES OF PRAYER

1. Hap's prayer.

"But Hap did yield to the desire of the inhabitants of the city for the establishment of a form of religious service. His group provided the Dalamations with the seven chants of worship and also gave them the daily praise-phrase and eventually taught them 'the Father's prayer,' which was:

"'Father of all, whose Son we honor, look down upon us with favor. Deliver us from the fear of all save you. Make us a pleasure to our divine teachers and forever put truth on our lips. Deliver us from violence and anger; give us respect for our elders and that which belongs to our neighbors. Give us this season green pastures and fruitful flocks to gladden our hearts. We pray for the hastening of the coming of the promised uplifter, and we would do your will on this world as others do on worlds beyond.'" P. 747.

2. John's prayer.

"'John indeed taught you a simple form of prayer: "O Father, cleanse us from sin, show us your glory, reveal your love, and let your spirit sanctify our hearts forever more, Amen." He taught this prayer that you might have something to teach the multitude. He did not intend that you should use such a set and formal petition as the expression of your own souls in prayer.

"'Prayer is entirely a personal and spontaneous expression of the attitude of the soul toward the spirit; prayer should be the communion of sonship and the expression of fellowship. Prayer, when indited by the spirit, leads to co-operative spiritual progress. The ideal prayer is a form of spiritual communion which leads to intelligent worship. True praying is the sincere attitude of reaching heavenward for the attainment of your ideals.'" P. 1618.

3. Other forms of prayer.

"From time to time, during the remainder of Jesus' sojourn on earth, he brought to the notice of the apostles several additional forms of prayer, but he did this only in illustration of other matters, and he enjoined that these 'parable prayers' should not be taught to the multitudes. Many of them were from other inhabited planets, but this fact Jesus did not reveal to the twelve. Among these prayers were the following

"Our Father in whom consist the universe realms,
    Uplifted be your name and all-glorious your character.
Your presence encompasses us, and your glory is manifested
    Imperfectly through us as it is in perfection shown on high.
Give us this day the vivifying forces of light,
    And let us not stray into the evil bypaths of our imagination,
For yours is the glorious indwelling, the everlasting power,
    And to us, the eternal gift of the infinite love of your Son.
Even so, and everlastingly true.

* * *

"Our creative Parent, who is in the center of the universe,
    Bestow upon us your nature and give to us your character.
Make us sons and daughters of yours by grace
    And glorify your name through our eternal achievement.
Your adjusting and controlling spirit give to live and dwell
        within us
That we may do your will on this sphere as angels do your
        bidding in light.
Sustain us this day in our progress along the path of truth.
    Deliver us from inertia, evil, and all sinful transgression.
Be patient with us as we show loving-kindness to our fellows.
    Shed abroad the spirit of your mercy in our creature
        hearts.
Lead us by your own hand, step by step, through the uncertain
        maze of life,
And when our end shall come, receive into your own bosom
        our faithful spirits.
Even so, not our desires but your will be done.

* * *

"Our perfect and righteous heavenly Father,
    This day guide and direct our journey.
Sanctify our steps and co-ordinate our thoughts.
    Ever lead us in the ways of eternal progress.
Fill us with wisdom to the fullness of power.
    And vitalize us with your infinite energy.
Inspire us with the divine consciousness of
    The presence and guidance of the seraphic hosts.

Guide us ever upward in the pathway of light;
>Justify us fully in the day of the great judgment.
Make us like yourself in eternal glory
>And receive us into your endless service on high.

* * *

"Our Father who is in the mystery,
>Reveal to us your holy character.
Give your children on earth this day
>To see the way, the light, and the truth.
Show us the pathway of eternal progress
>And give us the will to walk therein.
Establish within us your divine kingship
>And thereby bestow upon us the full mastery of self.
Let us not stray into paths of darkness and death;
>Lead us everlastingly beside the waters of life.
Hear these our prayers for your own sake;
>Be pleased to make us more and more like yourself.
At the end, for the sake of the divine Son,
>Receive us into the eternal arms.
Even so, not our will but yours be done.

* * *

"Glorious Father and Mother, in one parent combined,
>Loyal would we be to your divine nature.
Your own self to live again in and through us
>By the gift and bestowal of your divine spirit,
Thus reproducing you imperfectly in this sphere
>As you are perfectly and majestically shown on high.
Give us day by day your sweet ministry of brotherhood
>And lead us by moment in the pathway of loving service.
Be you ever and unfailingly patient with us
>Even as we show forth your patience to our children.
Give us the divine wisdom that does all things well
>And the infinite love that is gracious to every creature.
Bestow upon us your patience and loving-kindness
>That our charity may enfold the weak of the realm.
And when our career is finished, make it an honor to your name,
A pleasure to your good spirit, and a satisfaction to our soul helpers.

Not as we wish, our loving Father, but as you desire the eternal
>   good of your mortal children,
Even so may it be.

* * *

"Our all-faithful Source and all-powerful center,
>   Reverent and holy be the name of your all-gracious Son.
Your bounties and your blessing have descended upon us,
>   Thus empowering us to perform your will and execute your
>   bidding.
Give us moment by moment the sustenance of the tree of life;
>   Refresh us day by day with the living waters of the river
>   thereof.
Step by step lead us out of darkness and into the divine light.
>   Renew our minds by the transformations of the indwelling
>   spirit,
And when the mortal end shall finally come upon us,
>   Receive us to yourself and send us forth in eternity.
Crown us with celestial diadems of fruitful service,
>   And we shall glorify the Father, the Son, and the Holy
>   Influence.
Even so, throughout a universe without end.

* * *

"Our Father who dwells in the secret places of the universe,
>   Honored be your name, reverenced your mercy, and
>   respected your judgment.
Let the sun of righteousness shine upon us at noontime,
>   While we beseech you to guide our wayward steps in the
>   twilight.
Lead us by the hand in the ways of your own choosing
>   And forsake us not when the path is hard and the hours are
>   dark.
Forget us not as we so often neglect and forget you.
>   But be you merciful and love us as we desire to love you.
Look down upon us in kindness and forgive us in mercy
>   As we in justice forgive those who distress and injure us.
May the love, devotion, and bestowal of the majestic Son
>   Make available life everlasting with your endless mercy
>   and love.

May the God of universes bestow upon us the full measure of his spirit;

    Give us grace to yield to the leading of this spirit.

By the loving ministry of devoted seraphic hosts

    May the Son guide and lead us to the end of the age.

Make us ever and increasingly like yourself

    And at our end receive us into the eternal Paradise embrace.

Even so, in the name of the bestowal Son

    And for the honor and glory of the Supreme Father.

"Though the apostles were not at liberty to present these prayer lessons in their public teachings, they profited much from all of these revelations in their personal religious experiences. Jesus utilized these and other prayer models as illustrations in connection with the intimate instruction of the twelve, and specific permission has been granted for transcribing these seven specimen prayers into this record." P. 1621-4.

XII. JESUS'TEACHINGS ABOUT PRAYER

1. **Jesus' early praying.**

"During this year Joseph and Mary had trouble with Jesus about his prayers. He insisted on talking to his heavenly Father much as he would talk to Joseph, his earthly father. This departure from the more solemn and reverent modes of communication with Deity was a bit disconcerting to his parents, especially to his mother, but there was no persuading him to change; he would say his prayers just as he had been taught, after which he insisted on having 'just a little talk with my Father in heaven.'" P. 1360.

2. **Jesus' later prayer life.**

"Jesus brought to God, as a man of the realm, the greatest of all offerings: the consecration and dedication of his own will to the majestic service of doing the divine will. Jesus always and consistently interpreted religion wholly in terms of the Father's will. When you study the career of the Master, as concerns prayer or any other feature of the religious life, look not so much for what he taught as for what he did. Jesus never prayed as a religious duty. To him prayer was a sincere expression of spiritual attitude, a declaration of soul loyalty, a recital of personal devotion, an expression of thanksgiving, an avoidance of emotional tension, a prevention of conflict, an exaltation of intellection, an ennoblement of desire, a vindication of moral decision, an enrichment of thought, an invigoration of higher inclinations, a consecration of impulse, a clarification of viewpoint, a declaration of faith, a transcendental surrender of will, a sublime assertion of confidence, a revelation of courage, the proclamation of discovery, a confession of supreme devotion, the validation of consecration, a technique for the adjustment of difficulties, and the mighty mobilization of the combined soul powers to withstand all human tendencies toward selfishness, evil, and sin. He lived just such a life of prayerful consecration to the doing of his Father's will and ended his life triumphantly with just such a prayer. The secret of his unparalleled religious life was this consciousness of the presence of God; and he attained it by intelligent prayer and sincere worship—unbroken communion with God—and not by leadings, voices, visions, or extraordinary religious practices." P. 2088-9.

3. Jesus' discussion of prayer.

"1.   The conscious and persistent regard for iniquity in the heart of man gradually destroys the prayer connection of the human soul with the spirit circuits of communication between man and his Maker. Naturally God hears the petition of his child, but when the human heart deliberately and persistently harbors the concepts of, iniquity, there gradually ensues the loss of personal communion between the earth child and his heavenly Father.

"2.   That prayer which is inconsistent with the known and established laws of God is an abomination to the Paradise Deities. If man will not listen to the Gods as they speak to their creation in the laws of spirit, mind, and matter, the very act of such deliberate and conscious disdain by the creature turns the ears of spirit personalities away from hearing the personal petitions of such lawless and disobedient mortals. Jesus quoted to his apostles from the Prophet Zechariah: But they refused to hearken and pulled away the shoulder and stopped their ears that they should not hear. Yes, they made their hearts adamant like a stone, lest they should hear my law and the words which I sent by my spirit through the prophets; therefore did the results of their evil thinking come as a great wrath upon their guilty heads. And so it came to pass that they cried for mercy, but there was no ear open to hear.' And then Jesus quoted the proverb of the wise man who said: 'He who turns away his ear from hearing the divine law, even his prayer shall be an abomination.'

"3.   By opening the human end of the channel of the God-man communication, mortals make immediately available the ever-flowing stream of divine ministry to the creatures of the worlds. When man hears God's spirit speak within the human heart, inherent in such an experience is the fact that God simultaneously hears that man's prayer. Even the forgiveness of sin operates in this same unerring fashion. The Father in heaven has forgiven you even before you have thought to ask him, but such forgiveness is not available in your personal religious experience until such a time as you forgive your fellow men. God's forgiveness in *fact* is not conditioned upon your forgiving your fellows, but in *experience* it is exactly so conditioned. And this fact of the synchrony of divine and human forgiveness was thus recognized and linked together in the prayer which Jesus taught the apostles.

"4.   There is a basic law of justice in the universe which mercy is powerless to circumvent. The unselfish glories of Paradise are not possible of reception by a thoroughly selfish creature of the realms of time and space. Even the infinite love of God cannot force the salvation of eternal survival upon any mortal creature who does not choose to survive. Mercy has great latitude of bestowal, but, after all, there are mandates of justice which even love combined with mercy cannot effectively abrogate. Again, Jesus quoted from the Hebrew scriptures: 'I have called and you refused to hear; I stretched out my hand, but no man regarded. You have set at naught all my counsel, and you have rejected my reproof, and because of this rebellious attitude it becomes inevitable that you shall call upon me and fail to receive an answer. Having rejected the way of life, you may seek me diligently in your times of suffering, but you will not find me.'

"5.   They who would receive mercy must show mercy; judge not that you be not judged. With the spirit with which you judge others you also shall be judged. Mercy does not wholly abrogate universe fairness. In the end it will prove true: 'Whoso stops his ears to the cry of the poor, he also shall some day cry for help, and no one will hear him.' The sincerity of any prayer is the assurance of its being heard; the spiritual wisdom and universe consistency of any petition is the determiner of the time, manner, and degree of the answer. A wise father does not *literally* answer the foolish prayers of his ignorant and inexperienced children, albeit the children may derive much pleasure and real soul satisfaction from the making of such absurd petitions.

"6.   When you have become wholly dedicated to the doing of the will of the Father in heaven, the answer to all your petitions will be forthcoming because your prayers will be in full accordance with the Father's will, and the Father's will is ever manifest throughout his vast universe. What the true son desires and the infinite Father wills IS. Such a prayer cannot remain unanswered, and no other sort of petition can possibly be fully answered.

"7.   The cry of the righteous is the faith act of the child of God which opens the door of the Father's storehouse of goodness, truth, and mercy, and these good gifts have long been in waiting for the son's approach and personal appropriation. Prayer does not change the divine attitude toward man, but it does change man's attitude toward the changeless Father. The *motive* of the prayer gives it right of way to the divine ear, not the social, economic, or outward religious status of the one who prays.

"8. Prayer may not be employed to avoid the delays of time or to transcend the handicaps of space. Prayer is not designed as a technique for aggrandizing self or for gaining unfair advantage over one's fellows. A thoroughly selfish soul cannot pray in the true sense of the word. Said Jesus: 'Let your supreme delight be in the character of God, and he shall surely give you the sincere desires of your heart.' 'Commit your way to the Lord; trust in him, and he will act.' 'For the Lord hears the cry of the needy, and he will regard the prayer of the destitute.'

"9. 'I have come forth from the Father; if, therefore, you are ever in doubt as to what you would ask of the Father, ask in my name, and I will present your petition in accordance with your real needs and desires and in accordance with my Father's will.' Guard against the great danger of becoming self-centered in your prayers. Avoid praying much for yourself; pray more for the spiritual progress of your brethren. Avoid materialistic praying; pray in the spirit and for the abundance of the gifts of the spirit.

"10. When you pray for the sick and afflicted, do not expect that your petitions will take the place of loving and intelligent ministry to the necessities of these afflicted ones. Pray for the welfare of your families, friends, and fellows, but especially pray for those who curse you, and make loving petitions for those who persecute you. 'But when to pray, I will not say. Only the spirit that dwells within you may move you to the utterance of those petitions which are expressive of your inner relationship with the Father of spirits.'

"11. Many resort to prayer only when in trouble. Such a practice is thoughtless and misleading. True, you do well to pray when harassed, but you should also be mindful to speak as a son to your Father even when all goes well with your soul. Let your real petitions always be in secret. Do not let men hear your personal prayers. Prayers of thanksgiving are appropriate for groups of worshipers, but the prayer of the soul is a personal matter. There is but one form of prayer which is appropriate for all God's children, and that is: 'Nevertheless, your will be done.'

"12. All believers in this gospel should pray sincerely for the extension of the kingdom of heaven. Of all the prayers of the Hebrew scriptures he commented most approvingly on the petition of the Psalmist: 'Create in me a clean heart, O God, and renew a right spirit within me. Purge me from secret sins and keep back your servant from presumptuous transgression.' Jesus commented at great length on the relation of prayer to careless and offending speech, quoting: 'Set a watch, O Lord, before my mouth; keep the door of my lips.' 'The human tongue,' said Jesus, 'is a member which few men can tame, but the spirit within can transform this unruly member into a kindly voice of tolerance and an inspiring minister of mercy.'

"13. Jesus taught that the prayer for divine guidance over the pathway of earthly life was next in importance to the petition for a knowledge of the Father's will. In reality this means a prayer for divine wisdom. Jesus never taught that human knowledge and special skill could be gained by prayer. But he did teach that prayer is a factor in the enlargement of one's capacity to receive the presence of the divine spirit. When Jesus taught his associates to pray in the spirit and in truth, he explained that he referred to praying sincerely and in accordance with one's enlightenment, to praying wholeheartedly and intelligently, earnestly and steadfastly.

"14. Jesus warned his followers against thinking that their prayers would be rendered more efficacious by ornate repetitions, eloquent phraseology, fasting, penance, or sacrifices. But he did exhort his believers to employ prayer as a means of leading up through thanksgiving to true worship. Jesus deplored that so little of the spirit of thanksgiving was to be found in the prayers and worship of his followers. He quoted from the Scriptures on this occasion, saying: 'It is a good thing to give thanks to the Lord and to sing praises to the name of the Most High, to acknowledge his loving-kindness every morning and his faithfulness every night, for God has made me glad through his work. In everything I will give thanks according to the will of God.'

"15. And then Jesus said: 'Be not constantly overanxious about your common needs. Be not apprehensive concerning the problems of your earthly existence, but in all these things by prayer and supplication, with the spirit of sincere thanksgiving, let your needs be spread out before your Father who is in heaven.' Then he quoted from the Scriptures: 'I will praise the name of God with a song and will magnify him with thanksgiving. And this will please the Lord better than the sacrifice of an ox or bullock with horns and hoofs.'

"16. Jesus taught his followers that, when they had made their prayers to the Father, they should remain for a time in silent receptivity to afford the indwelling spirit the better opportunity to speak to the listening soul. The spirit of the Father speaks best to man when the human mind is in an attitude of true worship. We worship God by the aid of the Father's indwelling spirit and by the illumination of the human mind through the ministry of truth. Worship, taught Jesus, makes one increasingly like the being who is worshiped. Worship is a transforming experience whereby the finite gradually approaches and ultimately attains the presence of the Infinite." P. 1638-41. Zech. 7:11-13. Prov. 28:9; 1:24-28; 21:13. Ps. 21:2; 37:5; 72:12; 51:10, 11; 141:3; 140:3. Matt. 6:30-33. Ps. 69:30, 31.

XIII. DISTORTIONS OF PRAYER

1. Distortions of prayer.

"With those mortals who have not been delivered from the primitive bondage of fear, there is a real danger that all prayer may lead to a morbid sense of sin, unjustified convictions of guilt, real or fancied. But in modern times it is not likely that many will spend sufficient time at prayer to lead to this harmful brooding over their unworthiness or sinfulness. The dangers attendant upon the distortion and perversion of prayer consist in ignorance, superstition, crystallization, devitalization, materialism, and fanaticism." P. 995.

2. Misunderstanding prayer.

"But great sorrow later attended the misinterpretation of the Master's inferences regarding prayer. There would have been little difficulty about these teachings if his exact words had been remembered and subsequently truthfully recorded. But as the record was made, believers eventually regarded prayer in Jesus' name as a sort of supreme magic, thinking that they would receive from the Father anything they asked for. For centuries honest souls have continued to wreck their faith against this stumbling block. How long will it take the world of believers to understand that prayer is not a process of getting your way but rather a program of taking God's way, an experience of learning how to recognize and execute the Father's will? It is entirely true that, when your will has been truly aligned with his, you can ask anything conceived by that will-union, and it will be granted. And such a will-union is effected by and through Jesus even as the life of the vine flows into and through the living branches." P. 1946.

3. **Materialistic praying.**

"But the primitive mind was neither logical nor consistent. Early men did not perceive that material things were not the province of prayer. These simple-minded souls reasoned that food, shelter, rain, game, and other material goods enhanced the social welfare, and therefore they began to pray for these physical blessings. "While this constituted a perversion of prayer, it encouraged the effort to realize these material objectives by social and ethical actions. Such a prostitution of prayer, while debasing the spiritual values of a people, nevertheless directly elevated their economic, social, and ethical mores." P. 995.

4. **Prayer no escape from reality.**

"Do not be so slothful as to ask God to solve your difficulties, but never hesitate to ask him for wisdom and spiritual strength to guide and sustain you while you yourself resolutely and courageously attack the problems at hand." P. 999.

"Prayer must never be so prostituted as to become a substitute for action. All ethical prayer is a stimulus to action and a guide to the progressive striving for idealistic goals of superself-attainment." P. 997.

BIBLE TEACHING ABOUT PRAYER
I. PRAYER IN THE OLD TESTAMENT

1. **Prayers of supplication.**

"*And I besought the Lord at that time, saying....*" **Deut. 3:23**.

2. **Intercession.**

"*And Abraham said to God, 'Oh that Ishmael might live in thy sight!'*" **Gen. 17:18**.

3. **Adoration.**

"*That they may offer pleasing sacrifices to the God of heaven and pray for the life of the king.*" **Ezra 6:10**.

4. **Colloquy.**

   Gen. 15:1-8. Abraham and God talking.

5. **Vows.**

   "Then Jacob made a vow, saying, 'If God will be with me...'" **Gen. 28:20**.

6. **Thanksgiving.**

   "And you shall rejoice in all the good which the Lord your God has given to you and to your house." **Deut. 26:11**.

7. **Worship.**

   "O Lord, in distress they sought thee, they poured out a prayer when thy chastening was upon them." **Isa. 26:16**.

   "The prayer of the upright is his delight." **Prov. 15:8**.

   "He hears the prayer of the righteous." **Prov. 15:29**.

8. **Wisdom.**

   "Give thy servant therefore an understanding mind to govern thy people, that I may discern between good and evil." **1 Kings 3:9**.

9. **Guidance.**

   "Then David inquired of the Lord again. And the Lord answered him, 'Arise, go down to Keilah.'" **1 Sam. 23:4**.

10. **Forgiveness.**

    "Now therefore, I pray, pardon my sin...that I may worship the Lord." **1 Sam. 15:25**.

11. **Pouring out of soul.**

    "Trust in him at all times, O people; pour out your heart before him; God is a refuge for us." **Ps. 62:8**.

12. **The Psalms — a Book of Prayers.**

    Prayer Psalms 5, 17, 86, 90, 102, 142.

   NOTE: The Apocrypha is full of prayers.

II. PRAYER IN THE NEW TESTAMENT

"Let us draw near with a true heart in full assurance of faith." **Heb. 10:22**.

1. **Requests.**

   "If two of you agree on earth about anything they ask, it will be done for them by my Father in heaven." **Matt. 18:19**.

2. **Intercession.**

   "The Spirit intercedes for the saints according to the will of God." **Rom. 8:27**.

   "Pray for us also." **Col. 4:3**.

3. **Thanksgiving.**

   "I thank God through Jesus Christ for all of you." **Rom. 1:8**.

   "He took the seven loaves and the fish, and having given thanks, he broke them and gave them to the disciples." **Matt. 15:36**.

4. **Deliverance.**

   "Strive together with me in your prayers to God on my behalf, that I may be delivered." **Rom. 15:30**.

5. **Escape temptation.**

   "We pray God that you may not do wrong." **2 Cor. 13:7**.

   "And pray that you may not enter into temptation." **Matt. 26:41**.

6. **Temporal blessings.**

   Concerning his physical infirmity, Paul says: *"Three times I besought the Lord about this, that it should leave me."* **2 Cor. 12:8**.

7. **Spiritual assistance.**

   "Has set her hope on God, and continues in supplications and prayers night and day." **1 Tim. 5:5**.

8. **Ritual prayers.**

   a. *Healing.*
      "Is any one among you suffering? Let him pray." **Jas. 5:13**.
   b. *After baptism.*
      "And when Paul had laid his hands on them, the Holy Spirit came on them." **Acts 19:6**.
   c. *For converts.*
      "I do not cease to give thanks for you, remembering you in my prayers." **Eph. 1:16**.

9. **Time for prayer.**

   "About midnight Paul and Silas were praying and singing hymns." **Acts 16:25**.

   "Pray constantly." **1 Thess. 5:17**.

   "Peter went up on the housetop to pray, about the sixth hour." **Acts 10:9**.

   (The Jews prayed three times a day.)

10. **Place.**

    a.   *Temple.*

        "Peter and John were going up to the temple at the hour of prayer." **Acts 3:1**.

    b.   *By the riverside.*

        "We went outside the gate to the riverside, where we supposed there was a place of prayer." **Acts 16:13**.

    c.   *In private.*

        "When you pray, go into your room and shut the door and pray to your Father who is in secret." **Matt. 6:6**.

11. **Posture.**

    a.   *Standing.*

        "And wherever you stand praying." **Mark 11:25**.

    b.   *Kneeling.*

        "For this reason I bow my knees before the Father." **Eph. 3:14**.

    c.   *Prostrate.*

        "And going a little farther, he fell on his face and prayed." **Matt. 26:39**.

    d.   *Uplifted hands.*

        "In every place men should pray, lifting holy hands without anger." **1 Tim. 2:8**.

12. **Fasting, incense, etc.**

    "And the whole multitude of the people were praying outside at the hour of incense." **Luke 1:10**.

    "She did not depart from the temple, worshiping with fasting and prayer." **Luke 2:37**.

13. **Perverted prayer.**

    "And in praying do not heap up empty phrases as the Gentiles do; for they think that they will be heard for their many words." **Matt. 6:7**.

III. CHRIST'S PRAYER LIFE

"Jesus offered up prayers and supplications, with loud cries and tears." **Heb. 5:7**.

"He went out into the hills to pray; and all night he continued in prayer to God." **Luke 6:12**.

"He withdrew to the wilderness and prayed." **Luke 5:16**.

"And as he was praying, the appearance of his countenance was altered." **Luke 9:29**.

"And in the morning, a great while before day, he rose and went out to a lonelyplace, and there he prayed." **Mark 1:35**.

"And going a little farther, he fell on the ground and prayed that, if it were possible, the hour might pass from him." **Mark 14:35**.

A lengthy public prayer for his followers is found in **John 17**.

IV. THE LORD'S PRAYER

Found in Matthew and Luke. In Matthew it is part of the Sermon on the Mount. In Luke it appears much in the same connection as presented in *The Urantia Book*.

1. Matt. 6:9-15.

> *"Our Father who art in heaven,*
> *Hallowed be thy name.*
> *Thy kingdom come,*
> *Thy will be done,*
> *On earth as it is in heaven.*
> *Give us this day our daily bread,*
> *And forgive us our debts,*
> *As we also have forgiven our debtors.*
> *And lead us not into temptation,*
> *But deliver us from evil."*

2. Luke 11:2-4.

> *"Father, hallowed be thy name. Thy kingdom come. Give us each day our daily bread; and forgive us our sins, for we ourselves forgive every one who is indebted to us; and lead us not into temptation."*

> **NOTE**: The doxology—"For thine is the kingdom, and the power, and the glory"—is not found in the Standard Revised Version. In the King James Version, it appears only in Matthew.

8. WORSHIP

Worship in the Bible

TOPIC EIGHT

WORSHIP

I. WORSHIP DEFINED

1. **Worship is the pursuit of divine values.**

   "Worship, the sincere pursuit of divine values and the whole-hearted love of the divine Value-Giver." P. 195.

2. **We worship our highest concept of Deity.**

   "We crave the concept of the Infinite, but we worship the experience—idea of God, our anywhere and any—time capacity to grasp the personality and divinity factors of our highest concept of Deity." P. 59.

3. **Worship is personal communion with reality.**

   "True religious worship is not a futile monologue of self—deception. Worship is a personal communion with that which is divinely real, with that which is the very source of reality. Man aspires by worship to be better and thereby eventually attains the best." P. 2095.

II. PRIMITIVE WORSHIP

1. **Primitive nature worship.**

   "At one time or another mortal man has worshiped everything on the face of the earth, including himself. He has also worshiped about everything imaginable in the sky and beneath the surface of the earth. Primitive man feared all manifestations of power; he worshiped every natural phenomenon he could not comprehend. The observation of powerful natural forces, such as storms, floods, earthquakes, land-slides, volcanoes, fire, heat, and cold, greatly impressed the expanding mind of man. The inexplicable things of life are still termed 'acts of God' and 'mysterious dispensations of Providence.'" P. 944.

2. **Fear worship of power and mystery.**

   "Clouds, rain, and hail have all been feared and worshiped by numerous primitive tribes and by many of the early nature cults. Windstorms with thunder and lightning overawed early man. He was so impressed with these elemental disturbances that thunder was regarded as the voice of an angry god. The worship of fire and the fear of lightning were linked together and were widespread among many early groups." P. 947.

3. **The worship of plants.**

   "Plants were first feared and then worshiped because of the intoxicating liquors which were derived therefrom. Primitive man believed that intoxication rendered one divine. There was supposed to be something unusual and sacred about such an experience. Even in modern times alcohol is known as 'spirits.'" P. 945.

4. **Worship of the heavenly bodies.**

   "The worship of rocks, hills, trees, and animals naturally developed up through fearful veneration of the elements to the deification of the sun, moon, and stars. In India and elsewhere the stars were regarded as the glorified souls of great men who had departed from the life in the flesh. The Chaldean star cultists considered themselves to be the children of the sky father and the earth mother." P. 947.

5. **Progress beyond nature worship.**

   "In the evolution of the human species, worship in its primitive manifestations appears long before the mind of man is capable of formulating the more complex concepts of life now and in the hereafter which deserve to be called religion. Early religion was wholly intellectual in nature and was entirely predicated on associational circumstances. The objects of worship were altogether suggestive; they consisted of the things of nature which were close at hand, or which loomed large in the commonplace experience of the simple-minded primitive Urantians.

   "When religion once evolved beyond nature worship, it acquired roots of spirit origin but was nevertheless always conditioned by the social environment. As nature worship developed, man's concepts envisioned a division of labor in the supermortal world; there were nature spirits for lakes, trees, waterfalls, rain, and hundreds of other ordinary terrestrial phenomena." P. 944.

6. **Gifts and bribes as factors of worship.**

   "Gifts and bribes are given to men; but when tendered to the gods, they are described as being dedicated, made sacred, or are called sacrifices. Renunciation was the negative form of propitiation; sacrifice became the positive form. The act of propitiation included praise, glorification, flattery, and even entertainment. And it is the remnants of these positive practices of the olden propitiation cult that constitute the modern forms of divine worship. Present-day forms of worship are simply the ritualization of these ancient sacrificial techniques of positive propitiation." P. 978.

7. **Worship as insurance against misfortune.**

"And now the simple ghost cult is followed by the practices of the more advanced and relatively complex spirit-ghost cult, the service and worship of the higher spirits as they evolved in man's primitive imagination. Religious ceremonial must keep pace with spirit evolution and progress. The expanded cult was but the art of self-maintenance practiced in relation to belief in supernatural beings, self-adjustment to spirit environment. Industrial and military organizations were adjustments to natural and social environments. And as marriage arose to meet the demands of bisexuality, so did religious organization evolve in response to the belief in higher spirit forces and spiritual beings. Religion represents man's adjustment to his illusions of the mystery of chance. Spirit fear and subsequent worship were adopted as insurance against misfortune, as prosperity policies." P. 962.

III. THE EVOLUTION OF WORSHIP

1. **The slow evolution of worship.**

"The old cults were too egocentric; the new must be the outgrowth of applied love. The new cult must, like the old, foster sentiment, satisfy emotion, and promote loyalty; but it must do more: It must facilitate spiritual progress, enhance cosmic meanings, augment moral values, encourage social development, and stimulate a high type of personal religious living. The new cult must provide supreme goals of living which are both temporal and eternal—social and spiritual." P. 966.

2. **Mortals deified, then sainted.**

"Tribal chiefs died and were *deified*. Later, distinguished souls passed on and were *sainted*. Unaided evolution never originated gods higher than the glorified, exalted, and evolved spirits of deceased humans. In early evolution religion creates its own gods. In the course of revelation the Gods formulate religion. Evolutionary religion creates its gods in the image and likeness of mortal man; revelatory religion seeks to evolve and transform mortal man into the image and likeness of God." P. 948.

3. **Evolution of worship rituals.**

"Words become a part of ritual, such as the use of terms like amen and selah. The habit of swearing, profanity, represents a prostitution of former ritualistic repetition of holy names. The making of pilgrimages to sacred shrines is a very ancient ritual. The ritual next grew into elaborate ceremonies of purification, cleansing, and sanctification. The initiation ceremonies of the primitive tribal secret societies were in reality a crude religious rite. The worship technique of the olden mystery cults was just one long performance of accumulated religious ritual. Ritual finally developed into the modern types of social ceremonials and religious worship, services embracing prayer, song, responsive reading, and other individual and group spiritual devotions." P. 992.

4. **Man dares to bargain with God.**

"But the idea of making a covenant with the gods did finally arrive. *Evolutionary man eventually acquired such moral dignity that he dared to bargain with his gods.* And so the business of offering sacrifices gradually developed into the game of man's philosophic bargaining with God. And all this represented a new device for insuring against bad luck or, rather, an enhanced technique for the more definite purchase of prosperity. Do not entertain the mistaken idea that these early sacrifices were a free gift to the gods, a spontaneous offering of gratitude or thanksgiving; they were not expressions of true worship." P. 983.

5. **The long evolutionary struggle.**

"But at last the mind of primitive man was occupied with thoughts which transcended all of his inherent biologic urges; at last man was about to evolve an art of living based on something more than response to material stimuli. The beginnings of a primitive philosophic life policy were emerging. A supernatural standard of living was about to appear, for, if the spirit ghost in anger visits ill luck and in pleasure good fortune, then must human conduct be regulated accordingly. The concept of right and wrong had at last evolved; and all of this long before the times of any revelation on earth.

"With the emergence of these concepts, there was initiated the long and wasteful struggle to appease the ever-displeased spirits, the slavish bondage to evolutionary religious fear, that long waste of human effort upon tombs, temples, sacrifices, and priesthoods. It was a terrible and frightful price to pay, but it was worth all it cost, for man therein achieved a natural consciousness of relative right and wrong; human ethics was born!" P. 956.

6. **All religions teach worship.**

"All religions teach the worship of Deity and some doctrine of human salvation. The Buddhist religion promises salvation from suffering, unending peace; the Jewish religion promises salvation from difficulties, prosperity predicated on righteousness; the Greek religion promised salvation from disharmony, ugliness, by the realization of beauty; Christianity promises salvation from sin, sanctity; Mohammedanism provides deliverance from the rigorous moral standards of Judaism and Christianity. The religion of Jesus is salvation from self, deliverance from the evils of creature isolation in time and in eternity." P. 67.

IV. WHOM WE WORSHIP

1. It should be easy to worship God.

"I find it easy and pleasant to worship one who is so great and at the same time so affectionately devoted to the uplifting ministry of his lowly creatures. I naturally love one who is so powerful in creation and in the control thereof, and yet who is so perfect in goodness and so faithful in the loving-kindness which constantly overshadows us. I think I would love God just as much if he were not so great and powerful, as long as he is so good and merciful. We all love the Father more because of his nature than in recognition of his amazing attributes." P. 39.

2. Concept of Deity personality favors worship.

"When Jesus talked about 'the living God,' he referred to a personal Deity—the Father in heaven. The concept of the personality of Deity facilitates fellowship; it favors intelligent worship; it promotes refreshing trustfulness. Interactions can be had between nonpersonal things, but not fellowship. The fellowship relation of father and son, as between God and man, cannot be enjoyed unless both are persons. Only personalities can commune with each other, albeit this personal communion may be greatly facilitated by the presence of just such an impersonal entity as the Thought Adjuster." P. 31.

3. Worship must be voluntary.

"The Universal Father never imposes any form of arbitrary recognition, formal worship, or slavish service upon the intelligent will creatures of the universes. The evolutionary inhabitants of the worlds of time and space must of themselves—in their own hearts—recognize, love, and voluntarily worship him. The Creator refuses to coerce or compel the submission of the spiritual free wills of his material creatures. The affectionate dedication of the human will to the doing of the Father's will is man's choicest gift to

God; in fact, such a consecration of creature will constitutes man's only possible gift of true value to the Paradise Father. In God, man lives, moves, and has his being; there is nothing which man can give to God except this choosing to abide by the Father's will, and such decisions, effected by the intelligent will creatures of the universes, constitute the reality of that true worship which is so satisfying to the love—dominated nature of the Creator Father." P. 22.

V. WORSHIP IS COMMUNION WITH DEITY

1. The universal worship potential.

"However Urantia mortals may differ in their intellectual, social, economic, and even moral opportunities and endowments, forget not that their spiritual endowment is uniform and unique. They all enjoy the same divine presence of the gift from the Father, and they are all equally privileged to seek intimate personal communion with this indwelling spirit of divine origin, while they may all equally choose to accept the uniform spiritual leading of these Mystery Monitors." P. 63.

2. Worship deals directly with God.

"When you deal with the practical affairs of your daily life, you are in the hands of the spirit personalities having origin in the Third Source and Center; you are co-operating with the agencies of the Conjoint Actor. And so it is: You worship God; pray to, and commune with, the Son; and work out the details of your earthly sojourn in connection with the intelligences of the Infinite Spirit operating on your world and throughout your universe." P. 66.

3. Worship is a spiritual communion.

"The characteristic difference between a social occasion and a religious gathering is that in contrast with the secular the religious is pervaded by the atmosphere of *communion*. In this way human association generates a feeling of fellowship with the divine, and this is the beginning of group worship. Partaking of a common meal was the earliest type of social communion, and so did early religions provide that some portion of the ceremonial sacrifice should be eaten by the worshipers. Even in Christianity the Lord's Supper retains this mode of communion. The atmosphere of the communion provides a refreshing and comforting period of truce in the conflict of the self—seeking ego with the altruistic urge of the indwelling spirit Monitor. And this is the prelude to true worship—the practice of the presence of God which eventuates in the emergence of the brotherhood of man." P. 1133.

4. **Worship contact with the heavenly Father.**

"Although the approach to the Paradise presence of the Father must await your attainment of the highest finite levels of spirit progression, you should rejoice in the recognition of the ever-present possibility of immediate communion with the bestowal spirit of the Father so intimately associated with your inner soul and your spiritualizing self." P. 63.

VI. RELATIONS OF WORSHIP AND PRAYER

1. **The differentials of worship and prayer.**

"Supplications of all kinds belong to the realm of the Eternal Son and the Son's spiritual organization. Prayers, all formal communications, everything except adoration and worship of the Universal Father, are matters that concern a local universe; they do not ordinarily proceed out of the realm of the jurisdiction of a Creator Son. But worship is undoubtedly encircuited and dispatched to the person of the Creator by the function of the Father's personality circuit. We further believe that such registry of the homage of an Adjuster-indwelt creature is facilitated by the Father's spirit presence. There exists a tremendous amount of evidence to substantiate such a belief, and I know that all orders of Father fragments are empowered to register the bona fide adoration of their subjects acceptably in the presence of the Universal Father. The Adjusters undoubtedly also utilize direct prepersonal channels of communication with God, and they are likewise able to utilize the spirit-gravity circuits of the Eternal Son." P. 65.

2. **Worship is not self-seeking.**

"Worship is for its own sake; prayer embodies a self- or creature-interest element; that is the great difference between worship and prayer. There is absolutely no self-request or other element of personal interest in true worship; we simply worship God for what we comprehend him to be. Worship asks nothing and expects nothing for the worshiper. We do not worship the Father because of anything we may derive from such veneration; we render such devotion and engage in such worship as a natural and spontaneous reaction to the recognition of the Father's matchless personality and because of his lovable nature and adorable attributes." P. 65.

3. Worship tunes the soul to the Father's broadcasts.

"Prayer is the breath of the spirit life in the midst of the material civilization of the races of mankind. Worship is salvation for the pleasure-seeking generations of mortals.

"As prayer may be likened to recharging the spiritual batteries of the soul, so worship may be compared to the act of tuning in the soul to catch the universe broadcasts of the infinite spirit of the Universal Father." P. 1621.

4. Prayer can lead to worship.

"Prayer led Jesus up to the supercommunion of his soul with the Supreme Rulers of the universe of universes. Prayer will lead the mortals of earth up to the communion of true worship. The soul's spiritual capacity for receptivity determines the quantity of heavenly blessings which can be personally appropriated and consciously realized as an answer to prayer." P. 1621.

VII. FORMS, RITUALS, AND EMOTIONS

1. Source of the forms of worship.

"The early plan of Christian worship was largely taken over from the Jewish synagogue, modified by the Mithraic ritual; later on, much pagan pageantry was added. The backbone of the early Christian church consisted of Christianized Greek proselytes to Judaism." P. 2074.

2. Worship demands rituals.

"The Jewish religion persisted also because of its institutions. It is difficult for religion to survive as the private practice of isolated individuals. This has ever been the error of the religious leaders: Seeing the evils of institutionalized religion, they seek to destroy the technique of group functioning. In place of destroying all ritual, they would do better to reform it. In this respect Ezekiel was wiser than his contemporaries; though he joined with them in insisting on personal moral responsibility, he also set about to establish the faithful observance of a superior and purified ritual." P. 1076.

3. Concerning places of worship.

"When it is not possible to worship God in the tabernacles of nature, men should do their best to provide houses of beauty, sanctuaries of appealing simplicity and artistic embellishment, so that the highest of human emotions may be aroused in association with the intellectual approach to spiritual communion with God. Truth, beauty, and holiness are powerful and effective aids to true worship. But spirit communion is not promoted by mere massive ornateness and overmuch embellishment with man's elaborate and ostentatious art. Beauty is most religious when it is most simple and naturelike. How unfortunate that little children should have their first introduction to concepts of public worship in cold and barren rooms so devoid of the beauty appeal and so empty of all suggestion of good cheer and inspiring holiness! The child should be introduced to worship in nature's outdoors and later accompany his parents to public houses of religious assembly which are at least as materially attractive and artistically beautiful as the home in which he is daily domiciled." P. 1840.

4. **Origin of the worship impulse.**

"The impulse of worship largely originates in the spirit promptings of the higher mind adjutants, reinforced by the leadings of the Adjuster. But the urge to pray so often experienced by God-conscious mortals very often arises as the result of seraphic influence. The guarding seraphim is constantly manipulating the mortal environment for the purpose of augmenting the cosmic insight of the human ascender to the end that such a survival candidate may acquire enhanced realization of the presence of the indwelling Adjuster and thus be enabled to yield increased co-operation with the spiritual mission of the divine presence." P. 1245.

5. **The worshipful human emotions.**

"Many new emotions early appeared in these human twins. They experienced admiration for both objects and other beings and exhibited considerable vanity. But the most remarkable advance in emotional development was the sudden appearance of a new group of really human feelings, the worshipful group, embracing awe, reverence, humility, and even a primitive form of gratitude. Fear, joined with ignorance of natural phenomena, is about to give birth to primitive religion." P. 708.

VIII. THE ADJUTANT OF WORSHIP

1. **The primordial instinct for Deity.**

"*The adjutant of worship*—the appearance in animal consciousness of superanimal potentials for reality perception. This might be termed the primordial human instinct for Deity." P. 1003.

2. The spiritual impulse.

"*The spirit of worship*—the religious impulse, the first differential urge separating mind creatures into the two basic classes of mortal existence. The spirit of worship forever distinguishes the animal of its association from the soulless creatures of mind endowment. Worship is the badge of spiritual-ascension candidacy." P. 402.

3. Source of primitive worship urge.

"The evolution of religion from the preceding and primitive worship urge is not dependent on revelation. The normal functioning of the human mind under the directive influence of the sixth and seventh mind-adjutants of universal spirit bestowal is wholly sufficient to insure such development." P. 950.

4. Early action of the adjutant of worship.

"Nature worship may seem to have arisen naturally and spontaneously in the minds of primitive men and women, and so it did; but there was operating all this time in these same primitive minds the sixth adjutant spirit, which had been bestowed upon these peoples as a directing influence of this phase of human evolution. And this spirit was constantly stimulating the worship urge of the human species, no matter how primitive its first manifestations might be. The spirit of worship gave definite origin to the human impulse to worship, notwithstanding that animal fear motivated the expression of worshipfulness, and that its early practice became centered upon objects of nature." P. 948.

5. Wisdom admonishes worship urge.

"You must remember that feeling, not thinking, was the guiding and controlling influence in all evolutionary development. To the primitive mind there is little difference between fearing, shunning, honoring, and worshiping.

"When the worship urge is admonished and directed by wisdom— meditative and experiential thinking—it then begins to develop into the phenomenon of real religion. When the seventh adjutant spirit, the spirit of wisdom, achieves effective ministration, then in worship man begins to turn away from nature and natural objects to the God of nature and to the eternal Creator of all things natural." P. 948-9.

IX. WHAT WORSHIP DOES FOR US

1. What worship means to mortals.

"*Worship*—the spiritual domain of the reality of religious experience, the personal realization of divine fellowship, the recognition of spirit values, the assurance of eternal survival, the ascent from the status of servants of God to the joy and liberty of the sons of God. This is the highest insight of the cosmic mind, the reverential and worshipful form of the cosmic discrimination." P. 192.

2. **Reality results of worship.**

"This worshipful practice of your Master brings that relaxation which renews the mind; that illumination which inspires the soul; that courage which enables one bravely to face one's problems; that self-understanding which obliterates debilitating fear; and that consciousness of union with divinity which equips man with the assurance that enables him to dare to be Godlike. The relaxation of worship, or spiritual communion as practiced by the Master, relieves tension, removes conflicts, and mightily augments the total resources of the personality. And all this philosophy, plus the gospel of the kingdom, constitutes the new religion as I understand it." P. 1774.

3. **Worship yields spiritual strength.**

"One thing I am sure of: Emotional excitement is not the ideal spiritual stimulus. Excitement does not augment energy; it rather exhausts the powers of both mind and body. Whence then comes the energy to do these great things? Look to your Master. Even now he is out in the hills taking in power while we are here giving out energy. The secret of all this problem is wrapped up in spiritual communion, in worship. From the human standpoint it is a question of combined meditation and relaxation. Meditation makes the contact of mind with spirit; relaxation determines the capacity for spiritual receptivity. And this interchange of strength for weakness, courage for fear, the will of God for the mind of self, constitutes worship. At least, that is the way the philosopher views it." P. 1777.

4. **Worship of divine ideals.**

"Spiritual growth is first an awakening to needs, next a discernment of meanings, and then a discovery of values. The evidence of true spiritual development consists in the exhibition of a human personality motivated by love, activated by unselfish ministry, and dominated by the wholehearted worship of the perfection ideals of divinity. And this entire experience constitutes the reality of religion as contrasted with mere theological beliefs." P. 1095.

5. Worship the culmination of all.

"As mind pursues reality to its ultimate analysis, matter vanishes to the material senses but may still remain real to mind. When spiritual insight pursues that reality which remains after the disappearance of matter and pursues it to an ultimate analysis, it vanishes to mind, but the insight of spirit can still perceive cosmic realities and supreme values of a spiritual nature. Accordingly does science give way to philosophy, while philosophy must surrender to the conclusions inherent in genuine spiritual experience. Thinking surrenders to wisdom, and wisdom is lost in enlightened and reflective worship." P. 1228.

X. ADJUSTER'S PART IN WORSHIP

1. Spirit of worship antedates Adjusters.

"The Adjusters cannot invade the mortal mind until it has been duly prepared by the indwelling ministry of the adjutant mind-spirits and encircuited in the Holy Spirit. And it requires the co-ordinate function of all seven adjutants to thus qualify the human mind for the reception of an Adjuster. Creature mind must exhibit the worship outreach and indicate wisdom function by exhibiting the ability to choose between the emerging values of good and evil—moral choice." P. 1187.

2. Higher worship modern man's challenge.

"The great challenge to modern man is to achieve better communication with the divine Monitor that dwells within the human mind. Man's greatest adventure in the flesh consists in the well-balanced and sane effort to advance the borders of self-consciousness out through the dim realms of embryonic soul-consciousness in a wholehearted effort to reach the borderland of spirit-consciousness—contact with the divine presence. Such an experience constitutes God-consciousness, an experience mightily confirmative of the pre-existent truth of the religious experience of knowing God. Such spirit—consciousness is the equivalent of the knowledge of the actuality of sonship with God. Otherwise, the assurance of sonship is the experience of faith." P. 2097.

3. Worship mobilization of soul and Adjuster.

"Sincere worship connotes the mobilization of all the powers of the human personality under the dominance of the evolving soul and subject to the divine directionization of the associated Thought Adjuster. The mind of material limitations can never become highly conscious of the real significance of true worship. Man's realization of the reality of the worship experience is chiefly determined by the developmental status of his evolving immortal soul. The spiritual growth of the soul takes place wholly independently of the intellectual self-consciousness." P. 66.

4. **How the Adjuster conducts worship.**

"The worship experience consists in the sublime attempt of the betrothed Adjuster to communicate to the divine Father the inexpressible longings and the unutterable aspirations of the human soul—the conjoint creation of the God-seeking mortal mind and the God-revealing immortal Adjuster. Worship is, therefore, the act of the material mind's assenting to the attempt of its spiritualizing self, under the guidance of the associated spirit, to communicate with God as a faith son of the Universal Father.

The mortal mind consents to worship; the immortal soul craves and initiates worship; the divine Adjuster presence conducts such worship in behalf of the mortal mind and the evolving immortal soul. True worship, in the last analysis, becomes an experience realized on four cosmic levels: the intellectual, the morontial, the spiritual, and the personal—the consciousness of mind, soul, and spirit, and their unification in personality." P. 66.

XI. JESUS' TEACHINGS ABOUT WORSHIP

1. **Worship should be dynamic.**

"Jesus did not require of his followers that they should periodically assemble and recite a form of words indicative of their common beliefs. He only ordained that they should gather together to actually *do something*—partake of the communal supper of the remembrance of his bestowal life on Urantia." P. 1091.

2. **Religion of Jesus embraces highest worship.**

"The religion of Jesus transcends all our former concepts of the idea of worship in that he not only portrays his Father as the ideal of infinite reality but positively declares that this divine source of values and the eternal center of the universe is truly and personally attainable by every mortal creature who chooses to enter the kingdom of heaven on earth, thereby acknowledging the acceptance of sonship with God and brotherhood with man. That, I submit, is the highest concept of religion the world has ever known, and I pronounce that there can never be a higher since this gospel embraces the infinity of realities, the divinity of values, and the eternity of universal attainments. Such a concept constitutes the achievement of the experience of the idealism of the supreme and the ultimate." P. 1781.

3. **Jesus' teachings about worship.**

"At the evening conferences on Mount Gerizim, Jesus taught many great truths, and in particular he laid emphasis on the following:

"True religion is the act of an individual soul in its self-conscious relations with the Creator; organized religion is man's attempt to *socialize* the worship of individual religionists.

"Worship—contemplation of the spiritual—must alternate with service, contact with material reality. Work should alternate with play; religion should be balanced by humor. Profound philosophy should be relieved by rhythmic poetry. The strain of living—the time tension of personality—should be relaxed by the restfulness of worship. The feelings of insecurity arising from the fear of personality isolation in the universe should be antidoted by the faith contemplation of the Father and by the attempted realization of the Supreme.

"Prayer is designed to make man less thinking but more *realizing*; it is not designed to increase knowledge but rather to expand insight.

"Worship is intended to anticipate the better life ahead and then to reflect these new spiritual significances back onto the life which now is. Prayer is spiritually sustaining, but worship is divinely creative.

"Worship is the technique of looking to the *One* for the inspiration of service to the *many*. Worship is the yardstick which measures the extent of the soul's detachment from the material universe and its simultaneous and secure attachment to the spiritual realities of all creation.

"Prayer is self-reminding—sublime thinking; worship is self-forgetting—superthinking. Worship is effortless attention, true and ideal soul rest, a form of restful spiritual exertion.

"Worship is the act of a part identifying itself with the Whole; the finite with the Infinite; the son with the Father; time in the act of striking step with eternity. Worship is the act of the son's personal communion with the divine Father, the assumption of refreshing, creative, fraternal, and romantic attitudes by the human soul-spirit." P. 1616.

XII. WORSHIP ON PARADISE

1. The worship area of Paradise.

"On upper Paradise there are three grand spheres of activity, the *Deity presence*, the *Most Holy Sphere*, and the *Holy Area*. The vast region immediately surrounding the presence of the Deities is set aside as the Most Holy Sphere and is reserved for the functions of worship, trinitization, and high spiritual attainment. There are no material structures nor purely intellectual creations in this zone; they could not exist there. It is useless for me to undertake to portray to the human mind the divine nature and the beauteous grandeur of the Most Holy Sphere of Paradise. This realm is wholly spiritual, and you are almost wholly material. A purely spiritual reality is, to a purely material being, apparently nonexistent." P. 120.

2. Worship the highest joy of Paradise.

"All the arts of all the beings of the entire universe which are capable of intensifying and exalting the abilities of self-expression and the conveyance of appreciation, are employed to their highest capacity in the worship of the Paradise Deities. *Worship is the highest joy of Paradise existence*; it is the refreshing play of Paradise. What play does for your jaded minds on earth, worship will do for your perfected souls on Paradise. The mode of worship on Paradise is utterly beyond mortal comprehension, but the spirit of it you can begin to appreciate even down here on Urantia, for the spirits of the Gods even now indwell you, hover over you, and inspire you to true worship." P. 304.

3. The conductors of worship.

"It is the task of the conductors of worship so to teach the ascendant creatures how to worship that they may be enabled to gain this satisfaction of self-expression and at the same time be able to give attention to the essential activities of the Paradise regime. Without improvement in the technique of worship it would require hundreds of years for the average mortal who reaches Paradise to give full and satisfactory expression to his emotions of intelligent appreciation and ascendant gratitude. The conductors of worship open up new and hitherto unknown avenues of expression so that these wonderful children of the womb of space and the travail of time are enabled to gain the full satisfactions of worship in much less time." P. 304.

4. **The fullness of worship on Paradise.**

"Sometimes all Paradise becomes engulfed in a dominating tide of spiritual and worshipful expression. Often the conductors of worship cannot control such phenomena until the appearance of the threefold fluctuation of the light of the Deity abode, signifying that the divine heart of the Gods has been fully and completely satisfied by the sincere worship of the residents of Paradise, the perfect citizens of glory and the ascendant creatures of time. What a triumph of technique! What a fruition of the eternal plan and purpose of the Gods that the intelligent love of the creature child should give full satisfaction to the infinite love of the Creator Father!" P. 304-5.

5. **Worship is our highest delight.**

"Worship is the highest privilege and the first duty of all created intelligences. Worship is the conscious and joyous act of recognizing and acknowledging the truth and fact of the intimate and personal relationships of the Creators with their creatures. The quality of worship is determined by the depth of creature perception; and as the knowledge of the infinite character of the Gods progresses, the act of worship becomes increasingly all-encompassing until it eventually attains the glory of the highest experiential delight and the most exquisite pleasure known to created beings." P. 303.

6. **Destination of superior worshippers.**

"Those without Name and Number constitute the third and last group of the Trinitized Sons of Attainment; they are the ascendant souls who have developed the ability to worship beyond the skill of all the sons and daughters of the evolutionary races from the worlds of time and space." P. 246.

XIII. OBSTACLES AND WRONG CONCEPTS

1. **Modern obstacles to worship.**

"Modern man is adequately self-conscious of religion, but his worshipful customs are confused and discredited by his accelerated social metamorphosis and unprecedented scientific developments. Thinking men and women want religion redefined, and this demand will compel religion to re-evaluate itself.

"Modern man is confronted with the task of making more readjustments of human values in one generation than have been made in two thousand years. And this all influences the social attitude toward religion, for religion is a way of living as well as a technique of thinking." P. 1013.

2. **Mistaken concepts of worship.**

"Moral conduct is always an antecedent of evolved religion and a part of even revealed religion, but never the whole of religious experience. Social service is the result of moral thinking and religious living. Morality does not biologically lead to the higher spiritual levels of religious experience. The adoration of the abstract beautiful is not the worship of God; neither is exaltation of nature nor the reverence of unity the worship of God." P. 68.

3. **Worship as related to mysticism.**

"The more healthful attitude of spiritual meditation is to be found in reflective worship and in the prayer of thanksgiving. The direct communion with one's Thought Adjuster, such as occurred in the later years of Jesus' life in the flesh, should not be confused with these so-called mystical experiences. The factors which contribute to the initiation of mystic communion are indicative of the danger of such psychic states. The mystic status is favored by such things as: physical fatigue, fasting, psychic dissociation, profound aesthetic experiences, vivid sex impulses, fear, anxiety, rage, and wild dancing. Much of the material arising as a result of such preliminary preparation has its origin in the subconscious mind." P. 1100.

WORSHIP IN THE BIBLE
I. PRIVATE WORSHIP

"Praise the Lord. I will give thanks to the Lord with my whole heart." **Ps. 111:1.**

"Who worship God in spirit." **Phil. 3:3.**

"The true worshipers will worship the Father in spirit and truth." **John 4:23.**

"You shall worship the Lord your God, and him only shall you serve." **Luke 4:8.**

"I will give to the Lord the thanks due to his righteousness." **Ps. 7:17.**

"Seven times a day I praise thee." **Ps. 119:164.**

"And Joshua fell on his face to the earth, and worshiped." **Josh. 5:14.**

"Ascribe to the Lord the glory of his name; worship the Lord in holy array." **Ps. 29:2.**

"Then Job...fell upon the ground and worshiped." **Job 1:20.**

Psalms of Praise: 100, 104, 113-118, 136, 145, 150.

II. PUBLIC WORSHIP

"In the midst of the congregation I will praise thee." **Ps. 22:22**.

"Let the heavens praise thy wonders, O Lord, thy faithfulness in the assembly of the holy ones!" **Ps. 89:5**.

"I...will enter thy house, I will worship toward the holy temple." **Ps. 5:7**.

"Two men went up into the temple to pray." **Luke 18:10**.

"Not neglecting to meet together." **Heb. 10:25**.

"Let them extol him in the congregation of the people, and praise him in the assembly." **Ps. 107:32**.

Praise and adoration are a part of worship, but the word "adoration" does not appear in the King James version.

Praise represents an attitude ranging somewhere between prayer and worship, and is related to thanksgiving. Praise is connected with music—choirs.

9. PERSONALITY

The Psychology of Personality

PERSONALITY

I. DEITY PERSONALITY

1. God is an infinite personality.

"Do not permit the magnitude of God, his infinity, either to obscure or eclipse his personality. 'He who planned the ear, shall he not hear? He who formed the eye, shall he not see?' The Universal Father is the acme of divine personality; he is the origin and destiny of personality throughout all creation. God is both infinite and personal; he is an infinite personality. The Father is truly a personality, notwithstanding that the infinity of his person places him forever beyond the full comprehension of material and finite beings." P. 27. Ps. 94:9.

2. God is also much more than personality.

"God is much more than a personality as personality is understood by the human mind; he is even far more than any possible concept of a superpersonality. But it is utterly futile to discuss such incomprehensible concepts of divine personality with the minds of material creatures whose maximum concept of the reality of being consists in the idea and ideal of personality. The material creature's highest possible concept of the Universal Creator is embraced within the spiritual ideals of the exalted idea of divine personality. Therefore, although you may know that God must be much more than the human conception of personality, you equally well know that the Universal Father cannot possibly be anything less than an eternal, infinite, true, good, and beautiful personality." P. 27.

3. God not an egocentric personality.

"Divine personality is not self-centered; self-distribution and sharing of personality characterize divine freewill selfhood. Creatures crave association with other personal creatures; Creators are moved to share divinity with their universe children; the personality of the Infinite is disclosed as the Universal Father, who shares reality of being and equality of self with two co-ordinate personalities, the Eternal Son and the Conjoint Actor." P. 109.

4. How Deity personalizes.

"In this original transaction the theoretical I AM achieved the realization of personality by becoming the Eternal Father of the Original Son simultaneously with becoming the Eternal Source of the Isle of Paradise. Coexistent with the differentiation of the Son from the Father, and in the presence of Paradise, there appeared the person of the Infinite Spirit and the central universe of Havona. With the appearance of coexistent personal Deity, the Eternal Son and the Infinite Spirit, the Father escaped, as a personality, from otherwise inevitable diffusion throughout the potential of Total Deity. Thenceforth it is only in Trinity association with his two Deity equals that the Father fills all Deity potential, while increasingly experiential Deity is being actualized on the divinity levels of Supremacy, Ultimacy, and Absoluteness." P. 6.

II. WHAT IS PERSONALITY?

1. Personality a changeless reality.

"The personality of mortal man is neither body, mind, nor spirit; neither is it the soul. Personality is the one changeless reality in an otherwise ever-changing creature experience; and it unifies all other associated factors of individuality. The personality is the unique bestowal which the Universal Father makes upon the living and associated energies of matter, mind, and spirit, and which survives with the survival of the morontial soul." P. 9.

2. Mind is the arena of personality.

"Material mind is the arena in which human personalities live, are self-conscious, make decisions, choose God or forsake him, eternalize or destroy themselves." P. 1216.

3. Personality dimensions.

"The type of personality bestowed upon Urantia mortals has a potentiality of seven dimensions of self-expression or person-realization. These dimensional phenomena are realizable as three on the finite level, three on the absonite level, and one on the absolute level. On subabsolute levels this seventh or totality dimension is experiencible as the *fact* of personality. This supreme dimension is an associable absolute and, while not infinite, is dimensionally potential for subinfinite penetration of the absolute.

"The finite dimensions of personality have to do with cosmic length, depth, and breadth. Length denotes meaning; depth signifies value; breadth embraces insight—the capacity to experience unchallenge-able consciousness of cosmic reality." P. 1226.

4. Divine concept of personality.

"Never lose sight of the antipodal viewpoints of personality as it is conceived by God and man. Man views and comprehends person-ality, looking from the finite to the infinite; God looks from the infinite to the finite. Man possesses the lowest type of personality; God, the highest, even supreme, ultimate, and absolute. Therefore did the better concepts of the divine personality have patiently to await the appearance of improved ideas of human personality, especially the enhanced revelation of both human and divine personality in the Urantian bestowal life of Michael, the Creator Son." P. 30.

5. **Personality cannot be defined.**

"Though we can hardly undertake to define personality, we may attempt to narrate our understanding of the known factors which go to make up the ensemble of material, mental, and spiritual energies whose interassociation constitutes the mechanism wherein and whereon and wherewith the Universal Father causes his bestowed personality to function." P. 194.

6. **Divine spontaneity of personality.**

"The bestowal of creature personality confers relative liberation from slavish response to antecedent causation, and the personalities of all such moral beings, evolutionary or otherwise, are centered in the personality of the Universal Father. They are ever drawn towards his Paradise presence by that kinship of being which constitutes the vast and universal family circle and fraternal circuit of the eternal God. There is a kinship of divine spontaneity in all personality." P. 71.

III. SOURCE OF PERSONALITY

1. **God is personality.**

"Without God and except for his great and central person, there would be no personality throughout all the vast universe of universes. *God is personality*." P. 28.

2. **God the source of all personality.**

"The Universal Father is the secret of the reality of personality, the bestowal of personality, and the destiny of personality. The Eternal Son is the absolute personality, the secret of spiritual energy, morontia spirits, and perfected spirits. The Conjoint Actor is the spirit-mind personality, the source of intelligence, reason, and the universal mind. But the Isle of Paradise is nonpersonal and extraspiritual, being the essence of the universal body, the source and center of physical matter, and the absolute master pattern of universal material reality." P. 8.

3. **How we get our personality.**

    "Capacity for divine personality is inherent in the prepersonal Adjuster; capacity for human personality is potential in the cosmic-mind endowment of the human being. But the experiential personality of mortal man is not observable as an active and functional reality until after the material life vehicle of the mortal creature has been touched by the liberating divinity of the Universal Father, being thus launched upon the seas of experience as a self-conscious and a (relatively) self-determinative and self-creative personality. The material self is truly and *unqualifiedly personal.*" P. 71.

4. **The Father alone bestows personality.**

    "The bestowal of personality is the exclusive function of the Universal Father, the personalization of the living energy systems which he endows with the attributes of relative creative consciousness and the freewill control thereof. There is no personality apart from God the Father, and no personality exists except for God the Father. The fundamental attributes of human selfhood, as well as the absolute Adjuster nucleus of the human personality, are the bestowals of the Universal Father, acting in his exclusively personal domain of cosmic ministry." P. 70.

5. **God is bestower and conservator of every personality.**

    "The Universal Father is the God of personalities. The domain of universe personality, from the lowest mortal and material creature of personality status to the highest persons of creator dignity and divine status, has its center and circumference in the Universal Father. God the Father is the bestower and the conservator of every personality. And the Paradise Father is likewise the destiny of all those finite personalities who wholeheartedly choose to do the divine will, those who love God and long to be like him." P. 70.

6. **Personality is a universal mystery.**

    "Personality is one of the unsolved mysteries of the universes. We are able to form adequate concepts of the factors entering into the make-up of various orders and levels of personality, but we do not fully comprehend the real nature of the personality itself. We clearly perceive the numerous factors which, when put together, constitute the vehicle for human personality, but we do not fully comprehend the nature and significance of such a finite personality." P. 70.

IV. HUMAN PERSONALITY

1. Personality and selfhood.

"In the human organism the summation of its parts constitutes selfhood—individuality—but such a process has nothing whatever to do with personality, which is the unifier of all these factors as related to cosmic realities." P. 1227.

2. Personality relationships.

"Knowledge yields pride in the fact of personality; wisdom is the consciousness of the meaning of personality; religion is the experience of cognizance of the value of personality; revelation is the assurance of personality survival." P. 1122.

3. The psychic circles and personality.

"The psychic circles are not exclusively intellectual, neither are they wholly morontial; they have to do with personality status, mind attainment, soul growth, and Adjuster attunement. The successful traversal of these levels demands the harmonious functioning of the *entire personality*, not merely of some one phase thereof. The growth of the parts does not equal the true maturation of the whole; the parts really grow in proportion to the expansion of the entire self—the whole self—material, intellectual, and spiritual." P. 1209.

4. The quests of personality.

"Self-consciousness is in essence a communal consciousness: God and man, Father and son, Creator and creature. In human self-consciousness four universe-reality realizations are latent and inherent:

"1. The quest for knowledge, the logic of science.
"2. The quest for moral values, the sense of duty.
"3. The quest for spiritual values, the religious experience.
"4. The quest for personality values, the ability to recognize the reality of God as a personality and the concurrent realization of our fraternal relationship with fellow personalities." P. 196.

5. Human personality the shadow of the divine.

"Human personality is the time-space image-shadow cast by the divine Creator personality. And no actuality can ever be adequately comprehended by an examination of its shadow. Shadows should be interpreted in terms of the true substance." P. 29.

6. **Personality recognition by Census Directors.**

"The Census Directors are concerned with human beings—as with other will creatures—only to the extent of recording the fact of will function. They are not concerned with the records of your life and its doings; they are not in any sense recording personalities. The Census Director of Nebadon, number 81,412 of Orvonton, now stationed on Salvington, is at this very moment personally conscious and aware of your living presence here on Urantia; and he will afford the records confirmation of your death the moment you cease to function as a will creature." P. 267.

V. HOW PERSONALITY FUNCTIONS

1. **Personality functions on many universe levels.**

"The Universal Father bestows personality upon numerous orders of beings as they function on diverse levels of universe actuality. Urantia human beings are endowed with personality of the finite-mortal type, functioning on the level of the ascending sons of God." P. 194.

2. **Personality endows us with identity.**

"Personalities may be similar, but they are never the same. Persons of a given series, type, order, or pattern may and do resemble one another, but they are never identical. Personality is that feature of an individual which we *know*, and which enables us to identify such a being at some future time regardless of the nature and extent of changes in form, mind, or spirit status. Personality is that part of any individual which enables us to recognize and positively identify that person as the one we have previously known, no matter how much he may have changed because of the modification of the vehicle of expression and manifestation of his personality." P. 194.

3. **Two universal features of personality.**

"Creature personality is distinguished by two self-manifesting and characteristic phenomena of mortal reactive behavior: self-consciousness and associated relative free will.

"Self-consciousness consists in intellectual awareness of personality actuality; it includes the ability to recognize the reality of other personalities. It indicates capacity for individualized experience in and with cosmic realities, equivalating to the attainment of identity status in the personality relationships of the universe. Self-consciousness connotes recognition of the actuality of mind ministration and the realization of relative independence of creative and determinative free will." P. 194.

- 171 -

4. The domain of human personality.

"The relative free will which characterizes the self-consciousness of human personality is involved in:

"1. Moral decision, highest wisdom.

"2. Spiritual choice, truth discernment.

"3. Unselfish love, brotherhood service.

"4. Purposeful co-operation, group loyalty.

"5. Cosmic insight, the grasp of universe meanings.

"6. Personality dedication, wholehearted devotion to doing the Father's will.

"7. Worship, the sincere pursuit of divine values and the whole-hearted love of the divine Value-Giver." P. 194-5.

5. The attributes of personality.

"The Urantia type of human personality may be viewed as functioning in a physical mechanism consisting of the planetary modification of the Nebadon type of organism belonging to the electrochemical order of life activation and endowed with the Nebadon order of the Orvonton series of the cosmic mind of parental reproductive pattern. The bestowal of the divine gift of personality upon such a mind-endowed mortal mechanism confers the dignity of cosmic citizenship and enables such a mortal creature forthwith to become reactive to the constitutive recognition of the three basic mind realities of the cosmos:

"1. The mathematical or logical recognition of the uniformity of physical causation.

"2. The reasoned recognition of the obligation of moral conduct.

"3. The faith-grasp of the fellowship worship of Deity, associated with the loving service of humanity.

"The full function of such a personality endowment is the beginning realization of Deity kinship. Such a selfhood, indwelt by a prepersonal fragment of God the Father, is in truth and in fact a spiritual son of God. Such a creature not only discloses capacity for the reception of the gift of the divine presence but also exhibits reactive response to the personality-gravity circuit of the Paradise Father of all personalities." P. 195.

VI. ADJUSTERS AND PERSONALITY

1. Personality antedates the Adjusters.

"Personality is a unique endowment of original nature whose existence is independent of, and antecedent to, the bestowal of the

Thought Adjuster. Nevertheless, the presence of the Adjuster does augment the qualitative manifestation of personality. Thought Adjusters, when they come forth from the Father, are identical in nature, but personality is diverse, original, and exclusive; and the manifestation of personality is further conditioned and qualified by the nature and qualities of the associated energies of a material, mindal, and spiritual nature which constitute the organismal vehicle for personality manifestation." P. 194.

2. **Adjuster influences interpersonal relations.**

"The higher forms of intelligent intercommunication between human beings are greatly helped by the indwelling Adjusters. Animals do have fellow feelings, but they do not communicate concepts to each other; they can express emotions but not ideas and ideals. Neither do men of animal origin experience a high type of intellectual intercourse or spiritual communion with their fellows until the Thought Adjusters have been bestowed, albeit, when such evolutionary creatures develop speech, they are on the highroad to receiving Adjusters.

"Animals do, in a crude way, communicate with each other, but there is little or no *personality* in such primitive contact. Adjusters are not personality; they are prepersonal beings. But they do hail from the source of personality, and their presence does augment the qualitative manifestations of human personality; especially is this true if the Adjuster has had previous experience." P. 1198.

3. **Adjusters and personality potential.**

"The type of Adjuster has much to do with the potential for expression of the human personality. On down through the ages, many of the great intellectual and spiritual leaders of Urantia have exerted their influence chiefly because of the superiority and previous experience of their indwelling Adjusters." P. 1198.

VII. CHARACTERISTICS OF PERSONALITY

1. **Personality always seeks unification.**

"Personality inherently reaches out to unify all constituent realities. The infinite personality of the First Source and Center, the Universal Father, unifies all seven constituent Absolutes of Infinity; and the personality of mortal man, being an exclusive and direct bestowal of the Universal Father, likewise possesses the potential of unifying the constituent factors of the mortal creature. Such unifying creativity of all creature personality is a birthmark of its high and exclusive source and is further evidential of its unbroken contact with this same source through the personality circuit, by means of which the personality of the creature maintains direct and sustaining contact with the Father of all personality on Paradise." P. 640.

2. Facts about personality.

"While it would be presumptuous to attempt the definition of personality, it may prove helpful to recount some of the things which are known about personality:

"1. Personality is that quality in reality which is bestowed by the Universal Father himself or by the Conjoint Actor, acting for the Father.

"2. It may be bestowed upon any living energy system which includes mind or spirit.

"3. It is not wholly subject to the fetters of antecedent causation. It is relatively creative or cocreative.

"4. When bestowed upon evolutionary material creatures, it causes spirit to strive for the mastery of energy-matter through the mediation of mind.

"5. Personality, while devoid of identity, can unify the identity of any living energy system.

"6. It discloses only qualitative response to the personality circuit in contradistinction to the three energies which show both qualitative and quantitative response to gravity.

"7. Personality is changeless in the presence of change.

"8. It can make a gift to God—dedication of the free will to the doing of the will of God.

"9. It is characterized by morality—awareness of relativity of relationship with other persons. It discerns conduct levels and choosingly discriminates between them.

"10. Personality is unique, absolutely unique: It is unique in time and space; it is unique in eternity and on Paradise; it is unique when bestowed—there are no duplicates; it is unique during every moment of existence; it is unique in relation to God—he is no respecter of persons, but neither does he add them together, for they are nonaddable—they are associable but nontotalable.

"11. Personality responds directly to other-personality presence.

"12. It is one thing which can be added to spirit, thus illustrating the primacy of the Father in relation to the Son. (Mind does not have to be added to spirit.)

"13. Personality may survive mortal death with identity in the surviving soul. The Adjuster and the personality are changeless; the relationship between them (in the soul) is nothing but change, continuing evolution; and if this change (growth) ceased, the soul would cease.

"14. Personality is uniquely conscious of time, and this is something other than the time perception of mind or spirit." P. 1225-6.

VIII. RELIGION AND PERSONALITY

1. Religion springs from whole personality.

"The certainties of science proceed entirely from the intellect; the certitudes of religion spring from the very foundations of the *entire personality*. Science appeals to the understanding of the mind; religion appeals to the loyalty and devotion of the body, mind, and spirit, even to the whole personality." P. 1119.

2. Religion stabilizes the personality.

"It is difficult to identify and analyze the factors of a religious experience, but it is not difficult to observe that such religious practitioners live and carry on as if already in the presence of the Eternal. Believers react to this temporal life as if immortality already were within their grasp. In the lives of such mortals there is a valid originality and a spontaneity of expression that forever segregate them from those of their fellows who have imbibed only the wisdom of the world. Religionists seem to live in effective emancipation from harrying haste and the painful stress of the vicissitudes inherent in the temporal currents of time; they exhibit a stabilization of personality and a tranquillity of character not explained by the laws of physiology, psychology, and sociology." P. 1119-20.

3. Personality and the moral character.

"'*By their fruits you shall know them.*' Personality is basically changeless; that which changes—grows—is the moral character. The major error of modern religions is negativism. The tree which bears no fruit is 'hewn down and cast into the fire.' Moral worth cannot be derived from mere repression—obeying the injunction 'Thou shalt not.' Fear and shame are unworthy motivations for religious living. Religion is valid only when it reveals the fatherhood of God and enhances the brotherhood of men." P. 1572.

4. **Love enhances personality associations.**

"Love is the secret of beneficial association between personalities. You cannot really know a person as the result of a single contact. You cannot appreciatingly know music through mathematical deduction, even though music is a form of mathematical rhythm. The number assigned to a telephone subscriber does not in any manner identify the personality of that subscriber or signify anything concerning his character." P. 141.

5. **Spirit dominance of personality.**

"In the evolutionary superuniverses energy-matter is dominant except in personality, where spirit through the mediation of mind is struggling for the mastery. The goal of the evolutionary universes is the subjugation of energy-matter by mind, the co-ordination of mind with spirit, and all of this by virtue of the creative and unifying presence of personality. Thus, in relation to personality, do physical systems become subordinate; mind systems, co-ordinate; and spirit systems, directive.

"This union of power and personality is expressive on deity levels in and as the Supreme. But the actual evolution of spirit dominance is a growth which is predicated on the freewill acts of the Creators and creatures of the grand universe." P. 1275.

6. **The ultimate spirit conquest.**

"The Supreme is the divine channel through which flows the creative infinity of the triodities that crystallizes into the galactic panorama of space, against which takes place the magnificent personality drama of time: the spirit conquest of energy-matter through the mediation of mind." P. 1281.

IX. POTENTIALS OF PERSONALITY

1. **The potentials of personality.**

"Personality is a level of deified reality and ranges from the mortal and midwayer level of the higher mind activation of worship and wisdom up through the morontial and spiritual to the attainment of finality of personality status. That is the evolutionary ascent of mortal—and kindredcreature personality, but there are numerous other orders of universe personalities.

"Reality is subject to universal expansion, personality to infinite diversification, and both are capable of well-nigh unlimited Deity co-ordination and eternal stabilization. While the metamorphic range of nonpersonal reality is definitely limited, we know of no limitations to the progressive evolution of personality realities.

"On attained experiential levels all personality orders or values are associable and even cocreational. Even God and man can coexist in a unified personality, as is so exquisitely demonstrated in the present status of Christ Michael—Son of Man and Son of God." P. 8.

2. Personality the center of existence.

"All mortal concepts of reality are based on the assumption of the actuality of human personality; all concepts of superhuman realities are based on the experience of the human personality with and in the cosmic realities of certain associated spiritual entities and divine personalities. Everything nonspiritual in human experience, excepting personality, is a means to an end. Every true relationship of mortal man with other persons—human or divine—is an end in itself. And such fellowship with the personality of Deity is the eternal goal of universe ascension." P. 1228.

3. Cosmic unity of personality.

"The purpose of cosmic evolution is to achieve unity of personality through increasing spirit dominance, volitional response to the teaching and leading of the Thought Adjuster. Personality, both human and superhuman, is characterized by an inherent cosmic quality which may be called 'the evolution of dominance,' the expansion of the control of both itself and its environment." P. 1229.

4. Personality can eternalize its purpose.

"The personality of the mortal creature may eternalize by self-identification with the indwelling spirit through the technique of choosing to do the will of the Father. Such a consecration of will is tantamount to the realization of eternity-reality of purpose. This means that the purpose of the creature has become fixed with regard to the succession of moments; stated otherwise, that the succession of moments will witness no change in creature purpose. A million or a billion moments makes no difference. Number has ceased to have meaning with regard to the creature's purpose. Thus does creature choice plus God's choice eventuate in the eternal realities of the never-ending union of the spirit of God and the nature of man in the everlasting service of the children of God and of their Paradise Father." P. 1295.

5. **Personality action and Supreme reaction.**

"The progressing personality leaves a trail of actualized reality as it passes through the ascending levels of the universes. Be they mind, spirit, or energy, the growing creations of time and space are modified by the progression of personality through their domains. When man acts, the Supreme reacts, and this transaction constitutes the fact of progression." P. 1286.

X. JESUS' PERSONALITY

1. **Jesus was a unified personality.**

"Jesus was the perfectly unified human personality. And today, as in Galilee, he continues to unify mortal experience and to co-ordinate human endeavors. He unifies life, ennobles character, and simplifies experience. He enters the human mind to elevate, transform, and transfigure it. It is literally true: 'If any man has Christ Jesus within him, he is a new creature; old things are passing away; behold, all things are becoming new. P. 1103.

2. **Jesus a well-integrated personality.**

"The Son of Man was always a well-poised personality. Even his enemies maintained a wholesome respect for him; they even feared his presence. Jesus was unafraid. He was surcharged with divine enthusiasm, but he never became fanatical. He was emotionally active but never flighty. He was imaginative but always practical. He frankly faced the realities of life, but he was never dull or prosaic. He was courageous but never reckless; prudent but never cow-ardly. He was sympathetic but not sentimental; unique but not eccentric. He was pious but not sanctimonious. And he was so well-poised because he was so perfectly unified." P. 1102.

3. **Jesus had great respect for human personality.**

"Always respect the personality of man. Never should a righteous cause be promoted by force; spiritual victories can be won only by spiritual power. This injunction against the employment of material influences refers to psychic force as well as to physical force. Overpowering arguments and mental superiority are not to be employed to coerce men and women into the kingdom. Man's mind is not to be crushed by the mere weight of logic or overawed by shrewd eloquence. While emotion as a factor in human deci-sions cannot be wholly eliminated, it should not be directly appealed to in the teachings of those who would advance the cause of the kingdom. Make your appeals directly to the divine spirit that dwells within the minds of men. Do not appeal to fear, pity, or mere sentiment. In appealing to men, be fair; exercise self-control and exhibit due restraint; show proper respect for the personalities of your pupils. Remember that I have said: 'Behold, I stand at the door and knock, and if any man will open, I will come in.'

"In bringing men into the kingdom, do not lessen or destroy their self-respect. While overmuch self-respect may destroy proper humility and end in pride, conceit, and arrogance, the loss of self-respect often ends in paralysis of the will. It is the purpose of this gospel to restore self-respect to those who have lost it and to restrain it in those who have it. Make not the mistake of only condemning the wrongs in the lives of your pupils; remember also to accord generous recognition for the most praise-worthy things in their lives. Forget not that I will stop at nothing to restore self-respect to those who have lost it, and who really desire to regain it." P. 1765.

4. We should respect all personalities.

"Take care that you do not wound the self-respect of timid and fearful souls. Do not indulge in sarcasm at the expense of my simple-minded brethren. Be not cynical with my fear-ridden children. Idleness is destructive of self-respect; therefore, admonish your brethren ever to keep busy at their chosen tasks, and put forth every effort to secure work for those who find themselves without employment." P. 1765.

XI. SURVIVAL OF PERSONALITY

1. Survival of personality values.

"If mortal man fails to survive natural death, the real spiritual values of his human experience survive as a part of the continuing experience of the Thought Adjuster. The personality values of such a nonsurvivor persist as a factor in the personality of the actualizing Supreme Being. Such persisting qualities of personality are deprived of identity but not of experiential values accumulated during the mortal life in the flesh. The survival of identity is dependent on the survival of the immortal soul of morontia status and increasingly divine value. Personality identity survives in and by the survival of the soul." P. 195.

2. Personality as related to God.

"Man does not achieve union with God as a drop of water might find unity with the ocean. Man attains divine union by progressive reciprocal spiritual communion, by personality intercourse with the personal God, by increasingly attaining the divine nature through wholehearted and intelligent conformity to the divine will. Such a sublime relationship can exist only between personalities." P. 31.

3. Revelation enhances personality survival.

"A human being is also aware that he is a part of the ideational cosmos, but though concept may endure beyond a mortal life span, there is nothing inherent in concept which indicates the personal survival of the conceiving personality. Nor will the exhaustion of the possibilities of logic and reason ever reveal to the logician or to the reasoner the eternal truth of the survival of personality." P. 1116.

4. Destiny of nonsurviving personality.

"Throughout the grand universe the Supreme struggles for expression. His divine evolution is in measure predicated on the wisdom-action of every personality in existence. When a human being chooses eternal survival, he is cocreating destiny; and in the life of this ascending mortal the finite God finds an increased measure of personality self-realization and an enlargement of experiential sovereignty. But if a creature rejects the eternal career, that part of the Supreme which was dependent on this creature's choice experiences inescapable delay, a deprivation which must be compensated by substitutional or collateral experience; as for the personality of the nonsurvivor, it is absorbed into the oversoul of creation, becoming a part of the Deity of the Supreme." P. 1283.

The word "personality" does not appear in the Bible.

THE PSYCHOLOGY OF PERSONALITY

Psychology regards personality as being the sum of the individual's constitutional, ideational, affective, and responsive capacities. Personality is more than "charm," urbanity, and culture.

Personality is difficult to define—but it is recognized as functioning on diverse levels:

1. Physical level—the physique.
2. Intellectual level—the mind.
3. Emotional level—temperament.
4. Social level—ethical disposition.
5. Moral level—the character.
6. Spiritual level—religious experience.

I. ATTEMPTED DEFINITIONS

1. **Brown**: *"Personality is selfhood, self-consciousness, self-control, the power to know."*

2. **Kant**: *"That quality in every man which makes him worthwhile."*

3. **Wordsworth**: *"Personality refers not to any particular sort of activity, such as talking, remembering, thinking, or loving; but an individual can reveal his personality in the way he does any of these things."*

4. **Allport**: *"Personality is the dynamic organization within the individual of those psychological systems that determine his unique adjustments to his environment."*

II. CLASSIFICATION OF PERSONALITY

1. **Jung**: Introverts and extroverts—to which has been added ambiverts.

2. **Sheldon**: This is the better and more scientific classification:

    a. Extrovert type:
    1. **Endomorph.**
    2. **Mesomorph.**
    b. Introvert type—ectomorph.

    The *Endomorph* is the extrovert of emotion. There is a close connection with the vital internal organs.

    The *Mesomorph* is the extrovert of action. There is connection with the muscular system.

III. PSYCHIATRIC CLASSIFICATION

1. Asthenoid—Neurotic type.

2. Hysteroid.

3. Schizoid.

4. Cycloid.

5. Paranoid.

6. Epileptoid.

7. Psychopathic.

10. MIND AND SPIRIT

Mind and Spirit in the Bible

MIND AND SPIRIT

I. JESUS' DISCOURSE ON MIND

"My son, I have already told you much about the mind of man and the divine spirit that lives therein, but now let me emphasize that self-consciousness is a *reality*. When any animal becomes self-conscious, it becomes a primitive man. Such an attainment results from a co-ordination of function between impersonal energy and spirit-conceiving mind, and it is this phenomenon which warrants the bestowal of an absolute focal point for the human personality, the spirit of the Father in heaven.

"Ideas are not simply a record of sensations; ideas are sensations plus the reflective interpretations of the personal self; and the self is more than the sum of one's sensations. There begins to be something of an approach to unity in an evolving selfhood, and that unity is derived from the indwelling presence of a part of absolute unity which spiritually activates such a self-conscious animal-origin mind.

"No mere animal could possess a time self-consciousness. Animals possess a physiological co-ordination of associated sensation-recognition and memory thereof, but none experience a meaningful recognition of sensation or exhibit a purposeful association of these combined physical experiences such as is manifested in the conclusions of intelligent and reflective human interpretations. And this fact of self-conscious existence, associated with the reality of his subsequent spiritual experience, constitutes man a potential son of the universe and foreshadows his eventual attainment of the Supreme Unity of the universe.

"Neither is the human self merely the sum of the successive states of consciousness. Without the effective functioning of a consciousness sorter and associatore there would not exist sufficent unity to warrant the designation of a selfhood. Such an ununified mind could hardly attain conscious levels of human status. If the associations of consciousness were just an accident, the minds of all men would then exhibit the uncontrolled and random associations of certain phases of mental madness.

"A human mind, built up solely out of the consciousness of physical sensations, could never attain spiritual levels; this kind of material mind would be utterly lacking in a sense of moral values and would be without a guiding sense of spiritual dominance which is so essential to achieving harmonious personality unity in time, and which is inseparable from personality survival in eternity.

"The human mind early begins to manifest qualities which are super-material; the truly reflective human intellect is not altogether bound by the limits of time. That individuals so differ in their life performances indicates, not only the varying endowments of heredity and the different influences of the environment, but also the degree of unification with the indwelling spirit of the Father which has been achieved by the self, the measure of the identification of the one with the other.

"The human mind does not well stand the conflict of double allegiance. It is a severe strain on the soul to undergo the experience of an effort to serve both good and evil. The supremely happy and efficiently unified mind is the one wholly dedicated to the doing of the will of the Father in heaven. Unresolved conflicts destroy unity and may terminate in mind disruption. But the survival character of a soul is not fostered by attempting to secure peace of mind at any price, by the surrender of noble aspirations, and by the compromise of spiritual ideals; rather is such peace attained by the stalwart assertion of the triumph of that which is true, and this victory is achieved in the overcoming of evil with the potent force of good." P. 1479-80.

II. THE NATURE OF MIND

1. The nature of mind.

"*Mind* is a phenomenon connoting the presence-activity of *living ministry* in addition to varied energy systems; and this is true on all levels of intelligence. In personality, mind ever intervenes between spirit and matter; therefore is the universe illuminated by three kinds of light: material light, intellectual insight, and spirit luminosity." P. 9.

2. Mortal mind a cosmic loom.

"The material mind of mortal man is the cosmic loom that carries the morontia fabrics on which the indwelling Thought Adjuster threads the spirit patterns of a universe character of enduring values and divine meanings— a surviving soul of ultimate destiny and unending career, a potential finaliter.

"The human personality is identified with mind and spirit held together in functional relationship by life in a material body. This functioning relationship of such mind and spirit does not result in some combination of the qualities or attributes of mind and spirit but rather in an entirely new, original, and unique universe value of potentially eternal endurance, the *soul*." P. 1217-8.

3. **The seven adjutant mind-spirits.**

"The seven adjutant mind-spirits are the versatile mind ministers to the lower intelligent existences of a local universe. This order of mind is ministered from the local universe headquarters or from some world connected therewith, but there is influential direction of lower-mind function from the system capitals.

"On an evolutionary world much, very much, depends on the work of these seven adjutants. But they are mind ministers; they are not concerned in physical evolution, the domain of the Life Carriers. Nevertheless, the perfect integration of these spirit endowments with the ordained and natural procedure of the unfolding and inherent regime of the Life Carriers is responsible for the mortal inability to discern, in the phenomenon of mind, aught but the hand of nature and the outworking of natural processes, albeit you are occasionally somewhat perplexed in explaining all of everything connected with the natural reactions of mind as it is associated with matter. And if Urantia were operating more in accordance with the original plans, you would observe even less to arrest your attention in the phenomenon of mind." P. 738. Isa. 11:2, 3.

4. **The superconscious mind.**

"Only in the higher levels of the superconscious mind as it impinges upon the spirit realm of human experience can you find those higher concepts in association with effective master patterns which will contribute to the building of a better and more enduring civilization. Personality is inherently creative, but it thus functions only in the inner life of the individual." P. 1220.

5. **Marring of mortal mind.**

"Mind, on Urantia, is a compromise between the essence of thought perfection and the evolving mentality of your immature human nature. The plan for your intellectual evolution is, indeed, one of sublime perfection, but you are far short of that divine goal as you function in the tabernacles of the flesh. Mind is truly of divine origin, and it does have a divine destiny, but your mortal minds are not yet of divine dignity.

"Too often, all too often, you mar your minds by insincerity and sear them with unrighteousness; you subject them to animal fear and distort them by useless anxiety. Therefore, though the source of mind is divine, mind as you know it on your world of ascension can hardly become the object of great admiration, much less of adoration or worship. The contemplation of the immature and inactive human intellect should lead only to reactions of humility." P. 103.

6. **Comparative evaluation of human mind.**

"In the mind's eye conjure up a picture of one of your primitive ancestors of cave-dwelling times—a short, misshapen, filthy, snarling hulk of a man standing, legs spread, club upraised, breathing hate and animosity as he looks fiercely just ahead. Such a picture hardly depicts the divine dignity of man. But allow us to enlarge the picture. In front of this animated human crouches a saber-toothed tiger. Behind him, a woman and two children. Immediately you recognize that such a picture stands for the beginnings of much that is fine and noble in the human race, but the man is the same in both pictures. Only in the second sketch you are favored with a widened horizon. You therein discern the motivation of this evolving mortal. His attitude becomes, praiseworthy because you understand him. If you could only fathom the motives of your associates, how much better you would understand them. If you could only know your fellows, you would eventually fall in love with them." P. 1098.

III. CHARACTERISTIC FUNCTIONS OF MIND

1. The ability to learn.

"The acquisition of the potential of the ability to *learn* from experience marks the beginning of the functioning of the adjutant spirits, and they function from the lowliest minds of primitive and invisible existences up to the highest types in the evolutionary scale of human beings. They are the source and pattern for the otherwise more or less mysterious behavior and incompletely understood quick reactions of mind to the material environment. Long must these faithful and always dependable influences carry forward their preliminary ministry before the animal mind attains the human levels of spirit receptivity." P. 739.

2. Human mind functions.

"The evolution of mechanisms implies and indicates the concealed presence and dominance of creative mind. The ability of the mortal intellect to conceive, design, and create automatic mechanisms demonstrates the superior, creative, and purposive qualities of man's mind as the dominant influence on the planet. Mind always reaches out towards:

1. Creation of material mechanisms.
2. Discovery of hidden mysteries.
3. Exploration of remote situations.
4. Formulation of mental systems.
5. Attainment of wisdom goals.
6. Achievement of spirit levels.
7. The accomplishment of divine destinies—supreme, ultimate, and absolute." P.483.

3. Mind as a co-ordinator of realities.

"Mind is the technique whereby spirit realities become experiential to creature personalities. And in the last analysis the unifying possibilities of even human mind, the ability to co-ordinate things, ideas, and values, is supermaterial." P.140.

4. Far-flung relationships of mind.

"It is the purpose of education to develop and sharpen these innate endowments of the human mind; of civilization to express them; of life experience to realize them; of religion to ennoble them; and of personality to unify them." P. 192.

IV. MIND RELATED TO TIME AND SPACE

1. Mortal mind as related to time and space.

"Relationships to time do not exist without motion in space, but consciousness of time does. Sequentiality can consciousize time even in the absence of motion. Man's mind is less time-bound than space-bound because of the inherent nature of mind. Even during the days of the earth life in the flesh, though man's mind is rigidly space-bound, the creative human imagination is comparatively time free. But time itself is not genetically a quality of mind." P. 135.

2. Gravity relations of mind.

"As the mind of any personality in the universe becomes more spiritual—Godlike—it becomes less responsive to material gravity. Reality, measured by physical-gravity response, is the antithesis of reality as determined by quality of spirit content. Physical-gravity action is a quantitative determiner of nonspirit energy; spiritual-gravity action is the qualitative measure of the living energy of divinity." P. 140.

3. Relation of mind to energy and spirit.

"While mind is energy associated in purely material beings and spirit associated in purely spiritual personalities, innumerable orders of personality, including the human, possess minds that are associated with both energy and spirit. The spiritual aspects of creature mind unfailingly respond to the spirit-gravity pull of the Eternal Son; the material features respond to the gravity urge of the material universe." P. 104.

4. The differential functioning of mind.

"The greater the spirit-energy divergence, the greater the observable function of mind; the lesser the diversity of energy and spirit, the lesser the observable function of mind. Apparently, the maximum function of the cosmic mind is in the time universes of space. Here mind seems to function in a mid-zone between energy and spirit, but this is not true of the higher levels of mind; on Paradise, energy and spirit are essentially one." P. 104.

V. THE COSMIC MIND

1. The cosmic mind.

"*The cosmic mind.* This is the sevenfold diversified mind of time and space, one phase of which is ministered by each of the Seven Master Spirits to one of the seven superuniverses. The cosmic mind encompasses all finite-mind levels and co-ordinates experientially with the evolutionary- deity levels of the Supreme Mind and transcendentally with the existential levels of absolute mind—the direct circuits of the Conjoint Actor." P. 481.

2. **Evolutionary and cosmic minds.**

"When an evolving mind becomes attuned to the circuits of cosmic mind, when an evolving universe becomes stabilized after the pattern of the central universe, when an advancing spirit contacts the united ministry of the Master Spirits, when an ascending mortal personality finally attunes to the divine leading of the indwelling Adjuster, then has the actuality of the Supreme become real by one more degree in the universes; then has the divinity of Supremacy advanced one more step toward cosmic realization." P. 1278.

3. **"Kindred spirits" explained by cosmic mind.**

"The fact of the cosmic mind explains the kinship of various types of human and superhuman minds. Not only are kindred spirits attracted to each other, but kindred minds are also very fraternal and inclined towards co-operation the one with the other. Human minds are sometimes observed to be running in channels of astonishing similarity and inexplicable agreement." P. 191.

4. **Mind anticipates cause and effect.**

"The selective response of an animal is limited to the motor level of behavior. The supposed insight of the higher animals is on a motor level and usually appears only after the experience of motor trial and error. Man is able to exercise scientific, moral, and spiritual insight prior to all exploration or experimentation.

"Only a personality can know what it is doing before it does it; only personalities possess insight in advance of experience. A personality can look before it leaps and can therefore learn from looking as well as from leaping. A nonpersonal animal ordinarily learns only by leaping." P. 193.

VI. MIND IS SUPERMATERIAL

1. **The universe is divine-minded.**

"To assume that the universe can be known, that it is intelligible, is to assume that the universe is mind made and personality managed. Man's mind can only perceive the mind phenomena of other minds, be they human or superhuman. If man's personality can experience the universe, there is a divine mind and an actual personality somewhere concealed in that universe." P. 30.

2. Mind is not mechanistic.

"There exists a great cosmic gulf between matter and thought, and this gulf is immeasurably greater between material mind and spiritual love. Consciousness, much less self-consciousness, cannot be explained by any theory of mechanistic electronic association or materialistic energy phenomena." P. 1228.

3. Physics and chemistry cannot explain mind.

"Physics and chemistry alone cannot explain how a human being evolved out of the primeval protoplasm of the early seas. The ability to learn, memory and differential response to environment, is the endowment of mind. The laws of physics are not responsive to training; they are immutable and unchanging. The reactions of chemistry are not modified by education; they are uniform and dependable. Aside from the presence of the Unqualified Absolute, electrical and chemical reactions are predictable. But mind can profit from experience, can learn from reactive habits of behavior in response to repetition of stimuli." P. 738.

4. Will is superior to mind and matter.

"In the cosmic evolutionary laboratories mind is always dominant over matter, and spirit is ever correlated with mind. Failure of these diverse endowments to synchronize and co-ordinate may cause time delays, but if the individual really knows God and desires to find him and become like him, then survival is assured regardless of the handicaps of time. Physical status may handicap mind, and mental perversity may delay spiritual attainment, but none of these obstacles can defeat the whole-souled choice of will." P. 740.

5. Mind and spirit evolve the soul.

"There is a cosmic unity in the several mind levels of the universe of universes. Intellectual selves have their origin in the cosmic mind much as nebulae take origin in the cosmic energies of universe space. On the human (hence personal) level of intellectual selves the potential of spirit evolution becomes dominanat, with the assent of the mortal mind, because of the spiritual endowments of the human personality together with the creative presence of an entity-point of absolute value in such human selves. But such a spirit dominance of the material mind is conditioned upon two experiences: This mind must have evolved up through the ministry of the seven adjutant mind-spirits, and the material (personal) self must choose to co-operate with the indwelling Adjuster in creating and fostering the morontia self, the evolutionary and potentially immortal soul." P. 1216.

6. **Mind the arena of eternal choice.**

"Material mind is the arena in which human personalities live, are self-conscious, make decisions, choose God or forsake him, eternalize or destroy themselves." P. 1216.

VII. RELATIONS OF MIND AND SPIRIT

1. **The insight of spirit transcends mind.**

"The absolute mind is the mind of the Third Person; it is inseparable from the personality of God the Spirit. Mind, in functioning beings, is not separated from energy or spirit, or both. Mind is not inherent in energy; energy is receptive and responsive to mind; mind can be superimposed upon energy, but consciousness is not inherent in the purely material level. Mind does not have to be added to pure spirit, for spirit is innately conscious and identifying. Spirit is always intelligent, *minded* in some way. It may be this mind or that mind, it may be premind or supermind, even spirit mind, but it does the equivalent of thinking and knowing. The insight of spirit transcends, supervenes, and theoretically antedates the consciousness of mind." P. 102.

2. **Mind is meaning—spirit is value.**

"Cosmic force responds to mind even as cosmic mind responds to spirit. Spirit is divine purpose, and spirit mind is divine purpose in action. Energy is thing, mind is meaning, spirit is value. Even in time and space, mind establishes those relative relationships between energy and spirit which are suggestive of mutual kinship in eternity." P. 102.

3. **Mind functions in spirit and material realms.**

"Mind transmutes the values of spirit into the meanings of intellect; volition has power to bring the meanings of mind to fruit in both the material and spiritual domains. The Paradise ascent involves a relative and differential growth in spirit, mind, and energy. The personality is the unifier of these components of experiential individuality." P. 102.

4. **Correlation of spiritual influences.**

"The ministering personality of the guardian seraphim, the God presence of the indwelling Adjuster, the encircuited action of the Holy Spirit, and the Son-consciousness of the Spirit of Truth are all divinely correlated into a meaningful unity of spiritual ministry in and to a mortal personality. Though hailing from different sources and different levels, these celestial influences are all integrated in the enveloping and evolving presence of the Supreme Being." P. 1245.

5. **Mind is the instrument on which the will plays.**

"Mind is the cosmic instrument on which the human will can play the discords of destruction, or upon which this same human will can bring forth the exquisite melodies of God identification and consequent eternal survival. The Adjuster bestowed upon man is, in the last analysis, impervious to evil and incapable of sin, but mortal mind can actually be twisted, distorted, and rendered evil and ugly by the sinful machinations of a perverse and self-seeking human will. Likewise can this mind be made noble, beautiful, true, and good—actually great—in accordance with the spirit-illuminated will of a God-knowing human being." P. 1217.

6. **Ranges of mind stability.**

"Evolutionary mind is only fully stable and dependable when manifesting itself upon the two extremes of cosmic intellectuality—the wholly mechanized and the entirely spiritualized. Between the intellectual extremes of pure mechanical control and true spirit nature there intervenes that enormous group of evolving and ascending minds whose stability and tranquillity are dependent upon personality choice and spirit identification." P. 1217.

VIII. ADJUSTERS AND THE MIND

1. **Adjusters have no special functional mechanism.**

"The Thought Adjuster has no special mechanism through which to gain self-expression; there is no mystic religious faculty for the reception or expression of religious emotions. These experiences are made available through the naturally ordained mechanism of mortal mind. And therein lies one explanation of the Adjuster's difficulty in engaging in direct communication with the material mind of its constant indwelling." P. 1104.

2. **Adjusters work through material minds.**

"Though the work of Adjusters is spiritual in nature, they must, perforce, do all their work upon an intellectual foundation. Mind is the human soil from which the spirit Monitor must evolve the morontia soul with the cooperation of the indwelt personality." P. 1216.

3. **Mind relationships with Adjusters.**

"You as a personal creature have mind and will. The Adjuster as a prepersonal creature has premind and prewill. If you so fully conform to the Adjuster's mind that you see eye to eye, then your minds become one, and you receive the reinforcement of the Adjuster's mind. Subsequently, if your will orders and enforces the execution of the decisions of this new or combined mind, the Adjuster's prepersonal will attains to personality expression through your decision, and as far as that particular project is concerned, you and the Adjuster are one. Your mind has attained to divinity attunement, and the Adjuster's will has achieved personality expression." P. 1205.

4. **Co-operation with Adjusters.**

"But man does not passively, slavishly, surrender his will to the Adjuster. Rather does he actively, positively, and co-operatively choose to follow the Adjuster's leading when and as such leading consciously differs from the desires, and impulses of the natural mortal mind. The Adjusters manipulate but never dominate man's mind against his will; to the Adjusters the human will is supreme. And they so regard and respect it while they strive to achieve the spiritual goals of thought adjustment and character transformation in the almost limitless arena of the evolving human intellect." P. 1217.

5. **Human will is captain of the ship.**

"Mind is your ship, the Adjuster is your pilot, the human will is captain. The master of the mortal vessel should have the wisdom to trust the divine pilot to guide the ascending soul into the morontia harbors of eternal survival. Only by selfishness, slothfulness, and sinfulness can the will of man reject the guidance of such a loving pilot and eventually wreck the mortal career upon the evil shoals of rejected mercy and upon the rocks of embraced sin. With your consent, this faithful pilot will safely carry you across the barriers of time and the handicaps of space to the very source of the divine mind and on beyond, even to the Paradise Father of Adjusters." P. 1217.

IX. SPIRIT DOMINANCE

1. **Through mediation of mind, spirit seeks mastery.**

"In the evolutionary super-universes energy-matter is dominant except in personality, where spirit through the mediation of mind is struggling for the mastery. The goal of the evolutionary universes is the subjugation of energy-matter by mind, the co-ordination of mind with spirit, and all of this by virtue of the creative and unifying presence of personality. Thus, in relation to personality, do physical systems become subordinate; mind systems, co-ordinate; and spirit systems, directive." P. 1275.

2. Spirit dominance partnership of Creator and creature.

"This union of power and personality is expressive on deity levels in and as the Supreme. But the actual evolution of spirit dominance is a growth which is predicated on the freewill acts of the Creators and creatures of the grand universe." P. 1275.

3. Spirit dominance of survival minds.

"In the inner experience of man, mind is joined to matter. Such material-linked minds cannot survive mortal death. The technique of survival is embraced in those adjustments of the human will and those transformations in the mortal mind whereby such a God-conscious intellect gradually becomes spirit taught and eventually spirit led. This evolution of the human mind from matter association to spirit union results in the transmutation of the potentially spirit phases of the mortal mind into the morontia realities of the immortal soul. Mortal mind subservient to matter is destined to become increasingly material and consequently to suffer eventual personality extinction; mind yielded to spirit is destined to become increasingly spiritual and ultimately to achieve oneness with the surviving and guiding divine spirit and in this way to attain survival and eternity of personality existence." P. 26.

MIND AND SPIRIT IN THE BIBLE
I. MIND

1. Choosing right and wrong.

"To set the mind on the flesh is death, but to set the mind on the Spirit is life and peace." **Rom. 8:6.**

2. Consecrated mind.

"You shall love the Lord your God with...all your mind." **Matt. 22:37.**

"I...serve the law of God with my mind." **Rom. 7:25.**

3. Motivation.

"For if the readiness is there, it is acceptable according to what a man has, not according to what he has not." **2 Cor. 8:12.**

4. **Self-control.**

   "Therefore gird up your minds, be sober." **1 Peter 1:13**.

   "Likewise urge the younger men to control themselves." **Titus 2:6**.

   "Thou dost keep him in perfect peace, whose mind is stayed on thee." **Isa. 26:3**.

5. **Renewing of the mind.**

   "Do not be conformed to this world but be transformed by the renewal of your mind." **Rom. 12:2**.

6. **The futility of anxiety.**

   "Do not seek what you are to eat and what you are to drink, nor be of anxious mind." **Luke 12:29**.

   "When they deliver you up, do not be anxious how you are to speak or what you are to say." **Matt. 10:19**.

7. **The dishonest mind.**

   "For that person must not suppose that a double-minded man, unstable in all his ways, will receive anything from the Lord." **Jas. 1:8**.

8. The adjutant mind-spirits. **See Isa. 11:2.**

   1. Intuition.
   2. Understanding.
   3. Courage.
   4. Knowledge.
   5. Counsel.
   6. Worship.
   7. Wisdom.
   a. *Spirit of understanding.*
      "And out of my understanding a spirit answers me." **Job 20:3**.
   b. *Spirit of wisdom.*
      "But they could not withstand the wisdom and the Spirit with which he spoke." **Acts 6:10**.
      "And Joshua...was full of the spirit of wisdom." **Deut. 34:9**.
   Mind is an endowment.

   "Speak to all who have ability, whom I have endowed with an able mind." **Ex. 28:3**.

9. **The human-divine mind.**

   "Have this mind among yourselves, which you have in Christ Jesus." **Phil. 2:5**.

II. HEART

Heart, soul, and spirit are often used synonymously in the Bible. The word "heart" embraces human feelings and emotions.

1. **Serving God with a whole heart.**

   "And now...what does the Lord your God require of you, but to fear the Lord your God, to walk in all his ways, to love him, to serve the Lord your God with all your heart and with all your soul." **Deut. 10:12.**

2. **God judges by the heart.**

   "The Lord sees not as man sees...the Lord looks on the heart." **1 Sam. 16:7.**

3. **How to find God.**

   "You will seek the Lord your God, and you will find him, if you search after him with all your heart and with all your soul." **Deut. 4:29.**

4. **The pure in heart.**

   "Blessed are the pure in heart, for they shall see God." **Matt. 5:8.**

   "Create in me a clean heart, O God, and put a new and right spirit within me." **Ps. 51:10.**

5. **We should discipline the heart.**

   "The Lord saw that...every imagination of the thoughts of his heart was only evil continually." **Gen. 6:5.**

   "The heart is deceitful above all things, and desperately corrupt." **Jer. 17:9.**

   "Anxiety in a man's heart weighs him down." **Prov. 12:25.**

6. **Broken hearts.**

   "He heals the brokenhearted, and binds up their wounds." **Ps. 147:3.**

   "Hope deferred makes the heart sick." **Prov. 13:12.**

7. **Cheerful hearts.**

   "Making melody to the Lord with all your heart." **Eph. 5:19.**

   "A glad heart makes a cheerful countenance." **Prov. 15:13.**

8. **Importance of the emotions.**

   "I will give them a heart to know that I am the Lord; and they shall be my people." **Jer. 24:7.**

   "For where your treasure is, there will your heart be also." **Luke 12:34.**

   "For out of the abundance of the heart the mouth speaks." **Matt. 12:34.**

9. **Concerning hard hearts.**

   a. God hardens Pharaoh's heart.
       "I will harden Pharaoh's heart...he will not listen to you." **Ex. 7:3. 4.**

   b. Pharaoh hardens his own heart.
       "Pharaoh's heart is hardened, he refuses to let the people go." **Ex. 7:14.**

III. CONSCIENCE

Conscience is used in the New Testament 30 times. It seems to mean "joint knowledge."

1. **A good conscience.**

   "And Paul...said, "Brethren, I have lived before God in all good conscience up to this day."" **Acts 23:1.**

   "They must hold the mystery of the faith with a clear conscience." **l.Tim. 3:9.**

2. **A bad conscience.**

   "Let us draw near with a true heart in full assurance of faith, with our hearts sprinkled clean from an evil conscience." **Heb. 10:22.**

3. **The abused conscience.**

   "Eat food as really offered to an idol; and their conscience, being weak, is defiled." **l Cor. 8:7.**

   "By rejecting conscience, certain persons have made shipwreck of their faith." **l.Tim. 1:19.**

   "To the corrupt and unbelieving nothing is pure; their very minds and consciences are corrupted." **Titus 1:15.**

   "Through the pretentions of liars whose consciences are seared." **l Tim. 4:2.**

4. **Conscience as a guide.**

   "Eat whatever is set before you without raising any question on the ground of conscience." **l. Cor. 10:27.**

"Let each of you look not only to his own interests, but also to the interests of others." **Phil. 2:4.**

"By the open statement of the truth we would commend ourselves to every man's conscience." **2 Cor. 4:2.**

"If food is a cause of my brother's falling, I will never eat meat." **1 Cor. 8:13.**

IV. SPIRIT

1. Spirit of Deity.

"God is spirit." **John 4:24.**

"And the Spirit of God was moving over the face of the waters." **Gen. 1:2.**

2. Angels—ministering spirits.

"Are they not all ministering spirits sent forth to serve, for the sake of those who are to obtain salvation." **Heb. 1:14.**

3. The Spirits of the churches.

"Let him hear what the Spirit says to the churches." **Rev. 2:7.**

4. Divine spirit bestowed upon man.

"And it shall come to pass afterward, that I will pour out my spirit upon all flesh." **Joel 2:28.**

"The unspiritual man does not receive the gifts of the Spirit of God, for they are folly to him." **1 Cor. 2:14.**

5. The spirit of life and liberty.

"But he who sows to the Spirit will from the Spirit reap eternal life." **Gal. 6:8.**

"But the Spirit gives life." **2 Cor. 3:6.**

"The law of the Spirit of life in Christ Jesus has set me free from the law of sin and death." **Rom. 8:2.**

"Never flag in zeal, be aglow with the Spirit." **Rom. 12:11.**

"Where the Spirit of the Lord is, there is freedom." **2 Cor. 3:17.**

"It is the spirit that gives life." **John 6:63.**

"Not by might, nor by power, but by my Spirit says the Lord." **Zech. 4:6.**

6. Relation of spirit to the mind.

"And be renewed in the spirit of your minds." **Eph. 4:23.**

"Walk by the spirit." **Gal. 5:16**.

"Do not believe every spirit, but test the spirits to see whether they are of God." **1 John 4:1**.

"By this we know the spirit of truth and the spirit of error." **1 John 4:6**.

"I will pray with the spirit and I will pray with the mind also." **1 Cor. 14:15**.

7. **The spirit of sonship.**

   "For all who are led by the Spirit of God are the sons of God." **Rom. 8:14**.

   "You have received the spirit of sonship." **Rom. 8:15**.

   "The Spirit himself bearing witness with our spirit that we are children of God." **Rom. 8:16**.

8. **The spiritual birth.**

   "That which is born of the Spirit is spirit." **John 3:6**.

   "Jesus answered, 'Truly, truly, I say to you, unless one is born of water and the Spirit, he cannot enter the kingdom of God.'" **John 3:5**.

9. **The Spirit of truth.**

   "When the Spirit of truth comes, he will guide you into all the truth." **John 16:13**.

10. **Man's spirit—temperament.**

    a. *The poor in spirit.*
        "Blessed are the poor in spirit for theirs is the kingdom of heaven." **Matt. 5:3**.

    b. *Spirit and the flesh.*
        "The spirit indeed is willing, but the flesh is weak." **Matt. 26:41**.

    c. *Emotional control.*
        "Put a new and right spirit within me." **Ps. 51:10**.
        "He who rules his spirit is better than he who takes a city." **Prov. 16:32**.

    d. *Courage and confidence.*
        "But God did not give us a spirit of timidity but a spirit of power and love and self-control." **2 Tim. 1:7**.

    e. *Pride.*
        "Pride goes before destruction, and a haughty spirit before a fall." **Prov. 16:18**.

  f. Spirit depression.

   "A downcast spirit dries up the bones." **Prov. 17:22.**

   "Surely he has borne our griefs and carried our sorrows." **Isa. 53:4.**

11. **Old Testament doctrine about evil spirits.**

 "Now the Spirit of the Lord departed from Saul, and an evil spirit from the Lord tormented him." **1. Sam. 16:14.**

 (**Note**: Saul had a manic-depressive psychosis.)

 "Behold, the Lord has put a lying spirit in the mouth of these your prophets." **2 Chron. 18:22.**

12. **Perfection of the human spirit.**

 "And to the spirits of just men made perfect." **Heb. 12:23.**

 "The spirit searches everything, even the depths of God." **1 Cor. 2:10.**

 "God chose you ... to be saved, through sanctification by the Spirit and belief in the truth." **2 Thess. 2:13.**

13. **The indwelling spirit returns to God.**

 "The spirit of man is the lamp of the Lord." **Prov. 20:27.**

 "And the spirit returns to God who gave it." **Eccl. 12:7.**

14. **Wicked spirits.**

 "And in the synagogue there was a man who had the spirit of an unclean demon." **Luke 4:33.**

 "We are not contending against flesh and blood, but...against the spiritual hosts of wickedness in the heavenly places." **Eph. 6:12.**

 "Following the prince of the power of the air, the spirit that now is at work in the sons of disobedience." **Eph. 2:2.**

15. **Spirits in prison.**

 "For Christ also died for sins once for all...being put to death in the flesh but made alive in the spirit; in which he went and preached to the spirits in prison." **1. Pet. 3:18, 19.**

16. **The spirit of Jesus.**

 "And when Jesus was baptized...the heavens were opened and he saw the Spirit of God descending like a dove and alighting on him." **Matt. 3:16.**

"Then Jesus, crying with a loud voice, said, 'Father, into thy hands I commit my spirit!" **Luke 23:46**.

11. THOUGHT ADJUSTERS

Bible Texts Suggestive of Thought Adjusters

THOUGHT ADJUSTERS

I. ORIGIN OF THOUGHT ADJUSTERS

1. Adjusters proceed direct from the Universal Father.

"Though there are diverse opinions regarding the mode of the bestowal of Thought Adjusters, there exist no such differences concerning their origin; all are agreed that they proceed direct from the Universal Father, the First Source and Center. They are not created beings; they are fragmentized entities constituting the factual presence of the infinite God. Together with their many unrevealed associates, the Adjusters are undiluted and unmixed divinity, unqualified and unattenuated parts of Deity; they are of God, and as far as we are able to discern, *they are God.*" P. 1177.

2. Limited knowledge respecting Adjusters.

"As to the time of their beginning separate existences apart from the absoluteness of the First Source and Center, we do not know; neither do we know their number. We know very little concerning their careers until they arrive on the planets of time to indwell human minds, but from that time on we are more or less familiar with their cosmic progressions up to and including the consummation of their triune destinies: attainment of personality by fusion with some mortal ascender, attainment of personality by fiat of the Universal Father, or liberation from the known assignments of Thought Adjusters." P. 1177.

3. There is no limit to Adjuster creation.

"Although we do not know, we presume that Adjusters are being constantly individualized as the universe enlarges, and as the candidates for Adjuster fusion increase in numbers. But it may be equally possible that we are in error in attempting to assign a numerical magnitude to the Adjusters; like God himself, these fragments of his unfathomable nature may be existentially infinite." P. 1177.

4. Technique of Adjuster origin is unrevealed.

"The technique of the origin of the Thought Adjusters is one of the unrevealed functions of the Universal Father. We have every reason to believe that none of the other absolute associates of the First Source and Center have aught to do with the production of Father fragments. Adjusters are simply and eternally the divine gifts; they are of God and from God, and they are like God." P. 1177.

5. Adjusters are the gift of the absolute God.

"In their relationship to fusion creatures they reveal a supernal love and spiritual ministry that is profoundly confirmative of the declaration that God is spirit. But there is much that takes place in addition to this transcendent ministry that has never been revealed to Urantia mortals. Neither do we fully understand just what really transpires when the Universal Father gives of himself to be a part of the personality of a creature of time. Nor has the ascending progression of the Paradise finaliters as yet disclosed the full possibilities inherent in this supernal partnership of man and God. In the last analysis, the Father fragments must be the gift of the absolute God to those creatures whose destiny encompasses the possibility of the attainment of God as absolute." P. 1177-8.

II. NATURE OF THOUGHT ADJUSTERS

1. Adjusters are absolute essence of infinite Father.

"To say that a Thought Adjuster is divine is merely to recognize the nature of origin. It is highly probable that such purity of divinity embraces the essence of the potential of all attributes of Deity which can be contained within such a fragment of the absolute essence of the Universal presence of the eternal and infinite Paradise Father." P. 1180.

2. They are qualified absolute fragments of the Father.

"The actual source of the Adjuster must be infinite, and before fusion with the immortal soul of an evolving mortal, the reality of the Adjuster must border on absoluteness. Adjusters are not absolutes in the universal sense, in the Deity sense, but they are probably true absolutes within the potentialities of their fragmented nature. They are qualified as to universality but not as to nature; in extensiveness they are limited, but in intensiveness of meaning, value, and fact *they are absolute*. For this reason we sometimes denominate the divine gifts as the qualified absolute fragments of the Father." P. 1180.

3. Adjusters are essence of original Deity.

"Since Thought Adjusters are of the essence of original Deity, no one may presume to discourse authoritatively upon their nature and origin; I can only impart the traditions of Salvington and the beliefs of Uversa; I can only explain how we regard these Mystery Monitors and their associated entities throughout the grand universe." P. 1177.

4. **Adjusters are fragments of prepersonal Deity.**

"As the Universal Father fragmentizes his prepersonal Deity, so does the Infinite Spirit individuate portions of his premind spirit to indwell and actually to fuse with the evolutionary souls of the surviving mortals of the spirit-fusion series. But the nature of the Eternal Son is not thus fragmentable; the spirit of the Original Son is either diffuse or discretely personal. Son-fused creatures are united with individualized bestowals of the spirit of the Creator Sons of the Eternal Son." P. 1178.

5. **Adjusters are pure spirit—plus.**

"As Thought Adjusters are encountered in creature experience, they disclose the presence and leading of a spirit influence. The Adjuster is indeed a spirit, pure spirit, but spirit plus. We have never been able satisfactorily to classify Mystery Monitors; all that can certainly be said of them is that they are truly Godlike." P. 1182.

6. **Adjusters are pure spirits—presumably absolute.**

"We know that Thought Adjusters are spirits, pure spirits, presumably absolute spirits. But the Adjuster must also be something more than exclusive spirit reality. In addition to conjectured mindedness, factors of pure energy are also present. If you will remember that God is the source of pure energy and of pure spirit, it will not be so difficult to perceive that his fragments would be both. It is a fact that the Adjusters traverse space over the instantaneous and universal gravity circuits of the Paradise Isle." P. 1182.

7. **Adjusters are the real mind of God.**

"Because of the presence in your minds of the Thought Adjuster, it is no more of a mystery for you to know the mind of God than for you to be sure of the consciousness of knowing any other mind, human or superhuman. Religion and social consciousness have this in common: They are predicated on the consciousness of other-mindedness. The technique whereby you can accept another's idea as yours is the same whereby you may 'let the mind which was in Christ be also in you.'" P. 1123.

8. **Adjuster love is truly divine.**

"The endowment of imperfect beings with freedom entails inevitable tragedy, and it is the nature of the perfect ancestral Deity to universally and affectionately share these sufferings in loving companionship.

"As far as I am conversant with the affairs of a universe, I regard the love and devotion of a Thought Adjuster as the most truly divine affection in all creation. The love of the Sons in their ministry to the races is superb, but the devotion of an Adjuster to the individual is touchingly sublime, divinely Fatherlike. The Paradise Father has apparently reserved this form of personal contact with his individual creatures as an exclusive Creator prerogative. And there is nothing in all the universe of Universes exactly comparable to the marvelous ministry of these impersonal entities that so fascinatingly indwell the children of the evolutionary planets." P. 1203.

9. It is believed that Adjusters undergo training.

"The valor and wisdom exhibited by Thought Adjusters suggest that they have undergone a training of tremendous scope and range. Since they are not personalities, this training must be imparted in the educational institutions of Divinington. The unique Personalized Adjusters no doubt constitute the personnel of the Adjuster training schools of Divinington. And we do know that this central and supervising corps is presided over by the now Personalized Adjuster of the first Paradise Son of the Michael order to complete his sevenfold bestowal upon the races and peoples of his universe realms." P. 1180.

10. Adjusters are minded and possess selfhood.

"Since Adjusters can plan, work, and love, they must have powers of self-hood which are commensurate with mind. They are possessed of unlimited ability to communicate with each other, that is, all forms of Monitors above the first or virgin groups. As to the nature and purport of their intercommunications, we can reveal very little, for we do not know. And we further know that they must be minded in some manner else they could never be personalized.

"The mindedness of the Thought Adjuster is like the *mindedness* of the Universal Father and the Eternal Son—that which is ancestral to the *minds* of the Conjoint Actor." P. 1181.

11. Adjuster is man's infallible cosmic compass.

"The Adjuster is an absolute essence of an infinite being imprisoned within the mind of a finite creature which, depending on the choosing of such a mortal, can eventually consummate this temporary union of God and man and veritably actualize a new order of being for unending universe service. The Adjuster is the divine universe reality which factualizes the truth that God is man's

Father. The Adjuster is man's infallible cosmic compass, always and unerringly pointing the soul Godward." P. 1176-7.

12. Adjusters never cease their efforts.

"And yet, while the Adjusters utilize the material-gravity circuits, they are not subject thereto as is material creation. The Adjusters are fragments of the ancestor of gravity, not the consequentials of gravity; they have segmentized on a universe level of existence which is hypothetically antecedent to gravity appearance.

"Thought Adjusters have no relaxation from the time of their bestowal until the day of their release to start for Divinington upon the natural death of their mortal subjects. And those whose subjects do not pass through the protals of natural death do not even experience this temporary respite. Thought Adjusters do not require energy intake; they are energy, energy of the highest and most divine order." P. 1183

III. MISSION AND ASSIGNMENT OF ADJUSTERS

1. Adjusters are wisely and efficiently assigned.

"When Adjusters are dispatched for mortal service from Divinington, the are identical in the endowment of existential divinity, but they very in experiential qualities proportional to previous contact in and with evolutionary creatures. We cannot explain the basis of Adjuster assignment, but we conjecture that these divine gifts are bestowed in accordance with some wise and efficient policy of eternal fitness of adaptation to the indwelt personality. We do observe that the more experienced Adjuster is often the indweller of the higher type of human mind; human inheritance must therefore be a considerable factor in determining selection and assignment." P. 1185.

2. Adjusters are believed to be volunteers.

"Although we do not definitely know, we firmly believe that all Thought Adjusters are volunteers. But before ever they volunteer, they are in possession of full data respecting the candidate for indwelling. The seraphic drafts of ancestry and projected patterns of life conduct are transmitted via Paradise to the reserve corps of Adjusters on Divinington by the reflectivity technique extending inward from the capitals of the local universes to the headquarters of the superuniverses. This forecast covers not only the hereditary antecedents of the mortal candidate but also the estimate of probable intellectual endowment and spiritual capacity. The

Adjusters thus volunteer to indwell minds of whose intimate natures they have been fully apprised." P. 1185-6.

3. What the Adjuster wants to know.

"The volunteering Adjuster is particularly interested in three qualifications of the human candidate:

"1. *Intellectual capacity*. Is the mind normal? What is the intellectual potential, the intelligence capacity? Can the individual develop into a bona fide will creature? Will wisdom have an opportunity to function?

"2. *Spiritual perception*. The prospects of reverential development, the birth and growth of the religious nature. What is the potential of soul, the probable spiritual capacity of receptivity?

"3. *Combined intellectual and spiritual powers*. The degree to which these two endowments may possibly be associated, combined, so as to produce strength of human character and contribute to the certain evolution of an immortal soul of survival value." P. 1186.

4. Adjuster's transit speed.

"When once the Adjusters are actually dispatched from Divinington, practically no time intervenes between that moment and the hour of their appearance in the minds of their chosen subjects. The average transit time of an Adjuster from Divinington to Urantia is 117 hours, 42 minutes, and 7 seconds. Virtually all of this time is occupied with registration on Uversa." P. 1186.

5. Adjusters indispensable to Paradise ascension.

"The Adjusters accept a difficult assignment when they volunteer to indwell such composite beings as live on Urantia. But they have assumed the task of existing in your minds, there to receive the admonitions of the spiritual intelligences of the realms and then to undertake to redictate or translate these spiritual messages to the material mind; they are indispensable to the Paradise ascension." P. 1191.

6. Adjusters never fail in their assignment.

"One thing you can depend upon: The Adjusters will never lose anything committed to their care; never have we known these spirit helpers to default. Angels and other high types of spirit beings, not excepting the local universe type of Sons, may occasionally embrace evil, may sometimes depart from the divine way, but

Adjusters never falter. They are absolutely dependable, and this is equally true of all seven groups." P. 1191.

7. Adjuster arouses a hunger for perfection.

"The indwelling Thought Adjuster unfailingly arouses in man's soul a true and searching hunger for perfection together with a far-reaching curiosity which can be adequately satisfied only by communion with God, the divine source of that Adjuster. The hungry soul of man refuses to be satisfied with anything less than the personal realization of the living God. Whatever more God may be than a high and perfect moral personality, he cannot, in our hungry and finite concept, be anything less." P. 1119.

8. Adjuster is the cosmic window of the soul.

"All of man's truly religious reactions are sponsored by the early ministry of the adjutant of worship and are censored by the adjutant of wisdom. Man's first supermind endowment is that of personality encircuitment in the Holy Spirit of the Universe Creative Spirit; and long before either the bestowals of the divine Sons or the universal bestowal of the Adjusters, this influence functions to enlarge man's viewpoint of ethics, religion, and spirituality. Subsequent to the bestowals of the Paradise Sons the liberated Spirit of Truth makes mighty contributions to the enlargement of the human capacity to perceive religious truths. As evolution advances on an inhabited world, the Thought Adjusters increasingly participate in the development of the higher types of human religious insight. The Thought Adjuster is the cosmic window through which the finite creature may faithglimpse the certainties and divinities of limitless Deity, the Universal Father." P. 1129.

9. Adjusters overcome our planetary isolation.

"The isolation of a planet in no way affects the Adjusters and their ability to communicate with any part of the local universe, superuniverse, or the central universe. And this is the reason why contacts with the supreme and the self-acting Adjusters of the reserve corps of destiny are so frequently made on quarantined worlds. Recourse is had to such a technique as a means of circumventing the handicaps of planetary isolation. In recent years the archangels' circuit has functioned on Urantia, but that means of communication is largely limited to the transactions of the archangel corps itself." P. 1191.

10. Assignment of Personalized Adjusters.

"We really know very little about the nonpersonalized Adjusters; we only contact and communicate with the personalized orders. These are christened on Divinington and are always known by name and not by number. The Personalized Adjusters are permanently domiciled on Divinington; that sacred sphere is their home. They go out from that abode only by the will of the Universal Father. Very few are found in the domains of the local universes, but larger numbers are present in the central universe." P. 1180.

IV. PREREQUISITES OF ADJUSTER INDWELLING

1. Adjusters arrive on the first moral decision.

"Though the Adjusters volunteer for service as soon as the personality forecasts have been relayed to Divinington, they are not actually assigned until the human subjects make their first moral personality decision. The first moral choice of the human child is automatically indicated in the seventh mind-adjutant and registers instantly, by way of the local universe Creative Spirit, over the universal mind-gravity circuit of the Conjoint Actor in the presence of the Master Spirit of superuniverse jurisdiction, who forthwith dispatches this intelligence to Divinington. Adjusters reach their human subjects on Urantia, on the average, just prior to the sixth birthday. In the present generation it is running five years, ten months, and four days; that is, on the 2,134th day of terrestrial life." P. 1186-7.

2. Mission of adjutant spirits and Spirit of Truth.

"The Adjusters cannot invade the mortal mind until it has been duly prepared by the indwelling ministry of the adjutant mind-spirits and encircuited in the Holy Spirit. And it requires the co-ordinate function of all seven adjutants to thus qualify the human mind for the reception of an Adjuster. Creature mind must exhibit the worship outreach and indicate wisdom function by exhibiting the ability to choose between the emerging values of good and evil—moral choice.

"Thus is the stage of the human mind set for the reception of Adjusters, but as a general rule they do not immediately appear to indwell such minds except on those worlds where the Spirit of Truth is functioning as a spiritual co-ordinator of these different spirit ministries. If this spirit of the bestowal Sons is present, the Adjusters unfailingly come the instant the seventh adjutant mind-spirit begins to function and signalizes to the Universe Mother Spirit that it has achieved in potential the co-ordination of the associated six adjutants of prior ministry to such a mortal intellect. Therefore have the divine Adjusters been universally bestowed upon all normal minds of moral status on Urantia ever since the day of Pentecost." P. 1187.

3. Moral decision is the determining factor.

"Even with a Spirit of Truth endowed mind, the Adjusters cannot arbitrarily invade the mortal intellect prior to the appearance of moral decision. But when such a moral decision has been made, this spirit helper assumes jurisdiction direct from Divinington. There are no intermediaries or other intervening authorities or powers functioning between the divine Adjusters and their human subjects; God and man are directly related." P. 1187.

4. Determining factors of Adjuster bestowal.

"Before the times of the pouring out of the Spirit of Truth upon the inhabitants of an evolutionary world, the Adjusters' bestowal appears to be determined by many spirit influences and personality attitudes. We do not fully comprehend the laws governing such bestowals; we do not understand just what determines the release of the Adjusters who have volunteered to indwell such evolving minds. But we do observe numerous influences and conditions which appear to be associated with the arrival of the Adjusters in such minds prior to the bestowal of the Spirit of Truth, and they are:

"1. The assignment of personal seraphic guardians. If a mortal has not been previously indwelt by an Adjuster, the assignment of a personal guardian brings the Adjuster forthwith. There exists some very definite but unknown relation between the ministry of Adjusters and the ministry of personal seraphic guardians.

"2. The attainment of the third circle of intellectual achievement and spiritual attainment. I have observed Adjusters arrive in mortal minds upon the conquest of the third circle even before such an accomplishment could be signalized to the local universe personalities concerned with such matters.

"3. Upon the making of a supreme decision of unusual spiritual import. Such human behavior in a personal planetary crisis usually is attended by the immediate arrival of the waiting Adjuster.

"4. The spirit of brotherhood. Regardless of the attainment of the psychic circles and the assignment of personal guardians—in the absence of anything resembling a crisis decision—when an evolving mortal becomes dominated by the love of his fellows and consecrated to unselfish ministry to his brethren in the flesh, the waiting Adjuster unvaryingly descends to indwell the mind of such a mortal minister.

"5.   Declaration of intention to do the will of God. We observe that many mortals on the worlds of space may be apparently in readiness to receive Adjusters, and yet the Monitors do not appear. We go on watching such creatures as they live from day to day, and presently they quietly, almost unconsciously, arrive at the decision to begin the pursuit of the doing of the will of the Father in heaven. And then we observe the immediate dispatch of the Thought Adjusters.

"6.   Influence of the Supreme Being. On worlds where the Adjusters do not fuse with the evolving souls of the mortal inhabitants, we observe Adjusters sometimes bestowed in response to influences which are wholly beyond our comprehension. We conjecture that such bestowals are determined by some cosmic reflex action originating in the Supreme Being. As to why these Adjusters can not or do not fuse with these certain types of evolving mortal minds we do not know. Such transactions have never been revealed to us." P. 1187-8.

5.   **All created beings would welcome Adjusters.**

"There are no created beings that would not delight to be hosts to the Mystery Monitors, but no orders of beings are thus indwelt excepting evolutionary will creatures of finaliter destiny." P. 1184.

V. ADJUSTER'S RELATION TO HUMAN MIND

1.   **Adjusters indwell mortal minds.**

"Adjusters should not be thought of as living in the material brains of human beings. They are not organic parts of the physical creatures of the realms. The Thought Adjuster may more properly be envisaged as indwelling the mortal mind of man rather than as existing within the confines of a single physical organ. And indirectly and unrecognized the Adjuster is constantly communicating with the human subject, especially during those sublime experiences of the worshipful contact of mind with spirit in the superconsciousness." P. 1203.

2.   **Adjuster's manifold work in the mind.**

"I wish it were possible for me to help evolving mortals to achieve a better understanding and attain a fuller appreciation of the unselfish and superb work of the Adjusters living within them, who are so devoutly faithful to the task of fostering man's spiritual welfare. These Monitors are efficient ministers to the higher phases of men's minds; they are wise and experienced manipulators of the spiritual potential of the human intellect. These heavenly helpers are dedicated to the stupendous task of guiding you safely inward and upward to the celestial haven of happiness. These tireless toilers are consecrated to the future personification of the triumph of divine truth in your life everlasting. They are the watchful workers who pilot the God-conscious human mind away from the shoals of evil while expertly guiding the evolving soul of man towards the divine harbors of perfection on far-distant and eternal shores. The Adjusters are loving leaders, your safe and sure guides through the dark and uncertain mazes of your short earthly career; they are the patient teachers who so constantly urge their subjects forward in the paths of progressive perfection. They are the careful custodians of the sublime values of creature character. I wish you could love them more, co-operate with them more fully, and cherish them more affectionately." P. 1203.

3. **Adjuster is the mind's spiritual nucleus.**

    "Mortal man has a spirit nucleus. The mind is a personal-energy system existing around a divine spirit nucleus and functioning in a material environment. Such a living relationship of personal mind and spirit constitutes the universe potential of eternal personality. Real trouble, lasting disappointment, serious defeat, or inescapable death can come only after self-concepts presume fully to displace the governing power of the central spirit nucleus, thereby disrupting the cosmic scheme of personality identity." P. 142.

4. **How Thought Adjusters work.**

    "It is exceedingly difficult for the meagerly spiritualized, material mind of mortal man to experience marked consciousness of the spirit activities of such divine entities as the Paradise Adjusters. As the soul of joint mind and Adjuster creation becomes increasingly existent, there also evolves a new phase of soul consciousness which is capable of experiencing the presence, and of recognizing the spirit leadings and other supermaterial activities, of the Mystery Monitors.

"The entire experience of Adjuster communion is one involving "The entire experience of Adjuster communion is one involving moral status, mental motivation, and spiritual experience. The self-realization of such an achievement is mainly, though not exclusively, limited to the realms of soul consciousness, but the proofs are forthcoming and abundant in the manifestation of the fruits of the spirit in the lives of all such innerspirit contactors." P. 65.

5. Adjuster's relation to human emotions.

"Your transient and ever-changing emotions of joy and sorrow are in the main purely human and material reactions to your internal psychic climate and to your external material environment. Do not, therefore, look to the Adjuster for selfish consolation and mortal comfort. It is the business of the Adjuster to prepare you for the eternal adventure, to assure your survival. It is not the mission of the Mystery Monitor to smooth your ruffled feelings or to minister to your injured pride; it is the preparation of your soul for the long ascending career that engages the attention and occupies the time of the Adjuster." P. 1192.

6. Adjusters would deliver us from fear.

"The Thought Adjusters would like to change your feelings of fear to convictions of love and confidence; but they cannot mechanically and arbitrarily do such things; that is your task. In executing those decisions which deliver you from the fetters of fear, you literally supply the psychic fulcrum on which the Adjuster may subsequently apply a spiritual lever of uplifting and advancing illumination." P. 1192.

7. Their work is more or less of a mystery.

"I doubt that I am able to explain to you just what the Adjusters do in your minds and for your souls. I do not know that I am fully cognizant of what is really going on in the cosmic association of a divine Monitor and a human mind. It is all somewhat of a mystery to us, not as to the plan and purpose but as to the actual mode of accomplishment. And this is just why we are confronted with such difficulty in finding an appropriate name for these supernal gifts to mortal men." P. 1192.

8. Complex work of Adjuster in the mind.

"Adjusters are able to receive the continuous stream of cosmic intelligence coming in over the master circuits of time and space; they are in full touch with the spirit intelligence and energy of the universes. But these mighty indwellers are unable to transmit very much of this wealth of wisdom and truth to the minds of their mortal subjects because of the lack of commonness of nature and the absence of responsive recognition.

"The Thought Adjuster is engaged in a constant effort so to spiritualize your mind as to evolve your morontia soul; but you yourself are mostly unconscious of this inner ministry. You are quite incapable of distinguishing the product of your own material intellect from that of the conjoint activities of your soul and the Adjuster." P. 1207.

VI. ADJUSTERS AND PERSONALITY

1. **Adjusters are real entities—though not personal.**

   "Thought Adjusters are not personalities, but they are real entities; they are truly and perfectly individualized, although they are never, while indwelling mortals, actually personalized. Thought Adjusters are not true personalities; they are *true realities*, realities of the purest order known in the universe of universes—they are the divine presence. Though not personal, these marvelous fragments of the Father are commonly referred to as beings and sometimes, in view of the spiritual phases of their present ministry to mortals, as spirit entities." P. 1183.

2. **Adjusters individuation a universe mystery.**

   "If Thought Adjusters are not personalities having prerogatives of will and powers of choice, how then can they select mortal subjects and volunteer to indwell these creatures of the evolutionary worlds? This is a question easy to ask, but probably no being in the universe of universes has ever found the exact answer. Even my order of personality, the Solitary Messengers, does not fully understand the endowment of will, choice, and love in entities that are not personal." P. 1183.

3. **Adjuster volition must be on prepersonal level.**

   "We have often speculated that Thought Adjusters must have volition on all *prepersonal* levels of choice. They volunteer to indwell human beings, they lay plans for man's eternal career, they adapt, modify, and substitute in accordance with, circumstances, and these activities cannote genuine volition. They have affection for mortals, they function in universe crises, they are always waiting to act decisively in accordance with human choice, and all these are highly volitional reactions. In all situations not concerned with the domain of the human will, they unquestionably exhibit conduct which betokens the exercise of powers in every sense the equivalent of will, maximated decision." P. 1183.

4. Human will dominates Adjuster-human partnership.

"Why then, if Thought Adjusters possess volition, are they subservient to the mortal will? We believe it is because Adjuster volition, though absolute in nature, is prepersonal in manifestation. Human will functions on the personality level of universe reality, and throughout the cosmos the impersonal—the nonpersonal, the subpersonal, and the prepersonal—is ever responsive to the will and acts of existent personality." P. 1183.

5. Adjuster is your real and eternal self.

"Even though the spirit of a Son be poured out upon all flesh, even though a Son once dwelt with you in the likeness of mortal flesh, even though the seraphim personally guard and guide you, how can any of these divine beings of the Second and Third Centers ever hope to come as near to you or to understand you as fully as the Father, who has given a part of himself to be in you, to be your real and divine, even your eternal, self?" P. 139.

6. Recognition of Adjusters.

"There is a real proof of spiritual reality in the presence of the Thought Adjuster, but the validity of this presence is not demonstrable to the external world, only to the one who thus experiences the indwelling of God. The consciousness of the Adjuster is based on the intellectual reception of truth, the supermind perception of goodness, and the personality motivation to love." P. 1139.

VII. GOD IN MAN

1. A fragment of the living God lives in man.

"If the finite mind of man is unable to comprehend how so great and so majestic a God as the Universal Father can descend from his eternal abode in infinite perfection to fraternize with the individual human creature, then must such a finite intellect rest assurance of divine fellowship upon the truth of the fact that an actual fragment of the living God resides within the intellect of every normal-minded and morally conscious Urantia mortal. The indwelling Thought Adjusters are a part of the eternal Deity of the Paradise Father. Man does not have to go farther than his own inner experience of the soul's contemplation of this spiritual-reality presence to find God and attempt communion with him." P. 62.

2. A part of God dwells within us.

"The physical bodies of mortals are 'the temples of God.' Notwithstanding that the Sovereign Creator Sons come near the creatures of their inhabited worlds and 'draw all men to themselves'; though they 'stand at the door' of consciousness 'and knock' and delight to come in to all who will 'open the doors of their hearts'; although there does exist this intimate personal communion between the Creator Sons and their mortal creatures, nevertheless, mortal men have something from God himself which actually dwells within them; their bodies are the temples thereof." P. 26.

3. The Creator lives in the creature.

"The creature not only exists in God, but God also lives in the creature. 'We know we dwell in him because he lives in us; he has given us his spirit. This gift from the Paradise Father is man's inseparable companion.' 'He is the ever-present and all-pervading God.' 'The spirit of the everlasting Father is concealed in the mind of every mortal child.' 'Man goes forth searching for a friend while that very friend lives within his own heart.' 'The true God is not afar off; he is a part of us; his spirit speaks from within us.' The Father lives in the child. God is always with us. He is the guiding spirit of eternal destiny.'" P. 45.

4. Adjusters share our life experiences.

"Truly of the human race has it been said, 'You are of God' because 'he who dwells in love dwells in God, and God in him.' Even in wrongdoing you torment, the indwelling gift of God, for the Thought Adjuster must needs go through the consequences of evil thinking with the human mind of its incarceration." P. 45.

5. Adjusters actually indwell animal-origin beings.

"It is indeed a marvel of divine condescension for the exalted and perfect Adjusters to offer themselves for actual existence in the minds of material creatures, such as the mortals of Urantia, really to consummate a probationary union with the animal-origin beings of earth." P. 1192.

6. Adjusters are God's contact with man.

"In the mortal will creatures the Father is actually present in the indwelling Adjuster, a fragment of his prepersonal spirit; and the Father is also the source of the personality of such a mortal will creature.

"These Thought Adjusters, the bestowals of the Universal Father, are comparatively isolated; they indwell human minds but have no discernible connection with the ethical affairs of a local creation. They are not directly co-ordinated with the seraphic service nor with the administration of systems, constellations, or a local universe, not even with the rule of a Creator Son, whose will is the supreme law of his universe.

"The indwelling Adjusters are one of God's separate but unified modes of contact with the creatures of his all but infinite creation. Thus does he who is invisible to mortal man manifest his presence, and could he do so, he would show himself to us in still other ways, but such further revelation is not divinely possible." P. 363.

7. **Adjusters are the Father's love incarnate in man.**

"Although the Universal Father is personally resident on Paradise, at the very center of the universes, he is also actually present on the worlds of space in the minds of his countless children of time, for he indwells them as the Mystery Monitors. The eternal Father is at one and the same time farthest removed from, and most intimately associated with, his planetary mortal sons.

"The Adjusters are the actuality of the Father's love incarnate in the souls of men; they are the veritable promise of man's eternal career imprisoned within the mortal mind; they are the essence of man's perfected finaliter personality, which he can foretaste in time as he progressively masters the divine technique of achieving the living of the Father's will, step by step, through the ascension of universe upon universe until he actually attains the divine presence of his Paradise Father." P. 1176.

VIII. THE DIVINE PRESENCE

1. **The divine presence abides within us.**

"The divine presence cannot, however, be discovered anywhere in nature or even in the lives of God-knowing mortals so fully and so certainly as in your attempted communion with the indwelling Mystery Monitor, the Paradise Thought Adjuster. What a mistake to dream of God far off in the skies when the spirit of the Universal Father lives within your own mind!" P. 64.

2. **Adjuster is a part of infinite Deity.**

"The great God makes direct contact with mortal man and gives a part of his infinite and eternal and incomprehensible self to live and dwell within him. God has embarked upon the eternal adventure with man. If you yield to the leadings of the spiritual forces in you and around you, you cannot fail to attain the high destiny established by a loving God as the universe goal of his ascendant creatures from the evolutionary worlds of space." P. 64.

3. Adjusters the source of spirit insight.

"The divine nature may be perceived only with the eyes of the mind. But the mind that really discerns God, hears the indwelling Adjuster, is the pure mind. 'Without holiness no man may see the Lord.' All such inner and spiritual communion is termed spiritual insight. Such religious experiences result from the impress made upon the mind of man by the combined operations of the Adjuster and the Spirit of Truth as they function amid and upon the ideas, ideals, insights, and spirit strivings of the evolving sons of God." P. 1105.

4. Adjusters and God-consciousness.

"The realization of the recognition of spiritual values is an experience which is superideational. There is no word in any human language which can be employed to designate this 'sense,' 'feeling,' 'intuition,' or 'experience' which we have elected to call God-consciousness. The spirit of God that dwells in man is not personal—the Adjuster is prepersonal—but this Monitor presents a value, exudes a flavor of divinity, which is personal in the highest and infinite sense. If God were not at least personal, he could not be conscious, and if not conscious, then would he be infrahuman." P. 1130.

5. Adjuster is source of idealism of altruism.

"The early evolutionary mind gives origin to a feeling of social duty and moral obligation derived chiefly from emotional fear. The more positive urge of social service and the idealism of altruism are derived from the direct impulse of the divine spirit indwelling the human mind." P. 1133.

6. Spirit origin of man's spiritual impulses.

"It is fatal to man's idealism when he is taught that all of his altruistic impulses are merely the development of his natural herd instincts. But he is ennobled and mightily energized when he learns that these higher urges of his soul emanate from the spiritual forces that indwell his mortal mind.

"It lifts man out of himself and beyond himself when he once fully realizes that there lives and strives within him something which is eternal and divine. and so it is that a living faith in the superhuman origin of our ideals validates our belief that we are the sons of God and makes real our altruistic convictions, the feelings of the brotherhood of man." P. 1134.

7. **Adjuster attunement measure of spirituality.**

"Actual spiritual status is the measure of Deity attainment. Adjuster attunement. The achievement of finality of spirituality is equivalent to the attainment of the maximum of reality, the maximum of Godlikeness. Eternal life is the endless quest for infinite values." P. 1096.

8. **Mystery Monitors are patient indwellers.**

"In this universal bestowal of himself we have abundant proof of both the magnitude and the magnanimity of the Father's divine nature. If God has withheld aught of himself from the universal creation, then of that residue he is in lavish generosity bestowing the Thought Adjusters upon the mortals of the realms, the Mystery Monitors of time, who so patiently indwell the mortal candidates for life everlasting." P. 364.

IX. WHAT ADJUSTERS DO FOR US

1. **The three phases of Adjuster ministry.**

"On the evolutionary worlds, will creatures traverse three general developmental stages of being; From the arrival of the Adjuster to comparative full growth, about twenty years of age on Urantia, the Monitors are sometimes designated Thought Changers. From this time to the attainment of the age of discretion, about forty years, the Mystery Monitors are called Thought Adjusters. From the attainment of discretion to deliverance from the flesh, they are often referred to as Thought Controllers. These three phases of mortal life have no connection with the three stages of Adjuster progress in mind duplication and soul evolution." P. 1177.

2. **Adjusters impel belief in God.**

"Thus it may be seen that religious longings and spiritual urges are not of such a nature as would merely lead men to *want* to believe in God, but rather are they of such nature and power that men are profoundly impressed with the conviction that they *ought* to believe in God. The sense of evolutionary duty and the obligations consequent upon the illumination of revelation make such a profound impression upon man's moral nature that he finally reaches that position of mind and that attitude of soul where he concludes that he *has no right not to believe in God.* The higher and super-philosophic wisdom of such enlightened and disciplined individuals ultimately instructs them that to doubt God or distrust his goodness would be to prove untrue to the *realest* and *deepest* thing within the human mind and soul—the divine Adjuster." P. 1105.

3. **Adjusters the source of altruism.**

"The impulse of the spirit Monitor is realized in human conscious-ness as the urge to be altruistic, fellow-creature minded. At least this is the early and fundamental experience of the child mind. When the growing child fails of personality unification, the altruistic drive may become so overdeveloped as to work serious injury to the welfare of the self. A misguided conscience can become responsible for much conflict, worry, sorrow, and no end of human unhappiness." P. 1132.

4. **Adjuster makes real our cosmic insight.**

"The pursuit of knowledge constitutes science; the search for wisdom is philosophy; the love for God is religion; the hunger for truth *is* a revelation. But it is the indwelling Thought Adjuster that attaches the feeling of reality to man's spiritual insight into the cosmos." P. 1122.

5. **Adjusters are concerned with mortal survival.**

"Adjusters are interested in, and concerned with, your daily doings and the manifold details of your life just to the extent that these are influential in the determination of your significant temporal choices and vital spiritual decisions and, hence, are factors in the solution of your problem of soul survival and eternal progress. The Adjuster, while passive regarding purely temporal welfare, is divinely active concerning all the affairs of your eternal future." P. 1204.

6. **Interested in both temporal and eternal welfare.**

"Although the divine indwellers are chiefly concerned with your spiritual preparation for the next stage of the never-ending exist ence, they are also deeply interested in your temporal welfare and in your real achievements on earth. They are delighted to contribute to your health, happiness, and true prosperity. They are not indifferent to your success in all matters of planetary advancement which are not inimical to your future life of eternal progress." P. 1204.

7. They do not make life easy for us.

"The Mystery Monitors are not thought helpers; they are thought adjusters. They labor with the material mind for the purpose of constructing, by adjustment and spiritualization, a new mind for the new worlds and the new name of your future career. Their mission chiefly concerns the future life, not this life. They are called heavenly helpers, not earthly helpers. They are not interested in making the mortal career easy; rather are they concerned in making your life reasonably difficult and rugged, so that decisions will be stimulated and multiplied. The presence of a great Thought Adjuster does not bestow ease of living and freedom from strenuous thinking, but such a divine gift should confer a sublime peace of mind and a superb tranquillity of spirit." P. 1191-2.

8. Adjusters truly and divinely love us.

"The Adjuster is man's eternity possibility; man is the Adjuster's personality possibility. Your individual Adjusters work to spiritize you in the hope of eternalizing your temporal identity. The Adjusters are saturated with the beautiful and self-bestowing love of the Father of spirits. They truly and divinely love you; they are the prisoners of spirit hope confined within the minds of men. They long for the divinity attainment of your mortal minds that their loneliness may end, that they may be delivered with you from the limitations of material investiture and the habiliments of time." P. 1182.

9. Eternal partnership of Adjuster association.

"Your path to Paradise is the path of spirit attainment, and the Adjuster nature will faithfully unfold the revelation of the spiritual nature of the Universal Father. Beyond the Paradise ascent and in the postfinaliter stages of the eternal career, the Adjuster may possibly contact with the onetime human partner in other than spirit ministry; but the Paradise ascent and the finaliter career are the partnership between the God-knowing spiritualizing mortal and the spiritual ministry of the God-revealing Adjuster." P. 1182.

10. They create our longing to be Godlike.

"It is the Adjuster who creates within man that unquenchable yearning and incessant longing to be like God, to attain Paradise,

and there before the actual person of Deity to worship the infinite
source of the divine gift. The Adjuster is the living presence which
actually links the mortal son with his Paradise Father and draws
him nearer and nearer to the Father. The Adjuster is our compensa-
tory equalization of the enormous universe tension which is created
by the distance of man's removal from God and by the degree of his
partiality in contrast with the universality of the eternal Father." P.
1176.

11. Adjusters guide us to God.

"After all, the greatest evidence of the goodness of God and the
supreme reason for loving him is the indwelling gift of the Father—
the Adjuster who so patiently awaits the hour when you both shall
be eternally made one. Though you cannot find God by searching, if
you will submit to the leading of the indwelling spirit, you will be
unerringly guided, step by step, life by life, through universe upon
universe, and age by age, until you finally stand in the presence of
the Paradise personality of the Universal Father." P. 39.

12. They help to make us perfect.

"God, having commanded man to be perfect, even as he is perfect,
has descended as the Adjuster to become man's experiential
partner in the achievement of the supernal destiny which has been
thus ordained. The fragment of God which indwells the mind of
man is the absolute and unqualified assurance that man can find the
Universal Father in association with this divine Adjuster, which
came forth from God to find man and sonship him even in the days
of the flesh." P. 1176.

13. And they do enjoy communicating with us.

"The Adjusters are the eternal ancestors, the divine originals, of
your evolving immortal souls; they are the unceasing urge that
leads man to attempt the mastery of the material and present
existence in the light of the spiritual and future career. The Monitors are the prisoners of undying hope, the founts of everlasting
progression. And how they do enjoy communicating with their
subjects in more or less direct channels! How they rejoice when
they can dispense with symbols and other methods of indirection
and flash their messages straight to the intellects of their human
partners!" P. 1193.

X. THE OVER-ALL WORK OF ADJUSTERS

1. Adjusters have to do with the "image of God."

"The Mystery Monitors are undoubtedly the bestowal of the Universal Father, the reflection of the image of God abroad in the universe. A great teacher once admonished men that they should be renewed in the spirit of their minds; that they become new men who, like God, are created in righteousness and in the completion of truth. The Adjuster is the mark of divinity, the presence of God. The 'image of God' does not refer to physical likeness nor to the circumscribed limitations of material creature endowment but rather to the gift of the spirit presence of the Universal Father in the supernal bestowal of the Thought Adjusters upon the humble creatures of the universes," P. 1193.

2. Adjusters distinguish man from animals.

"The Adjuster is the wellspring of spiritual attainment and the hope of divine character within you. He is the power, privilege, and the possibility of survival, which so fully and forever distinguishes you from mere animal creatures. He is the higher and truly internal spiritual stimulus of thought in contrast with the external and physical stimulus, which reaches the mind over the nerve-energy mechanism of the material body." P. 1193.

3. Adjusters are creating survival values.

"These faithful custodians of the future career unfailingly duplicate every mental creation with a spiritual counterpart; they are thus slowly and surely re-creating you as you really are (only spiritually) for resurrection on the survival worlds. And all of these exquisite spirit recreations are being preserved in the emerging reality of your evolving and immortal soul, your morontia self. These realities are actually there, notwithstanding that the Adjuster is seldom able to exalt these duplicate creations sufficiently to exhibit them to the light of consciousness." P. 1193.

4. Adjuster the divine parent of the real you.

"And as you are the human parent, so is the Adjuster the divine parent of the real you, your higher and advancing self, your better morontial and future spiritual self. And it is this evolving morontial soul that the judges and censors discern when they decree your survival and pass you upward to new worlds and never-ending existence in eternal liaison with your faithful partner—God, the Adjuster." P. 1193.

5. **Adjusters insured the survival of religion.**

"Man evolved through the superstitions of mana, magic, nature worship, spirit fear, and animal worship to the various ceremonials whereby the religious attitude of the individual became the group reactions of the clan. And then these ceremonies became focalized and crystallized into tribal beliefs, and eventually these fears and faiths became personalized into gods. But in all of this religious evolution the moral element was never wholly absent. The impulse of the God within man was always potent. And these powerful influences—one human and the other divine—insured the survival of religion throughout the vicissitudes of the ages and that notwithstanding it was so often threatened with extinction by a thousand subversive tendencies and hostile antagonisms." P. 1132.

6. **Adjuster relation to other spirits.**

"Thought Adjusters appear to come and go quite independent of any and all other spiritual presences; they seem to function in accordance with universe laws quite apart from those which govern and control the performances of all other spirit influences. But regardless of such apparent independence, long-range observation unquestionably discloses that they function in the human mind in perfect synchrony and co-ordination with all other spirit ministries, including adjutant mind-spirits, Holy Spirit, Spirit of Truth, and other influences." P. 1190.

7. **Adjusters act in a crisis.**

"When it comes to the sharp and well-defined conflicts between the higher and lower tendencies of the races, between what *really is* right or wrong (not merely what you may call right and wrong), you can depend upon it that the Adjuster will always participate in some definite and active manner in such experiences. The fact that such Adjuster activity may be unconscious to the human partner does not in the least detract from its value and reality." P. 1192.

8. **Adjusters account for spiritual unity.**

"The unity of religious experience among a social or racial group derives from the identical nature of the God fragment indwelling the individual. It is this divine in man that gives origin to his unselfish interest in the welfare of other men. But since personality is unique—no two mortals being alike—it inevitably follows that no two human beings can similarly interpret the leadings and urges of the spirit of divinity which lives within their minds. A group of mortals can experience spiritual unity, but they can never attain philosophic uniformity. And this diversity of the interpretation of religious thought and experience is shown by the fact that twentieth-century theologians and philosophers have formulated upward of five hundred different definitions of religion. In reality, every human being defines religion in the terms of his own experiential interpretation of the divine impulses emanating from the God spirit that indwells him, and therefore must such an interpretation be unique and wholly different from the religious philosophy of all other human beings." P. 1129-30.

9. When Adjusters forsake human beings.

"The Adjuster remains with you in all disaster and through every sickness which does not wholly destroy the mentality. But how unkind knowingly to defile or otherwise deliberately to pollute the physical body, which must serve as the earthly tabernacle of this marvelous gift from God. All physical poisons greatly retard the efforts of the Adjuster to exalt the material mind, while the mental poisons of fear, anger, envy, jealousy, suspicion, and intolerance likewise tremendously interfere with the spiritual progress of the evolving soul." P. 1204.

10. Tremendous significance of the Adjuster.

"Can you really realize the true significance of the Adjuster's indwelling? Do you really fathom what it means to have an absolute fragment of the absolute and infinite Deity, the Universal Rather, indwelling and fusing with your finite mortal natures? When mortal man fuses with an actual fragment of the existential Cause of the total cosmos, no limit can ever be placed upon the destiny of such an unprecedented and unimaginable partnership. In eternity, man will be discovering not only the infinity of the objective Deity but also the unending potentiality of the subjective fragment of this same God. Always will the Adjuster be revealing to the mortal personality the wonder of God, and never can this supernal revelation come to an end, for the Adjuster is of God and as God to mortal man." P. 1181.

XI. ADJUSTERS AS RELATED TO HUMAN WILL

1. In everything we must be willing partners.

"They are persistent, ingenious, and perfect in their methods of work, but they never do violence to the volitional selfhood of their hosts. No human being will ever be spiritualized by a divine

Monitor against his will; survival is a gift of the Gods which must be desired by the creatures of time. In the final analysis, whatever the Adjuster has succeeded in doing for you, the records will show that the transformation has been accomplished with your co-operative consent; you will have been a willing partner with the Adjuster in the attainment of every step of the tremendous transformation of the ascension career." P. 1204-5.

2. **Adjuster always subservient to human will.**

"When Thought Adjusters indwell human minds, they bring with them the model careers, the ideal lives, as determined and foreordained by themselves and the Personalized Adjusters of Divinington, which have been certified by the Personalized Adjuster of Urantia. Thus they begin work with a definite and predetermined plan for the intellectual and spiritual development of their human subjects, but it is not incumbent upon any human being to accept this plan. You are all subjects of predestination, but it is not foreordained that you must accept this divine predestination; you are at full liberty to reject any part or all of the Thought Adjusters' program. It is their mission to effect such mind changes and to make such spiritual adjustments as you may willingly and intelligently authorize, to the end that they may gain more influence over the personality directionization; but under no circumstances do these divine Monitors ever take advantage of you or in any way arbitrarily influence you in your choices and decisions. The Adjusters respect your sovereignty of personality; *they are always subservient to your will.*" P. 1204.

3. **Adjuster is dependent on mind.**

"The Thought Adjuster has no special mechanism through which to gain self-expression; there is no mystic religious faculty for the reception or expression of religious emotions. These experiences are made available through the naturally ordained mechanism of mortal mind. And therein lies one explanation of the Adjuster's difficulty in engaging in direct communication with the material mind of its constant indwelling." P. 1104.

4. **Only conscious resistance hinders Adjusters.**

"Confusion, being puzzled, even sometimes discouraged and distracted, does not necessarily signify resistance to the leadings of the indwelling Adjuster. Such attitudes may sometimes connote lack of active co-operation with the divine Monitor and may, therefore somewhat delay spiritual progress, but such intellectual emotional difficulties do not in the least interfere with the certain survival of the God-knowing soul. Ignorance alone can never prevent survival; neither can confusional doubts nor fearful uncertainty. Only conscious resistance to the Adjuster's leading can prevent the survival of the evolving immortal soul." P. 1206.

5. **How will can co-operate with the Adjuster.**

"You must not regard co-operation with your Adjuster as a particularly conscious process, for it is not; but your motives and your decisions, your faithful determinations and your supreme desires, do constitute real and effective co-operation. You can consciously augment Adjuster harmony by:

"1. Choosing to respond to divine leading; sincerely basing the human life on the highest consciousness of truth, beauty, and goodness, and then co-ordinating these qualities of divinity through wisdom, worship, faith, and love.

"2. Loving God and desiring to be like him—genuine recognition of the divine fatherhood and loving worship of the heavenly Parent.

"3. Loving man and sincerely desiring to serve him—wholehearted recognition of the brotherhood of man coupled with an intelligent and wise affection for each of your fellow mortals.

"4. Joyful acceptance of cosmic citizenship—honest recognition of your progressive obligations to the Supreme Being, awareness of the interdependence of evolutionary man and evolving Deity. This is the birth of cosmic morality and the dawning realization of universal duty." P. 1206.

6. **Adjusters and the superconscious mind.**

"If one is disposed to recognize a theoretical subconscious mind as a practical working hypothesis in the otherwise unified intellectual life, then, to be consistent, one should postulate a similar and corresponding realm of ascending intellectual activity as the superconscious level, the zone of immediate contact with the indwelling spirit entity, the Thought Adjuster. The great danger in all these psychic speculations is that visions and other so-called mystic experiences, along with extraordinary dreams, may be regarded as divine communications to the human mind. In times past, divine beings have revealed themselves to certain God-knowing persons, not because of their mystic trances or morbid visions, but in spite of all these phenomena." P. 1099.

7. **Worship best method of contacting the Adjuster.**

"In contrast with conversion-seeking, the better approach to the morontia zones of possible contact with the Thought Adjuster would be through living faith and sincere worship, wholehearted and unselfish prayer. Altogether too much of the uprush of the memories of the unconscious levels of the human mind has been mistaken for divine revelations and spirit leadings." P. 1099.

8. **The great challenge.**

"The great challenge to modern man is to achieve better communication with the divine Monitor that dwells within the human mind. Man's greatest adventure in the flesh consists in the well-balanced and sane effort to advance the borders of self-consciousness out through the dim realms of embryonic soul-consciousness in a wholehearted effort to reach the borderland of spirit-consciousness—contact with the divine presence. Such an experience constitutes God-consciousness, an experience mightily confirmative of the pre-existent truth of the religious experience of knowing God. Such spirit-consciousness is the equivalent of the knowledge of the actuality of sonship with God. Otherwise, the assurance of sonship is the experience of faith." P. 2097.

XII. DETECTING THE PRESENCE OF ADJUSTERS

1. **The pilot light—the light of life.**

"There is a characteristic light, a spirit luminosity, which accompanies this divine presence, and which has become generally associated with thought Adjusters. In the universe of Nebadon this Paradise luminosity is widespreadly known as the 'pilot light'; on Uversa it is called the 'light of life.' On Urantia this phenomenon has sometimes been referred to as that 'true light which lights every man who comes into the world.'" P. 1181.

2. **When Personalized Adjusters are visible.**

"To all beings who have attained the Universal Father, the Personalized Thought Adjusters are visible. Adjusters of all stages, together with all other beings, entities, spirits, personalities, and spirit manifestations, are always discernible by those Supreme Creator Personalities who originate in the Paradise Deities, and who preside over the major governments of the grand universe." P. 1181.

3. Indicators of Adjuster presence.

"The actuality of the existence of God is demonstrated in human experience by the indwelling of the divine presence, the spirit Monitor sent from Paradise to live in the mortal mind of man and there to assist in evolving the immortal soul of eternal survival. The presence of this divine Adjuster in the human mind is disclosed by three experiential phenomena:

"1. The intellectual capacity for knowing God—God-consciousness.

"2. The spiritual urge to find God—God-seeking.

"3. The personality craving to be like God—the wholehearted desire to do the Father's will." P. 24.

4. Adjusters detected by Solitary Messengers.

"I may relate a further interesting fact: When a Solitary Messenger is on a planet whose inhabitants are indwelt by Thought Adjusters, as on Urantia, he is aware of a qualitative excitation in his detection-sensitivity to spirit presence. In such instances there is no quantitative excitation, only a qualitative agitation. When on a planet to which Adjusters do not come, contact with the natives does not produce any such reaction. This suggests that Thought Adjusters are in some manner related to, or are connected with, the Inspired Spirits of the Paradise Trinity. In some way they may possibly be associated in certain phases of their work; but we do not really know. They both originate near the center and source of all things, but they are not the same order of being. Thought Adjusters spring from the Father alone; Inspired Spirits are the offspring of the Paradise Trinity." P. 220.

XIII. THE PSYCHIC CIRCLES

1. The seven psychic circles.

"The sum total of personality realization on a material world is contained within the successive conquest of the seven psychic circles of mortal potentiality. Entrance upon the seventh circle marks the beginning of true human personality function. Completion of the first circle denotes the relative maturity of the mortal being. Though the traversal of the seven circles of cosmic growth does not equal fusion with the Adjuster, the mastery of these circles marks the attainment of those steps which are preliminary to Adjuster fusion.

"The Adjuster is your equal partner in the attainment of the seven circles—the achievement of comparative mortal maturity. The Adjuster ascends the circles with you from the seventh to the first but progresses to the status of supremacy and self-activity quite independent of the active co-operation of the mortal mind.

"The psychic circles are not exclusively intellectual, neither are they wholly morontial; they have to do with personality status, mind attainment, soul growth, and Adjuster attunement. The successful traversal of these levels demands the harmonious functioning of the *entire personality*, not merely of some one phase thereof. The growth of the parts does not equal the true maturation of the whole; the parts really grow in proportion to the expansion of the entire self—the whole self—material, intellectual, and spiritual.

"When the development of the intellectual nature proceeds faster than that of the spiritual, such a situation renders communication with the Thought Adjuster both difficult and dangerous. Likewise, overspiritual development tends to produce a fanatical and per-verted interpretation of the spirit leadings of the divine indweller. Lack of spiritual capacity makes it very difficult to transmit to such a material intellect the spiritual truths resident in the higher superconsciousness. It is to the mind of perfect pose, housed in a body of clean habits, stabilized neural energies, and balanced chemical function—when the physical, mental, and spiritual powers are in triune harmony of development—that a maximum of light and truth can be imparted with a minimum of temporal danger or risk to the real welfare of such a being. By such a balanced growth does man ascend the circles of planetary progression one by one, from the seventh to the first." P. 1209.

2. **Decisions advance both Adjuster and the self.**

"Every decision you make either impedes or facilitates the function of the Adjuster; likewise do these very decisions determine your advancement in the circles of human achievement. It is true that the supremacy of a decision, its crisis relationship, has a great deal to do with its circlemaking influence; nevertheless, numbers of deci-sions, frequent repetitions, persistent repetitions, are also essential to the habit-forming certainty of such reactions." P. 1210.

3. **Adjusters work in higher mind levels.**

"Adjusters work in the spheres of the higher levels of the human mind, unceasingly seeking to produce morontia duplicates of every concept of the mortal intellect. There are, therefore, two realities which impinge upon, and are centered in, the human mind circuits: one, a mortal self evolved from the original plans of the Life Carriers, the other, an immortal entity from the high spheres of Divinington, an indwelling gift from God. But the mortal self is also a personal self; it has personality." P. 1205.

4. **In relation to the problems and joys of living.**

"I cannot but observe that so many of you spend so much time and thought on mere trifles of living, while you almost wholly overlook the more essential realities of everlasting import, those very accomplishments which are concerned with the development of a more harmonious working agreement between you and your Adjusters. The great goal of human existence is to attune to the divinity of the indwelling Adjuster; the great achievement of mortal life is the attainment of a true and understanding consecration to the eternal aims of the divine spirit who waits and works within your mind. But a devoted and determined effort to realize eternal destiny is wholly compatible with a lighthearted and joyous life and with a successful and honorable career on earth. Co-operation with the Thought Adjuster does not entail self-torture, mock piety, or hypocritical and ostentatious self-abasement; the ideal life is one of loving service rather than an existence of fearful apprehension." P. 1206.

XIV. SELF-ACTING ADJUSTERS

1. **The scope of self-acting Adjusters.**

"You have been informed of the classification of Adjusters in relation to experience—virgin, advanced, and supreme. You should also recognize a certain functional classification—the self-acting Adjusters. A self-acting Adjuster is one who:

"1. Has had certained requisite experience in the evolving life of a will creature, either as a temporary indweller on a type of world where Adjusters are only loaned to mortal subjects or on an actual fusion planet where the human failed of survival. Such a Monitor is either an advanced or a supreme Adjuster.

"2. Has acquired the balance of spiritual power in a human who has made the third psychic circle and has had assigned to him a personal seraphic guardian.

"3. Has a subject who has made the supreme decision, has entered into a solemn and sincere betrothal with the Adjuster. The Adjuster looks beforehand to the time of actual fusion and reckons the union as an event of fact.

"4. Has a subject who has been mustered into one of the reserve corps of destiny on an evolutionary world of mortal ascension.

"5. At some time, during human sleep, has been temporarily detached from the mind of mortal incarceration to perform some exploit of liaison, contact, reregistration, or other extrahuman service associated with the spiritual administration of the world of assignment.

"6. Has served in a time of crisis in the experience of some human being who was the material complement of a spirit personality intrusted with the enactment of some cosmic achievement essential to the spiritual economy of the planet." P. 1196.

2. **The manifold doings of self-actors.**

"Self-acting Adjusters seem to possess a marked degree of will in all matters not involving the human personalities of their immediate indwelling, as is indicated by their numerous exploits both within and without the mortal subjects of attachment. Such Adjusters participate in numerous activities of the realm, but more frequently they function as undetected indwellers of the earthly tabernacles of their own choosing." P. 1196.

3. **Intercommunication of self-actors.**

"Undoubtedly these higher and more experienced types of Adjusters can communicate with those in other realms. But while self-acting Adjusters do thus intercommunicate, they do so only on the levels of their mutual work and for the purpose of preserving custodial data essential to the Adjuster ministry of the realms of their sojourn, though on occasions they have been known to function in interplanetary matters during times of crisis." P. 1196-7.

4. **Function of supreme and self-acting Adjusters.**

"Supreme and self-acting Adjusters can leave the human body at will. The indwellers are not an organic or biologic part of mortal life; they are divine superimpositions thereon. In the original life plans they were provided for, but they are not indispensable to material existence. Nevertheless it should be recorded that they very rarely, even temporarily, leave their mortal tabernacles after they once take up their indwelling.

"The superacting Adjusters are those who have achieved the conquest of their intrusted tasks and only await the dissolution of the material-life vehicle or the translation of the immortal soul." P. 1197.

5. Function of experienced Adjusters.

"The type of Adjuster has much to do with the potential for expression of the human personality. On down through the ages, many of the great intellectual and spiritual leaders of Urantia have exerted their influence chiefly because of the superiority and previous experience of their indwelling Adjusters." P. 1198.

6. Triumphs of self-acting Adjusters.

"Supreme and self-acting Adjusters are often able to contribute factors of spiritual import to the human mind when it flows freely in the liberated but controlled channels of creative imagination. At such times, and sometimes during sleep, the Adjuster is able to arrest the mental currents, to stay the flow, and then to divert the idea procession; and all this is done in order to effect deep spiritual transformations in the higher recesses of the superconsciousness. Thus are the forces and energies of mind more fully adjusted to the key of the contactual tones of the spiritual level of the present and the future.

"It is sometimes possible to have the mind illuminated, to hear the divine voice that continually speaks within you, so that you may become partially conscious of the wisdom, truth, goodness, and beauty of the potential personality constantly indwelling you." P. 1199.

XV. HOW ADJUSTERS GAIN EXPERIENCE

1. Adjusters in the child mind.

"The psychology of a child is naturally positive, not negative. So many mortals are negative because they were so trained. When it is said that the child is positive, reference is made to his moral impulses, those powers of mind whose emergence signals the arrival of the Thought Adjuster.

"In the absence of wrong teaching, the mind of the normal child moves positively, in the emergence of religious consciousness, toward moral righteousness and social ministry, rather than negatively, away from sin and guilt. There may or may not be conflict in the development of religious experience, but there are always present the inevitable decisions, effort, and function of the human will.

"Moral choosing is usually accompanied by more or less moral conflict. And this very first conflict in the child mind is between the urges of egoism and the impulses of altruism. The Thought Adjuster does not disregard the personality values of the egoistic motive but does operate to place a slight preference upon the altruistic impulse as leading to the goal of human happiness and to the joys of the kingdom of heaven." P. 1131.

2. **Great days of the Adjuster.**

"The great days in the individual careers of Adjusters are: first, when the human subject breaks through into the third psychic circle, thus insuring the Monitor's self-activity and increased range of function (provided the indweller was not already self-acting); then, when the human partner attains the first psychic circle, and they are thereby enabled to intercommunicate, at least to some degree; and last, when they are finally and eternally fused." P. 1212.

3. **The evolution of Adjusters.**

"The first stage of Adjuster evolution is attained in fusion with the surviving soul of a mortal being. Thus, while you are in nature evolving inward and upward from man to God, the Adjusters are in nature evolving outward and downward from God to man; and so will the final product of this union of divinity and humanity eternally be the son of man and the son of God." P. 1196.

4. **Adjuster experience in nonsurvivors.**

"But with those beings who are virtually disqualified for survival by disinheritance through the agency of unfit and inferior ancestors, many a virgin Adjuster has served a valuable preliminary experience in contacting evolutionary mind and thus has become better qualified for a subsequent assignment to a higher type of mind on some other world." P. 1198.

5. **Persistence of all true values.**

"Adjusters never fail; nothing worth surviving is ever lost; every meaningful value in every will creature is certain of survival, irrespective of the survival or nonsurvival of the meaning-discovering or evaluating personality. And so it is, a mortal creature may reject survival; still the life experience is not wasted; the eternal Adjuster carries the worthwhile features of such an apparent life of failure over into some other world and there bestows these surviving meanings and values upon some higher type of mortal mind, one of survival capacity. No worth-while experience ever happens in vain; no true meaning or real value ever perishes." P. 1200.

6.   Adjuster salvages values of nonsurvivors.

"And God-consciousness is equivalent to the integration of the self with the universe, and on its highest levels of spiritual reality. Only the spirit content of any value is imperishable. Even that which is true, beautiful, and good may not perish in human experience. If man does not choose to survive, then does the surviving Adjuster conserve those realities born of love and nurtured in service. And all these things are a part of the Universal Father. The Father is living love, and this life of the Father is in his Sons. And the spirit of the Father is in his Son's sons—mortal men. When all is said and done, the Father idea is still the highest human concept of God." P. 2097.

7.   Adjuster preserves values for next stage of existence.

"What the Thought Adjuster cannot utilize in your present life, those truths which he cannot successfully transmit to the man of his betrothal, he will faithfully preserve for use in the next stage of existence, just as he now carries over from circle to circle those items which he fails to register in the experience of the human subject, owing to the creature's inability, or failure, to give a sufficient degree of co-operation." P. 1191.

8.   Absolutely nothing takes the place of experience.

"Actual living experience has no cosmic substitute. The perfection of the divinity of a newly formed Thought Adjuster does not in any manner endow this Mystery Monitor with experienced ministrative ability. Experience is inseparable from a living existence; it is the one thing which no amount of divine endowment can absolve you from the necessity of securing by *actual living*. Therefore, in common with all beings living and functioning within the present sphere of the Supreme, Thought Adjusters must acquire experience; they must evolve from the lower, inexperienced, to the higher, more experienced, groups." P. 1195.

XVI. POTENTIALS OF ADJUSTER INDWELLING

1.   The potentials of Adjuster bestowal.

"The fact that he sends forth spirit messengers from himself to indwell the men and women of your world and other worlds in no wise lessens his ability to function as a divine and all-powerful spiritpersonality; and there is absolutely no limit to the extent or number of such spirit Monitors which he can and may send out. This giving of himself to his creatures creates a boundless, almost inconceivable future possibility of progressive and successive existences for these divinely endowed mortals. And this prodigal distribution of himself as these ministering spirit entities in no manner diminishes the wisdom and perfection of truth and knowledge which repose in the person of the all-wise, all-knowing, and all-powerful Father." P. 50.

2.   **Vast potentials of Adjuster endowment.**

"The Adjusters of prepersonal status indwell numerous types of mortal creatures, thus insuring that these same beings may survive mortal death to personalize as morontia creatures with the potential of ultimate spirit attainment. For, when such a creature mind of personality endowment is indwelt by a fragment of the spirit of the eternal God, the prepersonal bestowal of the personal Father, then does this finite personality possess the potential of the divine and the eternal and aspire to a destiny akin to the Ultimate, even reaching out for a realization of the Absolute." P. 70.

3.   **Adjusters crave divine perfection for you.**

"Your deepest nature—the divine Adjuster—creates within you a hunger and thirst for righteousness, a certain craving for divine perfection. Religion is the faith act of the recognition of this inner urge to divine attainment; and thus is brought about that soul trust and assurance of which you become conscious as the way of salvation, the technique of the survival of personality and all those values which you have come to look upon as being true and good." P. 1107.

4.   **The potentials of Adjuster fusion.**

"With man, the eventual fusion and resultant oneness with the indwelling Adjuster—the personality synthesis of man and the essence of God—constitute him, in potential, a living part of the Supreme and insure for such a onetime mortal being the eternal birthright of the endless pursuit of finality of universe service for and with the Supreme." P. 1112.

5.   **Adjusters the potential of eternal existence.**

"Your Adjuster is the potential of your new and next order of existence, the advance bestowal of your eternal sonship with God. By and with the consent of your will, the Adjuster has the power to subject the creature trends of the material mind to the transforming actions of the motivations and purposes of the emerging morontial soul." P. 1191.

XVII. ADJUSTER PROBLEMS AND HANDICAPS

1. **Seldom can the Adjuster speak to us.**

"Adjusters are playing the sacred and superb game of the ages; they are engaged in one of the supreme adventures of time in space. And how happy they are when your co-operation permits them to lend assistance in your short struggles of time as they continue to prosecute their larger tasks of eternity. But usually, when your Adjuster attempts to communicate with you, the message is lost in the material currents of the energy streams of human mind; only occasionally do you catch an echo, a faint and distant echo, of the divine voice." P. 1205.

2. **We can lessen the Adjuster's problem.**

"May I admonish you to heed the distant echo of the Adjuster's faithful call to your soul? The indwelling Adjuster cannot stop or even materially alter your career struggle of time; the Adjuster cannot lessen the hardships of life as you journey on through this world of toil. The divine indweller can only patiently forbear while you fight the battle of life as it is lived on your planet; but you could, if you only would—as you work and worry, as you fight and toil—permit the valiant Adjuster to fight with you and for you. You could be so comforted and inspired, so enthralled and intrigued, if you would only allow the Adjuster constantly to bring forth the pictures of the real motive, the final aim, and the eternal purpose of all this difficult, uphill struggle with the commonplace problems of your present material world." P. 1223.

3. **How we can aid the Adjuster.**

"Why do you not aid the Adjuster in the task of showing you the spiritual counterpart of all these strenuous material efforts? Why do you not allow the Adjuster to strengthen you with the spiritual truths of cosmic power while you wrestle with the temporal difficulties of creature existence? Why do you not encourage the heavenly helper to cheer you with the clear vision of the eternal outlook of universal life as you gaze in perplexity at the problems of the passing hour? Why do you refuse to be enlightened and inspired by the universe viewpoint while you toil amidst the handicaps of time and flounder in the maze of uncertainties which beset your mortal life journey? Why not allow the Adjuster to spiritualize your thinking, even though your feet must tread the material paths of earthly endeavor?" P. 1223.

4.   The recital of an Adjuster's problems.

"The higher human races of Urantia are complexly admixed; they are a blend of many races and stocks of different origin. This composite nature renders it exceedingly difficult for the Monitors to work efficiently during life and adds definitely to the problems of both the Adjuster and the guardian seraphim after death. Not long since I was present on Salvington and heard a guardian of destiny present a formal statement in extenuation of the difficulties of ministering to her mortal subject. This seraphim said:

"'Much of my difficulty was due to the unending conflict between the two natures of my subject: the urge of ambition opposed by animal indolence; the ideals of a superior people crossed by the instincts of an inferior race; the high purposes of a great mind antagonized by the urge of a primitive inheritance; the long-distance view of a far-seeing Monitor counteracted by the nearsightedness of a creature of time; the progressive plans of an ascending being modified by the desires and longings of a material nature; the flashes of universe intelligence cancelled by the chemical-energy mandates of the evolving race; the urge of angels opposed by the emotions of an animal; the training of an intellect annulled by the tendencies of instinct; the experience of the individual opposed by the accumulated propensities of the race; the aims of the best overshadowed by the drift of the worst; the flight of genius neutralized by the gravity of mediocrity; the progress of the good retarded by the inertia of the bad; the art of the beautiful be-smirched by the presence of evil; the buoyancy of health neutralized by the debility of disease; the fountain of faith polluted by the poisons of fear; the spring of joy embittered by the waters of sorrow; the gladness of anticipation disillusioned by the bitterness of realization; the joys of living ever threatened by the sorrows of death. Such a life on such a planet! And yet, because of the ever-present help and urge of the Thought Adjuster, this soul did achieve a fair degree of happiness and success and has even now ascended to the judgment halls of mansonia." P. 1223-4.

5.   Results of aborted Adjuster communication.

"There exists a vast gulf between the human and the divine, between man and God. The Urantia races are so largely electrically and chemically controlled, so highly animal like in their common behavior, so emotional in their ordinary reactions, that it becomes exceedingly difficult for the Monitors to guide and direct them. You are so devoid of courageous decisions and consecrated co-opera-tion that your indwelling Adjusters find it next to impossible to communicate directly with the human mind. Even when they do find it possible to flash a gleam of new truth to the evolving mortal soul, this spiritual revelation often so blinds the creature as to precipitate a convulsion of fanaticism or to initiate some other intellectual upheaval which results disastrously. Many a new religion and strange 'ism' has arisen from the aborted, imperfect, misunderstood, and garbled communications of the Thought Adjusters." P. 1207.

6. **Subconscious and superconscious in relation to Adjusters.**

"Certain abrupt presentations of thoughts, conclusions, and other pictures of mind are sometimes the direct or indirect work of the Adjuster; but far more often they are the sudden emergence into consciousness of ideas which have been grouping themselves together in the submerged mental levels, natural and everyday occurrences of normal and ordinary psychic function inherent in the circuits of the evolving animal mind. (In contrast with these subcon-scious emanations, the revelations of the Adjuster appear through the realms of the superconscious.)" P. 1207.

7. **What can't be done here, will be done over there.**

"Trust all matters of mind beyond the dead level of consciousness to the custody of the Adjusters. In due time, if not in this world then on the mansion worlds, they will give good account of their stewardship, and eventually will they bring forth those meanings and values intrusted to their care and keeping. They will resurrect every worthy treasure of the mortal mind if you survive." P. 1207.

8. **Manifold handicaps of the Adjuster.**

"But your unsteady and rapidly shifting mental attitudes often result in thwarting the plans and interrupting the work of the Adjusters. Their work is not only interfered with by the innate natures of the mortal races, but this ministry is also greatly retarded by your own preconceived opinions, settled ideas, and long-standing prejudices. Because of these handicaps, many times only their unfinished creations emerge into consciousness, and confusion of concept is inevitable. Therefore, in scrutinizing mental situations, safety lies only in the prompt recognition of each and every thought and experience for just what it actually and fundamentally is, disregarding entirely what it might have been." P. 1199.

9. **Do not identify conscience with Adjusters.**

"Do not confuse and confound the mission and influence of the Adjuster with what is commonly called conscience; they are not directly related. Conscience is a human and purely psychic reaction. It is not to be despised, but it is hardly the voice of God to the soul, which indeed the Adjuster's would be if such a voice could be heard. Conscience, rightly, admonishes you to do right; but the Adjuster, in addition, endeavors to tell you what truly is right; that is, when and as you are able to perceive the Monitor's leading." P. 1207-8.

10. **Relation of Adjusters to dreams.**

"Man's dream experiences, that disordered and disconnected parade of the un-co-ordinated sleeping mind, present adequate proof of the failure of the Adjusters to harmonize and associate the divergent factors of the mind of man. The Adjusters simply cannot, in a single lifetime, arbitrarily co-ordinate and synchronize two such unlike and diverse types of thinking as the human and the divine. When they do, as they sometimes have, such souls are translated directly to the mansion worlds without the necessity of passing through the experience of death.....

"It is extremely dangerous to postulate as to the Adjuster content of the dream life. The Adjusters do work during sleep, but your ordinary dream experiences are purely physiologic and psychologic phenomena. Likewise, it is hazardous to attempt the differentiation of the Adjusters' concept registry from the more or less continuous and conscious reception of the dictations of mortal conscience. These are problems which will have to be solved through individual discrimination and personal decision. But a human being would do better to err in rejecting an Adjuster's expression through believing it to be a purely human experience than to blunder into exalting a reaction of the mortal mind to the sphere of divine dignity. Remember, the influence of a Thought Adjuster is for the most part, though not wholly, a superconscious experience." P. 1208.

11. Dangerous ideas regarding the Adjuster's voice.

"In varying degrees and increasingly as you ascend the psychic circles, sometimes directly, but more often indirectly, you do communicate with your Adjusters. But it is dangerous to entertain the idea that every new concept originating in the human mind is the dictation of the Adjuster. More often, in beings of your order, that which you accept as the Adjuster's voice is in reality the emanation of your own intellect. This is dangerous ground, and every human being must settle these problems for himself in accordance with his natural human wisdom and superhuman insight." P. 1208.

XVIII. ATTAINMENT OF IMMORTALITY

1. Achievement of psychic circles is not Adjuster fusion.

"The achievement of the seven cosmic circles does not equal Adjuster fusion. There are many mortals living on Urantia who have attained their circles; but fusion depends on yet other greater and more sublime spiritual achievements, upon the attainment of a final and complete attunement of the mortal will with the will of God as it is resident in the Thought Adjuster." P. 1212.

2. Adjuster fusion can occur before physical death.

"When a human being has completed the circles of cosmic achievement, and further, when the final choosing of the mortal will permits the Adjuster to complete the association of human identity with the morontial soul during evolutionary and physical life, then do such consummated liaisons of soul and Adjuster go on independently to the mansion worlds, and there is issued the mandate from Uversa which provides for the immediate fusion of the Adjuster and the morontial soul. This fusion during physical life instantly consumes the material body; the human beings who might witness such a spectacle would only observe the translating mortal disappear 'in chariots of fire.'" P. 1212.

3. Translating Adjusters are usually highly experienced.

"Most Adjusters who have translated their subjects from Urantia were highly experienced and of record as previous indwellers of numerous mortals on other spheres. Remember, Adjusters gain valuable indwelling experience on planets of the loan order; it does not follow that Adjusters only gain experience for advanced work in those mortal subjects who fail to survive." P. 1212.

4. **The potentials of the oneness of Adjuster fusion.**

"Subsequent to mortal fusion the Adjusters share your destiny and experience; *they are you*. After the fusion of the immortal morontia soul and the associated Adjuster, all of the experience and all of the values of the one eventually become the possession of the other, so that the two are actually one entity. In a certain sense, this new being is of the eternal past as well as for the eternal future. All that was once human in the surviving soul and all that is experientially divine in the Adjuster now become the actual possession of the new and ever-ascending universe personality. But on each universe level the Adjuster can endow the new creature only with those attributes which are meaningful and of value on that level. An absolute *oneness* with the divine Monitor, a complete exhaustion of the endowment of an Adjuster, can only be achieved in eternity subsequent to the final attainment of the Universal Father, the Father of spirits, ever the source of these divine gifts." P. 1212.

5. **Few Urantians can expect translation.**

"But with the vast majority of Urantians the Adjuster must patiently await the arrival of death deliverance; must await the liberation of the emerging soul from the well-nigh complete domination of the energy patterns and chemical forces inherent in your material order of existence. The chief difficulty you experience in contacting with your Adjusters consists in this very inherent material nature. So few mortals are real thinkers; you do not spiritually develop and discipline your minds to the point of favorable liaison with the divine Adjusters. The ear of the human mind is almost deaf to the spiritual pleas which the Adjuster translates from the manifold messages of the universal broadcasts of love proceeding from the Father of mercies. The Adjuster finds it almost impossible to register these inspiring spirit leadings in an animal mind so completely dominated by the chemical and electrical forces inherent in your physical natures." P. 1213.

6. **Seldom can Adjusters speak to us.**

"Adjusters rejoice to make contact with the mortal mind; but they must be patient through the long years of silent sojourn during which they are unable to break through animal resistance and directly communicate with you. The higher the Thought Adjusters ascend in the scale of service, the more efficient they become. But never can they greet you, in the flesh, with the same full, sympathetic, and expressionful affection as they will when you discern them mind to mind on the mansion worlds....."

"While the voice of the Adjuster is ever within you, most of you will hear it seldom during a lifetime. Human beings below the third and second circles of attainment rarely hear the Adjuster's direct voice except in moments of supreme desire, in a supreme situation, and consequent upon a supreme decision." P. 1213.

7. A personal message from an Adjuster.

"During the making and breaking of a contact between the mortal mind of a destiny reservist and the planetary supervisors, sometimes the indwelling Adjuster is so situated that it becomes possible to transmit a message to the mortal partner. Not long since, on Urantia, such a message was transmitted by a self-acting Adjuster to the human associate, a member of the reserve corps of destiny. This message was introduced by these words: 'And now, without injury or jeopardy to the subject of my solicitous devotion and without intent to overchastise or discourage, for me, make record of this my plea to him.' Then followed a beautifully touching and appealing admonition. Among other things, the Adjuster pleaded 'that he more faithfully give me his sincere co-operation, more cheerfully endure the tasks of my emplacement, more faithfully carry out the program of my arrangement, more patiently go through the trials of my selection, more persistently and cheerfully tread the path of my choosing, more humbly receive credit that may accrue as a result of my ceaseless endeavors—thus transmit my admonition to the man of my indwelling. Upon him I bestow the supreme devotion and affection of a divine spirit. And say further to my beloved subject that I will function with wisdom and power until the very end, until the last earth struggle is over; I will be true to my personality trust. And I exhort him to survival, not to disappoint me, not to deprive me of the reward of my patient and intense struggle. On the human will our achievement of personality depends. Circle by circle I have patiently ascended this human mind, and I have testimony that I am meeting the approval of the chief of my kind. Circle by circle I am passing on to judgment. I await with pleasure and without apprehension the roll call of destiny; I am prepared to submit all to the tribunals of the Ancients of Days.'" P. 1213-14.

8. Adjuster is the potential of immortality.

"The sending of Adjusters, their indwelling, is indeed one of the unfathomable mysteries of God the Father. These fragments of the divine nature of the Universal Father carry with them the potential of creature immortality. Adjusters are immortal spirits, and union with them confers eternal life upon the soul of the fused mortal." P. 448.

XIX. THOUGHT ADJUSTERS AFTER DEATH

1. **At death Adjusters return to Divinington.**

    "When death of a material, intellectual, or spiritual nature occurs, the Adjuster bids farewell to the mortal host and departs for Divinington. From the headquarters of the local universe and the superuniverse a reflective contact is made with the supervisors of both governments, and the Monitor is registered out by the same number that recorded entry into the domains of time." P. 1231.

2. **At death Adjuster returns to the Father.**

    "When Thought Adjusters return to the Father, they go back to the realm of supposed origin, Divinington; and probably as a part of this experience, there is actual contact with the Father's Paradise personality as well as with the specialized manifestation of the Father's divinity which is reported to be situated on this secret sphere." P. 1179.

3. **Three kinds of death are recognized.**

    "1. *Spiritual (soul) death.* If and when mortal man has finally rejected survival, when he has been pronounced spiritually insolvent, morontially bankrupt, in the conjoint opinion of the Adjuster and the surviving seraphim, when such co-ordinate advice has been recorded on Uversa, and after the Censors and their reflective associates have verified these findings, thereupon do the rulers of Orvonton order the immediate release of the indwelling Monitor. But this release of the Adjuster in no way affects the duties of the personal or group seraphim concerned with that Adjuster-abandoned individual. This kind of death is final in its significance irrespective of the temporary continuation of the living energies of the physical and mind mechanisms. From the cosmic stand-point the mortal is already dead; the continuing life merely indicates the persistence of the material momentum of cosmic energies.

    "2. *Intellectual (mind) death.* When the vital circuits of higher adjutant ministry are disrupted through the aberrations of intellect or because of the partial destruction of the mechanism of the brain, and if these conditions pass a certain critical point of irreparability, the indwelling Adjuster is immediately released to depart for Divinington. On the universe records a mortal personality is considered to have met with death whenever the essential mind circuits of human willaction have been destroyed. And again, this is death, irrespective of the continuing function of the living mechanism of the physical body. The body minus the volitional mind is no longer human, but according to the prior choosing of the human will, the soul of such an individual may survive.

"3. *Physical (body and mind) death*. When death overtakes a human being, the Adjuster remains in the citadel of the mind until it ceases to function as an intelligent mechanism, about the time that the measureable brain energies cease their rhythmic vital pulsations. Following this dissolution the Adjuster takes leave of the vanishing mind, just as unceremoniously as entry was made years before, and proceeds to Divinington by way of Uversa." P. 1229-30.

4. Two factors survive death.

"After death the material body returns to the elemental world from which it was derived, but two nonmaterial factors of surviving personality persist: The pre-existent Thought Adjuster, with the memory transcription of the mortal career, proceeds to Divinington; and there also remains, in the custody of the destiny guardian, the immortal morontia soul of the deceased human. These phases and forms of soul, these once kinetic but now static formulas of identity, are essential to repersonalization on the morontia worlds; and it is the reunion of the Adjuster and the soul that reassembles the surviving personality, that reconsciousizes you at the time of the morontia awakening.

"For those who do not have personal seraphic guardians, the group custodians faithfully and efficiently perform the same service of identity safekeeping and personality resurrection. The seraphim, are indispensable to the reassembly of personality." P. 1230.

5. Personality and identity differentiated.

"Upon death the Thought Adjuster temporarily loses personality, but not identity; the human subject temporarily loses identity, but not personality; on the mansion worlds both reunite in eternal manifestation. Never does a departed Thought Adjuster return to earth as the being of former indwelling; never is personality manifested without the human will; and never does a dis-Adjusted human being after death manifest active identity or in any manner establish communication with the living beings of

earth. Such disAdjustered souls are wholly and absolutely unconscious during the long or short sleep of death. There can be no
exhibition of any sort of personality or ability to engage in communications with other personalities until after completion of survival.
Those who go to the mansion worlds are not permitted to send
messages back to their loved ones. It is the policy throughout the
universes to forbid such communication during the period of a
current dispensation." P. 1230.

6. **Thought Adjuster and memory.**

"The mortal-mind transcripts and the active creature-memory
patterns as transformed from the material levels to the spiritual are
the individual possession of the detached Thought Adjusters; these
spiritized factors of mind, memory, and creature personality are
forever a part of such Adjusters. The creature mind-matrix and the
passive potentials of identity are present in the morontia soul
intrusted to the keeping of the seraphic destiny guardians. And it is
the reuniting of the morontia-soul trust of the seraphim and the
spirit-mind trust of the Adjuster that reassembles creature personality and constitutes resurrection of a sleeping survivor." P. 533.

7. **Adjuster's memory discrimination.**

"Even with Adjuster-fusion candidates, only those human experiences which were of spiritual value are common possessions of the
surviving mortal and the returning Adjuster and hence are immediately remembered subsequent to mortal survival. Concerning
those happenings which were not of spiritual significance, even
these Adjuster-fusers must depend upon the attribute of recognition-response in the surviving soul. And since any one event may
have a spiritual connotation to one mortal but not to another, it
becomes possible for a group of contemporary ascenders from the
same planet to pool their store of Adjuster-remembered events and
thus to reconstruct any experience which they had in common, and
which was of spiritual value in the life of any one of them." P. 451.

XX. THOUGHT ADJUSTER FUSION

1. **The period of Adjuster courtship.**

"Today you are passing through the period of the courtship of your
Adjuster; and if you only prove faithful to the trust reposed in you
by the divine spirit who seeks your mind and soul in eternal union,
there will eventually ensue that morontia oneness, that supernal
harmony, that cosmic co-ordination, that divine attunement, that

celestial fusion, that never-ending blending of identity, that oneness of being which is so perfect and final that even the most experienced personalities can never segregate or recognize as separate identities the fusion partners—mortal man and divine Adjuster." P. 1204.

2. Fusion makes God and man one.

"Thought Adjuster fusion imparts eternal actualities to personality which were previously only potential. Among these new endowments may be mentioned: fixation of divinity quality, past-eternity experience and memory, immortality, and a phase of qualified potential absoluteness.

"When your earthly course in temporary form has been run, you are to awaken on the shores of a better world, and eventually you will be united with your faithful Adjuster in an eternal embrace. And this fusion constitutes the mystery of making God and man one, the mystery of finite creature evolution, but it is eternally true. Fusion is the secret of the sacred sphere of Ascendington, and no creature, save those who have experienced fusion with the spirit of Deity, can comprehend the true meaning of the actual values which are conjoined when the identity of a creature of time becomes eternally one with the spirit of Paradise Deity." P. 1237.

3. Fusion ends all danger of failure.

"When fusion with the Adjuster has been effected, there can be no future danger to the eternal career of such a personality. Celestial beings are tested throughout a long experience, but mortals pass through a relatively short and intensive testing on the evolutionary and morontia worlds." P. 1237.

4. Where fusion usually occurs.

"Fusion with the Adjuster is usually effected while the ascender is resident within his local system. It may occur on the planet of nativity as a transcendence of natural death; it may take place on any one of the mansion worlds or on the headquarters of the system; it may even be delayed until the time of the constellation sojourn; or, in special instances, it may not be consummated until the ascender is on the local universe capital." P. 1237.

5. Adoption of the new name.

"Human subjects are often known by the numbers of their Adjusters; mortals do not receive real universe names until after Adjuster fusion, which union is signalized by the bestowal of the new name upon the new creature by the destiny guardian." P. 1188.

6. **What Adjuster fusion means.**

"From the time of Adjuster fusion the status of the ascender is that of the evolutionary creature. The human member was the first to enjoy personality and, therefore, outranks the Adjuster in all matters concerned with the recognition of personality. The Paradise headquarters of this fused being is Ascendington, not Divinington, and this unique combination of God and man ranks as an ascending mortal all the way up to the Corps of the Finality.

"When once an Adjuster fuses with an ascending mortal, the number of that Adjuster is stricken from the records of the superuniverse. What happens on the records of Divinington, I do not know, but I surmise that the registry of that Adjuster is removed to the secret circles of the inner courts of Grandfanda, the acting head of the Corps of the Finality.

"With Adjuster fusion the Universal Father has completed his promise of the gift of himself to his material creatures; he has fulfilled the promise, and consummated the plan, of the eternal bestowal of divinity upon humanity. Now begins the human attempt to realize and to actualize the limitless possibilities that are inherent in the supernal partnership with God which has thus factualized." P. 1239.

7. **Fusion makes sonship a fact.**

"Your own races of surviving mortals belong to this group of the ascending Sons of God. You are now planetary sons, evolutionary creatures derived from the Life Carrier implantations and modified by the Adamic-life infusion, hardly yet ascending sons; but you are indeed sons of ascension potential—even to the highest heights of glory and divinity attainment—and this spiritual status of ascending sonship you may attain by faith and by freewill co-operation with the spiritualizing activities of the indwelling Adjuster. When you and your Adjusters are finally and forever fused, when you two are made one, even as in Christ Michael the Son of God and the Son of Man are one, then in fact have you become the ascending sons of God." P. 448-9.

8. **The Adjuster wins personality.**

"Has the triumphant Adjuster won personality by the magnificent service to humanity, or has the valiant human acquired immortality through sincere efforts to achieve Adjusterlikeness? It is neither; but they together have achieved the evolution of a member of one of the unique orders of the ascending personalities of the Supreme, one who will ever be found serviceable, faithful, and efficient, a candidate for further growth and development, ever ranging upward and never ceasing the supernal ascent until the seven circuits of Havona have been traversed and the onetime soul of earthly origin stands in worshipful recognition of the actual personality of the Father on Paradise." P. 1238.

9. **The potentials of Adjuster fusion.**

"Fusion with a fragment of the Universal Father is equivalent to a divine validation of eventual Paradise attainment, and such Adjuster-fused mortals are the only class of human beings who all traverse the Havona circuits and find God on Paradise. To the Adjuster-fused mortal the career of universal service is wide open. What dignity of destiny and glory of attainment await every one of you! Do you fully appreciate what has been done for you? Do you comprehend the grandeur of the heights of eternal achievement which are spread out before you?—even you who now trudge on in the lowly path of life through your so-called 'vale of tears'?" P. 449.

10. **Experience of nonfusion Adjusters.**

"An experiential Adjuster remains with a primitive human being throughout his entire lifetime in the flesh. The Adjusters contribute much to the advancement of primitive men but are unable to form eternal unions with such mortals. This transient ministry of the Adjusters accomplishes two things: First, they gain valuable and actual experience in the nature and working of the evolutionary intellect, an experience which will be invaluable in connection with later contacts on other worlds with beings of higher development. Second, the transient sojourn of the Adjusters contributes much towards preparing their mortal subjects for possible subsequent Spirit fusion. All God-seeking souls of this type achieve eternal life through the spiritual embrace of the Mother Spirit of the local universe, thus becoming ascending mortals of the local universe regime. Many persons from pre-Adamic Urantia were thus advanced to the mansion worlds of Satania." P. 446.

XXI. JESUS' THOUGHT ADJUSTER

1. Arrival of Jesus' Adjuster.

"In something more than a year after the return to Nazareth the boy Jesus arrived at the age of his first personal and wholehearted moral decision; and there came to abide with him a Thought Adjuster, a divine gift of the Paradise Father, which had aforetime served with Machiventa Melchizedek, thus gaining the experience of functioning in connection with the incarnation of a supermortal being living in the likeness of mortal flesh. This event occurred on February 11, 2 B.C. Jesus was no more aware of the coming of the divine Monitor than are the millions upon millions of other children who, before and since that day, have likewise received these Thought Adjusters to indwell their minds and work for the ultimate spiritualization of these minds and the eternal survival of their evolving immortal souls." P. 1357.

2. The personalization of Jesus' Adjuster.

"Ordinarily, when a mortal of the realm attains such high levels of personality perfection, there occur those preliminary phenomena of spiritual elevation which terminate in eventual fusion of the matured soul of the mortal with its associated divine Adjuster. And such a change was apparently due to take place in the personality experience of Jesus of Nazareth on that very day when he went down into the Jordan with his two brothers to be baptized by John. This ceremony was the final act of his purely human life on Urantia, and many superhuman observers expected to witness the fusion of the Adjuster with its indwelt mind, but they were all destined to suffer disappointment. Something new and even greater occurred. As John laid his hands upon Jesus to baptize him, the indwelling Adjuster took final leave of the perfected human soul of Joshua ben Joseph. And in a few moments this divine entity returned from Divinington as a Personalized Adjuster and chief of his kind throughout the entire local universe of Nebadon. Thus did Jesus observe his own former divine spirit descending on its return to him in personalized form. And he heard this same spirit of Paradise origin now speak, saying, 'This is my beloved Son in whom I am well pleased.' And John, with Jesus' two brothers, also heard these words. John's disciples, standing by the water's edge, did not hear these words, neither did they see the apparition of the Personalized Adjuster. Only the eyes of Jesus beheld the Personalized Adjuster." P. 1511.

3. **Experience and function of Jesus' Adjuster.**

   "The activities of Adjusters in your local universe are directed by the Personalized Adjuster of Michael of Nebadon, that very Monitor who guided him step by step when he lived his human life in the flesh of Joshua ben Joseph. Faithful to his trust was this extraordinary Adjuster, and wisely did this valiant Monitor direct the human nature, ever guiding the mortal mind of the Paradise Son in the choosing of the path of the Father's perfect will. This Adjuster had previously served with Machiventa Melchizedek in the days of Abraham and had engaged in tremendous exploits both previous to this indwelling and between these bestowal experiences." P. 1200.

4. **Function of Personalized Adjusters.**

   "We cannot state whether or not non-Adjuster Father fragments are personalizable, but you have been informed that personality is the sovereign freewill bestowal of the Universal Father. As far as we know, the Adjuster type of Father fragment attains personality only by the acquirement of personal attributes through service-ministry to a personal being. These Personalized Adjusters are at home on Divinington, where they instruct and direct their prepersonal associates.

   "Personalized Thought Adjusters are the untrammelled, unassigned, and sovereign stabilizers and compensators of the far-flung universe of universes. They combine the Creator and creature experience— existential and experiential. They are conjoint time and eternity beings. They associate the prepersonal and the personal in universe administration.

   "Personalized Adjusters are the all-wise and powerful executives of the Architects of the Master Universe. They are the personal agents of the full ministry of the Universal Father—personal, prepersonal, and superpersonal. They are the personal ministers of the extraordinary, the unusual, and the unexpected throughout all the realms of the transcendental absonite spheres of the domain of God the Ultimate, even to the levels of God the Absolute.

   "They are the exclusive beings of the universes who embrace within their being all the known relationships of personality; they are omnipersonal—they are before personality, they are personality, and they are after personality. They minister the personality of the Universal Father as in the eternal past, the eternal present, and the eternal future." P. 1201.

XXII. TABAMANTIA'S TRIBUTE TO ADJUSTERS

"It is interesting to note that local universe inspectors always address themselves, when carrying out a planetary examination, to the planetary chief of Thought Adjusters, just as they deliver charges to the chiefs of seraphim and to the leaders of other orders of beings attached to the administration of an evolving world. Not long since, Urantia underwent such a periodic inspection by Tabamantia, the sovereign supervisor of all life-experiment planets in the universe of Nebadon. And the records reveal that, in addition to his admonitions and indictments delivered to the various chiefs of superhuman personalities, he also delivered the following acknowledgment to the chief of Adjusters, whether located on the planet, on Salvington, Uversa, or Divinington, we do not definitely know, but he said:

"'Now to you, superiors far above me, I come as one placed in temporary authority over the experimental planetary series; and I come to express admiration and profound respect for this magnificent group of celestial ministers, the Mystery Monitors, who have volunteered to serve on this irregular sphere. No matter how trying the crises, you never falter. Not on the records of Nebadon nor before the commissions of Orvonton has there ever been offered an indictment of a divine Adjuster. You have been true to your trusts; you have been divinely faithful. You have helped to adjust the mistakes and to compensate for the shortcomings of all who labor on this confused planet. You are marvelous beings, guardians of the good in the souls of this backward realm. I pay you respect even while you are apparently under my jurisdiction as volunteer ministers. I bow before you in humble recognition of your exquisite unselfishness, your understanding ministry, and your impartial devotion. You deserve the name of the Godlike servers of the mortal inhabitants of this strife-torn, grief-stricken, and disease-afflicted world. I honor you! I all but worship you!'" P. 1189.

BIBLE TEXTS SUGGESTIVE OF THOUGHT ADJUSTERS

"*But it is the spirit in a man... that makes him understand.*" **Job 32:8.**

"*The spirit within me constrains me.*" **Job 32:18.**

"*Into thy hand I commit my spirit.*" **Ps. 31:5.**

"*The spirit of man is the lamp of the Lord.*" **Prov. 20:27.**

"*Who knows whether the spirit of man goes upward?*" **Eccl. 3:21.**

"And the spirit returns to God who gave it." **Eccl. 12:7**.

"I have put my spirit upon him." **Isa. 42:1**.

"Thus says the Lord, who…founded the earth and formed the spirit of man within him." **Zech. 12:1**.

"The heavens were opened and he saw the Spirit of God descending like a dove, and alighting on him." **Matt. 3:16**.

"As they were stoning Stephen, he prayed, 'Lord Jesus, receive my spirit.'" **Acts 7:59**.

"You are in the Spirit, if the Spirit of God really dwells in you." **Rom. 8:9**.

"Do you not know…that God's Spirit dwells in you?" **1 Cor. 3:16**.

12. TRUTH, BEAUTY, AND GOODNESS

Truth, Beauty, and Goodness in the Bible

TRUTH, BEAUTY, AND GOODNESS

I. MEANINGS AND VALUES OF TRUTH, BEAUTY, AND GOODNESS

1. Meanings of truth, beauty, and goodness.

"No matter what upheavals may attend the social and economic growth of civilization, religion is genuine and worth while if it fosters in the individual an experience in which the sovereignty of truth, beauty, and goodness prevails, for such is the true spiritual concept of supreme reality. And through love and worship this becomes meaningful as fellowship with man and sonship with God." P. 1089.

2. The charm and harmony of art.

"The discernment of supreme beauty is the discovery and integration of reality: The discernment of the divine goodness in the eternal truth, that is ultimate beauty. Even the charm of human art consists in the harmony of its unity." P. 43.

3. Truth, beauty, and goodness—discerning God in mind, matter, and spirit.

"Throughout this glorious age the chief pursuit of the ever-advancing mortals is the quest for a better understanding and a fuller realization of the comprehensible elements of Deity—truth, beauty, and goodness. This represents man's effort to discern God in mind, matter, and spirit. And as the mortal pursues this quest, he finds himself increasingly absorbed in the experimental study of philosophy, cosmology, and divinity." P. 646.

4. The achievement of cosmic art.

"Philosophy you somewhat grasp, and divinity you comprehend in worship, social service, and personal spiritual experience, but the pursuit of beauty—cosmology—you all too often limit to the study of man's crude artistic endeavors. Beauty, art, is largely a matter of the unification of contrasts. Variety is essential to the concept of beauty. The supreme beauty, the height of finite art, is the drama of the unification of the vastness of the cosmic extremes of Creator and creature. Man finding God and God finding man—the creature becoming perfect as is the Creator—that is the supernal achievement of the supremely beautiful, the attainment of the apex of cosmic art.

"Hence materialism, atheism, is the maximation of ugliness, the climax of the finite antithesis of the beautiful. Highest beauty consists in the panorama of the unification of the variations which have been born of pre-existent harmonious reality." P. 646.

II. INTERASSOCIATION OF TRUTH, BEAUTY, AND GOODNESS

1. **Interassociation of truth, beauty, and goodness.**

"All truth—material, philosophic, or spiritual—is both beautiful and good. All real beauty—material art or spiritual symmetry—is both true and good. All genuine goodness—whether personal morality, social equity, or divine ministry—is equally true and beautiful. Health, sanity, and happiness are integrations of truth, beauty, and goodness as they are blended in human experience. Such levels of efficient living come about through the unification of energy systems, idea systems, and spirit systems.

"Truth is coherent, beauty attractive, goodness stabilizing. And when these values of that which is real are co-ordinated in personality experience, the result is a high order of love conditioned by wisdom and qualified by loyalty. The real purpose of all universe education is to effect the better co-ordination of the isolated child of the worlds with the larger realities of his expanding experience. Reality is finite on the human level, infinite and eternal on the higher and divine levels." P. 43.

2. **Relations of truth, beauty, and goodness.**

"When reason once recognizes right and wrong, it exhibits wisdom; when wisdom chooses between right and wrong, truth and error, it demonstrates spirit leading. And thus are the functions of mind, soul, and spirit ever closely united and functionally interassociated. Reason deals with factual knowledge; wisdom, with philosophy and revelation; faith, with living spiritual experience. Through truth man attains beauty and by spiritual love ascends to goodness." P. 1142.

3. **Correlation of truth, beauty, and goodness.**

"Goodness is living, relative, always progressing, invariably a personal experience, and everlastingly correlated with the discernment of truth and beauty. Goodness is found in the recognition of the positive truth-values of the spiritual level, which must, in human experience, be contrasted with the negative counterpart—the shadows of potential evil." P. 1458.

III. AS RELATED TO PERSONALITY

1. Personal relations of truth, beauty, and goodness.

"The concept of truth might possibly be entertained apart from personality, the concept of beauty may exist without personality, but the concept of divine goodness is understandable only in relation to personality. Only a *person* can love and be loved. Even beauty and truth would be divorced from survival hope if they were not attributes of a personal God, a loving Father." P. 31.

2. Choice of truth, beauty, and goodness.

"The soul of survival value faithfully reflects both the qualitative and the quantitative actions and motivations of the material intellect, the former seat of the identity of selfhood. In the choosing of truth, beauty, and goodness, the mortal mind enters upon its premorontia universe career under the tutelage of the seven adjutant mind-spirits unified under the direction of the spirit of wisdom. Subsequently, upon the completion of the seven circles of premorontia attainment, the superimposition of the endowment of morontia mind upon adjutant mind initiates the prespiritual or morontia career of local universe progression." P. 1237.

3. Insight of the soul.

"In religion, Jesus advocated and followed the method of experience, even as modern science pursues the technique of experiment. We find God through the leadings of spiritual insight, but we approach this insight of the soul through the love of the beautiful, the pursuit of truth, loyalty to duty, and the worship of divine goodness. But of all these values, love is the true guide to real insight." P. 2076.

4. The perfection of truth, beauty, and goodness.

"The Master came to create in man a new spirit, a new will—to impart a new capacity for knowing the truth, experiencing compassion, and choosing goodness—the will to be in harmony with God's will, coupled with the eternal urge to become perfect, even as the Father in heaven is perfect." P. 1583.

5. Man earns appreciation of truth, beauty, and goodness.

"The full appreciation of truth, beauty, and goodness is inherent in the perfection of the divine universe. The inhabitants of the Havona worlds do not require the potential of relative value levels as a choice stimulus; such perfect beings are able to identify and choose the good in the absence of all contrastive and thought-compelling moral situations. But all such perfect beings are, in moral nature and spiritual status, what they are by virtue of the fact of existence. They have experientially earned advancement only within their inherent status. Mortal man earns even his status as an ascension candidate by his own faith and hope. Everything divine which the human mind grasps and the human soul acquires is an experiential attainment; it is a *reality* of personal experience and is therefore a unique possession in contrast to the inherent goodness and righteousness of the inerrant personalities of Havona." P. 52.

IV. ALL THREE SUMMED UP AS LOVE

1. **Truth, beauty, and goodness summed up as love.**

"Universal beauty is the recognition of the reflection of the Isle of Paradise in the material creation, while eternal truth is the special ministry of the Paradise Sons who not only bestow themselves upon the mortal races but even pour out their Spirit of Truth upon all peoples. Divine goodness is more fully shown forth in the loving ministry of the mainfold personalities of the Infinite Spirit. But love, the sum total of these three qualities, is man's perception of God as his spirit Father." P. 647-8.

2. **When love is only a sentiment.**

"Religious insight possesses the power of turning defeat into higher desires and new determinations. Love is the highest motivation which man may utilize in his universe ascent. But love, divested of truth, beauty, and goodness, is only a sentiment, a philosophic distortion, a psychic illusion, a spiritual deception. Love must always be redefined on successive levels of morontia and spirit progression." P. 2096.

3. **Love is the desire to do good to others.**

"To finite man truth, beauty, and goodness embrace the full revelation of divinity reality. As this love-comprehension of Deity finds spiritual expression in the lives of God-knowing mortals, there are yielded the fruits of divinity: intellectual peace, social progress, moral satisfaction, spiritual joy, and cosmic wisdom. The advanced mortals on a world in the seventh stage of light and life have learned that love is the greatest thing in the universe—and they know that God is love.

"Love is the desire to do good to others." P. 648.

V. AS RELATED TO DEITY

1. **Love, beauty, and goodness—a revelation of Deity.**

"The worlds settled in light and life are so fully concerned with the comprehension of truth, beauty, and goodness because these quality values embrace the revelation of Deity to the realms of time and space. The meanings of eternal truth make a combined appeal to the intellectual and spiritual natures of mortal man. Universal beauty embraces the harmonious relations and rhythms of the cosmic creation; this is more distinctly the intellectual appeal and leads towards unified and synchronous comprehension of the material universe. Divine goodness represents the revelation of infinite values to the finite mind, therein to be perceived and elevated to the very threshold of the spiritual level of human comprehension.

"Truth is the basis of science and philosophy, presenting the intellectual foundation of religion. Beauty sponsors art, music, and the meaningful rhythms of all human experience. Goodness embraces the sense of ethics, morality, and religion—experiential perfection-hunger.

"The existence of beauty implies the presence of appreciative creature mind just as certainly as the fact of progressive evolution indicates the dominance of the Supreme Mind. Beauty is the intellectual recognition of the harmonious time-space synthesis of the far-flung diversification of phenomenal reality, all of which stems from pre-existent and eternal oneness.

"Goodness is the mental recognition of the relative values of the diverse levels of divine perfection. The recognition of goodness implies a mind of moral status, a personal mind with ability to discriminate between good and evil. But the possession of goodness, greatness, is the measure of real divinity attainment." P. 646-7.

2. **Divinity comprehended as truth, beauty, and goodness.**

"Divinity is creature comprehensible as truth, beauty, and goodness; correlated in personality as love, mercy, and ministry; disclosed on impersonal levels as justice, power, and sovereignty." P. 3.

3. **As man's universe approach.**

"Even truth, beauty, and goodness—man's intellectual approach to the universe of mind, matter, and spirit—must be combined into one unified concept of a divine and supreme *ideal*. As mortal personality unifies the human experience with matter, mind, and spirit, so does this divine and supreme ideal become power-unified in Supremacy and then personalized as a God of fatherly love." P. 647.

VI. AS RELATED TO ADJUSTERS AND THE SUPREME

1. Adjusters and truth, beauty, and goodness.

"In a sense the Adjusters may be fostering a certain degree of planetary cross-fertilization in the domains of truth, beauty, and goodness. But they are seldom given two indwelling experiences on the same planet; there is no Adjuster now serving on Urantia who has been on this world previously. I know whereof I speak since we have their numbers and records in the archives of Uversa." P. 1199.

2. The Supreme and truth, beauty, and goodness.

"The final penetration of the truth, beauty, and goodness of the Supreme Being could only open up to the progressing creature those absonite qualities of ultimate divinity which lie beyond the concept levels of truth, beauty, and goodness." P. 1263.

VII. SPIRITUAL VALUES OF TRUTH, BEAUTY, AND GOODNESS

1. True spirit values of truth, beauty, and goodness.

"This same philosophy of the living flexibility and cosmic adaptability of divine truth to the individual requirements and capacity of every son of God, must be perceived before you can hope adequately to understand the Master's teaching and practice of nonresistance to evil. The Master's teaching is basically a spiritual pronouncement. Even the material implications of his philosophy cannot be helpfully considered apart from their spiritual correlations. The spirit of the Master's injunction consists in the nonresistance of all selfish reaction to the universe, coupled with the aggressive and progressive attainment of righteous levels of true spirit values: divine beauty, infinite goodness, and eternal truth—to know God and to become increasingly like him." P. 1950.

2. As related to Spirit ministry.

"Truth, beauty, and goodness are correlated in the ministry of the Spirit, the grandeur of Paradise, the mercy of the Son, and the experience of the Supreme. God the Supreme *is* truth, beauty, and goodness, for these concepts of divinity represent finite maximums of ideational experience. The eternal sources of these triune qualities of divinity are on superfinite levels, but a creature could only conceive of such sources as supertruth, superbeauty, and supergoodness." P. 1279.

3. Related to the environment of worship.

"It was also at Jericho, in connection with the discussion of the early religious training of children in habits of divine worship, that

Jesus impressed upon his apostles the great value of beauty as an influence leading to the urge to worship, especially with children. The Master by precept and example taught the value of worshiping the Creator in the midst of the natural surroundings of creation. He preferred to commune with the heavenly Father amidst the trees and among the lowly creatures of the natural world. He rejoiced to contemplate the Father through the inspiring spectacle of the starry realms of the Creator Sons." P. 1840.

4. **Paradise values of truth, beauty, and goodness.**

"Paradise values of eternity and infinity, of truth, beauty, and goodness, are concealed within the facts of the phenomena of the universes of time and space. But it requires the eye of faith in a spirit-born mortal to detect and discern these spiritual values." P. 2078.

5. **But nothing takes the place of faith.**

"The idealization and attempted service of truth, beauty, and goodness is not a substitute for genuine religious experience—spiritual reality. Psychology and idealism are not the equivalent of religious reality. The projections of the human intellect may indeed originate false gods—gods in man's image—but the true God-consciousness does not have such an origin. The God-consciousness is resident in the indwelling spirit. Many of the religious systems of man come from the formulations of the human intellect, but the God-consciousness is not necessarily a part of these grotesque systems of religious slavery." P. 2095.

TRUTH, BEAUTY, AND GOODNESS IN THE BIBLE
I. TRUTH

"True worshipers will worship the Father in spirit and truth." **John 4:23.**

"You will know the truth, and the truth will make you free." **John 8:32.**

"Jesus said to him, 'I am the way, and the truth, and the life.'" **John 14:6.**

"When the Spirit of truth comes, he will guide you into all the truth." **John 16:13.**

"Sanctify them in the truth; thy word is truth." **John 17:17.**

"Present yourself to God as one approved...rightly handling the word of truth." **2Tim. 2:15.**

"By this we know the spirit of truth and the spirit of error." **1 John 4:6.**

"Who have heard the word of truth, the gospel of your salvation." **Eph. 1:13.**

II. BEAUTY

"Out of Zion, the perfection of beauty, God shines forth." **Ps. 50:2**.

"Honor and majesty are before him; strength and beauty are in his sanctuary." **Ps. 96:6**.

"The Lord of Hosts will be a crown of glory, and a diadem of beauty." **Isa. 28:5**.

"I am perfect in beauty." **Eze. 27:3**.

III. GOODNESS

Many passages using the words "goodness" or "holiness" in the King James Version are rendered "faithfulness" in the Revised Version.

"Who is like thee, majestic in holiness." **Ex. 15:11**.

"God sits on his holy throne." **Ps. 47:8**.

"And give thanks to his holy name." **Ps. 97:12**.

"And designated Son of God in power according to the Spirit of holiness." **Rom. 1:4**.

"He disciplines us for our good, that we may share his holiness." **Heb. 12:10**.

"Holy, holy, holy is the Lord of hosts." **Isa. 6:3**.

"Thus says the high and lofty One who inhabits eternity, whose name is Holy." **Isa. 57:15**.

"You shall be holy, for I am holy." **1 Peter 1:16. (See also Lev. 19:2.)**

"Holy Father, keep them in thy name which thou hast given me." **John 17:11**.

13. EVOLUTION OF THE SOUL

Soul as Used in the Bible

EVOLUTION OF THE SOUL

I. VARIED CONCEPTS OF THE SOUL

1. **Primitive concepts of the soul.**

   "Early mortals usually failed to differentiate the concepts of an indwelling spirit and a soul of evolutionary nature. The savage was much confused as to whether the ghost soul was native to the body or was an external agency in possession of the body. The absence of reasoned thought in the presence of perplexity explains the gross inconsistencies of the savage view of souls, ghosts, and spirits." P. 954.

2. **Varied concepts of the soul.**

   "The concept of a soul and of an indwelling spirit is not new to Urantia; it has frequently appeared in the various systems of planetary beliefs. Many of the Oriental as well as some of the Occidental faiths have perceived that man is divine in heritage as well as human in inheritance. The feeling of the inner presence in addition to the external omnipresence of Deity has long formed a part of many Urantian religions. Men have long believed that there is something growing within the human nature, something vital that is destined to endure beyond the short span of temporal life.

   "Before man realized that his evolving soul was fathered by a divine spirit, it was thought to reside in different physical organs—the eye, liver, kidney, heart, and later, the brain. The savage associated the soul with blood, breath, shadows and with reflections of the self in water." P. 1215.

3. **The soul is a new reality.**

   "The soul of man is an experiential acquirement. As a mortal creature chooses to 'do the will of the Father in heaven,' so the indwelling spirit becomes the father of a *new reality* in human experience. The mortal and material mind is the mother of this same emerging reality. The substance of this new reality is neither material nor spiritual—it is *morontial*. This is the emerging and immortal soul which is destined to survive mortal death and begin the Paradise ascension." P. 8-9.

II. THE EVOLVING SOUL

1. **Evolution of the soul is by choice and consent.**

   "The mistakes of mortal mind and the errors of human conduct may markedly delay the evolution of the soul, although they cannot inhibit such a morontia phenomenon when once it has been initiated by the indwelling Adjuster with the consent of the creature will. But at any time prior to mortal death this same material and human will is empowered to rescind such a choice and to reject survival. Even after survival the ascending mortal still retains this prerogative of choosing to reject eternal life; at any time before fusion with the Adjuster the evolving and ascending creature can choose to forsake the will of the Paradise Father. Fusion with the Adjuster signalizes the fact that the ascending mortal has eternally and unreservedly chosen to do the Father's will." P. 1218-19.

2. The soul is at first wholly morontial.

"This immortal soul is at first wholly morontia in nature, but it possesses such a capacity for development that it invariably ascends to the true spirit levels of fusion value with the spirits of Deity, usually with the same spirit of the Universal Father that initiated such a creative phenomenon in the creature mind." P. 1219.

3. The soul is both human and divine.

"Both the human mind and the divine Adjuster are conscious of the presence and differential nature of the evolving soul—the Adjuster fully, the mind partially. The soul becomes increasingly conscious of both the mind and the Adjuster as associated identities, proportional to its own evolutionary growth. The soul partakes of the qualities of both the human mind and the divine spirit but persistently evolves toward augmentation of spirit control and divine dominance through the fostering of a mind function whose meanings seek to co-ordinate with true spirit value." P. 1219.

4. Soul evolution in relation to heredity.

"While the hereditary legacy of cerebral endowment and that of electrochemical overcontrol both operate to delimit the sphere of efficient Adjuster activity, no hereditary handicap (in normal minds) ever prevents eventual spiritual achievement. Heredity may interfere with the rate of personality conquest, but it does not prevent eventual consummation of the ascendant adventure. If you will co-operate with your Adjuster, the divine gift will, sooner or later, evolve the immortal morontia soul and, subsequent to fusion therewith, will present the new creature to the sovereign Master Son of the local universe and eventually to the Father of Adjusters on Paradise." P. 1199.

5. Technique of evolving the immortal soul.

"The material self has personality and identity, temporal identity; the prepersonal spirit Adjuster also has identity, eternal identity. This material personality and this spirit prepersonality are capable of so uniting their creative attributes as to bring into existence the surviving identity of the immortal soul.

"Having thus provided for the growth of the immortal soul and having liberated man's inner self from the fetters of absolute dependence on antecedent causation, the Father stands aside. Now, man having thus been liberated from the fetters of causation response, at least as pertains to eternal destiny, and provision having been made for the growth of the immortal self, the soul, it remains for man himself to will the creation or to inhibit the creation of this surviving and eternal self which is his for the choosing. No other being, force, creator, or agency in all the wide universe of universes can interfere to any degree with the absolute sovereignty of the mortal free will, as it operates within the realms of choice, regarding the eternal destiny of the personality of the choosing mortal. As pertains to eternal survival, God has decreed the sovereignty of the material and mortal will, and that decree is absolute." P. 71.

6. Faith and love are the measure of soul's evolution.

"The measure of the spiritual capacity of the evolving soul is your faith in truth and your love for man, but the measure of your human strength of character is your ability to resist the holding of grudges and your capacity to withstand brooding in the face of deep sorrow. Defeat is the true mirror in which you may honestly view your real self." P. 1740.

III. THE MORONTIA SOUL

1. Three factors in creation of morontia soul.

"There are three and not two factors in the evolutionary creation of such an immortal soul. These three antecedents of the morontia human soul are:

"1. *The human mind* and all cosmic influences antecedent thereto and impinging thereon.

"2. *The divine spirit* indwelling this human mind and all potentials inherent in such a fragment of absolute spirituality together with all associated spiritual influences and factors in human life.

"3. *The relationship between material mind and divine spirit*, which connotes a value and carries a meaning not found in either of the contributing factors to such an association. The reality of this unique relationship is neither material nor spiritual but morontial. It is the soul." P. 1218.

2. **Midwayers call the soul the mid-mind.**

"The midway creatures have long denominated this evolving soul of man the mid-mind in contradistinction to the lower or material mind and the higher or cosmic mind. This mid-mind is really a morontia phenomenon since it exists in the realm between the material and the spiritual. The potential of such a morontia evolution is inherent in the two universal urges of mind: the impulse of the finite mind of the creature to know God and attain the divinity of the Creator, and the impulse of the infinite mind of the Creator to know man and attain the *experience* of the creature." P. 1218.

3. **Creative soul potentials of human mind.**

"This supernal transaction of evolving the immortal soul is made possible because the mortal mind is first personal and second is in contact with superanimal realities; it possesses a supermaterial endowment of cosmic ministry which insures the evolution of a moral nature capable of making moral decisions, thereby effecting a bona fide creative contact with the associated spiritual ministries and with the indwelling Thought Adjuster.

"The inevitable result of such a contactual spiritualization of the human mind is the gradual birth of a soul, the joint offspring of an adjutant mind dominated by a human will that craves to know God, working in liaison with the spiritual forces of the universe which are under the overcontrol of an actual fragment of the very God of all creation—the Mystery Monitor. And thus does the material and mortal reality of the self transcend the temporal limitations of the physical-life machine and attain a new expression and a new identification in the evolving vehicle for selfhood continuity, the morontia and immortal soul." P. 1218.

4. **Survival of the morontia soul.**

"There is something real, something of human evolution, something additional to the Mystery Monitor, which survives death. This newly appearing entity is the soul, and it survives the death of both your physical body and your material mind. This entity is the conjoint child of the combined life and efforts of the human you in liaison with the divine you, the Adjuster. This child of human and divine parentage constitutes the surviving element of terrestrial origin; it is the morontia self, the immortal soul." P. 1234.

IV. MIND DETERMINES DESTINY OF SOUL

1. **Mind determines the destiny of the soul.**

"Mind is the cosmic instrument on which the human will can play the discords of destruction, or upon which this same human will can bring forth the exquisite melodies of God identification and consequent eternal survival. The Adjuster bestowed upon man is, in the last analysis, impervious to evil and incapable of sin, but mortal mind can actually be twisted, distorted, and rendered evil and ugly by the sinful machinations of a perverse and self-seeking human will. Likewise can this mind be made noble, beautiful, true, and good—actually great—in accordance with the spirit-illuminated will of a God-knowing human being." P. 1217.

2. **Human will is captain of the soul ship.**

"Mind is your ship, the Adjuster is your pilot, the human will is captain. The master of the mortal vessel should have the wisdom to trust the divine pilot to guide the ascending soul into the morontia harbors of eternal survival. Only by selfishness, slothfulness, and sinfulness can the will of man reject the guidance of such a loving pilot and eventually wreck the mortal career upon the evil shoals of rejected mercy and upon the rocks of embraced sin. With your consent, this faithful pilot will safely carry you across the barriers of time and the handicaps of space to the very source of the divine mind and on beyond, even to the Paradise Father of Adjusters." P. 1217.

V. INHERITANCE AND THE EVOLVED SOUL

1. **What the evolved soul inherits.**

"When the evolving soul and the divine Adjuster are finally and eternally fused, each gains all of the experiencible qualities of the other. This co-ordinate personality possesses all of the experiential memory of survival once held by the ancestral mortal mind and then resident in the morontia soul, and in addition thereto this potential finaliter embraces all the experiential memory of the Adjuster throughout the mortal indwellings of all time. But it will require an eternity of the future for an Adjuster ever completely to endow the personality partnership with the meanings and values which the divine Monitor carries forward from the eternity of the past." P. 1212-13.

2. **Surviving soul reflects past experience.**

"The soul of survival value faithfully reflects both the qualitative and the quantitative actions and motivations of the material intellect, the former seat of the identity of selfhood. In the choosing of truth, beauty, and goodness, the mortal mind enters upon its premorontia universe career under the tutelage of the seven adjutant mind-spirits unified under the direction of the spirit of wisdom. Subsequently, upon the completion of the seven circles of premorontia attainment, the superimposition of the endowment of morontia mind upon adjutant mind initiates the prespiritual or morontia career of local universe progression." P. 1237.

VI. MEMORY PROBLEMS OF THE EVOLVED SOUL

1. **Memory problems of the surviving soul.**

"Even with Adjuster-fusion candidates, only those human experiences which were of spiritual value are common possessions of the surviving mortal and the returning Adjuster and hence are immediately remembered subsequent to mortal survival. Concerning those happenings which were not of spiritual significance, even these Adjuster-fusers must depend upon the attribute of recognition-response in the surviving soul. And since any one event may have a spiritual connotation to one mortal but not to another, it becomes possible for a group of contemporary ascenders from the same planet to pool their store of Adjuster-remembered events and thus to reconstruct any experience which they had in common, and which was of spiritual value in the life of any one of them." P. 451.

2. **Continuity of the evolved soul.**

"Mortal mind, prior to death, is self-consciously independent of the Adjuster presence; adjutant mind needs only the associated material-energy pattern to enable it to operate. But the morontia soul, being superadjutant, does not retain self-consciousness without the Adjuster when deprived of the material-mind mechanism. This evolving soul does, however, possess a continuing character derived from the decisions of its former associated adjutant mind, and this character becomes active memory when the patterns thereof are energized by the returning Adjuster." P. 1236.

3. **Method of memory preservation.**

"The mortal-mind transcripts and the active creature-memory patterns as transformed from the material levels to the spiritual are the individual possession of the detached Thought Adjusters; these spiritized factors of mind, memory, and creature personality are forever a part of such Adjusters. The creature mind-matrix and the passive potentials of identity are present in the morontia soul intrusted to the keeping of the seraphic destiny guardians. And it is the reuniting of the morontia-soul trust of the seraphim and the spirit-mind trust of the Adjuster that reassembles creature personality and constitutes resurrection of a sleeping survivor." P. 533.

VII. SUPREME BEING AND SOUL EVOLUTION

1. Potential of evolved soul in the Supreme.

"Even the experience of man and Adjuster must find echo in the divinity of God the Supreme, for, as the Adjusters experience, they are like the Supreme, and the evolving soul of mortal man is created out of the pre-existent possibility for such experience within the Supreme." P. 1287.

2. Supreme Being Universal Mother of evolved soul.

"The morontia soul of an evolving mortal is really the son of the Adjuster action of the Universal Father and the child of the cosmic reaction of the Supreme Being, the Universal Mother. The mother influence dominates the human personality throughout the local universe childhood of the growing soul. The influence of the Deity parents becomes more equal after the Adjuster fusion and during the superuniverse career, but when the creatures of time begin the traversal of the central universe of eternity, the Father nature becomes increasingly manifest, attaining its height of finite manifestation upon the recognition of the Universal Father and the admission into the Corps of the Finality." P. 1288.

3. Partnership of God the Father and God the Supreme.

"All soul-evolving humans are literally the evolutionary sons of God the Father and God the Mother, the Supreme Being. But until such time as mortal man becomes soul-conscious of his divine heritage, this assurance of Deity kinship must be faith realized. Human life experience is the cosmic cocoon in which the universe endowments of the Supreme Being and the universe presence of the Universal Father (none of which are personalities) are evolving the morontia soul of time and the human-divine finaliter character of universe destiny and eternal service." P. 1289.

VIII.   JESUS TALKS ABOUT SOUL EVOLUTION

"'The soul is the self-reflective, truth-discerning, and spirit-perceiving part of man which forever elevates the human being above the level of the animal world. Self-consciousness, in and of itself, is not the soul.

Moral self-consciousness is true human self-realization and constitutes the foundation of the human soul, and the soul is that part of man which represents the potential survival value of human experience. Moral choice and spiritual attainment, the ability to know God and the urge to be like him, are the characteristics of the soul. The soul of man cannot exist apart from moral thinking and spiritual activity. A stagnant soul is a dying soul. But the soul of man is distinct from the divine spirit which dwells within the mind. The divine spirit arrives simultaneously with the first moral activity of the human mind, and that is the occasion of the birth of the soul.

"'The saving or losing of a soul has to do with whether or not the moral consciousness attains survival status through eternal alliance with its associated immortal spirit endowment. Salvation is the spiritualization of the self-realization of the moral consciousness, which thereby becomes possessed of survival value. All forms of soul conflict consist in the lack of harmony between the moral, or spiritual, self-consciousness and the purely intellectual self-consciousness.

"'The human soul, when matured, ennobled, and spiritualized, approaches the heavenly status in that it comes near to being an entity intervening between the material and the spiritual, the material self and the divine spirit. The evolving soul of a human being is difficult of description and more difficult of demonstration because it is not discoverable by the methods of either material investigation or spiritual proving. Material science cannot demonstrate the existence of a soul, neither can pure spirit-testing. Notwithstanding the failure of both material science and spiritual standards to discover the existence of the human soul, every morally conscious mortal *knows* of the existence of *his* soul as a *real* and actual personal experience.'" P. 1478-9.

SOUL AS USED IN THE BIBLE

In many passages where soul is found in the King James Version, it is translated as life, person, or being in the Revised Version.

I. SOUL AS COVERING ALL LIVING CREATURES

"In his hand is the life of every living thing and the breath of all mankind." **Job 12:10.** (King James Version reads: "soul of every living thing.")

II. HUMAN BEING—PERSON, INDIVIDUAL

"Breathed into his nostrils the breath of life; and man became a living being." *(Soul)* **Gen. 2:7.**

"No man cares for me."(My soul) **Ps. 142:4**.

"So those who received his word were baptized, and there were added that day about three thousand souls." **Acts 2:41**.

III. SOUL AS CONTRASTED WITH SPIRIT

"For the word of God is living and active, sharper than any two-edged sword, piercing to the division of soul and spirit." **Heb. 4:12**.

IV. SOUL AS THE EMOTIONAL LIFE

"But Hannah answered, '...I am a woman sorely troubled;...I have been pouring out my soul before the Lord.'" **1 Sam. 1:15**.

"Hungry and thirsty, their soul fainted within them." **Ps. 107:5**.

"Like cold water to a thirsty soul, so is good news from a far country." **Prov. 25:25**.

"Then he said to them, 'My soul is very sorrowful, even to death.'" **Matt. 26:38**.

V. SOUL AS RELATED TO SIN AND ATONEMENT

"You shall keep the sabbath...whoever does any work on it, that soul shall be cut off from among his people." **Ex. 31:14**.

"He has redeemed my soul from going down into the Pit." **Job 33:28**.

"But God will ransom my soul." **Ps. 49:15**.

"The soul that sins shall die." **Eze. 18:4**.

VI. SOUL AS RELIGIOUS EXPERIENCE

"My soul yearns for thee in the night." **Isa. 26:9**.

"And Mary said, 'My soul magnifies the Lord.'" **Luke 1:46**.

"You shall love the Lord your God with all your heart, and with all your soul, and with all your might." **Deut. 6:5**.

"He restores my soul." **Ps. 23:3**.

"And find rest for your souls." **Jer. 6:16**.

"Take my yoke upon you,...and you will find rest for your souls." **Matt. 11:29**.

VII. SOUL—ASSOCIATED WITH SPIRIT AND BODY

"And may your spirit and soul and body be kept sound and blameless." **1 Thess. 5:23**. (Paul recognized the threefold nature of man.)

VIII. THE SOUL AND SURVIVAL

"And as her soul was departing (for she died)." **Gen. 35:18.**

"For what will it profit a man, if he gains the whole world and forfeits his life?" (Soul, King James Version) **Matt. 16:26.**

14. ANGELS

Angels in the Bible

ANGELS

I. MANIFOLD SERVICES OF ANGELS

1. They enjoy a wide range of ministry.

"Angels are the ministering-spirit associates of the evolutionary and ascending will creatures of all space; they are also the colleagues and working associates of the higher hosts of the divine personalities of the spheres. The angels of all orders are distinct personalities and are highly individualized. They all have a large capacity for appreciation of the ministrations of the reversion directors. Together with the Messenger Hosts of Space, the ministering spirits enjoy seasons of rest and change; they possess very social natures and have an associative capacity far transcending that of human beings." P. 285.

2. In service, angels range from Urantia to Paradise.

"The individual members of the angelic orders are not altogether stationary as to personal status in the universe. Angels of certain orders may become Paradise Companions for a season; some become Celestial Recorders; others ascend to the ranks of the Technical Advisers. Certain of the cherubim may aspire to seraphic status and destiny, while evolutionary seraphim can achieve the spiritual levels of the ascending Sons of God." P. 285.

3. Angels function on both material and spiritual levels.

"The seraphim are so created as to function on both spiritual and literal levels. There are few phases of morontia or spirit activity which are not open to their ministrations. While in personal status angels are not so far removed from human beings, in certain functional performances seraphim far transcend them. They possess many powers far beyond human comprehension. For example: You have been told that the 'very hairs of your head are numbered,' and it is true they are, but a seraphim does not spend her time counting them and keeping the number corrected up to date. Angels possess inherent and automatic (that is, automatic as far as you could perceive) powers of knowing such things; you would truly regard a seraphim as a mathematical prodigy. Therefore, numerous duties which would be tremendous tasks for mortals are performed with exceeding ease by seraphim." P. 419. Matt. 10:30.

4. Angels do not judge us.

"Angels are superior to you in spiritual status, but they are not your judges or accusers. No matter what your faults, 'the angels, although greater in power and might, bring no accusation against you.' Angels do not sit in judgment on mankind, neither should individual mortals prejudge their fellow creatures." P. 419.

5.   Angels are not to be worshiped.

"You do well to love them, but you should not adore them; angels are not objects of worship. The great seraphim, Loyalatia, when your seer 'fell down to worship before the feet of the angel,' said: 'See that you do it not; I am a fellow servant with you and with your races, who are all enjoined to worship God.'" P. 419. Rev. 19:10; 22:9.

6.   In nature, angels are near humans.

"In nature and personality endowment the seraphim are just a trifle ahead of mortal races in the scale of creature existence. Indeed, when you are delivered from the flesh, you become very much like them. On the mansion worlds you will begin to appreciate the seraphim, on the constellation spheres to enjoy them, while on Salvington they will share their places of rest and worship with you. Throughout the whole morontia and subsequent spirit ascent, your fraternity with the seraphim will be ideal; your companionship will be superb." P. 419.

7.   Angels are mind stimulators.

"The guardian seraphim are not mind, though they do spring from the same source that also gives origin to mortal mind, the Creative Spirit. Seraphim are mind stimulators; they continually seek to promote circle-making decisions in human mind. They do this, not as does the Adjuster, operating from within and through the soul, but rather from the outside inward, working through the social, ethical, and moral environment of human beings. Seraphim are not the divine Adjuster lure of the Universal Father, but they do function as the personal agency of the ministry of the Infinite Spirit." P. 1245.

8.   Angels are teachers of mind and soul.

"Mortal man, subject to Adjuster leading, is also amenable to seraphic guidance. The Adjuster is the essence of man's eternal nature; the seraphim is the teacher of man's evolving nature—in this life the mortal mind, in the next the morontia soul. On the mansion worlds you will be conscious and aware of seraphic instructors, but in the first life men are usually unaware of them.

"Seraphim function as teachers of men by guiding the footsteps of the human personality into paths of new and progressive experiences. To accept the guidance of a seraphim rarely means attaining a life of ease. In following this leading you are sure to encounter, and if you have the courage, to traverse, the rugged hills of moral choosing and spiritual progress." P. 1245.

9. Angels prompt us to worship.

"The impulse of worship largely originates in the spirit promptings of the higher mind adjutants, reinforced by the leadings of the Adjuster. But the urge to pray so often experienced by God-conscious mortals very often arises as the result of seraphic influence. The guarding seraphim is constantly manipulating the mortal environment for the purpose of augmenting the cosmic insight of the human ascender to the end that such a survival candidate may acquire enhanced realization of the presence of the indwelling Adjuster and thus be enabled to yield increased co-operation with the spiritual mission of the divine presence." P. 1245.

10. Angels co-operate with Thought Adjusters.

"While there is apparently no communication between the indwelling Adjusters and the encompassing seraphim, they always seem to work in perfect harmony and exquisite accord. The guardians are most active at those times when the Adjusters are least active, but their ministry is in some manner strangely correlated. Such superb co-operation could hardly be either accidental or incidental." P. 1245.

11. Angels may attain their Corps of Completion.

"After attainment of the Father of spirits and admission to the seraphic service of completion, angels are sometimes assigned to the ministry of worlds settled in light and life. They gain attachment to the high trinitized beings of the universes and to the exalted services of Paradise and Havona. These seraphim of the local universes have experientially compensated the differential in divinity potential formerly setting them apart from the ministering spirits of the central and superuniverses. Angels of the Seraphic Corps of Completion serve as associates of the superuniverse seconaphim and as assistants to the high Paradise-Havona orders of supernaphim. For such angels the career of time is finished; henceforth and forever they are the servants of God, the consorts of divine personalities, and the peers of the Paradise finaliters." P. 441.

II. MINISTERING SPIRITS TO ASCENDERS

1. **Supernaphim to seraphim are all ministers.**

   "As the supernaphim in the central universe and the seconaphim in a superuniverse, so the seraphim, with the associated cherubim and sanobim, constitute the angelic corps of a local universe.

   "The seraphim are all fairly uniform in design. From universe to universe, throughout all seven of the superuniverses, they show a minimum of variation; they are the most nearly standard of all spirit types of personal beings. Their various orders constitute the corps of the skilled and common ministers of the local creations." P. 418.

2. **Angelic assistance for ascenders.**

   "All orders of the angelic hosts are devoted to the various universe services, and they minister in one way or another to the higher orders of celestial beings; but it is the supernaphim, seconaphim, and seraphim who, in large numbers, are employed in the further-ance of the ascending scheme of progressive perfection for the children of time. Functioning in the central, super-, and local universes, they form that unbroken chain of spirit ministers which has been provided by the Infinite Spirit for the help and guidance of all who seek to attain the Universal Father through the Eternal Son." P. 286.

3. **Angels are very close to mortals.**

   "Angels do not have material bodies, but they are definite and discrete beings; they are of spirit nature and origin. Though invisible to mortals, they perceive you as you are in the flesh without the aid of transformers or translators; they intellectually understand the mode of mortal life, and they share all of man's nonsensuous emotions and sentiments. They appreciate and greatly enjoy your efforts in music, art, and real humor. They are fully cognizant of your moral struggles and spiritual difficulties. They love human beings, and only good can result from your efforts to understand and love them." P. 419.

4. **Angels do not control human mind.**

   "Angels do not invade the sanctity of the human mind; they do not manipulate the will of mortals; neither do they directly contact with the indwelling Adjusters. The guardian of destiny influences you in every possible manner consistent with the dignity of your personality; under no circumstances do these angels interfere with the free action of the human will. Neither angels nor any other order of universe personality have power or authority to curtail or abridge the prerogatives of human choosing." P. 1245-6.

5. They figuratively "weep" over us.

"Angels are so near you and care so feelingly for you that they figuratively 'weep because of your willful intolerance and stubbornness.' Seraphim do not shed physical tears; they do not have physical bodies; neither do they possess wings. But they do have spiritual emotions, and they do experience feelings and sentiments of a spiritual nature which are in certain ways comparable to human emotions." P. 1246.

6. They minister regardless of our appeals.

"The seraphim act in your behalf quite independent of your direct appeals; they are executing the mandates of their superiors, and thus they function regardless of your passing whims or changing moods. This does not imply that you may not make their tasks either easier or more difficult, but rather that angels are not directly concerned with your appeals or with your prayers." P. 1246.

7. Co-operation with midwayers.

"Seraphim are able to function as material ministers to human beings under certain circumstances, but their action in this capacity is very rare. They are able, with the assistance of the midway creatures and the physical controllers, to function in a wide range of activities in behalf of human beings, even to make actual contact with mankind, but such occurrences are very unusual. In most instances the circumstances of the material realm proceed unaltered by seraphic action, although occasions have arisen, involving jeopardy to vital links in the chain of human evolution, in which seraphic guardians have acted, and properly, on their own initiative." P. 1246.

III. THE SERAPHIM

1. Classification of seraphim.

"As far as we are cognizant, the Infinite Spirit, as personalized on the local universe headquarters, intends to produce uniformly perfect seraphim, but for some unknown reason these seraphic offspring are very diverse. This diversity may be a result of the unknown interposition of evolving experiential Deity; if so, we cannot prove it. But we do observe that, when seraphim have been subjected to educational tests and training discipline, they unfailingly and distinctly classify into the following seven groups:

1. Supreme Seraphim.
2. Superior Seraphim.
3. Supervisor Seraphim.
4. Administrator Seraphim.
5. Planetary Helpers.
6. Transition Ministers.
7. Seraphim of the Future." P. 426.

2. **Organization of seraphim.**

"After the second millennium of sojourn at seraphic headquarters the seraphim are organized under chiefs into groups of twelve (12 pairs, 24 seraphim), and twelve such groups constitute a company (144 pairs, 288 seraphim), which is commanded by a leader. Twelve companies under a commander constitute a battalion (1,728 pairs or 3,456 seraphim), and twelve battalions under a director equal a seraphic unit (20,736 pairs or 41,472 individuals), while twelve units, subject to the command of a supervisor, constitute a legion numbering 248,832 pairs or 497,664 individuals. Jesus alluded to such a group of angels that night in the garden of Gethsemane when he said: 'I can even now ask my Father, and he will presently give me more than twelve legions of angels.'

"Twelve legions of angels comprise a host numbering 2,985,984 pairs or 5,971,968 individuals, and twelve such hosts (35,831,808 pairs or 71,663,616 individuals) make up the largest operating organization of seraphim, an angelic army. A seraphic host is commanded by an archangel or by some other personality of co-ordinate status, while the angelic armies are directed by the Brilliant Evening Stars or by other immediate lieutenants of Gabriel. And Gabriel is the 'supreme commander of the armies of heaven,' the chief executive of the Sovereign of Nebadon, 'the Lord God of hosts.'" P. 421. Matt. 26:53.

3. **Negative and positive seraphim.**

"Though not male and female as are the Material Sons and the mortal races, seraphim are negative and positive. In the majority of assignments it requires two angels to accomplish the task. When they are not encircuited, they can work alone; neither do they require complements of being when stationary. Ordinarily they retain their original complements of being, but not necessarily. Such associations are primarily necessitated by function; they are not characterized by sex emotion, though they are exceedingly personal and truly affectionate." P. 420.

IV. CHERUBIM AND SANOBIM

1. They are our nearest of spirit kin.

"In all essential endowments cherubim and sanobim are similar to seraphim. They have the same origin but not always the same destiny. They are wonderfully intelligent, marvelously efficient, touchingly affectionate, and almost human. They are the lowest order of angels, hence all the nearer of kin to the more progressive types of human beings on the evolutionary worlds." P. 422.

2. Why they usually work in pairs.

"Cherubim and sanobim are inherently associated, functionally united. One is an energy positive personality; the other, energy negative. The right-hand deflector, or positively charged angel, is the cherubim—the senior or controlling personality. The left-hand deflector, or negatively charged angel, is the sanobim—the complement of being. Each type of angel is very limited in solitary function; hence they usually serve in pairs. When serving independently of their seraphic directors, they are more than ever dependent on mutual contact and always function together." P. 422.

3. They are faithful seraphic helpers.

"Cherubim and sanobim are the faithful and efficient aids of the seraphic ministers, and all seven orders of seraphim are provided with these subordinate assistants. Cherubim and sanobim serve for ages in these capacities, but they do not accompany seraphim on assignments beyond the confines of the local universe." P. 422.

4. "Fourth creatures" of the cherubim.

"Cherubim and sanobim are by nature very near the morontia level of existence, and they prove to be most efficient in the borderland work of the physical, morontial, and spiritual domains. These children of the local universe Mother Spirit are characterized by 'fourth creatures' much as are the Havona Servitals and the conciliating commissions. Every fourth cherubim and every fourth sanobim are quasi-material, very definitely resembling the morontia level of existence.

"These angelic fourth creatures are of great assistance to the seraphim in the more literal phases of their universe and planetary activities. Such morontia cherubim also perform many indispensable borderline tasks on the morontia training worlds and are assigned to the service of the Morontia Companions in large numbers. They are to the morontia spheres about what the midway creatures are to the evolutionary planets. On the inhabited worlds these morontia cherubim frequently work in liaison with the midway creatures. Cherubim and midway creatures are distinctly separate orders of beings; they have dissimilar origins, but they disclose great similarity in nature and function." P. 422-3.

V. GUARDIAN ANGELS

1. Guardian angels are not a myth.

"The teaching about guardian angels is not a myth; certain groups of human beings do actually have personal angels. It was in recognition of this that Jesus, in speaking of the children of the heavenly kingdom, said: 'Take heed that you despise not one of these little ones, for I say to you, their angels do always behold the presence of the spirit of my Father.'" P. 1241. Matt. 18:10.

2. Assignment of guardian angels.

"Originally, the seraphim were definitely assigned to the separate Urantia races. But since the bestowal of Michael, they are assigned in accordance with human intelligence, spirituality, and destiny. Intellectually, mankind is divided into three classes:

"1. The subnormal minded—those who do not exercise normal will power; those who do not make average decisions. This class embraces those who cannot comprehend God; they lack capacity for the intelligent worship of Deity. The subnormal beings of Urantia have a corps of seraphim, one company, with one battalion of cherubim, assigned to minister to them and to witness that justice and mercy are extended to them in the life struggles of the sphere.

"2. The average, normal type of human mind. From the standpoint of seraphic ministry, most men and women are grouped in seven classes in accordance with their status in making the circles of human progress and spiritual development.

"3. The supernormal minded—those of great decision and undoubted potential of spiritual achievement; men and women who enjoy more or less contact with their indwelling Adjusters; members of the various reserve corps of destiny. No matter in what circle a human happens to be, if such an individual becomes enrolled in any of the several reserve corps

- 289 -

of destiny, right then and there, personal seraphim are assigned, and from that time until the earthly career is finished, that mortal will enjoy the continuous ministry and unceasing watchcare of a guardian angel. Also, when any human being makes *the* supreme decision, when there is a real betrothal with the Adjuster, a personal guardian is immediately assigned to that soul." P. 1241-2.

3.   **When guardians are assigned.**

"Seraphim are not known as guardians of destiny until such time as they are assigned to the association of a human soul who has realized one or more of three achievements: has made a supreme decision to become Godlike, has entered the third circle, or has been mustered into one of the reserve corps of destiny.

"In the evolution of races a guardian of destiny is assigned to the very first being who attains the requisite circle of conquest. On Urantia the first mortal to secure a personal guardian was Rantowoc, a wise man of the red race of long ago." P. 1242.

4.   **Guardians are volunteers.**

"All angelic assignments are made from a group of volunteering seaphim, and these appointments are always in accordance with human needs and with regards to the status of the angelic pair—in the light of seraphic experience, skill, and wisdom. Only seraphim of long service, the more experienced and tested types, are assigned as destiny guards. Many guardians have gained much valuable experience on those worlds which are of the non-Adjuster fusion series. Like the Adjusters, the seraphim attend these beings for a single lifetime and then are liberated for new assignment. Many guardians on Urantia have had this previous practiacal experience on other worlds." P. 1242-3.

5.   **Guardians' affection for mortals.**

"The angels develop an abiding affection for their human associates; and you would, if you could only visualize the seraphim, develop a warm affection for them. Divested of material bodies, given spirit forms, you would be very near the angels in many attributes of personality. They share most of your emotions and experience some additional ones. The only emotion actuating you which is somewhat difficult for them to comprehend is the legacy of animal fear that bulks so large in the mental life of the average inhabitant of Urantia. The angels really find it hard to understand why you will so persistently allow your higher intellectual powers, even your religious faith, to be so dominated by fear, so thoroughly demoralized by the thoughtless panic of dread and anxiety." P. 1243.

6. Reassignment of disappointed guardians.

"When human beings fail to survive, their personal or group guardians may repeatedly serve in similar capacities on the same planet. The seraphim develop a sentimental regard for individual worlds and entertain a special affection for certain races and types of mortal creatures with whom they have been so closely and intimately associated." P. 1243.

7. Life assignment of guardians.

"When a seraphic pair accept guardian assignment, they serve for the remainder of the life of that human being. The complement of being (one of the two angels) becomes the recorder of the undertaking. These complemental seraphim are the recording angels of the mortals of the evolutionary worlds. The records are kept by the pair of cherubim (a cherubim and a sanobim) who are always associated with the seraphic guardians, but these records are always sponsored by one of the seraphim." P. 1243.

8. They guard and guide—are not overlords.

"In the life of the flesh the intelligence of angels is not directly available to mortal men. They are not overlords or directors; they are simply guardians. The seraphim *guard* you; they do not seek directly to influence you; you must chart your own course, but these angels then act to make the best possible use of the course you have chosen. They do not (ordinarily) arbitrarily intervene in the routine affairs of human life. But when they receive instructions from their superiors to perform some unusual exploit, you may rest assured that these guardians will find some means of carrying out these mandates. They do not, therefore, intrude into the picture of human drama except in emergencies and then usually on the direct orders of their superiors. They are the beings who are going to follow you for many an age, and they are thus receiving an introduction to their future work and personality association." P. 1246.

9. Guardian angels after death.

"Having told you something of the ministry of seraphim during natural life, I will endeavor to inform you about the conduct of the guardians of destiny at the time of the mortal dissolution of their human associates. Upon your death, your records, identity specifications, and the morontia entity of the human soul—conjointly evolved by the ministry of mortal mind and the divine Adjuster—are faithfully conserved by the destiny guardian together with all other values related to your future existence, everything that constitutes you, the real you, except the identity of continuing existence represented by the departing Adjuster and the actuality of personality.

"The instant the pilot light in the human mind disappears, the spirit luminosity which seraphim associate with the presence of the Adjuster, the attending angel reports in person to the commanding angels, successively, of the group, company, battalion, unit, legion, and host; and after being duly registered for the final adventure of time and space, such an angel receives certification by the planetary chief of seraphim for reporting to the Evening Star (or other lieutenant of Gabriel) in command of the seraphic army of this candidate for universe ascension. And upon being granted permission from the commander of this highest organizational unit, such a guardian of destiny proceeds to the first mansion world and there awaits the consciousizing of her former ward in the flesh." P. 1246-7.

VI. MANSION WORLD MINISTRY

1. **Seraphic help on mansion worlds.**

"On the mansion worlds the seraphic evangels will help you to choose wisely among the optional routes to Edentia, Salvington, Uversa, and Havona. If there are a number of equally advisable routes, these will be put before you, and you will be permitted to select the one that most appeals to you. These seraphim then make recommendations to the four and twenty advisers on Jerusem concerning that course which would be most advantageous for each ascending soul." P. 552.

2. **Early contacts on the mansion worlds.**

"It is indeed an epoch in the career of an ascending mortal, this first awakening on the shores of the mansion world; there, for the first time, actually to see your long-loved and ever-present angelic companions of earth days; there also to become truly conscious of the identity and presence of the divine Monitor who so long indwelt your mind on earth. Such an experience constitutes a glorious awakening, a real resurrection.

- 292 -

"On the morontia spheres the attending seraphim (there are two of them) are your open companions. These angels not only consort with you as you progress through the career of the transition worlds, in every way possible assisting you in the acquirement of morontia and spirit status, but they also avail themselves of the opportunity to advance by study in the extension schools for evolutionary seraphim maintained on the mansion worlds.

"The human race was created just a little lower than the more simple types of the angelic orders. Therefore will your first assignment of the morontia life be as assistants to the seraphim in the immediate work awaiting at the time you attain personality consciousness subsequent to your liberation from the bonds of the flesh." P. 1248.

3. **Following us through the local universe.**

"Before leaving the mansion worlds, all mortals will have permanent seraphic associates or guardians. And as you ascend the morontia spheres, eventually it is the seraphic guardians who witness and certify the decrees of your eternal union with the Thought Adjusters. Together they have established your personality identities as children of the flesh from the worlds of time. Then, with your attainment of the mature morontia estate, they accompany you through Jerusem and the associated worlds of system progress and culture. After that they go with you to Edentia and its seventy spheres of advanced socialization, and subsequently will they pilot you to the Melchizedeks and follow you through the superb career of the universe headquarters worlds. And when you have learned the wisdom and culture of the Melchizedeks, they will take you on to Salvington, where you will stand face to face with the Sovereign of all Nebadon. And still will these seraphic guides follow you through the minor and major sectors of the superuniverse and on to the receiving worlds of Uversa, remaining with you until you finally enseconaphim for the long Havona flight." P. 1248.

4. **Through the superuniverse and on to Paradise.**

"Some of the destiny guardians of attachment during the mortal career follow the course of the ascending pilgrims through Havona. The others bid their long-time mortal associates a temporary farewell, and then, while these mortals traverse the circles of the central universe, these guardians of destiny achieve the circles of Seraphington. And they will be in waiting on the shores of Paradise when their mortal associates awaken from the last transit sleep of time into the new experiences of eternity. Such ascending seraphim subsequently enter upon divergent services in the finaliter corps and in the Seraphic Corps of Completion." P. 1248.

5. **Mansion world seraphic evangels.**

"These seraphic evangels are dedicated to the proclamation of the gospel of eternal progression, the triumph of perfection attainment. On the mansion worlds they proclaim the great law of the conservation and dominance of goodness: No act of good is ever wholly lost; it may be long thwarted but never wholly annulled, and it is eternally potent in proportion to the divinity of its motivation." P. 552.

VII. TRANSPORT SERAPHIM

1. **Source of conventional idea of angels.**

"Your conventional idea of angels has been derived in the following way: During moments just prior to physical death a reflective phenomenon sometimes occurs in the human mind, and this dimming consciousness seems to visualize something of the form of the attending angel, and this is immediately translated into terms of the habitual concept of angels held in that individual's mind.

"The erroneous idea that angels possess wings is not wholly due to olden notions that they must have wings to fly through the air. Human beings have sometimes been permitted to observe seraphim that were being prepared for transport service, and the traditions of these experiences have largely determined the Urantian concept of angels. In observing a transport seraphim being made ready to receive a passenger for interplanetary transit, there may be seen what are apparently double sets of wings extending from the head to the foot of the angel. In reality these wings are energy insulators—friction shields." P. 438.

2. **Preparations for seraphic transport.**

"When celestial beings are to be enseraphimed for transfer from one world to another, they are brought to the headquarters of the sphere and, after due registry, are inducted into the transit sleep. Meantime, the transport seraphim moves into a horizontal position immediately above the universe energy pole of the planet. While the energy shields are wide open, the sleeping personality is skillfully deposited, by the officiating seraphic assistants, directly on top of the transport angel. Then both the upper and lower pairs of shields are carefully closed and adjusted." P. 438.

3.   **The technique of seraphic transport.**

"And now, under the influence of the transformers and the transmitters, a strange metamorphosis begins as the seraphim is made ready to swing into the energy currents of the universe circuits. To outward appearance the seraphim grows pointed at both extremities and becomes so enshrouded in a queer light of amber hue that very soon it is impossible to distinguish the enseraphimed personality. When all is in readiness for departure, the chief of transport makes the proper inspection of the carriage of life, carries out the routine tests to ascertain whether or not the angel is properly encircuited, and then announces that the traveler is properly enseraphimed, that the energies are adjusted, that the angel is insulated, and that everything is in readiness for the departing flash. The mechanical controllers, two of them, next take their positions. By this time the transport seraphim has become an almost transparent, vibrating, torpedo-shaped outline of glistening luminosity. Now the transport dispatcher of the realm summons the auxiliary batteries of the living energy transmitters, usually one thousand in number; as he announces the destination of the transport, he reaches out and touches the near point of the seraphic carriage, which shoots forward with lightninglike speed, leaving a trail of celestial luminosity as far as the planetary atmospheric investment extends. In less than ten minutes the marvelous spectacle will be lost even to reinforced seraphic vision." P. 438-9.

VIII.   RELATION TO OTHER SPIRITS

1.   **They co-ordinate all impersonal spirit influences.**

"One of the most important things a destiny guardian does for her mortal subject is to effect a personal co-ordination of the numerous impersonal spirit influences which indwell, surround, and impinge upon the mind and soul of the evolving material creature. Human beings are personalities, and it is exceedingly difficult for nonpersonal spirits and prepersonal entities to make direct contact with such highly material and discretely personal minds. In the ministry of the guarding angel all of these influences are more or less unified and made more nearly appreciable by the expanding moral nature of the evolving human personality." P. 1244.

2. **Correlate manifold influences of Infinite Spirit.**

"More especially can and does this seraphic guardian correlate the manifold agencies and influences of the Infinite Spirit, ranging from the domains of the physical controllers and the adjutant mind-spirits up to the Holy Spirit of the Divine Minister and to the Omnipresent Spirit presence of the Paradise Third Source and Center. Having thus unified and made more personal these vast ministries of the Infinite Spirit, the seraphim then undertakes to correlate this integrated influence of the Conjoint Actor with the spirit presences of the Father and the Son." P. 1244.

3. **Combined love of the Father and mercy of the Son.**

"The Adjuster is the presence of the Father; the Spirit of Truth, the presence of the Sons. These divine endowments are unified and co-ordinated on the lower levels of human spiritual experience by the ministry of the guardian seraphim. The angelic servers are gifted in combining the love of the Father and the mercy of the Son in their ministry to mortal creatures." P. 1244.

4. **Custodian of mind patterns and soul realities.**

"And herein is revealed the reason why the seraphic guardian eventually becomes the personal custodian of the mind patterns, memory formulas, and soul realities of the mortal survivor during that interval between physical death and morontia resurrection. None but the ministering children of the Infinite Spirit could thus function in behalf of the human creature during this phase of transition from one level of the universe to another and higher level. Even when you engage in your terminal transition slumber, when you pass from time to eternity, a high supernaphim likewise shares the transit with you as the custodian of creature identity and the surety of personal integrity." P. 1244.

IX. SUPERNAPHIM AND SECONAPHIM

1. **Associates of the ascending career.**

"Each of these working groups contains angels of all seven created types, and a pilgrim of space is always tutored by secondary supernaphim of origin in the Master Spirit who presides over that pilgrim's superuniverse of nativity. When you mortals of Urantia attain Havona, you will certainly be piloted by supernaphim whose created natures—like your own evolved natures—are derived from the Master Spirit of Orvonton. And since your tutors spring from the Master Spirit of your own superuniverse, they are especially qualified to understand, comfort, and assist you in all your efforts to attain Paradise perfection." P. 289-90.

2. **Ascender ministry of supernaphim.**

"The secondary supernaphim are ministers to the seven planetary circuits of the central universe. Part are devoted to the service of the pilgrims of time, and one half of the entire order is assigned to the training of the Paradise pilgrims of eternity. These Paradise Citizens, in their pilgrimage through the Havona circuits, are also attended by volunteers from the Mortal Finality Corps, an arrangement that has prevailed since the completion of the first finaliter group." P. 289.

3. **Ascender ministry of seconaphim.**

"The seconaphim have their origin and headquarters on the capitals of the superuniverses, but with their liaison fellows they range from the shores of Paradise to the evolutionary worlds of space. They serve as valued assistants to the members of the deliberative assemblies of the super-governments and are of great help to the courtesy colonies of Uversa: the star students, millennial tourists, celestial observers, and a host of others, including the ascendant beings in waiting for Havona transport. The Ancients of Days take pleasure in assigning certain of the primary seconaphim to assist the ascending creatures domiciled on the four hundred ninety study worlds surrounding Uversa, and here also do many of the secondary and tertiary orders serve as teachers. These Uversa satellites are the finishing schools of the universes of time, presenting the preparatory course for the seven-circuited university of Havona." P. 317.

4. **The secoraphic living mirrors.**

"The primary seconaphim, of assignment to the Ancients of Days, are living mirrors in the service of these triune rulers. Think what it means in the economy of a superuniverse to be able to turn, as it were, to a living mirror and therein to see and therewith to hear the certain responses of another being a thousand or a hundred thousand light-years distant and to do all this instantly and unerringly. Records are essential to the conduct of the universes, broadcasts are serviceable, the work of the Solitary and other messengers is very helpful, but the Ancients of Days from their position midway between the inhabited worlds and Paradise—between man and God—can instantly look both ways, hear both ways, and *know* both ways.

"This ability—to hear and see, as it were, all things—can be perfectly realized in the superuniverses only by the Ancients of Days and only on their respective headquarters worlds. Even there limits are encountered: From Uversa, such communication is limited to the worlds and universes of Orvonton, and while inoperative between the superuniverses, this same reflective technique keeps each one of them in close touch with the centtral universe and with Paradise. The seven supergovernments, though individually segregated, are thus perfectly reflective of the authority above and are wholly sympathetic, as well as perfectly conversant, with the needs below." P. 307-8.

5. **Reflectivity of the seconaphim.**

    "Seconaphim of the secondary order are no less reflective than their primary fellows. Being classed as primary, secondary, and tertiary does not indicate a differential of status or function in the case of seconaphim; it merely denotes orders of procedure. Identical qualities are exhibited by all three groups in their activities.

    "The seven reflective types of secondary seconaphim are assigned to the services of the co-ordinate Trinity-origin associates of the Ancients of Days as follows:

    "To the Perfectors of Wisdom—the Voices of Wisdom, the Souls of Philosophy, and the Unions of Souls.

    "To the Divine Counselors—the Hearts of Counsel, the Joys of Existence, and the Satisfactions of Service.

    "To the Universal Censors—the Discerners of Spirits.

    "Like the primary order, this group is created serially; that is, the first-born was a Voice of Wisdom, and the seventh thereafter was similar, and so with the six other types of these reflective angels." P. 310.

X. SERAPHIC PLANETARY GOVERNMENT

1. **Planetary supervisors on Urantia.**

    "When the first governor general arrived on Urantia, concurrent with the outpouring of the Spirit of Truth, he was accompanied by twelve corps of special seraphim, Seraphington graduates, who were immediately assigned to certain special planetary services. These exalted angels are known as the master seraphim of planetary supervision and are, aside from the overcontrol of the planetary Most High observer, under the immediate direction of the resident governor general.

"These twelve groups of angels, while functioning under the general supervision of the resident governor general, are immediately directed by the seraphic council of twelve, the acting chiefs of each group. This council also serves as the volunteer cabinet of the resident governor general.

"As planetary chief of seraphim, I preside over this council of seraphic chiefs, and I am a volunteer supernaphim of the primary order serving on Urantia as the successor of the onetime chief of the angelic hosts of the planet who defaulted at the time of the Caligastia secession." P. 1254-5.

2. The twelve seraphic planetary corps.

"The twelve corps of the master seraphim of planetary supervision are functional on Urantia as follows:

1. *The epochal angels.* These are the angels of the current age, the dispensational group. These celestial ministers are intrusted with the oversight and direction of the affairs of each generation as they are designed to fit into the mosaic of the age in which they occur. The present corps of epochal angels serving on Urantia is the third group assigned to the planet during the current dispensation.

"2. *The progress angels.* These seraphim are intrusted with the task of initiating the evolutionary progress of the successive social ages. They foster the development of the inherent progressive trend of evolutionary creatures; they labor incessantly to make things what they ought to be. The group now on duty is the second to be assigned to the planet.

"3. *The religious guardians.* These are the 'angels of the churches,' the earnest contenders for that which is and has been. They endeavor to maintain the ideals of that which has survived for the sake of the safe transit of moral values from one epoch to another. They are the checkmates of the angels of progress, all the while seeking to translate from one generation to another the imperishable values of the old and passing forms into the new and therefore less stabilized patterns of thought and conduct. These angels do contend for spiritual forms, but they are not the source of ultrasectarianism and meaningless controversial divisions of professed religionists. The corps now functioning on Urantia is the fifth thus to serve. (Rev. 1:20)

"4. *The angels of nation life.* These are the 'angels of the trumpets,' directors of the political performances of Urantia national life. The group now functioning in the overcontrol of international relations is the fourth corps to serve on the planet. It is particularly through the ministry of this seraphic division that 'the Most Highs rule in the kingdoms of men.' (Rev. 8:2,6)

"5. *The angels of the races.* Those who work for the conservation of the evolutionary races of time, regardless of their political entanglements and religious groupings. On Urantia there are remnants of nine human races which have commingled and combined into the people of modern times. These seraphim are closely associated with the ministry of the race commissioners, and the group now on Urantia is the original corps assigned to the planet soon after the day of Pentecost.

"6. *The angels of the future.* These are the projection angels, who forecast a future age and plan for the realization of the better things of a new and advancing dispensation; they are the architects of the successive eras. The group now on the planet has thus functioned since the beginning of the current dispensation.

"7. *The angels of enlightenment.* Urantia is now receiving the help of the third corps of seraphim dedicated to the fostering of planetary education. These angels are occupied with mental and moral training as it concerns individuals, families, groups, schools, communities, nations, and whole races.

"8. *The angels of health.* These are the seraphic ministers assigned to the assistance of those mortal agencies dedicated to the promotion of health and the prevention of disease. The present corps is the sixth group to serve during this dispensation.

"9. *The home seraphim.* Urantia now enjoys the services of the fifth group of angelic ministers dedicated to the preservation and advancement of the home, the basic institution of human civilization.

"10. *The angels of industry.* This seraphic group is concerned with fostering industrial development and improving economic conditions among the Urantia peoples. This corps has been seven times changed since the bestowal of Michael.

"11. *The angels of diversion.* These are the seraphim who foster the values of play, humor, and rest. They ever seek to uplift man's recreational diversions and thus to promote the more profitable utilization of human leisure. The present corps is the third of that order to minister on Urantia.

"12. *The angels of superhuman ministry.* These are the angels of the angels, those seraphim who are assigned to the ministry of all other superhuman life on the planet, temporary or permanent. This corps has served since the beginning of the current dispensation." P. 1255-6.

3. How Most Highs rule the kingdoms of men.

"The Most Highs rule in the Kingdoms of men through many celestial forces and agencies but chiefly through the ministry of seraphim.

"At noon today the roll call of planetary angels, guardians, and others on Urantia was 501,234,619 pairs of seraphim.

"There were assigned to my command two hundred seraphic hosts—597,196,800 pairs of seraphim, or 1,194,393,600 individual angels. The registry, however, shows 1,002,469,238 individuals; it follows therefore that 191,924,362 angels were absent from this world on transport, messenger, and death duty. (On Urantia there are about the same number of cherubim as seraphim, and they are similarly organized.)" P. 1250.

XI. JESUS TALKS ABOUT ANGELS

"'The angelic hosts are a separate order of created beings; they are entirely different from the material order of mortal creatures, and they function as a distinct group of universe intelligences. Angels are not of that group of creatures called "the Sons of God" in the Scriptures; neither are they the glorified spirits of mortal men who have gone on to progress through the mansions on high. Angels are a direct creation, and they do not reproduce themselves. The angelic hosts have only a spiritual kinship with the human race. As man progresses in the journey to the Father in Paradise, he does traverse a state of being at one time analogous to the state of the angels, but mortal man never becomes an angel.

"'The angels never die, as man does. The angels are immortal unless, perchance, they become involved in sin as did some of them with the deceptions of Lucifer. The angels are the spirit servants in heaven, and they are neither all-wise nor all-powerful. But all of the loyal angels are truly pure and holy.

"'And do you not remember that I said to you once before that, if you had your spiritual eyes anointed, you would then see the heavens opened and behold the angels of God ascending and descending? It is by the ministry of the angels that one world may be kept in touch with other worlds, for have I not repeatedly told you that I have other sheep not of this fold? And these angels are not the spies of the spirit world who watch upon you and then go forth to tell the Father the thoughts of your heart and to report on the deeds of the flesh. The Father has no need of such service inasmuch as his own spirit lives within you. But these angelic spirits do function to keep one part of the heavenly creation informed concerning the doings of other and remote parts of the universe. And many of the angels, while functioning in the government of the Father and the universes of the Sons, are assigned to the service of the human races. When I taught you that many of these seraphim are ministering spirits, I spoke not in figurative language nor in poetic strains. And all this is true, regardless of your difficulty in comprehending such matters.

"'Many of these angels are engaged in the work of saving men, for have I not told you of the seraphic joy when one soul elects to forsake sin and begin the search for God? I did even tell you of the joy in the *presence of the angels* of heaven over one sinner who repents, thereby indicating the existence of other and higher orders of celestial beings who are likewise concerned in the spiritual welfare and with the divine progress of mortal man.

"'Also are these angels very much concerned with the means whereby man's spirit is released from the tabernacles of the flesh and his soul escorted to the mansions in heaven. Angels are the sure and heavenly guides of the soul of man during that uncharted and indefinite period of time which intervenes between the death of the flesh and the new life in the spirit abodes.'" P. 1841. John 1:51. Matt. 4:6. Luke 15:10.

ANGELS IN THE BIBLE
I. GENERAL

"Every one who acknowledges me before men, the Son of man also will acknowledge before the angels of God." **Luke 12:8.**

Speaking of this second coming, Jesus said: *"But of that day and hour no one knows, not even the angels of heaven."* **Matt. 24:36.**

Paul, referring to the second coming, says: *"When the Lord Jesus is revealed from heaven with his mighty angels in flaming fire."* **2 Thess. 1:7.**

II. NATURE OF ANGELS

"Then the Lord your God will come and all the holy ones with him." **Zech. 14:5**.

"Bless the Lord, O you his angels, you mighty ones who do his word." **Ps. 103:20**.

"For in the resurrection they...are like the angels in heaven." **Matt. 22:30**.

"There is joy before the angels of God over one sinner who repents." **Luke 15:10**.

"Then I fell down at his feet to worship him, but he said to me, 'You must not do that!'" **Rev. 19:10**.

"And his angels he charges with error." **Job 4:18**.

III. MISSION AND WORK OF ANGELS

"At night an angel of the Lord opened the prison doors and brought them out." **Acts 5:19**.

"The harvest is the close of the age, and the reapers are angels." **Matt. 13:39**.

"For the Son of man is to come with his angels in the glory of his Father." **Matt. 16:27**.

"An angel of the Lord descended from heaven and came and rolled back the stone, and sat upon it." **Matt. 28:2**.

Speaking of Herod, it says: *"An angel of the Lord smote him, because he did not give God the glory."* **Acts 12:23**.

IV. MINISTERING SPIRITS

"Are they not all ministering spirits sent forth to serve, for the sake of those who are to obtain salvation?" **Heb. 1:14**.

"And he dreamed that there was a ladder set up on the earth,...and behold, the angels of God were ascending and descending on it!" **Gen. 28:12**.

"You will see heaven opened, and the angels of God ascending and descending upon the Son of man." **John 1:51**.

"Do you think that I cannot appeal to my Father, and he will at once send me more than twelve legions of angels?" **Matt. 26:53**.

"And the angel of his presence saved them." **Isa. 63:9**.

V. GUIDING AND GUARDING ANGELS

"Behold, I send an angel before you, to guard you on the way." **Ex. 23:20.**

"Upon your walls, O Jerusalem, I have set watchmen." **Isa. 62:6.**

"If there be for him an angel, a mediator, one of the thousand, to declare to man what is right for him." **Job 33:23.**

VI.   PERSONAL CONTACT WITH ANGELS

"An angel of the Lord appeared to him in a dream." **Matt. 1:20.**

"And he set it before them, and he stood by them under the tree while they ate." **Gen. 18:8.**

"And behold, an angel touched him, and said to him, 'Arise and eat.'" **1 Kings 19:5.**

"Jacob went on his way, and the angels of God met him." **Gen. 32:1.**

"The angel who talked with me said to me, 'I will show you.'" **Zech. 1:9.**

"And behold, angels came and ministered to him." Matt. 4:11.

VII. GUARDIAN ANGELS

"For he will give his angels charge of you to guard you in all your ways." **Ps. 91:11.**

"For I tell you that in heaven their angels always behold the face of my Father." **Matt. 18:10.**

Speaking of Peter: *"They said, 'It is his angel.'"* **Acts 12:15.**

"In the presence of God...and of the elect angels, I charge you." **1 Tim. 5:21.**

VIII.   THE ANGEL OF THE LORD

(*The* angel of the Lord as contrasted with *an* angel of the Lord.)

"The angel of the Lord called to him from heaven, and said, 'Abraham, Abraham!'" **Gen. 22:11.**

"And the angel of the Lord appeared to him in a flame of fire out of the midst of a bush." **Ex. 3:2.**

Speaking of Balaam: *"And the angel of the Lord took his stand in the way as his adversary."* **Num. 22:22.**

"Now the angel of the Lord came and sat under the oak at Ophrah...as...Gideon was beating out the wheat." **Judges 6:11.**

"And the angel of the Lord said to her." **Gen. 16:11.**

"When Joseph woke from sleep, he did as the angel of the Lord commanded him." **Matt. 1:24.**

"And an angel of the Lord appeared to them, and the glory of the Lord shone around them." **Luke 2:9.**

IX. WICKED ANGELS

"Now war arose in heaven. Michael and his angels fighting against the dragon; and the dragon and his angels fought." **Rev. 12:7.**

"Depart from me...into the eternal fire prepared for the devil and his angels." **Matt. 25:41.**

"Then he showed me Joshua...standing before the angel of the Lord, and Satan standing at his right hand to accuse him." **Zech. 3:1.**

X. SPECIAL ANGELS

1. **Michael.**

   "Michael and his angels." **Rev. 12:7.**

   "But Michael, one of the chief princes, came to help me." **Dan. 10:13.**

   "There is none who contends by my side against these except Michael." **Dan. 10:21.**

   "At that time shall arise Michael, the great prince who has charge of your people." **Dan. 12:1.**

   "But when the archangel Michael contending with the devil..." **Jude 9.**

2. **Gabriel.**

   "Gabriel, make this man understand the vision." **Dan. 8:16.**

   "The angel Gabriel was sent from God to...Nazareth." **Luke 1:26.**

   "While I was speaking in prayer, the man Gabriel...came to me in swift flight." **Dan. 9:21.**

   "And the angel answered him, 'I am Gabriel, who stand in the presence of God.'" **Luke 1:19.**

3. **Soul transports.**

   "The poor man died and was carried by the angels to Abraham's bosom." **Luke 16:22.**

4. The mighty angel.

"Then I saw another mighty angel coming down from heaven, wrapped in a cloud, with a rainbow over his head, and his face was like the sun, and his legs like pillars of fire." **Rev. 10:1**.

5. Angels of the trumpets.

"Now the seven angels who had the seven trumpets made ready to blow them." **Rev. 8:6**.

6. Angels of the churches.

"The seven stars are the angels of the seven churches." **Rev. 1:20**.

7. The three messengers.

"Then I saw another angel flying in midheaven with an eternal gospel." **Rev. 14:6**.

"Another angel, a second, followed, saying, 'Fallen, fallen is Babylon the great.'" **Rev. 14:8**.

"And another angel, a third, followed, saying..." **Rev. 14:9**.

8. The angels of wrath.

"Then I heard a loud voice from the temple telling the seven angels, 'Go and pour out on the earth the seven bowls of the wrath of God.'" **Rev. 16:1**.

9. The angel of revelation.

"The revelation of Jesus Christ...and he made it known by sending his angel to his servant John." **Rev. 1:1**.

10. Seraphim.

"Above him stood the seraphim; each had six wings: with two he covered his face, and with two he covered his feet, and with two he flew." **Isa. 6:2**.

"Then flew one of the seraphim to me, having in his hand a burning coal which he had taken with tongs from the altar." **Isa. 6:6**.

15. THE PLAN OF SURVIVAL

Human survival will be presented in three sections.

Section One: The Plan of Salvation as found in the Bible—salvation as presented by the religion *about* Jesus.

Section Two: The Plan of Salvation as presented in *The Urantia Book*—the religion *of* Jesus.

Section Three: The Plan of Survival—as detailed in *The Urantia Book*.

15. THE PLAN OF SURVIVAL

SECTION ONE: THE PLAN OF SALVATION— BIBLE VERSION

1. THE FALL OF MAN.
2. ORIGINAL SIN.
3. MAN A CAPTIVE OF SIN.
4. MAN A CHILD OF THE DEVIL.
5. REDEMPTION ONLY THROUGH BLOOD.
6. CHRIST IS THE REDEEMER.
7. THE ATONEMENT DOCTRINE.
8. WE ARE ADOPTED SONS OF GOD.

SECTION TWO: THE PLAN OF SALVATION— *URANTIA BOOK* VERSION

GOD'S ETERNAL PURPOSE

CONSIDERATION OF MICHAEL'S INCARNATE BESTOWAL

1. TO EARN THE SUPREME AND UNLIMITED SOVEREIGNTY OF HIS UNIVERSE.
2. TO BECOME A MERCIFUL, WISE, AND UNDERSTANDING ADMINISTRATOR.
3. TO REVEAL THE FATHER IN HEAVEN AND TO DO HIS WILL.
4. TO PORTRAY THE MAXIMUM AUTHORITY OF THE PARADISE TRINITY.
5. TO TERMINATE THE LUCIFER REBELLION.
6. TO REVEAL THE WILL AND TO ENHANCE THE EVOLUTION OF GOD THE SUPREME.
7. TO PROVIDE FOR THE UNIVERSAL BESTOWAL OF THOUGHT ADJUSTERS.
8. TO PREPARE THE WAY FOR THE BESTOWAL OF THE SPIRIT OF TRUTH.
9. TO BECOME THE INSPIRATION FOR RELIGIOUS LIVING FOR ALL HIS UNIVERSE.
10. JESUS' DEATH ON THE CROSS.
    A. THE CROSS WAS MAN'S DOINGS, NOT GOD'S.
    B. CHRIST DID NOT DIE TO APPEASE AN ANGRY GOD.
    C. THE CROSS WAS NOT A SACRIFICE FOR MORTAL GUILT.

SECTION THREE: THE PLAN OF SURVIVAL— AS DETAILED IN *THE URANTIA BOOK*

SECTION ONE: THE PLAN OF SALVATION
As presented in the religion *about* Jesus

THE BIBLE VERSION

1. **The fall of man. Gen. 3.**

2. **Original sin.**

   "For as in Adam all die, so also in Christ shall all be made alive." 1 Cor. 15:22.

   "Sin came into the world through one man and death through sin." **Rom. 5:12.**

   "Because of one man's trespass, death reigned, through that one man." **Rom. 5:17.**

   "One man's trespass led to condemnation for all men." Rom. 5:18.

3. **Man a captive of sin.**

   "I see in my members another law...making me captive to the law of sin... With my flesh I serve the law of sin." **Rom. 7:23,25.**

4. **Man a child of the devil.**

   "And so we were by nature children of wrath." **Eph. 2:3.**

   "By this it may be seen who are the children of God, and who are the children of the devil." **1 John 3:10.**

5. **Redemption only through blood.**

   "Since, therefore, we are now justified by his blood, much more shall we be saved by him from the wrath of God." **Rom. 5:9.**

   "In him we have redemption through his blood." **Eph. 1:7.**

   "Without the shedding of blood there is no forgiveness of sins." **Heb. 9:22.**

   "For this is my blood of the covenant, which is poured out for many for the forgiveness of sins." **Matt. 26:28.**

6. **Christ is the Redeemer.**

   "For God so loved the world that he gave his only Son, that whoever believes in him should not perish but have eternal life." **John 3:16.**

"Sending his own Son in the likeness of sinful flesh and for sin." **Rom. 8:3**.

"They are justified...through the redemption which is in Christ Jesus, whom God put forward as an expiation by his blood." **Rom. 3:24,25**.

"Christ died for the ungodly." **Rom. 5:6**.

"Christ redeemed us... having become a curse for us." **Gal. 3:13**.

7. The atonement doctrine.

"Moses said, '...now I will go up to the Lord; perhaps I can make atonement for your sin.'" **Ex. 32:30**.

"We also rejoice in God through our Lord Jesus Christ through whom we have now received our reconciliation." **Rom. 5:11**. (This passage in the King James Version is the only use of the word atonement in the New Testament.)

"At the right time Christ died for the ungodly.""While we were yet sinners, Christ died for us." **Rom. 5:6,8**.

"Christ died for our sins." **1 Cor. 15:3**.

"Christ redeemed us from the curse of the law, having become a curse for us." **Gal. 3:13**.

8. We are adopted sons of God.

"To redeem those who were under the law, so that we might receive adoption as sons." **Gal. 4:5**.

"To all who received him...he gave power to become children of God." **John 1:12**.

SECTION TWO: THE PLAN OF SALVATION
As presented in the religion *of* Jesus

THE URANTIA BOOK VERSION

GOD'S ETERNAL PURPOSE

"There is in the mind of God a plan which embraces every creature of all his vast domains, and this plan is an eternal purpose of boundless opportunity, unlimited progress, and endless life." P. 365.

CONSIDERATION OF MICHAEL'S
INCARNATE BESTOWAL

1. **To earn the supreme and unlimited sovereignty of his universe.**

    "To live such identical lives as he imposes upon the intelligent beings of his own creation, thus to bestow himself in the likeness of his various orders of created beings, is a part of the price which every Creator Son must pay for the full and supreme sovereignty of his self-made universe of things and beings." P. 1323.

2. **To become a merciful, wise, and understanding administrator.**

    "These bestowals are not essential to the wise, just, and efficient management of a local universe, but they are absolutely necessary to a fair, merciful, and understanding administration of such a creation..." P. 1308.

3. **To reveal the Father in heaven and to do his will.**

    "'Your great mission to be realized and experienced in the mortal incarnation is embraced in your decision to live a life whole heartedly motivated to do the will of your Paradise Father, thus to *reveal God*, your Father, in the flesh and especially to the creatures of the flesh.'" P. 1328.

4. **To portray the maximum authority of the Paradise Trinity.**

    "...he was aspiring to the privilege of representing the maximum authority of the Paradise Trinity which can be exercised in the direct and personal administration of a local universe." P. 1324.

5. **To terminate the Lucifer rebellion.**

"On an afternoon in late summer, amid the trees and in the silence of nature, Michael of Nebadon won the unquestioned sovereignty of his universe. On that day he completed the task set for Creator Sons to live to the full the incarnated life in the likeness of mortal flesh... And when Jesus came down from his sojourn on Mount Hermon, the Lucifer rebellion in Satania and the Caligastia secession on Urantia were virtually settled." P. 1494.

6. **To reveal the will and to enhance the evolution of God the Supreme.**

"In passing through the experience of revealing the Seven Master Spirit wills of the Trinity, the Creator Son has passed through the experience of revealing the will of the Supreme...In this universe age he reveals the Supreme and participates in the actualization of the sovereignty of Supremacy." P. 1318.

7. **To provide for the universal bestowal of Thought Adjusters.**

"'Pour out upon the planet of your bestowal the Spirit of Truth and thus make all normal mortals of that isolated sphere immediately and fully accessible to the ministry of the segregated presence of our Paradise Father, the Thought Adjusters of the realms.'" P. 1328.

8. **To prepare the way for the bestowal of the Spirit of Truth.**

"'And this Spirit of Truth which I will bestow upon you shall guide and comfort you and shall eventually lead you into all truth.'" P. 1948.

"'This new teacher is the Spirit of Truth who will live with each one of you, in your hearts, and so will all the children of light be made one and be drawn toward one another.'" P. 1949.

9. **To become the inspiration for religious living for all his universe.**

"'Live the ideal religious life for the inspiration and edification of all your universe.'" P. 1328.

"'Rather shall your life in the flesh on Urantia be the *inspiration* for all lives upon all Nebadon worlds throughout all generations in the ages to come.'" P. 1328.

10. **Jesus' death on the cross.**

A. *The cross was man's doing, not God's.*
   "It was man and not God who planned and executed the death of Jesus on the cross." P. 2002.

B.   *The cross was not a sacrifice for mortal guilt.*

"The cross is not the symbol of the sacrifice of the innocent
Son of God in the place of guilty sinners and in order to
appease the wrath of an offended God…" P. 2019.

C.   *Man is not a child of the devil.*

"Mortal man was never the property of the archdeceivers.
Jesus did not die to ransom man from the clutch of the
apostate rulers and fallen princes of the spheres…Neither was
the Master's death on the cross a sacrifice which consisted in an
effort to pay God a debt which the race of mankind had come
to owe him." P. 2016.

11. Jesus' death was not an atonement.

"Jesus is not about to die as a sacrifice for sin. He is not going to
atone for the inborn moral guilt of the human race. Mankind has no
such racial guilt before God." P. 2003.

"The barbarous idea of appeasing an angry God, of propitiating an
offended Lord, of winning the favor of Deity through sacrifices and
penance and even by the shedding of blood, represents a religion
wholly puerile and primitive, a philosophy unworthy of an enlightened age of science and truth. Such beliefs are utterly repulsive to
the celestial beings and the divine rulers who serve and reign in the
universes. It is an affront to God to believe, hold, or teach that
innocent blood must be shed in order to win his favor or to divert
the fictitious divine wrath." P. 60.

"The erroneous supposition that the righteousness of God was
irreconcilable with the selfless love of the heavenly Father,
presupposed absence of unity in the nature of Deity and led directly
to the elaboration of the atonement doctrine, which is a philosophic
assault upon both the unity and free-willness of God." P. 41.

12. To establish the new and living way from man to God.

"Jesus is the new and living way from man to God, from the partial to
the perfect, from the earthly to the heavenly, from time to eternity." P.
1426.

"'I am the door, I am the new and living way, and whosoever wills
may enter to embark upon the endless truth-search for eternal
life.'" P. 1829.

"Jesus was and is the new and living way whereby man can come
into the divine inheritance which the Father has decreed shall be his
but for the asking." P. 1113.

13. **To restore the right of ascension to the mansion worlds on the third day.**

"But ever since the day of Pentecost, Urantia mortals again may proceed directly to the morontia spheres." P. 596.

14. **To portray mortal man as a son of God.**

"'Behold, what manner of love the Father has bestowed upon us that we should be called the sons of God.'" P. 448. 1 John 3:1.

15. **To enhance the perfection plan for mortal ascenders.**

"From the Universal Father who inhabits eternity there has gone forth the supreme mandate, 'Be you perfect, even as I am perfect.' In love and mercy the messengers of Paradise have carried this divine exortation down through the ages and out through the universes, even to such lowly animal-origin creatures as the human races of Urantia." P. 21.

"The very instant the Eternal Son accepted his Father's plan of perfection attainment for the creatures of the universes, the moment the ascension project became a Father-Son plan, that instant the Infinite Spirit became the conjoint administrator of the Father and the Son for the execution of their united and eternal purpose." P. 93.

16. **The three parts of the perfection plan.**

   A. *The Plan of Progressive Attainment.*
   "This provision for upstepping the creatures of time involves the Father's bestowal of the Thought Adjusters and the endowing of material creatures with the prerogatives of personality." P. 85.

   B. *The Bestowal Plan.*
   "This is the proposal of the Eternal Son and consists of his bestowal of the Sons of God upon the evolutionary creations, there to personalize and factualize, to incarnate and make real, the love of the Father and the mercy of the Son to the creatures of all universes." P. 85.

   C. *The Plan of Mercy Ministry.*
   "...the Infinite Spirit projected and put in operation the tremendous and universal enterprise of mercy ministry. This is the service so essential to the practical and effective operation of both the attainment and bestowal undertakings..." P. 85.

17. Mortal survival and the Paradise ascension.

A. *The Paradise journey.*

"Evolutionary mortals are born on the planets of space, pass through the morontia worlds, ascend the spirit universes, traverse the Havona spheres, find God, attain Paradise, and are mustered into the primary Corps of the Finality, therein to await the next assignment of universe service...And as we view this sublime spectacle, we all exclaim: What a glorious destiny for the animal-origin children of time, the material sons of space!" P. 354.

B. *Finding God.*

"The attainment of the Universal Father is the passport to eternity...The test of time is almost over; the race for eternity has been all but run. The days of uncertainty are ending; the temptation to doubt is vanishing; the injunction to be *perfect* has been obeyed. From the very bottom of intelligent existence the creature of time and material personality has ascended the evolutionary spheres of space, thus proving the feasibility of the ascension plan while forever demonstrating the justice and righteousness of the command of the Universal Father to his lowly creatures of the worlds: 'Be you perfect, even as I am perfect.'" P. 294-5.

18. Mortal destiny is the Paradise Corps of the Finality.

"The present known destiny of surviving mortals is the Paradise Corps of the Finality...At present the Paradise finaliters are working throughout the grand universe in many undertakings..." P. 1239.

19. Ultimate finaliter destiny.

"What an adventure! What a romance! A gigantic creation to be administered by the children of the Supreme, these personalized and humanized Adjusters, these Adjusterized and eternalized mortals, these mysterious combinations and eternal associations of the highest known manifestation of the essence of the First Source and Center and the lowest form of intelligent life capable of comprehending and attaining the Universal Father. We conceive that such amalgamated beings, such partnerships of Creator and creature, will become superb rulers, matchless administrators, and understanding and sympathetic directors of any and all forms of intelligent life which may come into existence throughout these future universes of the first outer space level." P. 1239.

20. **Concerning the statement of Jesus on the cross: "Father, into your hands I commend my spirit."**

"But there are those in the universe who hold that this soul-identity of Jesus now reposes in the 'bosom of the Father,' to be subsequently released for leadership of the Nebadon Corps of the Finality in their undisclosed destiny in connection with the uncreated universes of the unorganized realms of outer space." P. 2015.

SECTION THREE: THE PLAN OF SURVIVAL
As detailed in *The Urantia Book*

I. THE DIVINE PLAN OF PERFECTION

1. The eternal goal.

"The goal of eternity is ahead! The adventure of divinity attainment lies before you! The race for perfection is on! whosoever will may enter, and certain victory will crown the efforts of every human being who will run the race of faith and trust, depending every step of the way on the leading of the indwelling Adjuster and on the guidance of that good spirit of the Universe Son, which so freely has been poured out upon all flesh." P. 365.

2. The divine plan: "Be you perfect."

"The enlightened worlds all recognize and worship the Universal Father, the eternal maker and infinite upholder of all creation. The will creatures of universe upon universe have embarked upon the long, long Paradise journey, the fascinating struggle of the eternal adventure of attaining God the Father. The transcendent goal of the children of time is to find the eternal God, to comprehend the divine nature, to recognize the Universal Father. God-knowing creatures have only one supreme ambition, just one consuming desire, and that is to become, as they are in their spheres, like him as he is in his Paradise perfection of personality and in his universal sphere of righteous supremacy." P. 21.

3. Universe status of the perfection plan.

"The amazing plan for perfecting evolutionary mortals and, after their attainment of Paradise and the Corps of the Finality, providing further training for some undisclosed future work, does seem to be, at present, one of the chief concerns of the seven superuniverses and their many subdivisions; but this ascension scheme for spiritualizing and training the mortals of time and space is by no means the exclusive occupation of the universe intelligences. There are, indeed, many other fascinating pursuits which occupy the time and enlist the energies of the celestial hosts." P. 54.

4. Meaning of the perfection injunction.

"This magnificent and universal injunction to strive for the attainment of the perfection of divinity is the first duty, and should be the highest ambition, of all the struggling creature creation of the God of perfection. This possibility of the attainment of divine perfection is the final and certain destiny of all man's eternal spiritual progress.

"Urantia mortals can hardly hope to be perfect in the infinite sense, but it is entirely possible for human beings, starting out as they do on this planet, to attain the supernal and divine goal which the infinite God has set for mortal man; and when they do achieve this destiny, they will, in all that pertains to self-realization and mind attainment, be just as replete in their sphere of divine perfection as God himself is in his sphere of infinity and eternity. Such perfection may not be universal in the material sense, unlimited in intellectual grasp, or final in spiritual experience, but it is final and complete in all finite aspects of divinity of will, perfection of personality motivation, and God-consciousness.

"This is the true meaning of that divine command, 'Be you perfect, even as I am perfect,' which ever urges mortal man onward and beckons him inward in that long and fascinating struggle for the attainment of higher and higher levels of spiritual values and true universe meanings. This sublime search for the God of universes is the supreme adventure of the inhabitants of all the worlds of time and space." P. 22.

5. **No "short cuts" in the perfection plan.**

"Never, in all your ascent to Paradise, will you gain anything by impatiently attempting to circumvent the established and divine plan by short cuts, personal inventions, or other devices for improving on the way of perfection, to perfection, and for eternal perfection." P. 846.

6. **Infinite Spirit administrator of perfection plan.**

"The Infinite Spirit is the effective agent of the all-loving Father and the all-merciful Son for the execution of their conjoint project of drawing to themselves all truth-loving souls on all the worlds of time and space...the Infinite Spirit pledged all his resources of divine presence and of spirit personalities to the Father and the Son; he has dedicated *all* to the stupendous plan of exalting surviving will creatures to the divine heights of Paradise perfection." P. 93.

7. **This perfection becomes a personality possession.**

"Excepting perfect beings of Deity origin, all will creatures in the superuniverses are of evolutionary nature, beginning in lowly estate and climbing ever upward, in reality inward. Even highly spiritual personalities continue to ascend the scale of life by progressive translations from life to life and from sphere to sphere. And in the case of those who entertain the Mystery Monitors, there is indeed no limit to the possible heights of their spiritual ascent and universe attainment.

"The perfection of the creatures of time, when finally achieved, is wholly an acquirement, a bona fide personality possession. While the elements of grace are freely admixed, nevertheless, the creature attainments are the result of individual effort and actual living, personality reaction to the existing environment." P. 361.

8. **Man climbs from the bottom to the top.**

"The fact of animal evolutionary origin does not attach stigma to any personality in the sight of the universe as that is the exclusive method of producing one of the two basic types of finite intelligent will creatures. When the heights of perfection and eternity are attained, all the more honor to those who began at the bottom and joyfully climbed the ladder of life, round by round, and who, when they do reach the heights of glory, will have gained a personal experience which embodies an actual knowledge of every phase of life from the bottom to the top." P. 361.

9. **We are fortunate who begin at the bottom.**

"In all this is shown the wisdom of the Creators. It would be just as easy for the Universal Father to make all mortals perfect beings, to impart perfection by his divine word. But that would deprive them of the wonderful experience of the adventure and training associated with the long and gradual inward climb, an experience to be had only by those who are so fortunate as to begin at the very bottom of living existence." P. 361-2.

II. THE PROGRESSIVE ASCENSION PLAN

1. **Father and Son are united in "plan of progress."**

"The Eternal Son is in everlasting liaison with the Father in the successful prosecution of the *divine plan of progress*: the universal plan for the creation, evolution, ascension, and perfection of will creatures. And, in divine faithfulness, the Son is the eternal equal of the Father.

"The Father and his Son are as one in the formulation and prosecution of this gigantic attainment plan for advancing the material beings of time to the perfection of eternity. This project for the spiritual elevation of the ascendant souls of space is a joint creation of the

Father and the Son, and they are, with the co-operation of the Infinite Spirit, engaged in associative execution of their divine purpose." P. 85.

2. **Three parts of the divine perfection plan.**

"This divine plan of perfection attainment embraces three unique, though marvelously correlated, enterprises of universal adventure:

"1. *The Plan of Progressive Attainment.* This is the Universal Father's plan of evolutionary ascension, a program unreservedly accepted by the Eternal Son when he concurred in the Father's proposal, 'Let us make mortal creatures in our own image.' This provision for upstepping the creatures of time involves the Father's bestowal of the Thought Adjusters and the endowing of material creatures with the prerogatives of personality.

"2. *The Bestowal Plan.* The next universal plan is the great Father-revelation enterprise of the Eternal Son and his co-ordinate Sons. This is the proposal of the Eternal Son and consists of his bestowal of the Sons of God upon the evolutionary creations, there to personalize and factualize, to incarnate and make real, the love of the Father and the mercy of the Son to the creatures of all universes. Inherent in the bestowal plan, and as a provisional feature of this ministration of love, the Paradise Sons act as rehabilitators of that which misguided creature will has placed in spiritual jeopardy. Whenever and wherever there occurs a delay in the functioning of the attainment plan, if rebellion, perchance, should mar or complicate this enterprise, then do the emergency provisions of the bestowal plan become active forthwith. The Paradise Sons stand pledged and ready to function as retrievers, to go into the very realms of rebellion and there restore the spiritual status of the spheres. And such a heroic service a co-ordinate Creator Son did perform on Urantia in connection with his experiential bestowal career of sovereignty acquirement.

"3. *The Plan of Mercy Ministry.* When the attainment plan and the bestowal plan had been formulated and proclaimed, alone and of himself, the Infinite Spirit projected and put in operation the tremendous and universal enterprise of mercy ministry. This is the service so essential to the practical and effective operation of both the attainment and the bestowal undertakings, and the spiritual personalities of the Third Source and Center all partake of the spirit of mercy ministry which is so much a part of the nature of the Third Person of Deity. Not only in creation but also in administration, the Infinite Spirit functions truly and literally as the conjoint executive of the Father and the Son." P. 85.

3. **Eternal Son is trustee of perfection plan.**

"The Eternal Son is the personal trustee, the divine custodian, of the Father's universal plan of creature ascension. Having promulgated the universal mandate, 'Be you perfect, even as I am perfect,' the Father intrusted the execution of this tremendous undertaking to the Eternal Son; and the Eternal Son shares the fostering of this supernal enterprise with his divine co-ordinate, the Infinite Spirit. Thus do the Deities effectively co-operate in the work of creation, control, evolution, revelation, and ministration—and if required, in restoration and rehabilitation." P. 86.

4. **Survival, a chief business of the universe.**

"The entire organization of high spirits, angelic hosts, and midway fellows is enthusiastically devoted to the furtherance of the Paradise plan for the progressive ascension and perfection attainment of evolutionary mortals, one of the supernal businesses of the universe—the superb survival plan of bringing God down to man and then, by a sublime sort of partnership, carrying man up to God and on to eternity of service and divinity of attainment—alike for mortal and midwayer." P. 867.

5. **Conditions of mortal survival.**

"As to the chances of mortal survival, let it be made forever clear: All souls of every possible phase of mortal existence will survive provided they manifest willingness to co-operate with their indwelling Adjusters and exhibit a desire to find God and to attain divine perfection, even though these desires be but the first faint flickers of the primitive comprehension of that 'true light which lights every man who comes into the world.'" P. 447. John 1:9.

6. **All-triumphant ascension plan.**

"Man is spiritually indwelt by a surviving Thought Adjuster. If such a human mind is sincerely and spiritually motivated, if such a human soul desires to know God and become like him, honestly wants to do the Father's will, there exists no negative influence of mortal deprivation nor positive power of possible interference which can prevent such a divinely motivated soul from securely ascending to the portals of Paradise.

"The Father desires all his creatures to be in personal communion with him. He has on Paradise a place to receive all those whose survival status and spiritual nature make possible such attainment. Therefore settle in your philosophy now and forever: To each of you and to all of us, God is approachable, the Father is attainable, the way is open; the forces of divine love and the ways and means of divine administration are all inter-locked in an effort to facilitate the advancement of every worthy intelligence of every universe to the Paradise presence of the Universal Father." P. 63.

III. THE MORTAL-SURVIVAL PLAN

1. **Objective of the mortal-survival plan.**

    "The mortal-survival plan has a practical and serviceable objective; you are not the recipients of all this divine labor and painstaking training only that you may survive just to enjoy endless bliss and eternal ease. There is a goal of transcendent service concealed beyond the horizon of the present universe age. If the Gods designed merely to take you on one long and eternal joy excursion, they certainly would not so largely turn the whole universe into one vast and intricate practical training school, requisition a substantial part of the celestial creation as teachers and instructors, and then spend ages upon ages piloting you, one by one, through this gigantic universe school of experiential training. The further-ance of the scheme of mortal progression seems to be one of the chief businesses of the present organized universe, and the majority of innumerable orders of created intelligences are either directly or indirectly engaged in advancing some phase of this progressive perfection plan." P. 558.

2. **The path of mortal ascent.**

    "This sevenfold Deity personalization in time and space and to the seven superuniverses enables mortal man to attain the presence of God, who is spirit. This sevenfold Deity, to finite time-space creatures sometime power-personalizing in the Supreme Being, is the functional Deity of the mortal evolutionary creatures of the Paradise-ascension career. Such an experiential discovery-career of the realization of God begins with the recognition of the divinity of the Creator Son of the local universe and ascends through the superuniverse Ancients of Days and by way of the person of one of the Seven Master Spirits to the attainment of the discovery and recognition of the divine personality of the Universal Father on Paradise." P. 11-12.

3. The mortal survival experience.

"While the mortal survivors of time and space are denominated *ascending pilgrims* when accredited for the progressive ascent to Paradise, these evolutionary creatures occupy such an important place in these narratives that we here desire to present a synopsis of the following seven stages of the ascending universe career:

"1. Planetary Mortals.

"2. Sleeping Survivors.

"3. Mansion World Students.

"4. Morontia Progressors.

"5. Superuniverse Wards.

"6. Havona Pilgrims.

"7. Paradise Arrivals.

"The following narrative presents the universe career of an Adjuster-indwelt mortal. The Son- and Spirit-fused mortals share portions of this career, but we have elected to tell this story as it pertains to the Adjuster-fused mortals, for such a destiny may be anticipated by all of the human races of Urantia.

"1. *Planetary Mortals.* Mortals are all animal-origin evolutionary beings of ascendant potential. In origin, nature, and destiny these various groups and types of human beings are not wholly unlike the Urantia peoples. The human races of each world receive the same ministry of the Sons of God and enjoy the presence of the ministering spirits of time. After natural death all types of ascenders fraternize as one morontia family on the mansion worlds.

"2. *Sleeping Survivors.* All mortals of survival status, in the custody of personal guardians of destiny, pass through the portals of natural death and, on the third period, personalize on the mansion worlds. Those accredited beings who have, for any reason, been unable to attain that level of intelligence mastery and endowment of spirituality which would entitle them to personal guardians, cannot thus immediately and directly go to the mansion worlds. Such surviving souls must rest in unconscious sleep until the judgment day of a new epoch, a new dispensation, the coming of a Son of God to call the rolls of the age and adjudicate the realm, and this is the general practice throughout all Nebadon. It was said of Christ Michael that, when he ascended on high at the conclusion of his work on earth, 'He led a great multitude of captives.' And these captives were the sleeping survivors from the days of Adam to the day of the Master's resurrection on Urantia. (Eph. 4:8.)

"The passing of time is of no moment to sleeping mortals; they are wholly unconscious and oblivious to the length of their rest. On reassembly of personality at the end of an age, those who have slept five thousand years will react no differently than those who have rested five days. Aside from this time delay these survivors pass on through the ascension regime identically with those who avoid the longer or shorter sleep of death.

"These dispensational classes of world pilgrims are utilized for group morontia activities in the work of the local universes. There is a great advantage in the mobilization of such enormous groups; they are thus kept together for long periods of effective service.

"3. *Mansion World Students*. All surviving mortals who reawaken on the mansion worlds belong to this class.

"The physical body of mortal flesh is not a part of the reassembly of the sleeping survivor; the physical body has returned to dust. The seraphim of assignment sponsors the new body, the morontia form, as the new life vehicle for the immortal soul and for the indwelling of the returned Adjuster. The Adjuster is the custodian of the spirit transcript of the mind of the sleeping survivor. The assigned seraphim is the keeper of the surviving identity—the immortal soul—as far as it has evolved. And when these two, the Adjuster and the seraphim, reunite their personality trusts, the new individual constitutes the resurrection of the old personality, the survival of the evolving morontia identity of the soul. Such a reassociation of soul and Adjuster is quite properly called a resurrection, a reassembly of personality factors; but even this does not entirely explain the reappearance of the surviving *personality*. Though you will probably never understand the fact of such an inexplicable transaction, you will sometime experientially know the truth of it if you do not reject the plan of mortal survival.

"The plan of initial mortal detention on seven worlds of progressive training is nearly universal in Orvonton. In each local system of approximately one thousand inhabited planets there are seven mansion worlds, usually satellites or subsatellites of the system capital. They are the receiving worlds for the majority of ascending mortals.

"Sometimes all training worlds of mortal residence are called universe 'mansions,' and it was to such spheres that Jesus alluded when he said: 'In my Father's house are many mansions.' From here on, within a given group of spheres like the mansion worlds, ascenders will progress individually from one sphere to another and from one phase of life to another, but they will always advance from one stage of universe study to another in class formation. (John 14:2.)

"4. *Morontia Progressors.* From the mansion worlds on up through the spheres of the system, constellation, and the universe, mortals are classed as morontia progressors; they are traversing the transition spheres of mortal ascension. As the ascending mortals progress from the lower to the higher of the morontia worlds, they serve on countless assignments in association with their teachers and in company with their more advanced and senior brethren.

"Morontia progression pertains to continuing advancement of intellect, spirit, and personality form. Survivors are still three-natured beings. Throughout the entire morontia experience they are wards of the local universe. The regime of the superuniverse does not function until the spirit career begins.

"Mortals acquire real spirit identity just before they leave the local universe headquarters for the receiving worlds of the minor sectors of the superuniverse. Passing from the final morontia stages to the first or lowest spirit status is but a slight transition. The mind, personality, and character are unchanged by such an advance; only does the form undergo modification. But the spirit form is just as real as the morontia body, and it is equally discernible.

"Before departing from their native local universes for the superuniverse receiving worlds, the mortals of time are recipients of spirit confirmation from the Creator Son and the local universe Mother Spirit. From this point on, the status of the ascending mortal is forever settled. Superuniverse wards have never been known to go astray. Ascending seraphim are also advanced in angelic standing at the time of their departure from the local universes.

"5. *Superuniverse Wards.* All ascenders arriving on the training worlds of the superuniverses become the wards of the Ancients of Days; they have traversed the morontia life of the local universe and are now accredited spirits. As young spirits they begin the ascension of the superuniverse system of training and culture, extending from the receiving spheres of their minor sector in through the study worlds of the ten major sectors and on to the higher cultural spheres of the superuniverse headquarters.

"There are three orders of student spirits in accordance with their sojourn upon the minor sector, major sectors, and the superuniverse headquarters worlds of spirit progression. As morontia ascenders studied and worked on the worlds of the local universe, so spirit ascenders continue to master new worlds while they practice at giving out to others that which they have imbibed at the experiential founts of wisdom. But going to school as a spirit being in the superuniverse career is very unlike anything that has ever entered the imaginative realms of the material mind of man.

"Before leaving the superuniverse for Havona, these ascending spirits receive the same thorough course in superuniverse management that they received during their morontia experience in local universe supervision. Before spirit mortals reach Havona, their chief study, but not exclusive occupation, is the mastery of local and superuniverse administration. The reason for all of this experience is not now fully apparent, but no doubt such training is wise and necessary in view of their possible future destiny as members of the Corps of the Finality.

"The superuniverse regime is not the same for all ascending mortals. They receive the same general education, but special groups and classes are carried through special courses of instruction and are put through specific courses of training.

"6. *Havona Pilgrims.* When spirit development is complete, even though not replete, then the surviving mortal prepares for the long flight to Havona, the haven of evolutionary spirits. On earth you were a creature of flesh and blood; through the local universe you were a morontia being; through the superuniverse you were an evolving spirit; with your arrival on the receiving worlds of Havona your spiritual education begins in reality and in earnest; your eventual appearance on Paradise will be as a perfected spirit.

"The journey from the superuniverse headquarters to the Havona receiving spheres is always made alone. From now on no more class or group instruction will be administered. You are through with the technical and administrative training of the evolutionary worlds of time and space. Now begins your *personal education*, your individual spiritual training. From first to last, throughout all Havona, the instruction is personal and threefold in nature: intellectual, spiritual, and experiential.

"The first act of your Havona career will be to recognize and thank your transport seconaphim for the long and safe journey. Then you are presented to those beings who will sponsor your early Havona activities. Next you go to register your arrival and prepare your message of thanksgiving and adoration for dispatch to the Creator Son of your local universe, the universe Father who made possible your sonship career. This concludes the formalities of the Havona arrival; whereupon you are accorded a long period of leisure for free observation, and this affords opportunity for looking up your friends, fellows, and associates of the long ascension experience. You may also consult the broadcasts to ascertain who of your fellow pilgrims have departed for Havona since the time of your leaving Uversa.

"The fact of your arrival on the receiving worlds of Havona will be duly transmitted to the headquarters of your local universe and personally conveyed to your seraphic guardian, wherever that seraphim may chance to be.

The ascendant mortals have been thoroughly trained in the affairs of the evolutionary worlds of space; now they begin their long and profitable contact with the created spheres of perfection. What a preparation for some future work is afforded by this combined, unique, and extraordinary experience! But I cannot tell you about Havona; you must see these worlds to appreciate their glory or to understand their grandeur.

"7. *Paradise Arrivals.* On reaching Paradise with residential status, you begin the progressive course in divinity and absonity. Your residence on Paradise signifies that you have found God, and that you are to be mustered into the Mortal Corps of the Finality. Of all the creatures of the grand universe, only those who are Father fused are mustered into the Mortal Corps of the Finality. Only such individuals take the finaliter oath. Other beings of Paradise perfection or attainment may be temporarily attached to this finality corps, but they are not of eternal assignment to the unknown and unrevealed mission of this accumulating host of the evolutionary and perfected veterans of time and space.

"Paradise arrivals are accorded a period of freedom, after which they begin their associations with the seven groups of the primary supernaphim. They are designated Paradise graduates when they have finished their course with the conductors of worship and then, as finaliters, are assigned on observational and co-operative service to the ends of the far-flung creation. As yet there seems to be no specific or settled employment for the Mortal Corps of Finaliters, though they serve in many capacities on worlds settled in light and life.

"If there should be no future or unrevealed destiny for the Mortal Corps of the Finality, the present assignment of these ascendant beings would be altogether adequate and glorious. Their present destiny wholly justifies the universal plan of evolutionary ascent. But the future ages of the evolution of the spheres of outer space will undoubtedly further elaborate, and with more repleteness divinely illuminate, the wisdom and loving-kindness of the Gods in the execution of their divine plan of human survival and mortal ascension." P. 340-4.

IV. LIFE IN THE FLESH

1. Ascension during "light and life."

"The translated souls of the flowering ages of the settled spheres do not pass through the mansion worlds. Neither do they sojourn, as students, on the morontia worlds of the system or constellation. They do not pass through any of the earlier phases of morontia life. They are the only ascending mortals who so nearly escape the morontia transition from material existence to semispirit status. The initial experience of such *Son seized* mortals in the ascension career is in the services of the progression worlds of the universe headquarters. And from these study worlds of Salvington they go back as teachers to the very worlds they passed by, subsequently going on inward to Paradise by the established route of mortal ascension." P. 624.

2. Work of Adjusters for ascenders.

"The Thought Adjuster will recall and rehearse for you only those memories and experiences which are a part of, and essential to, your universe career. If the Adjuster has been a partner in the evolution of aught in the human mind, then will these worth-while experiences survive in the eternal consciousness of the Adjuster. But much of your past life and its memories, having neither spiritual meaning nor morontia value, will perish with the material brain; much of material experience will pass away as onetime scaffolding which, having bridged you over to the morontia level, no longer serves a purpose in the universe. But personality and the relationships between personalities are never scaffolding; mortal memory of personality relationships has cosmic value and will persist. On the mansion worlds you will know and be known, and more, you will remember, and be remembered by, your onetime associates in the short but intriguing life on Urantia." P. 1235.

3. Paradise path of mortal ascenders.

"On Urantia you pass through a short and intense test during your initial life of material existence. On the mansion worlds and up through your system, constellation, and local universe, you traverse the morontia phases of ascension. On the training worlds of the superuniverse you pass through the true spirit stages of progression and are prepared for eventual transit to Havona. On the seven circuits of Havona your attainment is intellectual, spiritual, and experiential. And there is a definite task to be achieved on each of the worlds of each of these circuits." P. 158.

4. Paradise the destiny of all survivors.

"After all, to mortals the most important thing about eternal Paradise is the fact that this perfect abode of the Universal Father is the real and far-distant destiny of the immortal souls of the mortal and material sons of God, the ascending creatures of the evolutionary worlds of time and space. Every God-knowing mortal who has espoused the career of doing the Father's will has already embarked upon the long, long Paradise trail of divinity pursuit and perfection attainment. And when such an animal-origin being does stand, as countless numbers now do, before the Gods on Paradise, having ascended from the lowly spheres of space, such an achievement represents the reality of a spiritual transformation bordering on the limits of supremacy." P. 127.

V. THE INEVITABILITIES

1. **Evolutionary creature life is beset by inevitabilities.**

"The uncertainties of life and the vicissitudes of existence do not in any manner contradict the concept of the universal sovereignty of God. All evolutionary creature life is beset by certain *inevitabilities*. Consider the following:

"1.   Is *courage*—strength of character—desirable? Then must man be reared in an environment which necessitates grappling with hardships and re-acting to disappointments.

"2.   Is *altruism*—service of one's fellows—desirable? Then must life experience provide for encountering situations of social inequality.

"3.   Is *hope*—the grandeur of trust—desirable? Then human existence must constantly be confronted with insecurities and recurrent uncertainties.

"4.   Is *faith*—the supreme assertion of human thought—desirable? Then must the mind of man find itself in that troublesome predicament where it ever knows less than it can believe.

"5.   Is the *love of truth* and the willingness to go wherever it leads, desirable? Then must man grow up in a world where error is present and falsehood always possible.

"6.   Is *idealism*—the approaching concept of the divine—desirable? Then must man struggle in an environment of relative goodness and beauty, surroundings stimulative of the irrepressible reach for better things.

"7.   Is *loyalty*—devotion to highest duty—desirable? Then must man carry on amid the possibilities of betrayal and desertion. The valor of devotion to duty consists in the implied danger of default.

"8.   Is *unselfishness*—the spirit of self-forgetfulness—desirable? Then must mortal man live face to face with the incessant clamoring of an inescapable self for recognition and honor. Man could not dynamically choose the divine life if there were no self-life to forsake. Man could never lay saving hold on righteousness if there were no potential evil to exalt and differentiate the good by contrast.

"9.   Is *pleasure*—the satisfaction of happiness—desirable? Then must man live in a world where the alternative of pain and the likelihood of suffering are ever-present experiential possibilities." P. 51.

"The creatures of Havona are naturally brave, but they are not courageous in the human sense. They are innately kind and considerate, but hardly altruistic in the human way. They are expectant of a pleasant future, but not hopeful in the exquisite manner of the trusting mortal of the uncertain evolutionary spheres. They have faith in the stability of the universe, but they are utter strangers to that saving faith whereby mortal man climbs from the status of an animal up to the portals of Paradise. They love the truth, but they know nothing of its soul-saving qualities. They are idealists, but they were born that way; they are wholly ignorant of the ecstasy of becoming such by exhilarating choice. They are loyal, but they have never experienced the thrill of wholehearted and intelligent devotion to duty in the face of temptation to default. They are unselfish, but they never gained such levels of experience by the magnificent conquest of a belligerent self. They enjoy pleasure, but they do not comprehend the sweetness of the pleasure escape from the pain potential." P. 52.

2.   **But this mortal man is a son of God.**

"It is a solemn and supernal fact that such lowly and material creatures as Urantia human beings are the sons of God, faith children of the Highest. 'Behold, what manner of love the Father has bestowed upon us that we should be called the sons of God.' 'As many as received him, to them gave he the power to recognize that they are the sons of God.' While 'it does not yet appear what you shall be,' even now 'you are the faith sons of God'; 'for you have not received the spirit of bondage again to fear, but you have received the spirit of sonship, whereby you cry, "our Father."' Spoke the prophet of old in the name of the eternal God: 'Even to them will I give in my house a place and a name better than sons; I will give them an everlasting name, one that shall not be cut off.' 'And because you are sons, God has sent forth the spirit of his Son into your hearts.'" P. 448. 1 John 3:1. John 1:12. 1 John 3:2. Rom. 8:15. Isa. 56:5. 1 John 4:13.

3.   **Survival choice is indomitable.**

"Eternal survival of personality is wholly dependent on the choosing of the mortal mind, whose decisions determine the survival potential of the immortal soul. When the mind believes God and the soul knows God, and when, with the fostering Adjuster, they all *desire* God, then is survival assured. Limitations of intellect, curtailment of education, deprivation of culture, impoverishment of social status, even inferiority of the human standards of morality resulting from the unfortunate lack of educational, cultural, and social advantages, cannot invalidate the presence of the divine spirit in such unfortunate and humanly handicapped but believing individuals. The indwelling of the Mystery Monitor constitutes the inception and insures the possibility of the potential of growth and survival of the immortal soul." P. 69-70.

VI. JESUS' BESTOWAL

1. Purpose of Jesus' bestowal.

"A Creator Son did not incarnate in the likeness of mortal flesh and bestow himself upon the humanity of Urantia to reconcile an angry God but rather to win all mankind to the recognition of the Father's love and to the realization of their sonship with God. After all, even the great advocate of the atonement doctrine realized something of this truth, for he declared that 'God was in Christ reconciling the world to himself.'" P. 1083. 2. Cor. 5:19.

2. The new concept of the Messiah.

"The new and vital feature of Peter's confession was the clear-cut recognition that Jesus was the Son of God, of his unquestioned divinity. Ever since his baptism and the wedding at Cana these apostles had variously regarded him as the Messiah, but it was not a part of the Jewish concept of the national deliverer that he should be *divine*. The Jews had not taught that the Messiah would spring from divinity; he was to be the 'anointed one,' but hardly had they contemplated him as being 'the Son of God.' In the second confession more emphasis was placed upon the *combined nature*, the supernal fact that he was the Son of Man *and* the Son of God, and it was upon this great truth of the union of the human nature with the divine nature that Jesus declared he would build the kingdom of heaven.

"Jesus had sought to live his life on earth and complete his bestowal mission as the Son of Man. His followers were disposed to regard him as the expected Messiah. Knowing that he could never fulfill their Messianic expectations, he endeavored to effect such a modification of their concept of the Messiah as would enable him partially to meet their expectations. But he now recognized that such a plan could hardly be carried through successfully. He therefore elected boldly to disclose the third plan—openly to announce his divinity, acknowledge the truthfulness of Peter's confession, and directly proclaim to the twelve that he was a Son of God.

"For three years Jesus had been proclaiming that he was the 'Son of Man,' while for these same three years the apostles had been increasingly insistent that he was the expected Jewish Messiah. He now disclosed that he was the Son of God, and upon the concept of the *combined nature* of the Son of Man and the Son of God, he determined to build the kingdom of heaven. He had decided to refrain from further efforts to convince them that he was not the Messiah. He now proposed boldly to reveal to them what he is, and then to ignore their determination to persist in regarding him as the Messiah." P. 1748.

VII. DEATH AND RESURRECTION

1. Spirit returns to God who gave it.

"When you are through down here, when your course has been run in temporary form on earth, when your trial trip in the flesh is finished, when the dust that composes the mortal tabernacle 'returns to the earth whence it came'; then, it is revealed, the indwelling 'Spirit shall return to God who gave it.' There sojourns within each moral being of this planet a fragment of God, a part and parcel of divinity. It is not yet yours by right of possession, but it is designedly intended to be one with you if you survive the mortal existence." P. 26. Eccl. 12:7.

2. Relation of Adjusters to death.

"Subsequent to physical death, except in individuals translated from among the living, the released Adjuster goes immediately to the home sphere of Divinington. The details of what transpires on that world during the time of awaiting the factual reappearance of the surviving mortal depend chiefly on whether the human being ascends to the mansion worlds in his own individual right or awaits a dispensational summoning of the sleeping survivors of a planetary age." P. 1231.

3. Survival without delay.

"If the human individual survives without delay, the Adjuster, so I am instructed, registers at Divinington, proceeds to the Paradise presence of the Universal Father, returns immediately and is embraced by the Personalized Adjusters of the superuniverse and local universe of assignment, receives the recognition of the chief Personalized Monitor of Divinington, and then, at once, passes into the 'realization of identity transition,' being summoned therefrom on the third period and on the mansion world in the actual personality form made ready for the reception of the surviving soul of the earth mortal as that form has been projected by the guardian of destiny." P. 1232.

4. The mansonia resurrection halls.

"From the Temple of New Life there extend seven radial wings, the resurrection halls of the mortal races. Each of these structures is devoted to the assembly of one of the seven races of time. There are one hundred thousand personal resurrection chambers in each of these seven wings terminating in the circular class assembly halls, which serve as the awakening chambers for as many as one million individuals. There halls are surrounded by the personality assembly chambers of the blended races of the normal post-Adamic worlds. Regardless of the technique which may be employed on the individual worlds of time in connection with special or dispensational resurrections, the real and conscious reassembly of actual and complete personality takes place in the resurrection halls of mansonia number one. Throughout all eternity you will recall the profound memory impressions of your first witnessing of these resurrection mornings." P. 533.

5. The reconstruction of survivors.

"During the transit of surviving mortals from the world of origin to the mansion worlds, whether they experience personality reassembly on the third period or ascend at the time of a group resurrection, the record of personality constitution is faithfully preserved by the archangels on their worlds of special activities. These beings are not the custodians of personality (as the guardian seraphim are of the soul), but it is nonetheless true that every identifiable factor of personality is effectually safeguarded in the custody of these dependable trustees of mortal survival. As to the exact whereabouts of mortal personality during the time intervening between death and survival, we do not know.

"The situation which makes repersonalization possible is brought about in the resurrection halls of the morontia receiving planets of a local universe. Here in these life-assembly chambers the supervising authorities provide that relationship of universe energy—morontial, mindal, and spiritual—which makes possible the reconsciousizing of the sleeping survivor. The reassembly of the constituent parts of a onetime material personality involves:

"1.   The fabrication of a suitable form, a morontia energy pattern, in which the new survivor can make contact with nonspiritual reality, and within which the morontia variant of the cosmic mind can be encircuited.

"2.   The return of the Adjuster to the waiting morontia creature. The Adjuster is the eternal custodian of your ascending identity; your Monitor is the absolute assurance that you yourself and not another will occupy the morontia form created for your personality awakening. And the Adjuster will be present at your personality reassembly to take up once more the role of Paradise guide to your surviving self.

"3.   When these prerequisites of repersonalization have been assembled, the seraphic custodian of the potentialities of the slumbering immortal soul, with the assistance of numerous cosmic personalities, bestows this morontia entity upon and in the awaiting morontia mind-body form while committing this evolutionary child of the Supreme to eternal association with the waiting Adjuster. And this completes the repersonalization, reassembly of memory, insight, and consciousness—identity." P. 1234-5.

VIII. SURVIVAL OF SELF—PERSONALITY

1.   The self must choose to survive as a personality.

"Selfhood is a cosmic reality whether material, morontial, or spiritual. The actuality of the *personal* is the bestowal of the Universal Father acting in and of himself or through his manifold universe agencies. To say that a being is personal is to recognize the relative individuation of such a being within the cosmic organism. The living cosmos is an all but infinitely integrated aggregation of real units, all of which are relatively subject to the destiny of the whole. But those that are personal have been endowed with the actual choice of destiny acceptance or of destiny rejection." P. 1232.

2.   In nonsurvivors, personality enters the Supreme.

"That which comes from the Father is like the Father eternal, and this is just as true of personality, which God gives by his own freewill choice, as it is of the divine Thought Adjuster, an actual fragment of God. Man's personality is eternal but with regard to identity a conditioned eternal reality. Having appeared in response to the Father's will, personality will attain Deity destiny, but man must choose whether or not he will be present at the attainment of such destiny. In default of such choice, personality attains experiential Deity directly, becoming a part of the Supreme Being. The cycle is foreordained, but man's participation therein is optional, personal, and experiential." P. 1232.

3. Experience the keynote of survival.

"Nothing in the entire universe can substitute for the fact of experience on nonexistential levels. The infinite God is, as always, replete and complete, infinitely inclusive of all things except evil and creature experience. God cannot do wrong; he is infallible. God cannot experientially know what he has never personally experienced; God's preknowledge is existential. Therefore does the spirit of the Father descend from Paradise to participate with finite mortals in every bona fide experience of the ascending career; it is only by such a method that the existential God could become in truth and in fact man's experiential Father. The infinity of the eternal God encompasses the potential for finite experience, which indeed becomes actual in the ministry of the Adjuster fragments that actually share the life vicissitude experiences of human beings." P. 1185.

4. The permanency of personality.

"The evolutionary planets are the spheres of human origin, the initial worlds of the ascending mortal career. Urantia is your starting point; here you and your divine Thought Adjuster are joined in temporary union. You have been endowed with a perfect guide; therefore, if you will sincerely run the race of time and gain the final goal of faith, the reward of the ages shall be yours; you will be eternally united with your indwelling Adjuster. Then will begin your real life, the ascending life, to which your present mortal state is but the vestibule. Then will begin your exalted and progressive mission as finaliters in the eternity which stretches out before you. And throughout all of these successive ages and stages of evolutionary growth, there is one part of you that remains absolutely unaltered, and that is personality—permanence in the presence of change." P. 1225.

5. Custodians of identity and survival values.

"The guardian seraphim is the custodial trustee of the survival values of mortal man's slumbering soul as the absent Adjuster is the identity of such an immortal universe being. When these two collaborate in the resurrection halls of mansonia in conjunction with the newly fabricated morontia form, there occurs the reassembly of the constituent factors of the personality of the mortal ascender.

"The Adjuster will identify you; the guardian seraphim will repersonalize you and then re-present you to the faithful Monitor of your earth days.

"And even so, when a planetary age ends, when those in the lower circles of mortal achievement are forgathered, it is their group guardians who reassemble them in the resurrection halls of the mansion spheres, even as your record tells: 'And he shall send his angels with a great voice and shall gather together his elect from one end of the realm to another.'" P. 1247. Matt. 24:31.

IX. THE MANSION WORLDS

1. Deficiency ministry of first mansion world.

"Almost the entire experience of mansion world number one pertains to deficiency ministry, Survivors arriving on this first of the detention spheres present so many and such varied defects of creature character and deficiencies of mortal experience that the major activities of the realm are occupied with the correction and cure of these manifold legacies of the life in the flesh on the material evolutionary worlds of time and space." P. 533.

2. Life continuation on mansion worlds.

"On the mansion worlds the resurrected mortal survivors resume their lives just where they left off when overtaken by death. When you go from Urantia to the first mansion world, you will notice considerable change, but if you had come from a more normal and progressive sphere of time, you would hardly notice the difference except for the fact that you were in possession of a different body; the tabernacle of flesh and blood has been left behind on the world of nativity." P. 532.

3. Must make up our earth failures.

"Those things which you might have learned on earth, but which you failed to learn, must be acquired under the tutelage of these faithful and patient teachers. There are no royal roads, short cuts, or easy paths to Paradise. Irrespective of the individual variations of the route, you master the lessons of one sphere before you proceed to another; at least this is true after you once leave the world of your nativity." P. 551.

4. Cosmic awakening on mansion worlds.

"A real birth of cosmic consciousness takes place on mansonia number five. You are becoming universe minded. This is indeed a time of expanding horizons. It is beginning to dawn upon the enlarging minds of the ascending mortals that some stupendous and magnificent, some supernal and divine, destiny awaits all who complete the progressive Paradise ascension, which has been so laboriously but so joyfully and auspiciously begun. At about this point the average mortal ascender begins to manifest bona fide experiential enthusiasm for the Havona ascent. Study is becoming voluntary, unselfish service natural, and worship spontaneous. A real morontia character is budding; a real morontia creature is evolving." P. 537.

5. Confirmation of Adjuster fusion.

"The union of the evolving immortal soul with the eternal and divine Adjuster is signalized by the seraphic summoning of the supervising super-angel for resurrected survivors and of the archangel of record for those going to judgement on the third day; and then, in the presence of such a survivor's morontia associates, these messengers of confirmation speak: 'This is a beloved son in whom I am well pleased.' This simple ceremony marks the entrance of an ascending mortal upon the eternal career of Paradise service.

"Immediately upon the confirmation of Adjuster fusion the new morontia being is introduced to his fellows for the first time by his new name and is granted the forty days of spiritual retirement from all routine activities wherein to commune with himself and to choose some one of the optional routes to Havona and to select from the differential techniques of Paradise attainment." P. 538. Rev. 2:17; 3:12; 14:1.

6. Is there a second probation?

"If ever there is doubt as to the advisability of advancing a human identity to the mansion worlds, the universe governments invariably rule in the personal interests of that individual; they unhesitatingly advance such a soul to the status of a transitional being, while they continue their observations of the emerging morontia intent and spiritual purpose. Thus divine justice is certain of achievement, and divine mercy is accorded further opportunity for extending its ministry.

"The governments of Orvonton and Nebadon do not claim absolute perfection for the detail working of the universal plan of mortal repersonalization, but they do claim to, and actually do, manifest patience, tolerance, understanding, and merciful sympathy. We had rather assume the risk of a system rebellion than to court the hazard of depriving one struggling mortal from any evolutionary world of the eternal joy of pursuing the ascending career.

"This does not mean that human beings are to enjoy a second opportunity in the face of the rejection of a first, not at all. But it does signify that all will creatures are to experience one true opportunity to make one undoubted, self-conscious, and final choice. The sovereign Judges of the universes will not deprive any being of personality status who has not finally and fully made the eternal choice; the soul of man must and will be given full and ample opportunity to reveal its true intent and real purpose." P. 1233.

X. THE MORONTIA LIFE

1. **Resurrection launches us on morontia career.**

"Mortal death is a technique of escape from the material life in the flesh; and the mansonia experience of progressive life through seven worlds of corrective training and cultural education represents the introduction of mortal survivors to the morontia career, the transition life which intervenes between the evolutionary material existence and the higher spirit attainment of the ascenders of time who are destined to achieve the portals of eternity." P. 540.

2. **Morontia life really begins on Jerusem.**

"The mortal personality initiated on the evolutionary worlds and tabernacled in the flesh—indwelt by the Mystery Monitors and invested by the Spirit of Truth—is not fully mobilized, realized, and unified until that day when such a Jerusem citizen is given clearance for Edentia and proclaimed a true member of the morontia corps of Nebadon—an immortal survivor of Adjuster association, a Paradise ascender, a personality of morontia status, and a true child of the Most Highs." P. 540.

3. **Seven times morontians sleep and are resurrected.**

"Seven times do those mortals who pass through the entire mansonia career experience the adjustment sleep and the resurrection awakening. But the last resurrection hall, the final awakening chamber, was left behind on the seventh mansion world. No more will a form-change necessitate the lapse of consciousness or a break in the continuity of personal memory." P. 540.

4. The survival of young children.

"Children who die when too young to have Thought Adjusters are repersonalized on the finaliter world of the local systems concomitant with the arrival of either parent on the mansion worlds. A child acquires physical entity at mortal birth, but in the matter of survival all Adjusterless children are reckoned as still attached to their parents.

"In due course Thought Adjusters come to indwell these little ones, while the seraphic ministry to both groups of the probationary-dependent orders of survival is in general similar to that of the more advanced parent or is equivalent to that of the parent in case only one survives. Those attaining the third circle, regardless of the status of their parents, are accorded personal guardians.

"Similar probation nurseries are maintained on the finaliter spheres of the constellation and the universe headquarters for the Adjusterless children of the primary and secondary modified orders of ascenders." P. 570.

5. Parental experience is required of all ascenders.

"On the seven mansion worlds ascending mortals are afforded ample opportunities for compensating any and all experiential deprivations suffered on their worlds of origin, whether due to inheritance, environment, or unfortunate premature termination of the career in the flesh. This is in every sense true except in the mortal sex life and its attendant adjustments. Thousands of mortals reach the mansion worlds without having benefited particularly from the disciplines derived from fairly average sex relations on their native spheres. The mansion world experience can provide little opportunity for compensating these very personal deprivations. Sex experience in a physical sense is past for these ascenders, but in close association with the Material Sons and Daughters, both individually and as members of their families, these sex-deficient mortals are enabled to compensate the social, intellectual, emotional, and spiritual aspects of their deficiency. Thus are all those humans whom circumstances or bad judgment deprived of the benefits of advantageous sex association on the evolutionary worlds, here on the system capitals afforded full opportunity to acquire these essential mortal experiences in close and loving association with the supernal Adamic sex creatures of permanent residence on the system capitals.

"No surviving mortal, midwayer, or seraphim may ascend to Paradise, attain the Father, and be mustered into the Corps of the Finality without having passed through that sublime experience of achieving parental relationship to an evolving child of the worlds or some other experience analogous and equivalent thereto. The relationship of child and parent is fundamental to the essential concept of the Universal Father and his universe children. Therefore does such an experience become indispensable to the experiential training of all ascenders.

"The ascending midway creatures and the evolutionary seraphim must pass through this parenthood experience in association with the Material Sons and Daughters of the system headquarters. Thus do such nonreproducing ascenders obtain the experience of parenthood by assisting the Jerusem Adams and Eves in rearing and training their progeny.

"All mortal survivors who have not experienced parenthood on the evolutionary worlds must also obtain this necessary training while sojourning in the homes of the Jerusem Material Sons and as parental associates of these superb fathers and mothers. This is true except in so far as such mortals have been able to compensate their deficiencies on the system nursery located on the first transitional-culture world of Jerusem." P. 516.

XI. SPIRIT PLAY AND RECREATION

1. **All ascenders continue to play.**

"The principles of Urantian play life are philosophically sound and continue to apply on up through your ascending life, through the circuits of Havona to the eternal shores of Paradise. As ascendant beings you are in possession of personal memories of all former and lower existences, and without such identity memories of the past there would be no basis for the humor of the present, either mortal laughter or morontia mirth. It is this recalling of past experiences that provides the basis for present diversion and amusement. And so you will enjoy the celestial equivalents of your earthly humor all the way up through your long morontia, and then increasingly spiritual, careers. And that part of God (the Adjuster) which becomes an eternal part of the personality of an ascendant mortal contributes the overtones of divinity to the joyous expressions, even spiritual laughter, of the ascending creatures of time and space." P. 550.

2. The manifold functions of humor.

"Humor should function as an automatic safety valve to prevent the building up of excessive pressures due to the monotony of sustained and serious self-contemplation in association with the intense struggle for developmental progress and noble achievement. Humor also functions to lessen the shock of the unexpected impact of fact or of truth, rigid unyielding fact and flexible ever-living truth. The mortal personality, never sure as to which will next be encountered, through humor swiftly grasps—sees the point and achieves insight—the unexpected nature of the situation be it fact or be it truth." P. 549.

3. Those who most need relaxation.

"The need for the relaxation and diversion of humor is greatest in those orders of ascendant beings who are subjected to sustained stress in their upward struggles. The two extremes of life have little need for humorous diversions. Primitive men have no capacity therefor, and beings of Paradise perfection have no need thereof. The hosts of Havona are naturally a joyous and exhilarating assemblage of supremely happy personalities. On Paradise the quality of worship obviates the necessity for reversion activities. But among those who start their careers far below the goal of Paradise perfection, there is a large place for the ministry of the reversion directors." P. 549.

4. Increased spirituality lessens need for diversion.

"The higher the mortal species, the greater the stress and the greater the capacity for humor as well as the necessity for it. In the spirit world the opposite is true: The higher we ascend, the less the need for the diversions of reversion experiences. But proceeding down the scale of spirit life from Paradise to the seraphic hosts, there is an increasing need for the mission of mirth and the ministry of merriment. Those beings who most need the refreshment of periodic reversion to the intellectual status of previous experiences are the higher types of the human species, the morontians, angels, and the Material Sons, together with all similar types of personality." P. 549.

XII. IN THE LOCAL UNIVERSE

1. Records of the local universe career.

"*The Worlds of the Archangels.* The seventh group of the encircling Salvington worlds, with their associated satellites, is assigned to the archangels. Sphere number one and all of its six tributary satellites are occupied by the personality record keepers. This enormous corps of recorders busy themselves with keeping straight the record of each mortal of time from the moment of birth up through the universe career until such an individual either leaves Salvington for the superuniverse regime or is 'blotted out of recorded existence' by the mandate of the Ancients of Days.

"It is on these worlds that personality records and identification sureties are classified, filed, and preserved during that time which intervenes between mortal death and the hour of repersonalization, the resurrection from death." P. 409.

2. Ever-changing spiritual ascent.

"Before ascending mortals leave the local universe to embark upon their spirit careers, they will be satiated respecting every intellectual, artistic, and social longing or true ambition which ever characterised their mortal or morontia planes of existence. This is the achievement of equality of the satisfaction of self-expression and self-realization but not the attainment of identical experiential status nor the complete obliteration of characteristic individuality in skill, technique, and expression. But the new spirit differential of personal experiental attainment will not become thus leveled off and equalized until after you have finished the last circle of the Havona career. And then will the Paradise residents be confronted with the necessity of adjusting to that absonite differential of personal experience which can be leveled off only by the group attainment of the ultimate of creature status— the seventh-stage-spirit destiny of the mortal finaliters." P. 508.

3. The visions of John and Paul.

"John the Revelator saw a vision of the arrival of a class of advancing mortals from the seventh mansion world to their first heaven, the glories of Jerusem. He recorded: 'And I saw as it were a sea of glass mingled with fire; and those who had gained the victory over the beast that was originally in them and over the image that persisted through the mansion worlds and finally over the last mark and trace, standing on the sea of glass, having the harps of God, and singing the song of deliverance from mortal fear and death.' (Perfected space communication is to be had on all these worlds; and your anywhere reception of such communications is made possible by carrying the 'harp of God,' a morontia contrivance compensating for the inability to directly adjust the immature morontia sensory mechanism to the reception of space communications.)

"Paul also had a view of the ascendant-citizen corps of perfecting mortals on Jerusem, for he wrote: 'But you have come to Mount Zion and to the city of the living God, the heavenly Jerusalem, and to an innumerable company of angels, to the grand assembly of Michael, and to the spirits of just men being made perfect.'" P. 539. Rev. 15:2-4. Heb. 12:22-23.

XIII. SUPERUNIVERSE ASCENT

1. **Going through the superuniverse.**

   "You will early see the Perfections of days when you advance to the headquarters of Splandon after your sojourn on the worlds of your minor sector, for these exalted rulers are closely associated with the seventy major sector worlds of higher training for the ascendant creatures of time. The Perfections of Days, in person, administer the group pledges to the ascending graduates of the major sector schools.

   "The work of the pilgrims of time on the worlds surrounding a major sector headquarters is chiefly of an intellectual nature in contrast with the more physical and material character of the training on the seven educational spheres of a minor sector and with the spiritual undertakings on the four hundred ninety university worlds of a superuniverse headquarters.

   "Although you are entered only upon the registry of the major sector of Splandon, which embraces the local universe of your origin, you will have to pass through every one of the ten major divisions of our superuniverse. You will see all thirty of the Orvonton Perfections of Days before you reach Uversa." P. 211.

2. **Achievements of the superuniverse.**

   "That, then, is the primary or elementary course which confronts the faith-tested and much-traveled pilgrims of space. But long before reaching Havona, these ascendant children of time have learned to feast upon uncertainty, to fatten upon disappointment, to enthuse over apparent defeat, to invigorate in the presence of difficulties, to exhibit indomitable courage in the face of immensity, and to exercise unconquerable faith when confronted with the challenge of the inexplicable. Long since, the battle cry of these pilgrims became: 'In liaison with God, nothing—absolutely nothing—is impossible.'" P. 291.

3. **Ascenders sponsored by Seventh Master Spirit.**

"It is Master Spirit Number Seven who, in his multiple capacities, personally sponsors the progress of the ascension candidates from the worlds of time in their attempts to achieve comprehension of the undivided Deity of Supremacy. Such comprehension involves a grasp of the existential sovereignty of the Trinity of Supremacy so co-ordinated with a concept of the growing experiential sovereignty of the Supreme Being as to constitute the creature grasp of the unity of Supremacy. Creature realization of these three factors equals Havona comprehension of Trinity reality and endows the pilgrims of time with the ability eventually to penetrate the Trinity, to discover the three infinite persons of Deity." P. 188.

XIV. PASSING THROUGH HAVONA

1. **Pilgrims arrive with perfection of purpose.**

"When, through and by the ministry of all the helper hosts of the universal scheme of survival, you are finally deposited on the receiving world of Havona, you arrive with only one sort of perfection—*perfection of purpose*. Your purpose has been thoroughly proved; your faith has been tested. You are known to be disappointment proof. Not even the failure to discern the Universal Father can shake the faith or seriously disturb the trust of an ascendant mortal who has passed through the experience that all must traverse in order to attain the perfect spheres of Havona. By the time you reach Havona, your sincerity has become sublime. Perfection of purpose and divinity of desire, with steadfastness of faith, have secured your entrance to the settled abodes of eternity; your deliverance from the uncertainties of time is full and complete; and now must you come face to face with the problems of Havona and the immensities of paradise, to meet which you have so long been in training in the experiential epochs of time on the world schools of space." P. 290.

2. **Executing the perfection command.**

"The pilgrim lands on the receiving planet of Havona, the pilot world of the seventh circuit, with only one endowment of perfection, perfection of purpose. The Universal Father has decreed: 'Be you perfect, even as I am perfect.' That is the astounding invitation-command broadcast to the finite children of the worlds of space. The promulgation of that injunction has set all creation astir in the co-operative effort of the celestial beings to assist in bringing about the fulfillment and realization of that tremendous command of the First Great Source and Center." P. 290.

3. Being guided through Havona.

"The Graduate Guides are engaged in piloting the pilgrims of time through the seven circuits of Havona worlds. The guide who greets you upon your arrival on the receiving world of the outer Havona circuit will remain with you throughout your entire career on the heavenly circuits. Though you will associate with countless other personalities during your so journ on a billion worlds, your Graduate Guide will follow you to the end of your Havona progression and will witness your entrance into the terminal slumber of time, the sleep of eternity transit to the Paradise goal, where, upon awakening, you will be greeted by the Paradise Companion assigned to welcome you and perhaps to remain with you until you are initiated as a member of the Mortal Corps of the Finality." P. 270.

4. Experiences on the second Havona circuit.

"For the successful pilgrims on the second circuit the stimulus of evolutionary uncertainty is over, but the adventure of the eternal assignment has not yet begun; and while the sojourn on this circle is wholly pleasurable and highly profitable, it lacks some of the anticipative enthusiasm of the former circles. Many are the pilgrims who, at such a time, look back upon the long, long struggle with a joyous envy, really wishing they might somehow go back to the worlds of time and begin it all over again, just as you mortals, in approaching advanced age, sometimes look back over the struggles of youth and early life and truly wish you might live your lives over once again." P. 296.

5. Meeting Havona helpers and Paradise pilgrims.

"The first of the seven groups of secondary supernaphim to be encountered are the pilgrim helpers, those beings of quick under-standing and broad sympathy who welcome the much-traveled ascenders of space to the stabilized worlds and settled economy of the central universe. Simultaneously these high ministers begin their work for the Paradise pilgrims of eternity, the first of whom arrived on the pilot world of the inner Havona circuit concomitantly with the landing of Grandfanda on the pilot world of the outer circuit. Back in those far-distant days the pilgrims from Paradise and the pilgrims of time first met on the receiving world of circuit number four." P. 291.

6. **Grandfanda's arrival in Havona.**

"'And Malvorian, the first of this order, did greet and instruct the pilgrim discoverer of Havona and did conduct him from the outer circuits of initial experience, step by step and circuit by circuit, until he stood in the very presence of the Source and Destiny of all personality, subsequently crossing the threshold of eternity to Paradise.'

"At that far-distant time I was attached to the service of the Ancients of Days on Uversa, and we all rejoiced in the assurance that, eventually, pilgrims from our superuniverse would reach Havona. For ages we had been taught that the evolutionary creatures of space would attain Paradise, and the thrill of all time swept through the heavenly courts when the first pilgrim actually arrived.

"The name of this pilgrim discoverer of Havona is *Grandfanda*, and he hailed from planet 341 of system 84 in constellation 62 of local universe 1,131 situated in superuniverse number one. His arrival was the signal for the establishment of the broadcast service of the universe of universes. Theretofore only the broadcasts of the superuniverses and the local universes had been in operation, but the announcement of the arrival of Grandfanda at the portals of Havona signalized the inauguration of the 'space reports of glory,' so named because the initial universe broadcast reported the Havona arrival of the first of the evolutionary beings to attain entrance upon the goal of ascendant existence." P. 270.

XV. FINDING DEITY

1. **Contacting the Supreme.**

"Ascenders of space are designated 'spiritual graduates' when translated from the seventh to the sixth circle and are placed under the immediate supervision of the supremacy guides. These guides should not be confused with the Graduate Guides—belonging to the Higher Personalities of the Infinite Spirit— who, with their servital associates, minister on all circuits of Havona to both ascending and descending pilgrims. The supremacy guides function only on the sixth circle of the central universe.

"It is in this circle that the ascenders achieve a new realization of Supreme Divinity. Through their long careers in the evolutionary universes the pilgrims of time have been experiencing a growing awareness of the reality of an almighty overcontrol of the time-space creations. Here, on this Havona circuit, they come near to encountering the central universe source of time-space unity—the spiritual reality of God the Supreme." P. 292.

2. Finding the Infinite Spirit.

"Trinity guides are the tireless ministers of the fifth circle of the Havona training of the advancing pilgrims of time and space. The spiritual graduates are here designated 'candidates for the Deity adventure' since it is on this circle, under the direction of the Trinity guides, that the pilgrims receive advanced instruction concerning the divine Trinity in preparation for the attempt to achieve the personality recognition of the Infinite Spirit. And here the ascending pilgrims discover what true study and real mental effort mean as they begin to discern the nature of the still-more-taxing and far-more-arduous spiritual exertion that will be required to meet the demands of the high goal set for their achievement on the worlds of this circuit." P. 292.

3. Preparing to meet the Eternal Son.

"The fourth Havona circuit is sometimes called the 'circuit of the Sons.' From the worlds of this circuit the ascending pilgrims go to Paradise to achieve an understanding contact with the Eternal Son, while on the worlds of this circuit the descending pilgrims achieve a new comprehension of the nature and mission of the Creator Sons of time and space. There are seven worlds in this circuit on which the reserve corps of the Paradise Michaels maintain special service schools of mutual ministry to both the ascending and descending pilgrims; and it is on these worlds of the Michael Sons that the pilgrims of time and the pilgrims of eternity arrive at their first truly mutual understanding of one another. In many respects the experiences of this circuit are the most intriguing of the entire Havona sojourn." P. 293.

4. Preparing to recognize the Universal Father.

"When the pilgrim soul attains the third circle of Havona, he comes under the tutelage of the Father guides, the older, highly skilled, and most experienced of the superaphic ministers. On the worlds of this circuit the Father guides maintain schools of wisdom and colleges of technique wherein all the beings inhabiting the central universe serve as teachers. Nothing is neglected which would be of service to a creature of time in this transcendent adventure of eternity attainment.

"The attainment of the Universal Father is the passport to eternity, notwithstanding the remaining circuits to be traversed. It is therefore a momentous occasion on the pilot world of circle number three when the transit trio announce that the last venture of time is about to ensue; that another creature of space seeks entry to Paradise through the portals of eternity." P. 294-5.

5. **Guidance on these Paradise excursions.**

"When an ascendant soul actually starts for Paradise, he is accompanied only by the transist trio: the superaphic circle associate, the Graduate Guide, and the ever-present servital associate of the latter. These excursions from the Havona circles to Paradise are trial trips; the ascenders are not yet of Paradise status. They do not achieve residential status on Paradise until they have passed through the terminal rest of time subsequent to the attainment of the Universal Father and the final clearance of the Havona circuits. Not until after the divine rest do they partake of the the 'essence of divinity' and the 'spirit of supremacy' and thus really begin to function in the circle of eternity and in the presence of the Trinity.

"The ascender's companions of the transit trio are not required to enable him to locate the geographic presence of the spiritual luminosity of the Trinity, rather to afford all possible assistance to a pilgrim in his difficult task of recognizing, discerning, and comprehending the Infinite Spirit sufficiently to constitute personality recognition. Any ascendant pilgrim on Paradise can discern the geographic or locational presence of the Trinity, the great majority are able to contact the intellectual reality of the Deities, especially the Third Person, but not all can recognize or even partially comprehend the reality of the spiritual presence of the Father and the Son. Still more difficult is even the minimum spiritual comprehension of the Universal Father." P. 293.

XVI. FINAL PREPARATION FOR PARADISE DESTINY

1. **Comprehension the passport to Paradise.**

"*Ability to comprehend is the mortal passport to Paradise.* Willingness to believe is the key to Havona. The acceptance of sonship, co-operation with the indwelling Adjuster, is the price of evolutionary survival." P. 290.

2.   Making ready for the Paradise journey.

"Near the end of the first-circle sojourn the ascending pilgrims first meet the instigators of rest of the primary order of supernaphim. These are the angels of Paradise coming out to greet those who stand at the threshold of eternity and to complete their preparation for the transition slumber of the last resurrection. You are not really a child of paradise until you have traversed the inner circle and have experienced the resurrection of eternity from the terminal sleep of time. The perfected pilgrims begin this rest, go to sleep, on the first circle of Havona, but they awaken on the shores of Paradise. Of all who ascend to the eternal Isle, only those who thus arrive are the children of eternity; the other go as visitors, as guests without residential status." P. 297.

3.   The final pre-Paradise sleep.

"And now, at the culmination of the Havona career, as you mortals go to sleep on the pilot world of the inner circuit, you go not alone to your rest as you did on the worlds of your origin when you close your eyes in the natural sleep of mortal death, nor as you did when you entered the preparatory for the journey to Havona. Now, as you prepare for the attainment rest, there moves over by your side your long-time associate of the first circle, the majestic complement of rest, who prepares to enter the rest as one with you, as the pledge of Havona that your transition is complete, and that you await only the final touches of perfection.

"Your first transition was indeed death, the second an ideal sleep, and now the third metamorphosis is the true rest, the relaxation of the ages." P. 297.

4.   The terminal rest of time.

"But the last metamorphic sleep is something more than those previous transition slumbers which have marked the successive status attainments of the ascendant career; thereby do the creatures of time and space traverse the innermost margins of the temporal and the spatial to attain residential status in the time less and spaceless abodes of Paradise. The instigators and the complements of rest are just as essential to this transcending metamorphosis as are the seraphim and associated beings to the mortal creature's survival of death." P. 299.

5. The last grand stretch of faith.

"You enter the rest on the final Havona circuit and are eternally resurrected on Paradise. And as you there spiritually repersonalize, you will immediately recognize the instigator of rest who welcomes you to the enternal shores as the very primary supernaphim who produced the final sleep on the innermost circuit of Havona; and you will recall the last grand stretch of faith as you once again made ready to commend the keeping of your identity into the Universal Father." P. 299.

6. The eternity arrival on Paradise.

"The last rest of time has been enjoyed; the last transition sleep has been experienced; now you awake to life everlasting on the shores of the eternal abode. 'And there shall be no more sleep. The presence of God and his Son are before you, and you are eternally his servants; you have seen his face, and his name is your spirit. There shall be no night there; and they need no light of the sun, for the Great Source and Center gives them light; they shall live forever and ever. And God shall wipe away all tears from their eyes; there shall be no more death, neither sorrow nor crying, neither shall there be any more pain, for the former things passed away.'" P. 299. Rev. 22:5; 7:17; 21:4.

XVII. PARADISE

1. The scope of Paradise destiny.

"What an adventure! What a romance! A gigantic creation to be administered by the children of the Supreme, these personalized and humanized Adjusters, these Adjusterized and eternalized mortals, these mysterious combinations and eternal associations of the highest known manifestation of the essence of the First Source and Center and the lowest form of intelligent life capable of comprehending and attaining the Universal Father. We conceive that such amalgamated beings, such partnerships of Creator and creature. will become superb rulers, matchless administrators, and understanding and sympathetic directors of any and all forms of intelligent life which may come into existence throughout these future universes of the first outer space level.

"True it is, you mortals are of earthly, animal origin; your frame is indeed dust. But if you actually will, if you really desire, surely the heritage of the ages is yours, and you shall someday serve throughout the universes in your true characters—children of the Supreme God of experience and divine sons of the Paradise Father of all personalities." P. 1239-40.

2. **Paradise companionship for ascenders.**

"Mortals come from races that are very social. The Creators well know that it is 'not good for man to be alone,' and provision is accordingly made for companionship, even on Paradise.

"If you, as an ascendant mortal, should reach Paradise in the company of the companion or close associate of your earthly career, or if your seraphic guardian of destiny should chance to arrive with you or were waiting for you, then no permanent companion would be assigned you. But if you arrive alone, a companion will certainly welcome you as you awaken on the Isle of Light from the terminal sleep of time. Even if it is known that you will be accompanied by someone of ascendant association, temporary companions will be designated to welcome you to the eternal shores and to escort you to the reservation made ready for the reception of you and your associates. You may be certain of being warmly welcomed when you experience the resurrection into eternity on the everlasting shores of Paradise.

"Reception companions are assigned during the terminal days of the ascenders' sojourn on the last circuit of Havona, and they carefully examine the records of mortal origins and eventful ascent through the worlds of space and the circles of Havona. When they greet the mortals of time, they are already well versed in the careers of thes arriving pilgrims and immediately prove to be sympathetic and intriguing companions.

"During your prefinaliter sojourn on Paradise, if for any reason you should be temporarily separated from your associate of the ascending career—mortal or seraphic—a Paradise Companion would be forthwith assigned for counsel and companionship. When once assigned to an ascendant mortal of solitary residence on Paradise, the companion remains with this person until he either is rejoined by his ascedant associates or is duly mustered into the Corps of the Finality." P. 283-4.

XVIII. THE CORPS OF THE FINALITY

1. **Entering the Corps of the Finality.**

"After the attainment of the supreme satisfaction of the fullness of worship, you are qualified for admission to the Corps of the Finality.

The ascendant career is well-nigh finished, and the seventh jubilee prepares for celebration. The first jubilee marked the mortal agreement with the Thought Adjuster when the purpose to survive was sealed; the second was the awakening in the morontia life; the third was the fusion with the Thought Adjuster; the fourth was the awakening in Havona; the fifth celebrated the finding of the Universal Father; and the sixth jubilee was the association of the Paradise awakening from the final transit slumber of time. The seventh jubilee marks entrance into the mortal finaliter corps and the beginning of the eternity service. The attainment of the seventh stage of a spirit realization by a finaliter will probably signalize the celebration of the first of the jubilees of eternity." P. 305.

2. **Taking the finaliter oath.**

"Although all mortals who attain Paradise frequently fraternize with the Transcendentalers as they do with the Paradise Citizens, it develops that man's first serious contact with a Transcendentaler occurs on that eventful occasion when, as a member of a new finaliter group, the mortal ascender stands in the finaliter receiving circle as the Trinity oath of eternity is administered by the chief of Transcendentalers, the presiding head of the Architects of the Master Universe." P. 351.

3. **Beginning of the end of the long ascension.**

"Step by step, life by life, world by world, the ascendant career has been mastered, and the goal of Deity has been attained. Survival is complete in perfection, and perfection is replete in the supremacy of divinity. Time is lost in eternity; space is swallowed up in worship-ful identity and harmony with the Universal Father. The broadcasts of Havona flash forth the space reports of glory, the good news that is very truth the conscientious creatures of animal nature and material origin have, through evolutionary ascension, become in reality and eternally the perfected sons of God." P. 295

4. **Finaliter destiny in outer space.**

"We believe that the mortals of Adjuster fusion, together with their finaliter associates, are destined to function in some manner in the administration on the universes of the first outer space level. We have not the slightest doubt that in due time these enormous galaxies will become inhabited universes. And we are equally convinced that among the administrators thereof will be found the Paradise finaliters whose natures are the cosmic consequence of the blending of creatures and Creator." P. 1239.

5. The high destiny of the finaliters.

"The Perfectors of Wisdom will always require this complement of experiential wisdom for the completion of their administrative sagacity. But it has been postulated that a high and hitherto unattained level of wisdom may possibly be achieved by the paradise finaliters *after* they are sometime inducted into the seventh stage of spirit existence. If this inference is correct, then would such perfected beings of evolutionary ascent undoubtedly become the most effective universe administrators ever to be known in all creation. I believe that such is the high destiny of finaliters." P. 216.

16. EVIL AND SIN

THE BIBLE ON EVIL AND SIN

   I. EVIL.
  II. SIN.
 III. GUILT.
 IV. SANCTIFICATION.

THE URANTIA BOOK

    I. DEFINITIONS OF EVIL AND SIN.
   II. GOD'S ATTITUDE TOWARDS SIN.
  III. OLDEN CONCEPTS OF EVIL AND SIN.
  IV. MAN MUST BE FALLIBLE IF FREE.
   V. NATURE'S IMPERFECTIONS.
  VI. REBELLION—THE PENALTY OF SIN.
 VII. REMOTE REPERCUSSIONS OF SIN.
VIII. LIBERTY—TRUE AND FALSE.
  IX. GUILT—SECURITY AGAINST SIN.
   X. FORGIVENESS OF SIN.
  XI. INTERVAL BETWEEN SIN AND THE PENALTY.
 XII. ORIGINAL SIN.
XIII. JESUS TALKS ABOUT GOOD AND EVIL.

EVIL AND SIN

THE BIBLE ON EVIL AND SIN

I. EVIL

There are three kinds of evil presented in the Bible:

1. Physical evil.
2. Moral evil.
3. Mixed evil.

1. Physical evil.

"I form light and create darkness, I make weak and create woe, I am the Lord, who do all these things." **Isa. 45:7**.

"Does evil befall a city, unless the Lord has done it?" **Amos 3:6**.

"Behold, I will bring evil upon the house of Jeroboam...and will utterly consume the house of Jeroboam." **1 Kings 14:10**.

"When the angel stretched forth his hand toward Jerusalem to destroy it, the Lord repented of the evil, and said to the angel...'It is enough; now stay your hand.'" **2 Sam. 24:16**.

"No evil shall befall you." **Ps. 91:10**.

2. Moral evil.

"The fear of the Lord is hatred of evil." **Prov. 8:13**.

"Do not be overcome by evil, but overcome evil with good." **Rom. 12:21**.

"Wash yourselves; make yourselves clean; remove the evil of your doings." **Isa. 1:16**.

"And lead us not into temptation, but deliver us from evil." **Matt. 6:13**.

"But the evil I do not want is what I do." **Rom. 7:19**.

"Let him turn away from evil and do right...the face of the Lord is against those that do evil." **1 Peter 3:11-12**.

3. Mixed evil.

"And the Lord will take away from you all sickness; and none of the evil diseases of Egypt...will he inflict upon you." **Deut. 7:15**.

"For the love of money is the root of all evils." **1 Tim. 6:10**.

"And God sent an evil spirit between Abimelech and the men of Shechem." **Judges 9:23**.

"And on the morrow an evil spirit from God rushed upon Saul, and he raved within his house." **1 Sam. 18:10**. (**Note**: Today, we would diagnose Saul as being a manic-depressive. This also explains his suicide on Gilboa.)

"But the Lord hardened the heart of Pharaoh, and he did not listen to them." **Ex. 9:12**.

"Whenever they marched out, the hand of the Lord was against them for evil, as the Lord had warned." **Judges 2:15**.

(**Note**: The concept of evil is hazy through all of the Old Testament. About 100 B.C. it begins to clarify in some books of the Apocrypha, and was later linked up with sin and the atonement by Paul.)

The change in the doctrine of the origin of evil is shown in the episode of David taking a census of the Hebrew nation—see:

"The anger of the Lord was kindled against Israel and he incited David against them, saying, 'Go number Israel and Judah.'" **2 Sam. 24:1**.

"Satan stood up against Israel, and incited David to number Israel." **1 Chron. 21:1**.

II. SIN

1. **Definitions.**

   "Everyone who commits sin is guilty of lawlessness; sin is lawlessness." **1 John 3:4**.

   "Whatever does not proceed from faith is sin." **Rom. 14:23**.

   "If you show partiality, you commit sin." **Jas. 2:9**.

   "All wrongdoing is sin." **1 John 5:17**.

2. **Sin determined by enlightenment.**

   "If anyone sins unwittingly..." **Lev. 4:2**.

   "If I had not come and spoken to them, they would not have sin; but now they have no excuse for their sin." **John 15:22**.

3. **Deliberate and knowing sin is fatal.**

   "For if we sin deliberately after receiving the knowledge of the truth, there no longer remains a sacrifice for sins." **Heb. 10:26**.

"There is sin which is mortal; I do not say that one is to pray for that."
1 John 5:16.

4. **Besetting sins.**

"Let us also lay aside every weight, and sin which clings so closely, and let us run with perseverance the race that is set before us." **Heb. 12:1.**

5. **Original sin.**

"For as in Adam all die, so also in Christ shall all be made alive."
1 Cor. 15:22.

But Jesus did not recognize original guilt and sin. **See:**

"Jesus answered, 'It was not that this man sinned, or his parents, but that the works of God might be made manifest.'" **John 9:3.**

Paul taught innate carnal sin.

"Let not sin therefore reign in your mortal bodies, to make you obey their passions." **Rom. 6:12.**

6. **The atonement.**

"He who commits sin is of the devil; for the devil has sinned from the beginning." **1 John 3:8.**

"For our sake he made him to be sin who knew no sin, so that in him we might become the righteousness of God." **2 Cor. 5:21.**

"Without the shedding of blood there is no forgiveness of sins." **Heb. 9:22.**

7. **The penalty of sin.**

"For the wages of sin is death." **Rom. 6:23.**

8. **Forgiveness of sin.**

"I will forgive their iniquity, and I will remember their sin no more."
Jer. 31:34.

"For thou, O Lord, art good and forgiving." **Ps. 86:5.**

"If we confess our sins, he is faithful and just, and will forgive our sins and cleanse us from all unrighteousness." **1 John 1:9.**

III. GUILT

Guilt is seldom mentioned in the Bible.

1. **Having to do with the mores.**

   "If anyone touches an unclean thing...he shall be guilty." **Lev. 5:2.**

2. **Guilt from sins of ignorance.**

   "If anyone sins...though he does not know it, yet he is guilty." **Lev. 5:17.**

   "For whoever keeps the whole law but fails in one point has become guilty of all of it." **Jas. 2:10.**

IV. SANCTIFICATION

1. **Taught in the Old Testament.**

   "They gathered their brethren, and sanctified themselves." **2 Chron. 29:15.**

2. **God wills sanctification.**

   "For this is the will of God, your sanctification." **1 Thess. 4:3.**

3. **Truth sanctifies.**

   "Sanctify them in the truth; thy word is truth." **John 17:17.**

   "I commend you to God and to the word of his grace, which is able to build you up and to give you the inheritance among all those who are sanctified." **Acts 20:32.**

4. **Sanctified in Jesus' name.**

   "But you were washed, you were sanctified, you were justified in the name of the Lord Jesus Christ." **1 Cor. 6:11.**

   "Chosen and destined by God the Father and sanctified by the Spirit for obedience to Jesus Christ." **1 Peter 1:2.**

5. **The sinless new birth.**

   "No one born of God commits sin." **1 John 3:9.**

   "Whoever has suffered in the flesh has ceased from sin." **1 Peter 4:1.**

   "I am writing this to you so that you may not sin." **1 John 2:1.**

6. **Forgiveness and sanctification.**

   "That they may receive forgiveness of sins and a place among those who are sanctified by faith." **Acts 26:18.**

   NOTE: The Father has said: "Be you perfect." Such bliss may be partially realized on worlds settled in light and life—and on Paradise.

THE URANTIA BOOK
I. DEFINITIONS OF EVIL AND SIN

1. **Jesus' definition of evil, sin, and iniquity.**

   "'Evil is the unconscious or unintended transgression of the divine law, the Father's will. Evil is likewise the measure of the imperfectness of obedience to the Father's will.

   "'Sin is the conscious, knowing, and deliberate transgression of the divine law, the Father's will. Sin is the measure of unwillingness to be divinely led and spiritually directed.

   "'Iniquity is the willful, determined, and persistent transgression of the divine law, the Father's will. Iniquity is the measure of the continued rejection of the Father's loving plan of personality survival and the Sons' merciful ministry of salvation.'" P. 1660.

2. **Diverse concepts of sin.**

   "There are many ways of looking at sin, but from the universe philosophic viewpoint sin is the attitude of a personality who is knowingly resisting cosmic reality. Error might be regarded as a misconception or distortion of reality. Evil is a partial realization of, or maladjustment to, universe realities. But sin is a purposeful resistance to divine reality—a conscious choosing to oppose spiritual progress—while iniquity consists in an open and persistent defiance of recognized reality and signifies such a degree of personality disintegration as to border on cosmic insanity." P. 754.

3. **How error and evil progress to sin and iniquity.**

   "Error suggests lack of intellectual keenness; evil, deficiency of wisdom; sin, abject spiritual poverty; but iniquity is indicative of vanishing personality control.

   "And when sin has so many times been chosen and so often been repeated, it may become habitual. Habitual sinners can easily become iniquitous, become wholehearted rebels against the universe and all of its divine realities. While all manner of sins may be forgiven, we doubt whether the established iniquiter would ever sincerely experience sorrow for his misdeeds or accept forgiveness for his sins." P. 755.

4. Sin isolates from universe reality.

"Every impulse of every electron, thought, or spirit is an acting unit in the whole universe. Only sin is isolated and evil gravity resisting on the mental and spiritual levels. The universe is a whole; no thing or being exists or lives in isolation. Self-realization is potentially evil if it is antisocial. It is literally true: 'No man lives by himself.' Cosmic socialization constitutes the highest from of personality unification. Said Jesus: 'He who would be greatest among you, let him become server of all.'" P. 647. Luke 22:26.

5. The problem of sin.

"The problem of sin is not self-existent in the finite world. The fact of finiteness is not evil or sinful. The finite world was made by an infinite Creator—it is the handiwork of his divine Sons—and therefore it must be good. It is the misuse, distortion, and perversion of the finite that gives origin to evil and sin." P. 1222.

6. Sin as redefined.

"*Sin must be redefined as deliberate disloyalty to Deity*. There are degrees of disloyalty: the partial loyalty of indecision; the divided loyalty of confliction; the dying loyalty of indifference; and the death of loyalty exhibited in devotion to godless ideals." P. 984.

II. GOD'S ATTITUDE TOWARD SIN

1. God does not create evil.

"'It is not strange that you ask such questions seeing that you are beginning to know the Father as I know him, and not as the early Hebrew prophets so dimly saw him. You well know how our forefathers were disposed to see God in almost everything that happened. They looked for the hand of God in all natural occurrences and in every unusual episode of human experience. They connected God with both good and evil. They thought he softened the heart of Moses and hardened the heart of Pharaoh. When man had a strong urge to do something, good or evil, he was in the habit of accounting for these unusual emotions by remarking: "The Lord spoke to me saying, do thus and so, or go here and there." Accordingly, since men so often and so violently ran into temptation, it became the habit of our forefathers to believe that God led them

thither for testing, punishing, or strengthening. But you, indeed, now
know better. You know that men are all too often led into temptation
by the urge of their own selfishness and by the impulses of their
animal natures. When you are in this way tempted, I admonish you
that, while you recognize temptation honestly and sincerely for just
what it is, you intelligently redirect the energies of spirit, mind, and
body, which are seeking expression, into higher channels and toward
more idealistic goals. In this way may you transform your tempta-
tions into the highest types of uplifting mortal ministry while you
almost wholly avoid these wasteful and weakening conflicts between
the animal and spiritual natures.'" P. 1738.

2. Origin of evil and sin.

"The Gods neither create evil nor permit sin and rebellion.
Potential evil is time-existent in a universe embracing differential
levels of perfection meanings and values. Sin is potential in all
realms where imperfect beings are endowed with the ability to
choose between good and evil. The very conflicting presence of
truth and untruth, fact and falsehood, constitutes the potentiality of
error. The deliberate choice of evil constitutes sin; the willful
rejection of truth is error; the persistent pursuit of sin and error is
iniquity." P. 613.

3. God loves the sinner—hates the sin.

"God loves the sinner and *hates* the sin: such a statement is true
philosophically, but God is a transcendent personality, and persons
can only love and hate other persons. Sin is not a person. God loves
the sinner because he is a personality reality (potentially eternal),
while towards sin God strikes no personal attitude, for sin is not a
spiritual reality; it is not personal; therefore does only the justice of
God take cognizance of its existence. The love of God saves the
sinner; the law of God destroys the sin. This attitude of the divine
nature would apparently change if the sinner finally identified
himself wholly with sin just as the same mortal mind may also fully
identify itself with the indwelling spirit Adjuster. Such a sin-
identified mortal would then become wholly unspiritual in nature
(and therefore personally unreal) and would experience eventual
extinction of being. Unreality, even incompleteness of creature
nature, cannot exist forever in a progressingly real and increasingly
spiritual universe." P. 41.

4. **Adjusters in relation to sin and evil.**

"No matter what the previous status of the inhabitants of a world, subsequent to the bestowal of a divine Son and after the bestowal of the Spirit of Truth upon all humans, the Adjusters flock to such a world to indwell the minds of all normal will creatures. Following the completion of the mission of a Paradise bestowal Son, these Monitors truly become the 'kingdom of heaven within you.' Through the bestowal of the divine gifts the Father makes the closest possible approach to sin and evil, for it is literally true that the Adjuster must coexist in the mortal mind even in the very midst of human unrighteousness. The indwelling Adjusters are particularly tormented by those thoughts which are purely sordid and selfish; they are distressed by irreverence for that which is beautiful and divine, and they are virtually thwarted in their work by many of man's foolish animal fears and childish anxieties." P. 1193.

5. **How the Creator deals with sin.**

"In all their dealings with intelligent beings, both the Creator Son and his Paradise Father are love dominated. It is impossible to comprehend many phases of the attitude of the universe rulers toward rebels and rebellion—sin and sinners—unless it be remembered that God as a Father takes precedence over all other phases of Deity manifestation in all the dealings of divinity with humanity. It should also be recalled that the Paradise Creator Sons are all mercy motivated." P. 618.

6. **The universal mission of evil.**

"The infinite goodness of the Father is beyond the comprehension of the finite mind of time; hence must there always be afforded a contrast with comparative evil (not sin) for the effective exhibition of all phases of relative goodness. Perfection of divine goodness can be discerned by mortal imperfection of insight only because it stands in contrastive association with relative imperfection in the relationships of time and matter in the motions of space." P. 58.

7. **Returning good for evil.**

"Then asked Nathaniel: 'Master, shall we give no place to justice? The law of Moses says, "An eye for an eye, and a tooth for a tooth." What shall we say?' And Jesus answered: 'You shall return good for evil. My messengers must not strive with men, but be gentle toward all. Measure for measure shall not be your rule. The rulers of men may have such laws, but not so in the kingdom; mercy always shall determine your judgments and love your conduct. And if these are hard sayings, you can even now turn back. If you find the requirements of apostleship too hard, you may return to the less rigorous pathway of discipleship.'" P. 1577.

III. OLDEN CONCEPTS OF EVIL AND SIN

1. **Olden concepts of sin.**

"As the savage mind evolved to that point where it envisaged both good and bad spirits, and when the taboo received the solemn sanction of evolving religion, the stage was all set for the appearance of the new conception of sin. The idea of sin was universally established in the world before revealed religion ever made its entry. It was only by the concept of sin that natural death became logical to the primitive mind. Sin was the transgression of taboo, and death was the penalty of sin." P. 975.

2. **Sin was at first ritual, not rational.**

"Sin was ritual, not rational; an act, not a thought. And this entire concept of sin was fostered by the lingering traditions of Dilmun and the days of a little paradise on earth. The tradition of Adam and the Garden of Eden also lent substance to the dream of a onetime 'golden age' of the dawn of the races. And all this confirmed the ideas later expressed in the belief that man had his origin in a special creation, that he started his career in perfection, and that transgression of the taboos—sin—brought him down to his later sorry plight." P. 975.

3. **Olden concept of the blood sacrifice.**

"The Hebrews believed that 'without the shedding of blood there could be no remission of sin.' They had not found deliverance from the old and pagan idea that the Gods could not be appeased except by the sight of blood, though Moses did make a distinct advance when he forbade human sacrifices and substituted therefor, in the primitive minds of his childlike Bedouin followers, the ceremonial sacrifice of animals." P. 60. Matt. 26:28. Heb. 9;22.

4. **Evolution of vice, crime, and sin.**

"The habitual violation of a taboo became a vice; primitive law made vice a crime; religion made it a sin. Among the early tribes the violation of a taboo was a combined crime and sin. Community calamity was always regarded as punishment for tribal sin. To those who believed that prosperity and righteousness went together, the apparent prosperity of the wicked occasioned so much worry that it was necessary to invent hells for the punishment of taboo violators; the numbers of these places of future punishment have varied from one to five." P. 976.

5. **Sacrifice, sin, and atonement.**

"The earliest idea of the sacrifice was that of a neutrality assessment levied by ancestral spirits; only later did the idea of atonement develop. As man got away from the notion of the evolutionary origin of the race, as the traditions of the days of the Planetary Prince and the sojourn of Adam filtered down through time, the concept of sin and of original sin became widespread, so that sacrifice for accidental and personal sin evolved into the doctrine of sacrifice for the atonement of racial sin. The atonement of the sacrifice was a blanket insurance device which covered even the resentment and jealousy of an unknown god." P. 978.

IV. MAN MUST BE FALLIBLE IF FREE

1. **Only perfect beings are both sinless and free.**

"Throughout the universe, every unit is regarded as a part of the whole. Survival of the part is dependent on co-operation with the plan and purpose of the whole, the wholehearted desire and perfect willingness to do the Father's divine will. The only evolutionary world without error (the possibility of unwise judgment) would be a world without *free* intelligence. In the Havona universe there are a billion perfect worlds with their perfect inhabitants, but evolving man must be fallible if he is to be free. Free and inexperienced intelligence cannot possibly at first be uniformly wise. The possibility of mistaken judgment (evil) becomes sin only when the human will consciously endorses and knowingly embraces a deliberate immoral judgment." P. 52.

2. **Error in relation to spiritual concepts.**

"The element of error present in human religious experience is directly proportional to the content of materialism which contaminates the spiritual concept of the Universal Father. Man's prespirit progression in the universe consists in the experience of divesting himself of these erroneous ideas of the nature of God and of the reality of pure and true spirit. Deity is more than spirit, but the spiritual approach is the only one possible to ascending man." P. 1123.

3. **Source of evil tendencies.**

"'Many times, when you have done evil, you have thought to charge up your acts to the influence of the evil one when in reality you have but been led astray by your own natural tendencies. Did not the Prophet Jeremiah long ago tell you that the human heart is deceitful above all things and sometimes even desperately wicked? How easy for you to become self-deceived and thereby fall into foolish fears, divers lusts, enslaving pleasures, malice, envy, and even vengeful hatred!'" P. 1609-10. Jer. 17:9.

4. **The mischief of our "besetting sins."**

"Almost every human being has some one thing which is held on to as a pet evil, and which the entrance into the kingdom of heaven requires as a part of the price of admission. If Matadormus had parted with his wealth, it probably would have been put right back into his hands for administration as treasurer of the seventy. For later on, after the establishment of the church at Jerusalem, he did obey the Master's injunction, although it was then too late to enjoy membership in the seventy, and he became the treasurer of the Jerusalem church, of which James the Lord's brother in the flesh was the head." P. 1802.

5. **The default of Adam and Eve.**

"And as the Material Son and Daughter thus communed in the moonlit Garden, 'the voice in the Garden' reproved them for disobedience. And that voice was none other than my own announcement to the Edenic pair that they had transgressed the Garden covenant; that they had disobeyed the instructions of the Melchizedeks; that they had defaulted in the execution of their oaths of trust to the sovereign of the universe.

"Eve had consented to participate in the practice of good and evil. Good is the carrying out of the divine plans; sin is a deliberate transgression of the divine will; evil is the misadaptation of plans and the maladjustment of techniques resulting in universe disharmony and planetary confusion." P. 842.

V. NATURE'S IMPERFECTIONS

1. **Sin mars the face of nature.**

"And nature is marred, her beautiful face is scarred, her features are seared, by the rebellion, the misconduct, the misthinking of the myriads of creatures who are a part of nature, but who have contributed to her disfigurement in time. No, nature is not God. Nature is not an object of worship." P. 57.

2. **Nature is perfection divided by incompletion.**

"Nature is the perfection of Paradise divided by the incompletion, evil, and sin of the unfinished universes. This quotient is thus expressive of both the perfect and the partial, of both the eternal and the temporal. Continuing evolution modifies nature by augmenting the content of Paradise perfection and by diminishing the content of the evil, error, and disharmony of relative reality." P. 57.

3. **Nature is not a true portrayal of God.**

"God is not personally present in nature or in any of the forces of nature, for the phenomenon of nature is the superimposition of the imperfections of progressive evolution and, sometimes, the consequences of insurrectionary rebellion, upon the Paradise foundations of God's universal law. As it appears on such a world as Urantia, nature can never be the adequate expression, the true representation, the faithful portrayal, of an all-wise and infinite God." P. 57.

VI. REBELLION—THE PENALTY OF SIN

1. **The beginnings of sin.**

"Lucifer is now the fallen and deposed Sovereign of Satania. Self-contemplation is most disastrous, even to the exalted personalities of the celestial world. Of Lucifer it was said: 'Your heart was lifted up because of your beauty; you corrupted your wisdom because of your brightness.' Your olden prophet saw his sad estate when he wrote: 'How are you fallen from heaven, O Lucifer, son of the morning! How are you cast down, you who dared to confuse the worlds!'" P. 601. Eze. 28:17. Isa. 14:12.

2. **Internal origins of sin.**

"There were no peculiar or special conditions in the system of Satania which suggested or favored rebellion. It is our belief that the idea took origin and form in Lucifer's mind, and that he might have instigated such a rebellion no matter where he might have been stationed. Lucifer first announced his plans to Satan, but it required several months to corrupt the mind of his able and brilliant associate. However, when once converted to the rebel theories, he became a bold and earnest advocate of 'self-assertion and liberty.'" P. 602.

3. Obscure causes of rebellion.

"It is very difficult to point out the exact cause or causes which finally culminated in the Lucifer rebellion. We are certain of only one thing, and that is: Whatever these first beginnings were, they had their origin in Lucifer's mind. There must have been a pride of self that nourished itself to the point of self-deception, so that Lucifer for a time really persuaded himself that his contemplation of rebellion was actually for the good of the system, if not of the universe. By the time his plans had developed to the point of disillusionment, no doubt he had gone too far for his original and mischief-making pride to permit him to stop. At some point in this experience he became insincere, and evil evolved into deliberate and willful sin. That this happened is proved by the subsequent conduct of this brilliant executive. He was long offered opportunity for repentance, but only some of his subordinates ever accepted the proffered mercy. The Faithful of Days of Edentia, on the request of the Constellation Fathers, in person presented the plan of Michael for the saving of these flagrant rebels, but always was the mercy of the Creator Son rejected and rejected with increasing contempt and disdain." P. 603.

4. The evil of disturbing cosmic timing.

"Lucifer similarly sought to disrupt the time governor operating in restraint of the premature attainment of certain liberties in the local system. A local system settled in light and life has experientially achieved those viewpoints and insights which make feasible the operation of many techniques that would be disruptive and destructive in the pre-settled eras of that very realm." P. 1302.

5. Fate of identification with sin.

"When this sentence is finally confirmed, the sin-identified being instantly becomes as though he had not been. There is no resurrection from such a fate; it is everlasting and eternal. The living energy factors of identity are resolved by the transformations of time and the metamorphoses of space into the cosmic potentials whence they once emerged. As for the personality of the iniquitous one, it is deprived of a continuing life vehicle by the creature's failure to make those choices and final decisions which would have assured eternal life. When the continued embrace of sin by the associated mind culminates in complete self-identification with iniquity, then upon the cessation of life, upon cosmic dissolution, such an isolated personality is absorbed into the oversoul of creation, becoming a part of the evolving experience of the Supreme Being. Never again does it appear as a personality; its identity becomes as though it had never been. In the case of an Adjuster-indwelt personality, the experiential spirit values survive in the reality of the continuing Adjuster." P. 37.

6. **Willful sin is automatically suicidal.**

"In any universe contest between actual levels of reality, the personality of the higher level will ultimately triumph over the personality of the lower level. This inevitable outcome of universe controversy is inherent in the fact that divinity of quality equals the degree of reality or actuality of any will creature. Undiluted evil, complete error, willful sin, and unmitigated iniquity are inherently and automatically suicidal. Such attitudes of cosmic unreality can survive in the universe only because of transient mercy-tolerance pending the action of the justice-determining and fairness-finding mechanisms of the universe tribunals of righteous adjudication." P. 37.

7. **The ever-loyal Amadonites.**

"These *Amadonites* were derived from the group of 144 loyal Andonites to which Amadon belonged, and who have become known by his name. This group comprised thirty-nine men and one hundred and five women. Fifty-six of this number were of immortality status, and all (except Amadon) were translated along with the loyal members of the staff. The remainder of this noble band continued on earth to the end of their mortal days under the leadership of Van and Amadon. They were the biologic leaven which multiplied and continued to furnish leadership for the world down through the long dark ages of the post-rebellion era." P. 759.

8. **The hero of the Lucifer rebellion.**

"The Lucifer rebellion was withstood by many courageous beings on the various worlds of Satania; but the records of Salvington portray Amadon as the outstanding character of the entire system in his glorious rejection of the flood tides of sedition and in his unswerving devotion to Van—they stood together unmoved in their loyalty to the supremacy of the invisible Father and his Son Michael." P. 761.

"Amadon is the outstanding human hero of the Lucifer rebellion. This male descendant of Andon and Fonta was one of the one hundred who contributed life plasm to the Prince's staff, and ever since that event he had been attached to Van as his associate and human assistant. Amadon elected to stand with his chief throughout the long and trying struggle. And it was an inspiring sight to behold this child of the evolutionary races standing unmoved by the sophistries of Daligastia while throughout the seven-year struggle he and his loyal associates resisted with unyielding fortitude all of the deceptive teachings of the brilliant Caligastia." P. 757.

"From Edentia up through Salvington and even on to Uversa, for seven long years the first inquiry of all subordinate celestial life regarding the Satania rebellion, ever and always, was: 'What of Amadon of Urantia, does he still stand unmoved?'" P. 762.

9. **Michael terminates Lucifer rebellion.**

"The bestowal of Michael terminated the Lucifer rebellion in all Satania aside from the planets of the apostate Planetary Princes. And this was the significance of Jesus' personal experience, just before his death in the flesh, when he one day exclaimed to his disciples, 'And I beheld Satan fall as lightning from heaven.' He had come with Lucifer to Urantia for the last crucial struggle." P. 609. Luke 10:18.

10. **Relation of evil and sin.**

"Since the triumph of Christ, all Norlatiadek is being cleansed of sin and rebels. Sometime before Michael's death in the flesh the fallen Lucifer's associate, Satan, sought to attend such an Edentia conclave, but the solidification of sentiment againts the archrebels had reached the point where the doors of sympathy were so well-nigh universally closed that there could be found no standing ground for the Satania adversaries. When there exists no open door for the reception of evil, there exists no opportunity for the entertainment of sin. The doors of the hearts of all Edentia closed against Satan; he was unanimously rejected by the assembled System Sovereigns, and it was at this time that the Son of Man 'beheld Satan fall as lightning from heaven.'" P. 490.

VII. REMOTE REPERCUSSIONS OF SIN

1. **Impersonal consequences of sin may be collective.**

"The personal (centripetal) consequences of the creature's willful and persistent rejection of light are both inevitable and individual and are of concern only to Deity and to that personal creature. Such a soul-destroying harvest of iniquity is the inner reaping of the iniquitous will creature.

"But not so with the external repercussions of sin: The impersonal (centrifugal) consequences of embraced sin are both inevitable and collective, being of concern to every creature functioning within the affect-range of such events." P. 760-1.

2. **Effects of rebellion on Urantia's state.**

"By fifty thousand years after the collapse of the planetary adminis-tration, earthly affairs were so disorganized and retarded that the human race had gained very little over the general evolutionary status existing at the time of Caligastia's arrival three hundred and fifty thousand years previously. In certain respects progress had been made; in other directions much ground had been lost." P. 761.

3. **Spiritual and physical results of sin.**

"Sin is never purely local in its effects. The administrative sectors of the universes are organismal; the plight of one personality must to a certain extent be shared by all. Sin, being an attitude of the person toward reality, is destined to exhibit its inherent negativistic harvest upon any and all related levels of universe values. But the full consequences of erroneous thinking, evil-doing, or sinful planning are experienced only on the level of actual performance. The transgression of universe law may be fatal in the physical realm without seriously involving the mind or impairing the spiritual experience. Sin is fraught with fatal conse-quences to personality survival only when it is the attitude of the whole being, when it stands for the choosing of the mind and the willing of the soul." P. 761.

4. **Sin of another cannot rob you of survival.**

"Evil and sin visit their consequences in material and social realms and may sometimes even retard spiritual progress on certain levels of universe reality, but never does the sin of any being rob another of the realization of the divine right of personality survival. Eternal survival can be jeopardized only by the decisions of the mind and the choice of the soul of the individual himself." P. 761.

5. **What sin does and does not do.**

"Sin on Urantia did very little to delay biologic evolution, but it did operate to deprive the mortal races of the full benefit of the Adamic inheritance. Sin enormously retards intellectual development, moral growth, social progress, and mass spiritual attainment. But it does not prevent the highest spiritual achievement by any individual who chooses to know God and sincerely do his divine will." P. 761.

6. **Warnings against sin.**

"But for ages the seven prison worlds of spiritual darkness in Satania have constituted a solemn warning to all Nebadon, eloquently and effectively proclaiming the great truth 'that the way of the transgressor is hard'; 'that within every sin is concealed the seed of its own destruction'; that 'the wages of sin is death.'" P. 611-12. Prov. 13:15. Rom. 6:23.

VIII. LIBERTY—TRUE AND FALSE

1. **Foundations of true and false liberty.**

"Of all the perplexing problems growing out of the Lucifer rebellion, none has occasioned more difficulty than the failure of immature evolutionary mortals to distinguish between true and false liberty.

"True liberty is the quest of the ages and the reward of evolutionary progress. False liberty is the subtle deception of the error of time and the evil of space. Enduring liberty is predicated on the reality of justice—intelligence, maturity, fraternity, and equity." P. 613.

2. **Cosmic results of true and false liberty.**

"Liberty is a self-destroying technique of cosmic existence when its motivation is unintelligent, unconditioned, and uncontrolled. True liberty is progressively related to reality and is ever regardful of social equity, cosmic fairness, universe fraternity, and divine obligations.

"Liberty is suicidal when divorced from material justice, intellectual fairness, social forbearance, moral duty, and spiritual value. Liberty is nonexistent apart from cosmic reality, and all personality reality is proportional to its divinity relationships." P. 613.

3. **Self-motivated license equals bondage.**

"Unbridled self-will and unregulated self-expression equal unmitigated selfishness, the acme of ungodliness. Liberty without the associated and ever-increasing conquest of self is a figment of egoistic mortal imagination. Self-motivated liberty is a conceptual illusion, a cruel deception. License masquerading in the garments of liberty is the forerunner of abject bondage." P. 613.

4. **The fallacy of false liberty.**

"The Caligastia scheme for the immediate reconstruction of human society in accordance with his ideas of individual freedom and group liberties, proved a swift and more or less complete failure.

Society quickly sank back to its old biologic level, and the forward struggle began all over, starting not very far in advance of where it was at the beginning of the Caligastia regime, this upheaval having left the world in confusion worse confounded." P. 759.

5. Liberty without license.

"Someday man should learn how to enjoy liberty without license, nourishment without gluttony, and pleasure without debauchery. Self-control is a better human policy of behavior regulation than is extreme self-denial. Nor did Jesus ever teach these unreasonable views to his followers." P. 977.

IX. GUILT—SECURITY AGAINST SIN

1. The nature of the guilt feeling.

"The sense of guilt (not the consciousness of sin) comes either from interrupted spiritual communion or from the lowering of one's moral ideals. Deliverance from such a predicament can only come through the realization that one's highest moral ideals are not necessarily synonymous with the will of God. Man cannot hope to live up to his highest ideals, but he can be true to his purpose of finding God and becoming more and more like him." P. 1133.

2. Jesus destroyed the basis of guilt.

"Jesus swept away all of the ceremonials of sacrifice and atonement. He destroyed the basis of all this fictitious guilt and sense of isolation in the universe by declaring that man is a child of God; the creature-Creator relationship was placed on a child-parent basis. God becomes a loving Father to his mortal sons and daughters. All ceremonials not a legitimate part of such an intimate family relationship are forever abrogated." P. 1133.

3. Human mind secure against Satanic invasion.

"But even so, no fallen spirit ever did have the power to invade the minds or to harass the souls of the children of God. Neither Satan nor Caligastia could ever touch or approach the faith sons of God; faith is an effective armor against sin and iniquity. It is true: 'He who is born of God keeps himself, and the wicked one touches him not.'" P. 610. 1 John 5:18.

4. Ascendant experience security against sin.

"It was over two years of system time from the beginning of the 'war in heaven' until the installation of Lucifer's successor. But at last the new Sovereign came, landing on the sea of glass with his staff. I was among the reserves mobilized on Edentia by Gabriel, and I well remember the first message of Lanaforge to the Constellation Father of Norlatiadek. It read: 'Not a single Jerusem citizen was lost. Every ascendant mortal survived the fiery trial and emerged from the crucial test triumphant and altogether victorious.' And on to Salvington, Uversa, and Paradise went this message of assurance that the survival experience of mortal ascension is the greatest security against rebellion and the surest safeguard against sin. This noble Jerusem band of faithful mortals numbered just 187,432,811." P. 608-9.

5. **Origin and nature of guilt feelings.**

"The sense or feeling of guilt is the consciousness of the violation of the mores; it is not necessarily sin. There is no real sin in the absence of conscious disloyalty to Deity.

"The possibility of the recognition of the sense of guilt is a badge of transcendent distinction for mankind. It does not mark man as mean but rather sets him apart as a creature of potential greatness and ever-ascending glory. Such a sense of unworthiness is the initial stimulus that should lead quickly and surely to those faith conquests which translate the mortal mind to the superb levels of moral nobility, cosmic insight, and spiritual living; thus are all the meanings of human existence changed from the temporal to the eternal, and all values are elevated from the human to the divine." P. 984.

X. FORGIVENESS OF SIN

1. **Ancient man gained peace by sacrifice.**

"Ancient man only attained consciousness of favor with God through sacrifice. Modern man must develop new techniques of achieving the self-consciousness of salvation. The consciousness of sin persists in the mortal mind, but the thought patterns of salvation therefrom have become outworn and antiquated. The reality of the spiritual need persists, but intellectual progress has destroyed the olden ways of securing peace and consolation for mind and soul." P. 984.

2. **The confession of sin.**

"The confession of sin is a manful repudiation of disloyalty, but it in no wise mitigates the time-space consequences of such disloyalty. But confession—sincere recognition of the nature of sin—is essential to religious growth and spiritual progress." P. 984.

3. About receiving forgiveness.

"The forgiveness of sin by Deity is the renewal of loyalty relations following a period of the human consciousness of the lapse of such relations as the consequence of conscious rebellion. The forgiveness does not have to be sought, only received as the consciousness of re-establishment of loyalty relations between the creature and the Creator. And all the loyal sons of God are happy, service-loving, and ever-progressive in the Paradise ascent." P. 985.

4. Evil, guilt, and forgiveness.

"Said Jesus: 'My disciples must not only cease to do evil but learn to do well; you must not only be cleansed from all conscious sin, but you must refuse to harbor even the feelings of guilt. If you confess your sins, they are forgiven; therefore must you maintain a conscience void of offense.'" P. 1736. 1 Peter 3:11. Rom. 12:21.

5. Unforgivable sins.

"'Say what you will about the Son of Man, and it shall be forgiven you; but he who presumes to blaspheme against God shall hardly find forgiveness. When men go so far as knowingly to ascribe the doings of God to the forces of evil, such deliberate rebels will hardly seek forgiveness for their sins.'" P. 1820. Matt. 12:31.

6. Sin of blasphemy against God.

"Then said Jesus: 'How can Satan cast out Satan? A kingdom divided against itself cannot stand; if a house be divided against itself, it is soon brought to desolation. Can a city withstand a siege if it is not united? If Satan casts out Satan, he is divided against himself; how then shall his kingdom stand? But you should know that no one can enter into the house of a strong man and despoil his goods except he first overpower and bind that strong man. And so, if I by the power of Beelzebub cast out devils, by whom do your sons cast them out? Therefore shall they be your judges. But if I, by the spirit of God, cast out devils, then has the kingdom of God truly come upon you. If you were not blinded by prejudice and misled by fear and pride, you would easily perceive that one who is greater than devils stands in your midst. You compel me to declare that he who is not with me is against me, while he who gathers not with me scatters abroad. Let me utter a solemn warning to you who would presume, with your eyes open and with premeditated malice, knowingly to ascribe the works of God to the doings of devils! Verily, verily, I say to you, all your sins shall be forgiven, even all of your blasphemies, but whosoever shall blaspheme against God with deliberation and wicked intention shall never obtain forgiveness. Since such persistent workers of iniquity will never seek nor receive forgiveness, they are guilty of the sin of eternally rejecting divine forgiveness.'" P. 1714. Luke 11:17-18.

XI. INTERVAL BETWEEN SIN AND THE PENALTY

1. **Saving interval between sin and penalty.**

"Although conscious and wholehearted identification with evil (sin) is the equivalent of nonexistence (annihilation), there must always intervene between the time of such personal identification with sin and the execution of the penalty—the automatic result of such a willful embrace of evil—a period of time of sufficient length to allow for such an adjudication of such an individual's universe status as will prove entirely satisfactory to all related universe personalities, and which will be so fair and just as to win the approval of the sinner himself." P. 615.

2. **The wisdom of delay.**

"Of the many reasons known to me as to why Lucifer and his confederates were not sooner interned or adjudicated, I am permitted to recite the following:

"1. Mercy requires that every wrongdoer have sufficient time in which to formulate a deliberate and fully chosen attitude regarding his evil thoughts and sinful acts.

"2. Supreme justice is dominated by a Father's love; therefore will justice never destroy that which mercy can save. Time to accept salvation is vouchsafed every evildoer.

"3. No affectionate father is ever precipitate in visiting punishment upon an erring member of his family. Patience cannot function independently of time.

"4. While wrongdoing is always deleterious to a family, wisdom and love admonish the upright children to bear with an erring brother during the time granted by the affectionate father in which the sinner may see the error of his way and embrace salvation.

"5. Regardless of Michael's attitude toward Lucifer, notwithstanding his being Lucifer's Creator-father, it was not in the province of the Creator Son to exercise summary jurisdiction over the apostate System Sovereign because he had not then completed his bestowal career, thereby attaining unqualified sovereignty of Nebadon.

"6. The Ancients of Days could have immediately annihilated these rebels, but they seldom execute wrongdoers without a full hearing. In this instance they refused to overrule the Michael decisions.

"7. It is evident that Immanuel counseled Michael to remain aloof from the rebels and allow rebellion to pursue a natural course of self-obliteration. And the wisdom of the Union of Days is the time reflection of the united wisdom of the Paradise Trinity.

"8. The Faithful of Days on Edentia advised the Constellation Fathers to allow the rebels free course to the end that all sympathy for these evildoers should be the sooner uprooted in the hearts of every present and future citizen of Norlatiadek— every mortal, morontia, or spirit creature.

"9. On Jerusem the personal representative of the Supreme Executive of Orvonton counseled Gabriel to foster full opportunity for every living creature to mature a deliberate choice in those matters involved in the Lucifer Declaration of Liberty. The issues of rebellion having been raised, the Paradise emergency adviser of Gabriel portrayed that, if such full and free opportunity were not given all Norlatiadek creatures, then would the Paradise quarantine against all such possible halfhearted or doubt-stricken creatures be extended in self-protection against the entire constellation. To keep open the Paradise doors of ascension to the beings of Norlatiadek, it was necessary to provide for the full development of rebellion and to insure the complete determination of attitude on the part of all beings in any way concerned therewith.

"10. The Divine Minister of Salvington issued as her third independent proclamation a mandate directing that nothing be done to half cure, cowardly suppress, or otherwise hide the hideous visage of rebels and rebellion. The angelic hosts were directed to work for full disclosure and unlimited opportunity for sin-expression as the quickest technique of achieving the perfect and final cure of the plague of evil and sin.

"11. An emergency council of ex-mortals consisting of Mighty Messengers, glorified mortals who had had personal experience with like situations, together with their colleagues, was organized on Jerusem. They advised Gabriel that at least three times the number of beings would be led astray if arbitary or summary methods of suppression were attempted. The entire

Uversa corps of counselors concurred in advising Gabriel to permit the rebellion to take its full and natural course; even if it should require a million years to wind up the consequences.

"12. Time, even in a universe of time, is relative: If a Urantia mortal of average length of life should commit a crime which precipitated world-wide pandemonium, and if he were apprehended, tried, and executed within two or three days of the commission of the crime, would it seem a long time to you? And yet that would be nearer a comparison with the length of Lucifer's life even if his adjudication, now begun, should not be completed for a hundred thousand Urantia years. The relative lapse of time from the viewpoint of Uversa, where the litigation is pending, could be indicated by saying that the crime of Lucifer was being brought to trial within two and a half seconds of its commission. From the Paradise viewpoint the adjudication is simultaneous with the enactment." P. 617-18.

XII. ORIGINAL SIN

1. Original sin—racial guilt.

"Primitive man regarded himself as being in debt to the spirits, as standing in need of redemption. As the savages looked at it, in justice the spirits might have visited much more bad luck upon them. As time passed, this concept developed into the doctrine of sin and salvation. The soul was looked upon as coming into the world under forfeit—original sin. The soul must be ransomed; a scapegoat must be provided. The head-hunter, in addition to practicing the cult of skull worship, was able to provide a substitute for his own life, a scapeman." P. 974.

2. Doctrine of total depravity.

"The doctrine of the total depravity of man destroyed much of the potential of religion for effecting social repercussions of an uplifting nature and of inspirational value. Jesus sought to restore man's dignity when he declared that all men are the children of God." P. 1091.

3. Personal and racial concepts of sin.

"*Sin—punishment for taboo violation.* In comparatively recent times it has been believed that sickness is a punishment for sin, personal or racial. Among peoples traversing this level of evolution the prevailing theory is that one cannot be afflicted unless one has violated a taboo. To regard sickness and suffering as 'arrows of the

Almighty within them' is typical of such beliefs. The Chinese and
Mesopotamians long regarded disease as the result of the action of
evil demons, although the Chaldeans also looked upon the stars as
the cause of suffering. This theory of disease as a consequence of
divine wrath is still prevalent among many reputedly civilized
groups of Urantians." P. 990.

4. **Personal and group sins.**

"'No more should you fear that God will punish a nation for the sin
of an individual; neither will the Father in heaven punish one of his
believing children for the sins of a nation, albeit the individual
member of any family must often suffer the material consequences
of family mistakes and group transgressions. Do you not realize that
the hope of a better nation—or a better world—is bound up in the
progress and enlightenment of the individual?'" P. 1630.

5. **Salvation not jeopardized by another's sin.**

"But one thing should be made clear: If you are made to suffer the evil
consequences of the sin of some member of your family, some fellow
citizen or fellow mortal, even rebellion in the system or elsewhere—
no matter what you may have to endure because of the wrongdoing of
your associates, fellows, or superiors—you may rest secure in the
eternal assurance that such tribulations are transient afflictions. None
of these fraternal consequences of misbehavior in the group can ever
jeopardize your eternal prospects or in the least degree deprive you of
your divine right of Paradise ascension and God attainment." P. 619.

XIII. JESUS TALKS ABOUT GOOD AND EVIL

1. **Answering Gadiah's question about good and evil.**

"Jesus' last visit with Gadiah had to do with a discussion of good and
evil. This young Philistine was much troubled by a feeling of
injustice because of the presence of evil in the world alongside the
good. He said: 'How can God, if he is infinitely good, permit us to
suffer the sorrows of evil; after all, who creates evil?' It was still
believed by many in those days that God creates both good and evil,
but Jesus never taught such error. In answering this question, Jesus
said: 'My brother, God is love; therefore he must be good, and his
goodness is so great and real that it cannot contain the small and
unreal things of evil. God is so positively good that there is absolutely no place in him for negative evil. Evil is the immature
choosing and the unthinking misstep of those who are resistant to

goodness, rejectful of beauty, and disloyal to truth. Evil is only the misadaptation of immaturity or the disruptive and distorting influence of ignorance. Evil is the inevitable darkness which follows upon the heels of the unwise rejection of light. Evil is that which is dark and untrue, and which, when consciously embraced and willfully endorsed, becomes sin.

"'Your Father in heaven, by endowing you with the power to choose between truth and error, created the potential negative of the positive way of light and life; but such errors of evil are really nonexistent until such a time as an intelligent creature wills their existence by mischoosing the way of life. And then are such evils later exalted into sin by the knowing and deliberate circuits of such a willful and rebellious creature. This is why our Father in heaven permits the good and the evil to go along together until the end of life, just as nature allows the wheat and the tares to grow side by side until the harvest.' Gadiah was fully satisfied with Jesus' answer to his question after their subsequent discussion had made clear to his mind the real meaning of these momentous statements." P. 1429. Matt. 13:30.

2. Jesus talks about error and evil.

"Error (evil) is the penalty of imperfection. The qualities of imperfection or facts of misadaptation are disclosed on the material level by critical observation and by scientific analysis; on the moral level, by human experience. The presense of evil constitutes proof of the inaccuracies of mind and the immaturity of the evolving self. Evil is, therefore, also a measure of imperfection in universe interpretation. The possibility of making mistakes is inherent in the acquisition of wisdom, the scheme of progressing from the partial and temporal to the complete and eternal, from the relative and imperfect to the final and perfected. Error is the shadow of relative imcompleteness which must of necessity fall across man's ascending universe path to Paradise perfection. Error (evil) is not an actual universe quality; it is simply the observation of a relativity in the relatedness of the imperfection of the incomplete finite to the ascending levels of the Supreme and Ultimate.

"Although Jesus told all this to the lad in language best suited to his comprehension, at the end of the discussion Ganid was heavy of eye and was soon lost in slumber. They rose early the next morning to go aboard the boat bound for Lasea on the Island of Crete. But before they embarked, the lad had still further questions to ask about evil, to which Jesus replied:

"Evil is a relativity concept. It arises out of the observation of the imperfections which appear in the shadow cast by a finite universe of things and beings as such a cosmos obscures the living light of the universal expression of the eternal realities of the Infinite One.

"Potential evil is inherent in the necessary incompleteness of the revelation of God as a time-space limited expression of infinity and eternity. The fact of the partial in the presence of the complete constitutes relativity of reality, creates necessity for intellectual choosing, and establishes value levels of spirit recognition and response. The incomplete and finite concept of the infinite which is held by the temporal and limited creature mind is, in and of itself, *potential evil*. But the augmenting error of unjustified deficiency in reasonable spiritual rectification of these originally inherent intellectual disharmonies and spiritual insufficiencies, is equivalent to the realization of *actual evil*.

"All static, dead, concepts are potentially evil. The finite shadow of relative and living truth is continually moving. Static concepts invariably retard science, politics, society, and religion. Static concepts may represent a certain knowledge, but they are deficient in wisdom and devoid of truth. But do not permit the concept of relativity so to mislead you that you fail to recognize the co-ordination of the universe under the guidance of the cosmic mind, and its stabilized control by the energy and spirit of the Supreme." P. 1435-6.

3.   Jesus talks to Mardus about good and evil.

"Mardus was the acknowledged leader of the Cynics of Rome, and he became a great friend of the scribe of Damascus. Day after day he conversed with Jesus, and night upon night he listened to his supernal teaching. Among the more important discussions with Mardus was the one designed to answer this sincere Cynic's question about good and evil. In substance, and in twentieth-century phraseology, Jesus said:

"My brother, good and evil are merely words symbolizing relative levels of human comprehension of the observable universe. If you are ethically lazy and socially indifferent, you can take as your standard of good the current social usages. If you are spiritually indolent and morally unprogressive, you may take as your standards of good the religious practices and traditions of your contemporaries.

But the soul that survives time and emerges into eternity must make a living and personal choice between good and evil as they are determined by the true values of the spiritual standards established by the divine spirit which the Father in heaven has sent to dwell within the heart of man. This indwelling spirit is the standard of personality survival.

"Goodness, like truth, is always relative and unfailingly evil-contrasted. It is the perception of these qualities of goodness and truth that enables the evolving souls of men to make those personal decisions of choice which are essential to eternal survival." P. 1457-8.

"As you ascend the universe scale of creature development, you will find increasing goodness and diminishing evil in perfect accordance with your capacity for goodness-experience and truth-discernment. The ability to entertain error or experience evil will not be fully lost until the ascending human soul achieves final spirit levels." P. 1458.

"Until you attain Paradise levels, goodness will always be more of a quest than a possession, more of a goal than an experience of attainment. But even as you hunger and thirst for righteousness, you experience increasing satisfaction in the partial attainment of goodness. The presence of goodness and evil in the world is in itself positive proof of the existence and reality of man's moral will, the personality, which thus identifies these values and is also able to choose between them." P. 1458.

"The *possibility* of evil is necessary to moral choosing, but not the actuality thereof. A shadow is only relatively real. Actual evil is not necessary as a personal experience. Potential evil acts equally well as a decision stimulus in the realms of moral progress on the lower levels of spiritual development. Evil becomes a reality of personal experience only when a moral mind makes evil its choice." P. 1458.

4.   **Jesus talks to Thomas about evil and sin.**

"Do not make the mistake of confusing *evil* with the *evil one*, more correctly the *iniquitous one*. He whom you call the evil one is the son of self-love, the high administrator who knowingly went into deliber- ate rebellion against the rule of my Father and his loyal Sons. But I have already vanquished these sinful rebels. Make clear in your mind these different attitudes toward the Father and his universe. Never forget these laws of relation to the Father's will:

"'Evil is the unconscious or unintended transgression of the divine law, the Father's will. Evil is likewise the measure of the imperfectness of obedience to the Father's will.

"'Sin is the conscious, knowing, and deliberate transgression of the divine law, the Father's will. Sin is the measure of unwillingness to be divinely led and spiritually directed.

"'Iniquity is the willful, determined, and persistent transgression of the divine law, the Father's will. Iniquity is the measure of the continued rejection of the Father's loving plan of personality survival and the Sons' merciful ministry of salvation.

"'By nature, before the rebirth of the spirit, mortal man is subject to inherent evil tendencies, but such natural imperfections of behavior are neither sin nor iniquity. Mortal man is just beginning his long ascent to the perfection of the Father in Paradise. To be imperfect or partial in natural endowment is not sinful. Man is indeed subject to evil, but he is in no sense the child of the evil one unless he has knowingly and deliberately chosen the paths of sin and the life of iniquity. Evil is inherent in the natural order of this world, but sin is an attitude of conscious rebellion which was brought to this world by those who fell from spiritual light into gross darkness.

"'You are confused, Thomas, by the doctrines of the Greeks and the errors of the Persians. You do not understand the relationships of evil and sin because you view mankind as beginning on earth with a perfect Adam and rapidly degenerating, through sin, to man's present deplorable estate. But why do you refuse to comprehend the meaning of the record which discloses how Cain, the son of Adam, went over into the land of Nod and there got himself a wife? And why do you refuse to interpret the meaning of the record which portrays the sons of God finding wives for themselves among the daughters of men?

"'Men are, indeed, by nature evil, but not necessarily sinful. The new birth—the baptism of the spirit—is essential to deliverance from evil and necessary for entrance into the kingdom of heaven, but none of this detracts from the fact that man is the son of God. Neither does this inherent presence of potential evil mean that man is in some mysterious way estranged from the Father in heaven so that, as an alien, foreigner, or stepchild, he must in some manner seek for legal adoption by the Father.

TOPICAL STUDIES IN *THE URANTIA BOOK*

All such notions are born, first, of your misunderstanding of the Father and, second, of your ignorance of the origin, nature, and destiny of man.'" P. 1660.

"'Thomas, have you not read about this in the Scriptures, where it is written: "You are the children of the Lord your God." "I will be his Father and he shall be my son." "I have chosen him to be my son—I will be his Father." "Bring my sons from far and my daughters from the ends of the earth; even every one who is called by my name, for I have created them for my glory." "You are the sons of the living God." "They who have the spirit of God are indeed the sons of God." While there is a material part of the human father in the natural child, there is a spiritual part of the heavenly Father in every faith son of the kingdom.'" P. 1661. Gen. 4:16. 1 Chron. 28:6. 1 Chron. 17:13. Isa. 43:6-7. Hosea 1:10. Rom. 8:14.

17. THE HOLY SPIRIT

    I. THE HOLY SPIRIT IN A LOCAL UNIVERSE.
   II. WORK OF THE HOLY SPIRIT.
 III. HOLY SPIRIT'S INFLUENCE ON PERSONALITY.
 IV. RELATION OF HOLY SPIRIT TO ALL OTHER SPIRITS.

Holy Spirit in the Bible

     I. SPIRIT CREATIVE FUNCTIONS.
    II. IMPARTING INTELLIGENCE AND ABILITY.
   III. SPIRITUAL ENDOWMENT.
   IV. THE DIVINE PRESENCE.
    V. POURED OUT UPON ALL FLESH.
   VI. MAN'S ATTITUDE TOWARD THE SPIRIT.
  VII. AS A PENTECOSTAL EXPERIENCE.
  VII. SPIRIT OF THE THIRD PERSON OF THE TRINITY.

THE HOLY SPIRIT

I. THE HOLY SPIRIT IN A LOCAL UNIVERSE

1. **The Mother Spirit is confined to the local universe.**

   "The Universe Mother Spirit, however, never leaves the local universe headquarters world. The spirit of the Creator Son may and does function independently of the personal presence of the Son, but not so with her personal spirit. The Holy Spirit of the Divine Minister would become nonfunctional if her personal presence should be removed from Salvington. Her spirit presence seems to be fixed on the universe headquarters world, and it is this very fact that enables the spirit of the Creator Son to function independently of the whereabouts of the Son. The Universe Mother Spirit acts as the universe focus and center of the Spirit of Truth as well as of her own personal influence, the Holy Spirit." P. 378.

2. **Holy Spirit's work in the local universe.**

   "So it is with mortal man: The Mother Spirit of Salvington knows you fully, for the Holy Spirit on your world 'searches all things,' and whatsoever the divine Spirit knows of you is immediately available whenever the secoraphic discerners reflect with the Spirit concerning the Spirit's knowledge of you. It should, however, be mentioned that the knowledge and plans of the Father fragments are not reflectible. The discerners can and do reflect the presence of the Adjusters (and the Censors pronounce them divine), but they cannot decipher the content of the mindedness of the Mystery Monitors." P. 313. 1. Cor. 2:10.

3. **The Divine Minister acting for the Creator Son.**

   "When a Michael Son is absent from his universe, its government is directed by the first-born native being, the Bright and Morning Star, the local universe chief executive. The advice and counsel of the Union of Days is invaluable at such times. During these absences a Creator Son is able to invest the associated Mother Spirit with the overcontrol of his spiritual presence on the inhabited worlds and in the hearts of his mortal children. And the Mother Spirit of a local universe remains always at its headquarters, extending her fostering care and spiritual ministry to the uttermost parts of such an evolutionary domain." P. 237.

4. **Local universe spirit circuits.**

   "There are three distinct spirit circuits in the local universe of Nebadon:

"1. The bestowal spirit of the Creator Son, the Comforter, the Spirit of Truth.

"2. The spirit circuit of the Divine Minister, the Holy Spirit.

"3. The intelligence-ministry circuit, including the more or less unified activities but diverse functioning of the seven adjutant mind-spirits." P. 377.

II. WORK OF THE HOLY SPIRIT

1. **A source of continual spiritual strength.**

    "The divine Spirit is the source of continual ministry and encouragement to the children of man. Your power and achievement is 'according to his mercy, through the renewing of the Spirit.' Spiritual life, like physical energy, is consumed. Spiritual effort results in relative spiritual exhaustion. The whole ascendant experience is real as well as spiritual; therefore, it is truly written, 'It is the Spirit that quickens.' 'The Spirit gives life.'" P. 380. Titus 3:5. John 6:63. 2 Cor. 3:6.

2. **The Spirit imparts life to doctrine.**

    "The dead theory of even the highest religious doctrines is powerless to transform human character or to control mortal behaviour. What the world of today needs is the truth which your teacher of old declared: 'Not in word only but also in power and in the Holy Spirit.' The seed of theoretical truth is dead, the highest moral concepts without effect, unless and until the divine Spirit breathes upon the forms of truth and quickens the formulas of righteousness." P. 380. 1 Cor. 4:20.

3. **"You are the temple of God."**

    "Those who have received and recognized the indwelling of God have been born of the Spirit. 'You are the temple of God, and the spirit of God dwells in you.' It is not enough that this spirit be poured out upon you; the divine Spirit must dominate and control every phase of human experience." P. 381. 1 Cor. 3:16-17.

4. **Holy Spirit as the "water of life."**

    "It is the presence of the divine Spirit, the water of life, that prevents the consuming thirst of mortal discontent and that indescribable hunger of the unspiritualized human mind. Spirit-motivated beings 'never thirst, for this spiritual water shall be in them a well of satisfaction springing up into life everlasting.' Such divinely watered souls are all but independent of material environment as regards the joys of living and the satisfactions of earthly existence. They are spiritually illuminated and refreshed, morally strengthened and endowed." P. 381. John 4:14.

5. **Ministration to man's spiritual nature.**

"In every mortal there exists a dual nature: the inheritance of animal tendencies and the high urge of spirit endowment. During the short life you live on Urantia, these two diverse and opposing urges can seldom be fully reconciled; they can hardly be harmonized and unified; but throughout your lifetime the combined Spirit ever ministers to assist you in subjecting the flesh more and more to the leading of the Spirit. Even though you must live your material life through, even though you cannot escape the body and its necessities, nonetheless, in purpose and ideals you are empowered increasingly to subject the animal nature to the mastery of the Spirit. There truly exists within you a conspiracy of spiritual forces, a confederation of divine powers, whose exclusive purpose is to effect your final deliverance from material bondage and finite handicaps.

"The purpose of all this ministration is, 'That you may be strengthened with power through His spirit in the inner man.' And all this represents but the preliminary steps to the final attainment of the perfection of faith and service, that experience wherein you shall be 'filled with all the fullness of God,' 'for all those who are led by the spirit of God are the sons of God.'" P. 381. Eph. 3:19. Rom. 8:14.

6. **The Spirit leads—never drives.**

"The Spirit never *drives*, only leads. If you are a willing learner, if you want to attain spirit levels and reach divine heights, if you sincerely desire to reach the eternal goal, then the divine Spirit will gently and lovingly lead you along the pathway of sonship and spiritual progress. Every step you take must be one of willingness, intelligent and cheerful co-operation. The domination of the Spirit is never tainted with coercion nor compromised by compulsion.

"And when such a life of spirit guidance is freely and intelligently accepted, there gradually develops within the human mind a positive consciousness of divine contact and assurance of spirit communion; sooner or later 'the Spirit bears witness with your spirit (the Adjuster) that you are a child of God.' Already has your own Thought Adjuster told you of your kinship to God so that the record testifies that the Spirit bears witness '*with* your spirit,' not *to* your spirit." P. 381. Rom. 8:16.

7.   The fruits of the spirit are joy and peace.

"The consciousness of the spirit domination of a human life is presently attended by an increasing exhibition of the characteristics of the Spirit in the life reactions of such a spirit-led mortal, 'for the fruits of the spirit are love, joy, peace, long-suffering, gentleness, goodness, faith, meekness, and temperance.' Such spirit-guided and divinely illuminated mortals, while they yet tread the lowly paths of toil and in human faithfulness perform the duties of their earthly assignments, have already begun to discern the lights of eternal life as they glimmer on the faraway shores of another world; already have they begun to comprehend the reality of that inspiring and comforting truth, 'The kingdom of God is not meat and drink but righteousness, peace, and joy in the Holy Spirit.' And throughout every trial and in the presence of every hardship, spirit-born souls are sustained by that hope which. transcends all fear because the love of God is shed abroad in all hearts by the presence of the divine Spirit." P. 381-2. Gal. 5:22. Rom. 14:17.

III. HOLY SPIRIT'S INFLUENCE ON PERSONALITY

1.   Influence of Holy Spirit on personality.

"Revelation as an epochal phenomenon is periodic; as a personal human experience it is continuous. Divinity functions in mortal personality as the Adjuster gift of the Father, as the Spirit of Truth of the Son, and as the Holy Spirit of the Universe Spirit, while these three supermortal endowments are unified in human experiential evolution as the ministry of the Supreme." P. 1107.

2.   Holy Spirit imparts soul intelligence.

"Faith-insight, or spiritual intuition, is the endowment of the cosmic mind in association with the Thought Adjuster, which is the Father's gift to man. Spiritual reason, soul intelligence, is the endowment of the Holy Spirit, the Creative Spirit's gift to man. Spiritual philosophy, the wisdom of spirit realities, is the endowment of the Spirit of Truth, the combined gift of the bestowal Sons to the children of men. And the co-ordination and interassociation of these spirit endowments constitute man a spirit personality in potential destiny." P. 1108.

IV. RELATION OF HOLY SPIRIT TO OTHER SPIRITS

1.   Holy Spirit and the adjutant mind-spirits.

"Man possessed a religion of natural origin as a part of his evolutionary experience long before any systematic revelations were made on Urantia. But this religion of *natural* origin was, in itself, the product of man's superanimal endowments. Evolutionary religion arose slowly throughout the millenniums of mankind's experiential career through the ministry of the following influences operating within, and impinging upon, savage, barbarian, and civilized man:

"1. *The adjutant of worship*—the appearance in animal consciousness of superanimal potentials for reality perception. This might be termed the primordial human instinct for Deity.

"2. *The adjutant of wisdom*—the manifestation in a worshipful mind of the tendency to direct its adoration in higher channels of expression and toward ever-expanding concepts of Deity reality.

"3. *The Holy Spirit*—this is the initial supermind bestowal, and it unfailingly appears in all bona fide human personalities. This ministry to a worship-craving and wisdom-desiring mind creates the capacity to self-realize the postulate of human survival, both in theologic concept and as an actual and factual personality experience." P. 1003.

2.   Holy Spirit's preparation for Adjusters.

"When mind is thus endowed with the ministry of the Holy Spirit, it possesses the capacity for (consciously or unconsciously) choosing the spiritual presence of the Universal Father—the Thought Adjuster. But it is not until a bestowal Son has liberated the Spirit of Truth for planetary ministry to all mortals that all normal minds are automatically prepared for the reception of the Thought Adjusters. The Spirit of Truth works as one with the presence of the spirit of the Divine Minister. This dual spirit liaison hovers over the worlds, seeking to teach truth and to spiritually enlighten the minds of men, to inspire the souls of the creatures of the ascending races, and to lead the peoples dwelling on the evolutionary planets ever towards their Paradise goal of divine destiny." P. 379.

3.   Relation to all other Spirits.

"The presence of the Holy Spirit of the Universe Daughter of the Infinite Spirit, of the Spirit of Truth of the Universe. Son of the Eternal Son, and of the Adjuster-spirit of the Paradise Father in or with an evolutionary mortal, denotes symmetry of spiritual endowment and ministry and qualifies such a mortal consciously to realize the faith-fact of sonship with God." P. 380.

HOLY SPIRIT IN THE BIBLE

Holy Spirit, Holy Ghost, and the Spirit of God are used somewhat interchangeably in the Bible. These designations cover the references in *The Urantia Book* of the following different Spirit realities:

1. Personality circuit of the Universal Father.

2. The spirit circuit of the Eternal Son.

3. The omnipresence of the Infinite Spirit.

4. The Thought Adjuster bestowals of the Father.

5. The Holy Spirit presence of the local universe Mother Spirit.

7. The Spirit of Truth.

8. The seven adjutant mind-spirits of the local universe mind endowment.

I. SPIRIT CREATIVE FUNCTIONS

"And the Spirit of God was moving over the face of the waters." **Gen. 1:2**.

"When thou sendest forth thy spirit, they are created; and thou renewest the face of the ground." **Ps. 104:30**.

"The spirit of God has made me, and the breath of the Almighty gives me life." **Job. 33:4**.

II. IMPARTING INTELLIGENCE AND ABILITY

"And he has filled him with the Spirit of God, with ability, with intelligence, with knowledge, and with all craftsmanship." **Ex. 35:31**.

"Thou gavest thy good Spirit to instruct them." **Neh. 9:20**.

"But it is the spirit in a man, the breath of the Almighty, that makes him understand." **Job. 32:8**.

"But the Counselor, the Holy Spirit, whom the Father will send in my name, he will teach you all things." **John 14:26**.

III. SPIRITUAL ENDOWMENT

"The spirit of man is the lamp of the Lord, searching all his innermost parts." **Prov. 20:27**.

"And Peter said to them, 'Repent and be baptized…and you shall receive the gift of the Holy Spirit.'" **Acts 2:38**.

"Let thy good spirit lead me on a level path." **Ps. 143:10**.

"The spirit of the Lord speaks by me, his word is upon my tongue." **2 Sam. 23:2**.

"The spirit of the Lord God is upon me, because the Lord has anointed me." **Isa. 61:1**. *"But you shall receive power when the Holy Spirit has come upon you."* **Acts 1:8**.

"But as for me, I am filled with power, with the Spirit of the Lord." **Micah 3:8**.

IV. THE DIVINE PRESENCE

"For the Spirit searches everything, even the depths of God." **1 Cor. 2:10.**

"In him you also, who…were sealed with the promised Holy Spirit." **Eph. 1:13.**

"Whither shall I go from thy Spirit? Or whither shall I flee from thy presence?" **Ps. 139:7.**

"Create in me a clean heart, O God, and put a new and right spirit within me." **Ps. 51:10.**

V. POURED OUT UPON ALL FLESH

"I will pour out my spirit on all flesh." **Joel 2:28.**

"I will pour out my Spirit; and they shall prophesy." **Acts 2:18.**

"The Holy Spirit fell on all who heard the word." **Acts 10:44.**

VI. MAN'S ATTITUDE TOWARD THE SPIRIT

"Then he said to me, '…not by might, nor by power, but by my Spirit, says the Lord of hosts.'" **Zech. 4:6.**

"How much more will the heavenly Father give the Holy Spirit to those who ask him?" **Luke 11:13.**

"Do not grieve the Holy Spirit of God, in whom you were sealed for the day of redemption." **Eph. 4:30.**

"Do not quench the Spirit." **1 Thess. 5:19.**

"But they rebelled and grieved his Holy Spirit." **Isa. 63:10.**

"So that the offerings of the Gentiles may be acceptable, sanctified by the Holy Spirit." **Rom. 15:16.**

VII. AS A PENTECOSTAL EXPERIENCE

"And when Paul laid his hands upon them, the Holy Spirit came on them." **Acts 19:6.**

"And the Spirit is the witness, because the Spirit is the truth." **1 John 5:7.**

"And they were all filled with the Holy Spirit." **Acts 2:4.**

"And they were all filled with the Holy Spirit and spoke the word of God with boldness." **Acts 4:31.**

VIII. SPIRIT OF THE THIRD PERSON OF THE TRINITY

"Go therefore and make disciples of all nations, baptizing them in the name of the Father and of the Son and of the Holy Spirit." **Matt. 28:19.**

"But he who blasphemes against the Holy Spirit will not be forgiven." **Luke 12:10.**

"And Jesus returned in the power of the Spirit." **Luke 4:14.**

"Now the Lord is the Spirit, and where the Spirit of the Lord is, there is freedom." **2 Cor. 3:17.**

"And having received from the Father the promise of the Holy Spirit, he has poured out this which you see and hear." **Acts 2:33.**

"The grace of the Lord Jesus Christ and the love of God and the fellowship of the Holy Spirit be with you all." **2 Cor. 13:14.**

"And when Jesus was baptized...behold, the heavens were opened and he saw the Spirit of God descending like a dove, and alighting on him." **Matt. 3:16.**

18. THE SPIRIT OF TRUTH

    I.   THE PROMISED HELPER.

    II.   WORK OF THE SPIRIT OF TRUTH.

    III.   FUNCTIONS OF THE SPIRIT OF TRUTH.

    IV.   SPECIAL MINISTRY OF THE SPIRIT OF TRUTH.

    V.   BESTOWAL OF THE SPIRIT OF TRUTH.

    VI.   SIGNIFICANCE OF THE SPIRIT OF TRUTH.

    VII.   WHAT HAPPENED AT PENTECOST.

The Spirit of Truth in the Bible

    I.   JESUS PROMISES TO SEND THE SPIRIT OF TRUTH.

    II.   THE SPIRIT OF TRUTH COMES.

    III.   THE WORK OF THE SPIRIT OF TRUTH.

THE SPIRIT OF TRUTH

I. THE PROMISED HELPER

1. Jesus promises to send the new helper.

"Jesus continued to teach, saying: 'When I have gone to the Father, and after he has fully accepted the work I have done for you on earth, and after I have received the final sovereignty of my own domain, I shall say to my Father: Having left my children alone on earth, it is in accordance with my promise to send them another teacher. And when the Father shall approve, I will pour out the Spirit of Truth upon all flesh. Already is my Father's spirit in your hearts, and when this day shall come, you will also have me with you even as you now have the Father. This new gift is the spirit of living truth. The unbelievers will not at first listen to the teachings of this spirit, but the sons of light will all receive him gladly and with a whole heart. And you shall know this spirit when he comes even as you have known me, and you will receive this gift in your hearts, and he will abide with you. You thus perceive that I am not going to leave you without help and guidance. I will not leave you desolate. Today I can be with you only in person. In the times to come I will be with you and all other men who desire my presence, wherever you may be, and with each of you at the same time. Do you not discern that it is better for me to go away; that I leave you in the flesh so that I may the better and the more fully be with you in the spirit?'" P. 1948. Acts 2:17.

2. The new helper leads us into all truth.

"'In just a few hours the world will see me no more; but you will continue to know me in your hearts even until I send you this new teacher, the Spirit of Truth. As I have lived with you in person, then shall I live in you; I shall be one with your personal experience in the spirit kingdom. And when this has come to pass, you shall surely know that I am in the Father, and that, while your life is hid with the Father in me, I am also in you. I have loved the Father and have kept his word; you have loved me, and you will keep my word. As my Father has given me of his spirit, so will I give you of my spirit. And this Spirit of Truth which I will bestow upon you shall guide and comfort you and shall eventually lead you into all truth.'" P. 1948. John 16:13.

3. Helps us to remember what Jesus taught.

"'I am telling you these things while I am still with you that you may be the better prepared to endure those trials which are even now right upon us. And when this new day comes, you will be indwelt by the Son as well as by the Father. And these gifts of heaven will ever work the one with the other even as the Father and I have wrought on earth and before your very eyes as one person, the Son of Man. And this spirit friend will bring to your remembrance everything I have taught you.'" P. 1948.

4. The new helper is the "Spirit of Truth."

"The new helper which Jesus promised to send into the hearts of believers, to pour out upon all flesh, is the *Spirit of Truth*. This divine endowment is not the letter or law of truth, neither is it to function as the form or expression of truth. The new teacher is the *conviction of truth*, the consciousness and assurance of true meanings on real spirit levels. And this new teacher is the spirit of living and growing truth, expanding, unfolding, and adaptative truth." P. 1949.

5. The new helper vitalizes the golden rule.

"The golden rule, when divested of the superhuman insight of the Spirit of Truth, becomes nothing more than a rule of high ethical conduct. The golden rule, when literally interpreted, may become the instrument of great offense to one's fellows. Without a spiritual discernment of the golden rule of wisdom you might reason that, since you are desirous that all men speak the full and frank truth of their minds to you, you should therefore fully and frankly speak the full thought of your mind to your fellow beings. Such and unspiritual interpretation of the golden rule might result in untold unhappiness and no end of sorrow." P. 1949-50.

II. WORK OF THE SPIRIT OF TRUTH

1. Work of the Spirit of Truth.

"'Now that I am leaving you, seeing that the hour has come when I am about to go to the Father, I am surprised that none of you have asked me, Why do you leave us? Nevertheless, I know that you ask such questions in your hearts. I will speak to you plainly, as one friend to another. It is really profitable for you that I go away. If I go not away, the new teacher cannot come into your hearts. I must be divested of this mortal body and be restored to my place on high before I can send this spirit teacher to live in your souls and lead your spirits into the truth. And when my spirit comes to indwell you, he will illuminate the difference between sin and righteousness and will enable you to judge wisely in your hearts concerning them.'" P. 1951.

2. **Makes a reality of our sonship.**

"'While you cannot observe the divine spirit at work in your minds, there is a practical method of discovering the degree to which you have yielded the control of your soul powers to the teaching and guidance of this indwelling spirit of the heavenly Father, and that is the degree of your love for your fellow men. This spirit of the Father partakes of the love of the Father, and as it dominates man, it unfailingly leads in the directions of divine worship and loving regard for one's fellows. At first you believe that you are sons of God because my teaching has made you more conscious of the inner leadings of our Father's indwelling presence; but presently the Spirit of Truth shall be poured out upon all flesh, and it will live among men and teach all men, even as I now live among you and speak to you the words of truth. And this Spirit of Truth, speaking for the spiritual endowments of your souls, will help you to know that you are the sons of God. It will unfailingly bear witness with the Father's indwelling presence, your spirit, then dwelling in all men as it now dwells in some, telling you that you are in reality the sons of God.'" P. 1642.

3. **Draws truth seekers toward the Creator Son.**

"The Creator Sons are endowed with a spirit of universe presence in many ways analogous to that of the Seven Master Spirits of Paradise. This is the Spirit of Truth which is poured out upon a world by a bestowal Son after he receives spiritual title to such a sphere. This bestowed Comforter is the spiritual force which ever draws all truth seekers towards Him who is the personification of truth in the local universe. This spirit is an inherent endowment of the Creator Son, emerging from his divine nature just as the master circuits of the grand universe are derived from the personality presences of the Paradise Deities." P. 377.

4. **Mother Spirit universe focus of Spirit of Truth.**

"The Creator Son may come and go; his personal presence may be in the local universe or elsewhere; yet the Spirit of Truth functions undisturbed, for this divine presence, while derived from the personality of the Creator Son, is functionally centered in the person of the Divine Minister.

"The Universe Mother Spirit, however, never leaves the local universe headquarters world. The spirit of the Creator Son may and does function independently of the personal presence of the Son, but not so with her personal spirit. The Holy Spirit of the Divine Minister would become nonfunctional if her personal presence should be removed from Salvington. Her spirit presence seems to be fixed on the universe headquarters world, and it is this very fact that enables the spirit of the Creator Son to function independently of the where-abouts of the Son. The Universe Mother Spirit acts as the universe focus and center of the Spirit of Truth as well as of her own personal influence, the Holy Spirit." P. 377-8.

III. FUNCTIONS OF THE SPIRIT OF TRUTH

1. **Functions of the Spirit of Truth.**

"Though the Spirit of Truth is poured out upon all flesh, this spirit of the Son is almost wholly limited in function and power by man's personal reception of that which constitutes the sum and substance of the mission of the bestowal Son. The Holy Spirit is partly independent of human attitude and partially conditioned by the decisions and co-operation of the will of man. Nevertheless, the ministry of the Holy Spirit becomes increasingly effective in the sanctification and spiritualization of the inner life of those mortals who the more fully *obey* the divine leadings." P. 379.

2. **Transformation by the Spirit of Truth.**

"'By the old way you seek to suppress, obey, and conform to the rules of living; by the new way you are first *transformed* by the Spirit of Truth and thereby strengthened in your inner soul by the constant spiritual renewing of your mind, and so are you endowed with the power of the certain and joyous performance of the gracious, acceptable, and perfect will of God. Forget not—it is your personal faith in the exceedingly great and precious promises of God that ensures your becoming partakers of the divine nature. Thus by your faith and the spirit's transformation, you become in reality the temples of God, and his spirit actually dwells within you. If, then, the spirit dwells within you, you are no longer bondslaves of the flesh but free and liberated sons of the spirit. The new law of the spirit endows you with the liberty of self-mastery in place of the old law of the fear of self-bondage and the slavery of self-denial.'" P. 1609.

3. **Sure guidance of the Spirit of Truth.**

"Having started out on the way of life everlasting, having accepted the assignment and received your orders to advance, do not fear the dangers of human forgetfulness and mortal inconstancy, do not be troubled with doubts of failure or by perplexing confusion, do not falter and question your status and standing, for in every dark hour, at every crossroad in the forward struggle, the Spirit of Truth will always speak, saying, 'This is the way.'" P. 383.

IV. SPECIAL MINISTRY OF THE SPIRIT OF TRUTH

1. Spirit of Truth detects "spiritual flavor."

"Intellectual self-consciousness can discover the beauty of truth, its spiritual quality, not only by the philosophic consistency of its concepts, but more certainly and surely by the unerring response of the ever-present Spirit of Truth. Happiness ensues from the recognition of truth because it can be *acted out*; it can be lived. Disappointment and sorrow attend upon error because, not being a reality, it cannot be realized in experience. Divine truth is best known by its *spiritual flavor*." P. 42.

2. Compensates human handicaps.

"In all our efforts to enlarge and spiritualize the human concept of God, we are tremendously handicapped by the limited capacity of the mortal mind. We are also seriously handicapped in the execution of our assignment by the limitations of language and by the poverty of material which can be utilized for purposes of illustration or comparison in our efforts to portray divine values and to present spiritual meanings to the finite, mortal mind of man. All our efforts to enlarge the human concept of God would be well-nigh futile except for the fact that the mortal mind is indwelt by the bestowed Adjuster of the Universal Father and is pervaded by the Truth Spirit of the Creator Son. Depending, therefore, on the presence of these divine spirits within the heart of man for assistance in the enlargement of the concept of God, I cheerfully undertake the execution of my mandate to attempt the further portrayal of the nature of God to the mind of man." P. 33.

3. Fraternizes with the Adjusters.

"This supper of remembrance, when it is partaken of by those who are Son-believing and God-knowing, does not need to have associated with its symbolism any of man's puerile misinterpretations regarding the meaning of the divine presence, for upon all such occasions the Master is *really present*. The remembrance supper is the believer's symbolic rendezvous with Michael. When you become thus spirit-conscious, the Son is actually present, and his spirit fraternizes with the indwelling fragment of his Father." P. 1942.

V. BESTOWAL OF THE SPIRIT OF TRUTH

1. **According to Jesus' promise the Spirit comes.**

"About one o'clock, as the one hundred and twenty believers were engaged in prayer, they all became aware of a strange presence in the room. At the same time these disciples all became conscious of a new and profound sense of spiritual joy, security, and confidence. This new consciousness of spiritual strength was immediately followed by a strong urge to go out and publicly proclaim the gospel of the kingdom and the good news that Jesus had risen from the dead.

"Peter stood up and declared that this must be the coming of the Spirit of Truth which the Master had promised them and proposed that they go to the temple and begin the proclamation of the good news committed to their hands. And they did just what Peter suggested." P. 2059. Acts, Chap. 2.

2. **Religion of Jesus becomes a religion about Jesus.**

"These men had been trained and instructed that the gospel which they should preach was the fatherhood of God and the sonship of man, but at just this moment of spiritual ecstasy and personal triumph, the best tidings, the greatest news, these men could think of was the *fact* of the risen Master. And so they went forth, endowed with power from on high, preaching glad tidings to the people—even salvation through Jesus—but they unintentionally stumbled into the error of substituting some of the facts associated with the gospel for the gospel message itself. Peter unwittingly led off in this mistake, and others followed after him on down to Paul, who created a new religion out of the new version of the good news.

"The gospel of the kindgom is: the fact of the fatherhood of God, coupled with the resultant truth of the sonship-brotherhood of men. Christianity, as it developed from that day, is: the fact of God as the Father of the Lord Jesus Christ, in association with the experience of believer-fellowship with the risen and glorified Christ." P. 2059.

3. **Believers are enthralled by the new gospel.**

"It is not strange that these spirit-infused men should have seized upon this opportunity to express their feelings of triumph over the forces which had sought to destroy their Master and end the influence of his teachings. At such a time as this it was easier to remember their personal association with Jesus and to be thrilled with the assurance that the Master still lived, that their friendship had not ended, and that the spirit had indeed come upon them even as he had promised.

"These believers felt themselves suddenly translated into another world, a new existence of joy, power, and glory. The Master had told them the kingdom would come with power, and some of them thought they were beginning to discern what he meant.

"And when all of this is taken into consideration, it is not difficult to understand how these men came to preach a *new gospel about Jesus* in the place of their former message of the fatherhood of God and the brotherhood of men." P. 2059.

VI. SIGNIFICANCE OF THE SPIRIT OF TRUTH

1. **New spirit solvent for human difficulties.**

"Jesus lived on earth and taught a gospel which redeemed man from the superstition that he was a child of the devil and elevated him to the dignity of a faith son of God. Jesus' message, as he preached it and lived it in his day, was an effective solvent for man's spiritual difficulties in that day of its statement. And now that he has personally left the world, he sends in his place his Spirit of Truth, who is designed to live in man and, for each new generation, to restate the Jesus message so that every new group of mortals to appear upon the face of the earth shall have a new and up-to-date version of the gospel, just such personal enlightenment and group guidance as will prove to be an effective solvent for man's ever-new and varied spiritual difficulties." P. 2060.

2. **You are not conscious of the spirit.**

"Do not make the mistake of expecting to become strongly intellectually conscious of the outpoured Spirit of Truth. The spirit never creates a consciousness of himself, only a consciousness of Michael, the Son. From the beginning Jesus taught that the spirit would not speak of himself. The proof, therefore, of your fellowship with the Spirit of Truth is not to be found in your consciousness of this spirit but rather in your experience of enhanced fellowship with Michael." P. 2061.

"The spirit also came to help men recall and understand the words of the Master as well as to illuminate and reinterpret his life on earth.

"Next, the Spirit of Truth came to help the believer to witness to the realities of Jesus' teachings and his life as he lived it in the flesh, and as he now again lives it anew and afresh in the individual believer of each passing generation of the spirit-filled sons of God.

"Thus it appears that the Spirit of Truth comes really to lead all believers into all truth, into the expanding knowledge of the experience of the living and growing spiritual consciousness of the reality of eternal and ascending sonship with God." P. 2061.

4. Baptism of the spirit.

"The term 'baptism of the spirit,' which came into such general use about this time, merely signified the conscious reception of this gift of the Spirit of Truth and the personal acknowledgment of this new spiritual power as an augmentation of all spiritual influences previously experienced by God-knowing souls." P. 2061.

5. The sevenfold spirit influence.

"In a way, mankind is subject to the double influence of the sevenfold appeal of the universe spirit influences. The early evolutionary races of mortals are subject to the progressive contact of the seven adjutant mindspirits of the local universe Mother Spirit. As man progresses upward in the scale of intelligence and spiritual perception, there eventually come to hover over him and dwell within him the seven higher spirit influences. And these seven spirits of the advancing worlds are:

"1. The bestowed spirit of the Universal Father—the Thought Adjusters.

"2. The spirit presence of the Eternal Son—the spirit gravity of the universe of universes and the certain channel of all spirit communion.

"3. The spirit presence of the Infinite Spirit—the universal spirit-mind of all creation, the spiritual source of the intellectual kinship of all progressive intelligences.

"4. The spirit of the Universal Father and the Creator Son—the Spirit of Truth, generally regarded as the spirit of the Universe Son.

"5. The spirit of the Infinite Spirit and the Universe Mother Spirit—the Holy Spirit, generally regarded as the spirit of the Universe Spirit.

"6. The mind-spirit of the Universe Mother Spirit—the seven adjutant mind-spirits of the local universe.

"7. The spirit of the Father, Sons, and Spirits—the new-name spirit of the ascending mortals of the realms after the fusion of the mortal spirit-born soul with the Paradise Thought Adjuster and after the subsequent attainment of the divinity and glorification of the status of the Paradise Corps of the Finality.

"And so did the bestowal of the Spirit of Truth bring to the world and its peoples the last of the spirit endowment designed to aid in the ascending search for God." P. 2062.

VII. WHAT HAPPENED AT PENTECOST

1. Jesus lives in truth-taught believers.

"Many queer and strange teachings became associated with the early narra- tives of the day of Pentecost. In subsequent times the events of this day, on which the Spirit of Truth, the new teacher, came to dwell with mankind, have become confused with the foolish outbreaks of rampant emo- tionalism. The chief mission of this outpoured spirit of the Father and the Son is to teach men about the truths of the Father's love and the Son's mercy. These are the truths of divinity which men can comprehend more fully than all the other divine traits of character. The Spirit of Truth is concerned primarily with the revelation of the Father's spirit nature and the Son's moral character. The Creator Son, in the flesh, revealed God to men; the Spirit of Truth, in the heart, reveals the Creator Son to men. When man yields the 'fruits of the spirit' in his life, he is simply showing forth the traits which the Master manifested in his own earthly life. When Jesus was on earth, he lived his life as one personal- ity—Jesus of Nazareth. As the indwelling spirit of the 'new teacher,' the Master has, since Pentecost, been able to live his life anew in the experience of every truth-taught believer." P. 2062.

2. Pentecost broke national and racial fetters.

"On the day of Pentecost the religion of Jesus broke all national re- strictions and racial fetters. It is forever true, 'Where the spirit of the Lord is, there is liberty.' On this day the Spirit of Truth became the personal gift from the Master to every mortal. This spirit was bestowed for the purpose of qualifying believers more effectively to preach the gospel of the kingdom, but they mistook the experi- ence of receiving the outpoured spirit for a part of the new gospel which they were unconsciously formulating." P. 2063. 2 Cor. 3:17.

3. The Spirit of Truth was bestowed upon all believers.

"Do not overlook the fact that the Spirit of Truth was bestowed upon all sincere believers; this gift of the spirit did not come only to the apostles. The one hundred and twenty men and women assembled in the upper chamber all received the new teacher, as did all the honest of heart throughout the whole world. This new teacher was bestowed upon mankind, and every soul received him in accordance with the love for truth and the capacity to grasp and comprehend spiritual realities. At last, true religion is delivered from the custody of priests and all sacred classes and finds its real manifestation in the individual souls of men." P. 2063.

4. Scope of the spirit's influence.

"The religion of Jesus fosters the highest type of human civilization in that it creates the highest type of spiritual personality and proclaims the sacredness of that person.

"The coming of the Spirit of Truth on Pentecost made possible a religion which is neither radical nor conservative; it is neither the old nor the new; it is to be dominated neither by the old nor the young. The fact of Jesus' earthly life provides a fixed point for the anchor of time, while the bestowal of the Spirit of Truth provides for the everlasting expansion and endless growth of the religion which he lived and the gospel which he proclaimed. The spirit guides into all truth; he is the teacher of an expanding and always-growing religion of endless progress and divine unfolding. This new teacher will be forever unfolding to the truth-seeking believer that which was so divinely folded up in the person and nature of the Son of Man." P. 2063-4.

5. Jesus' religion free from all racial and religious influences.

"The manifestations associated with the bestowal of the 'new teacher,' and the reception of the apostles' preaching by the men of various races and nations gathered together at Jerusalem, indicate the universality of the religion of Jesus. The gospel of the kingdom was to be identified with no particular race, culture, or language. This day of Pentecost witnessed the great effort of the spirit to liberate the religion of Jesus from its inherited Jewish fetters. Even after this demonstration of pouring out the spirit upon all flesh, the apostles at first endeavored to impose the requirements of Judaism upon their converts. Even Paul had trouble with his

Jerusalem brethren because he refused to subject the gentiles to these Jewish practices. No revealed religion can spread to all the world when it makes the serious mistake of becoming permeated with some national culture or associated with established racial, social, or economic practices." P. 2064.

6. **Pentecost was free from all sacred environment.**

"The bestowal of the Spirit of Truth was independent of all forms, cere- monies, sacred places, and special behavior by those who received the fullness of its manifestation. When the spirit came upon those assembled in the upper chamber, they were simply sitting there, having just been engaged in silent prayer. The spirit was bestowed in the country as well as in the city. It was not necessary for the apostles to go apart to a lonely place for years of solitary meditation in order to receive the spirit. For all time, Pentecost disassociates the idea of spiritual experience from the notion of especially favorable environments." P. 2064.

7. **Liberation and magnification of Jesus' teachings.**

"Pentecost, with its spiritual endowment, was designed forever to loose the religion of the Master from all dependence upon physical force; the teachers of this new religion are now equipped with spiritual weapons. They are to go out to conquer the world with unfailing forgiveness, matchless good will, and abounding love. They are equipped to overcome evil with good, to vanquish hate by love, to destroy fear with a courageous and living faith in truth. Jesus had already taught his followers that his religion was never passive; always were his disciples to be active and positive in their ministry of mercy and in their manifestations of love. No longer did these believers look upon Yahweh as 'the Lord of Hosts.' They now regarded the eternal Deity as the 'God and Father of the Lord Jesus Christ.' They made that progress, at least, even if they did in some measure fail fully to grasp the truth that God is also the spiritual Father of every individual." P. 2064. Col. 1:3. Rom. 15:6. John 14:23.

8. **The secret of a better civilization.**

"Pentecost endowed mortal man with the power to forgive personal injuries, to keep sweet in the midst of the gravest injustice, to remain unmoved in the face of appalling danger, and to challenge the evils of hate and anger by the fearless acts of love and forbearance. Urantia has passed through the ravages of great and destructive wars in its history. All participants in these terrible struggles met with defeat. There was but one victor; there was only one who came out of these embittered struggles with an enhanced reputation— that was Jesus of Nazareth and his gospel of overcoming evil with good. The secret of a better civilization is bound up in the Master's teachings of the brotherhood of man, the good will of love and mutual trust." P. 2064.

THE SPIRIT OF TRUTH IN THE BIBLE

Throughout the New Testament the Spirit of Truth is confused with the Holy Spirit.

I. JESUS PROMISES TO SEND THE SPIRIT OF TRUTH

"If I do not go away, the Counselor will not come to you; but if I go, I will send him to you." **John 16:7**.

"And I will pray the Father, and he will give you another Counselor...even the Spirit of truth...you know him, for he dwells with you, and will be in you." **John 14:16,17**.

II. THE SPIRIT OF TRUTH COMES

"In those days Peter stood up among the brethren (the company of persons was in all about a hundred and twenty)." **Acts 1:15**.

"When the day of Pentecost had come, they were all together in one place... And they were all filled with the Holy Spirit." **Acts 2:1,4**.

Peter, referring to Pentecost, quotes Joel: *"In the last days...I will pour out my Spirit upon all flesh."* **Acts 2:17**.

"Being therefore exalted at the right hand of God, and having received from the Father the promise of the Holy Spirit, he has poured out this which you see and hear." **Acts 2:33.**

"And Peter said to them: 'Repent, and be baptized every one of you in the name of Jesus Christ for the forgiveness of your sins, and you shall receive the gift of the Holy Spirit." **Acts 2:38**.

III. THE WORK OF THE SPIRIT OF TRUTH

"When the Counselor comes...he will bear witness to me." **John 15:26**.

"When the Spirit of truth comes, he will guide you into all the truth." **John 16:13**.

*"The Counselor...whom the Father will send in my name, he will teach you all things, and bring to your remembrance all that I have said to you."***John 14:26.**

*"The Spirit is the truth."***1 John 5:7.**

19. PROVIDENCE

I. CONFUSED THINKING ABOUT THE DOINGS OF GOD.
II. PROVIDENCE THE DOMAIN OF THE CONJOINT ACTOR AND THE SUPREME BEING.
III. FUNCTIONS OF PROVIDENCE.
IV. JESUS AND THE MYSTERIOUS DISPENSATION OF PROVIDENCE.

The Bible on Providence

I. PROVIDENCE IN THE OLD TESTAMENT.
II. PROVIDENCE IN THE NEW TESTAMENT.

PROVIDENCE

I. CONFUSED THINKING ABOUT THE DOINGS OF GOD

1. Sometimes we must share the family discipline.

"We are all a part of the family of God, and we must therefore sometimes share in the family discipline. Many of the acts of God which so disturb and confuse us are the result of the decisions and final rulings of all-wisdom, empowering the Conjoint Actor to execute the choosing of the infallible will of the infinite mind, to enforce the decisions of the personality of perfection, whose survey, vision, and solicitude embrace the highest and eternal welfare of all his vast and far-flung creation." P. 48.

2. Why we so misunderstand God's doings.

"Thus it is that your detached, sectional, finite, gross, and highly materialistic viewpoint and the limitations inherent in the nature of your being constitute such a handicap that you are unable to see, comprehend, or know the wisdom and kindness of many of the divine acts which to you seem fraught with such crushing cruelty, and which seem to be characterized by such utter indifference to the comfort and welfare, to the planetary happiness and personal prosperity, of your fellow creatures. It is because of the limits of human vision, it is because of your circumscribed understanding and finite comprehension, that you misunderstand the motives, and pervert the purposes, of God. But many things occur on the evolu- tionary worlds which are not the personal doings of the Universal Father." P. 48.

3. The nature of genuine providence.

"For ages the inhabitants of Urantia have misunderstood the providence of God. There is a providence of divine outworking on your world, but it is not the childish, arbitrary, and material ministry many mortals have conceived it to be. The providence of God consists in the interlocking activities of the celestial beings and the divine spirits who, in accordance with cosmic law, unceasingly labor for the honor of God and for the spiritual advancement of his universe children." P. 54.

4. The concept of progressive providence.

"Can you not advance in your concept of God's dealing with man to that level where you recognize that the watchword of the universe is *progress*? Through long ages the human race has struggled to reach its present position. Throughout all these millenniums

Providence has been working out the plan of progressive evolution. The two thoughts are not opposed in practice, only in man's mistaken concepts. Divine providence is never arrayed in opposition to true human progress, either temporal or spiritual. Providence is always consistent with the unchanging and perfect nature of the supreme Lawmaker." P. 54.

II. PROVIDENCE THE DOMAIN OF THE CONJOINT ACTOR AND SUPREME BEING

1. The domain of Conjoint Actor and Supreme Being.

"While you envisage the Father as an original creator and the Son as a spiritual administrator, you should think of the Third Source and Center as a universal co-ordinator, a minister of unlimited co-operation. The Conjoint Actor is the correlator of all actual reality; he is the Deity repository of the Father's thought and the Son's word and in action is eternally regardful of the material absoluteness of the central Isle. The Paradise Trinity has ordained the universal order of *progress*, and the providence of God is the domain of the Conjoint Creator and the evolving Supreme Being. No actual or actualizing reality can escape eventual relationship with the Third Source and Center." P. 99.

2. How Moses regarded Providence.

"Moses was a believer in Providence; he had become thoroughly tainted with the doctrines of Egypt concerning the supernatural control of the Nile and the other elements of nature. He had a great vision of God, but he was thoroughly sincere when he taught the Hebrews that, if they would obey God, 'He will love you, bless you, and multiply you. He will multiply the fruit of your womb and the fruit of your land—the corn, wine, oil, and your flocks. You shall be prospered above all people, and the Lord your God will take away from you all sickness and will put none of the evil diseases of Egypt upon you.' He even said: 'Remember the Lord your God, for it is he who gives you the power to get wealth.' 'You shall lend to many nations, but you shall not borrow. You shall reign over many nations, but they shall not reign over you.'" P. 1058. Deut. 7:12-15.

III. FUNCTIONS OF PROVIDENCE

1. Man does have relative powers of choice.

"Providence does not mean that God has decided all things for us and in advance. God loves us too much to do that, for that would be nothing short of cosmic tyranny. Man does have relative powers of choice. Neither is the divine love that shortsighted affection which-would pamper and spoil the children of men." P. 1304.

2. Providence is a function.

"The Gods have attributes but the Trinity has functions, and like the Trinity, providence *is* a function, the composite of the other-than-personal overcontrol of the universe of universes, extending from the evolutionary levels of the Sevenfold synthesizing in the power of the Almighty on up through the transcendental realms of the Ultimacy of Deity." P. 1304.

3. Providence functions with regard to totals.

"God loves each creature as a child, and that love overshadows each crea- ture throughout all time and eternity. Providence functions with regard to the total and deals with the function of any creature as such function is related to the total. Providential intervention with regard to any being is indicative of the importance of the *function* of that being as concerns the evolutionary growth of some total; such total may be the total race, the total nation, the total planet, or even a higher total. It is the importance of the function of the creature that occasions providential intervention, not the impor-tance of the creature as a person." P. 1304-5.

4. Our mistaken ideas about providence.

"Nevertheless, the Father as a person may at any time interpose a fatherly hand in the stream of cosmic events all in accordance with the will of God and in consonance with the wisdom of God and as motivated by the love of God.

"But what man calls providence is all too often the product of his own imagination, the fortuitous juxtaposition of the circumstances of chance. There is, however, a real and emerging providence in the finite realm of universe existence, a true and actualizing correlation of the energies of space, the motions of time, the thoughts of intellect, the ideals of char- acter, the desires of spiritual natures, and the purposive volitional acts of evolving personalities. The circumstances of the material realms find final finite integration in the interlocking presences of the Supreme and the Ultimate." P. 1305.

5. How easy to misunderstand providence.

"Some of the amazingly fortuitous conditions occasionally prevail-ing on the evolutionary worlds may be due to the gradually emerging presence of the Supreme, the foretasting of his future universe activities. Most of what a mortal would call providential is not; his judgment of such matters is very handicapped by lack of farsighted vision into the true meanings of the circumstances of life. Much of what a mortal would call good luck might really be bad luck; the smile of fortune that bestows unearned leisure and undeserved wealth may be the greatest of human afflictions; the apparent cruelty of a perverse fate that heaps tribulation upon some suffering mortal may in reality be the tempering fire that is transmuting the soft iron of immature personality into the tempered steel of real character." P. 1305.

6. Providence of the overcontrol of Supremacy.

"There is a providence in the evolving universes, and it can be discovered by creatures to just the extent that they have attained capacity to perceive the purpose of the evolving universes. Complete capacity to discern universe purposes equals the evolutionary completion of the creature and may otherwise be expressed as the attainment of the Supreme within the limits of the present state of the incomplete universes.

"The love of the Father operates directly in the heart of the individual, independent of the actions or reactions of all other individuals; the relationship is personal—man and God. The impersonal presence of Deity (Almighty Supreme and Paradise Trinity) manifests regard for the whole, not for the part. The providence of the overcontrol of Supremacy becomes increasingly apparent as the successive parts of the universe progress in the attainment of finite destinies." P. 1305.

7. In the age of light and life providence becomes actual.

"On a planet of this advanced order, providence has become an actuality, the circumstances of life are correlated, but this is not only because man has come to dominate the material problems of his world; it is also because he has begun to live according to the trend of the universes; he is following the pathway of Supremacy to the attainment of the Universal Father." P. 1306.

8. As of now, providence can only be partial.

"The kingdom of God is in the hearts of men, and when this kingdom becomes actual in the heart of every individual on a world, then God's rule has become actual on that planet; and this is the attained sovereignty of the Supreme Being.

"To realize providence in time, man must accomplish the task of achieving perfection. But man can even now foretaste this providence in its eternity meanings as he ponders the universe fact that all things, be they good or evil, work together for the advancement of God-knowing mortals in their quest for the Father of all." P. 1306.

9. **Spiritual insight detects providence.**

"Providence becomes increasingly discernible as men reach upward from the material to the spiritual. The attainment of completed spiritual insight enables the ascending personality to detect harmony in what was thereto- fore chaos. Even morontia mota represents a real advance in this direc- tion." P. 1306-7.

10. **Providence and the incomplete Supreme.**

"Providence is in part the overcontrol of the incomplete Supreme manifested in the incomplete universes, and it must therefore ever be:

"1. *Partial*—due to the incompleteness of the actualization of the Supreme Being, and

"2. *Unpredictable*—due to the fluctuations in creature attitude, which ever varies from level to level, thus causing apparently variable reciprocal response in the Supreme." P. 1307.

11. **What providence really means.**

"When men pray for providential intervention in the circumstances of life, many times the answer to their prayer is their own changed attitudes toward life. But providence is not whimsical, neither is it fantastic nor magical. It is the slow and sure emergence of the mighty sovereign of the finite universes, whose majestic presence the evolving creatures occasionally detect in their universe progressions. Providence is the sure and certain march of the galaxies of space and the personalities of time toward the goals of eternity, first in the Supreme, then in the Ultimate, and perhaps in the Absolute. And in infinity we believe there is the same providence, and this is the will, the actions, the purpose of the Paradise Trinity thus motivating the cosmic panorama of universes upon universes." P. 1307.

12. **When providence becomes actual.**

"As the systems, constellations, universes, and superuniverses become settled in light and life, the Supreme increasingly emerges as the meaningful correlator of all that is transpiring, while the Ultimate gradually emerges as the transcendental unifier of all things." P. 1305.

IV. JESUS AND THE MYSTERIOUS DISPENSATION OF PROVIDENCE

"As Jesus mingled with the people, they found him entirely free from the super- stitions of that day. He was free from religious prejudices; he was never intolerant. He had nothing in his heart resembling social antagonism. While he complied with the good in the religion of his fathers, he did not hesitate to disregard man-made traditions of superstition and bondage. He dared to teach that catastrophes of nature, accidents of time, and other calamitous happenings are not visitations of divine judgments or mysterious dispensations of Providence. He denounced slavish devotion to meaningless ceremonials and exposed the fallacy of materialistic worship. He boldly proclaimed man's spiritual freedom and dared to teach that mortals of the flesh are indeed and in truth sons of the living God." P. 1671.

THE BIBLE ON PROVIDENCE
I. PROVIDENCE IN THE OLD TESTAMENT

While the word Providence does not appear in the Old Testament, the idea prevails throughout these writings as the concept of the "chosen people."

"You meant evil against me, but God meant it for good." **Gen. 50:20**.

"I will set apart the land of Goshen...so that no swarms of flies shall be there." **Ex. 8:22**.

"I will put none of the diseases upon you which I put upon the Egyptians." **Ex. 15:26**.

"And in this place I will give prosperity, says the Lord of hosts." **Hag. 2:9**.

"Look to Abraham...for when he was but one...I blessed him and made him many." **Isa. 51:2**.

"But for you who fear my name the sun of righteousness shall rise with healing in its wings." **Mal. 4:2**.

II. PROVIDENCE IN THE NEW TESTAMENT

In the New Testament the word Providence occurs once—in the King James Version—**Acts 24:2**. *"Seeing that by thee we enjoy great quietness, and that very worthy deeds are done unto this nation by thy providence."* (In the Revised Version Providence is rendered "provision.")

"Look at the birds of the air; they neither sow nor reap nor gather into barns, and yet your heavenly Father feeds them." **Matt. 6:26**.

"Are not two sparrows sold for a penny? And not one of them will fall to the ground without your Father's will." **Matt. 10:29**.

"But Jesus answered them, 'My Father is working still, and I am working.'" **John 5:17.**

"We know that in everything God works for good with those who love him, who are called according to his purpose." **Rom. 8:28**.

20. THE MORONTIA LIFE

Morontia in the Bible
Morontia Progression through the Local Universe

THE MORONTIA LIFE

I. MORONTIA DEFINED

1. Morontia is the realm between the material and the spiritual.

"*Morontia* is a term designating a vast level intervening between the material and the spiritual. It may designate personal or impersonal realities, living or nonliving energies. The warp of morontia is spiritual; its woof is physical." P. 9.

"Much of the reality of the spiritual worlds is of the morontia order, a phase of universe reality wholly unknown on Urantia. The goal of personality existence is spiritual, but the morontia creations always intervene, bridging the gulf between the material realms of mortal origin and the superuniverse spheres of advancing spiritual status. It is in this realm that the Master Spirits make their great contribution to the plan of man's Paradise ascension." P. 189.

II. THE MORONTIA TEMPLE

1. Morontia temples belong to the era of light and life.

"The presence of a morontia temple at the capital of an inhabited world is the certificate of the admission of such a sphere to the settled ages of light and life. Before the Teacher Sons leave a world at the conclusion of their terminal mission, they inaugurate this final epoch of evolutionary attainment; they preside on that day when the 'holy temple comes down upon earth.' This event, signalizing the dawn of the era of light and life, is always honored by the personal presence of the Paradise bestowal Son of that planet, who comes to witness this great day. There in this temple of unparalleled beauty, this bestowal Son of Paradise proclaims the long-time Planetary Prince as the new Planetary Sovereign and invests such a faithful Lanonandek Son with new powers and extended authority over planetary affairs. The System Sovereign is also present and speaks in confirmation of these pronouncements.

"A morontia temple has three parts: Centermost is the sanctuary of the Paradise bestowal Son. On the right is the seat of the former Planetary Prince, now Planetary Sovereign; and when present in the temple, this Lanonandek Son is visible to the more spiritual individuals of the realm. On the left is the seat of the acting chief of finaliters attached to the planet." P. 622.

2. Construction of the morontia temple.

"Although the planetary temples have been spoken of as 'coming down from heaven,' in reality no actual material is transported from the system headquarters. The architecture of each is worked out in miniature on the system capital, and the Morontia Power Supervisors subsequently bring these approved plans to the planet. Here, in association with the Master Physical Controllers, they proceed to build the morontia temple according to specifications." P. 622. Rev. 21:10.

3. Description of the temple.

"The average morontia temple seats about three hundred thousand specta- tors. These edifices are not used for worship, play, or for receiving broadcasts; they are devoted to the special ceremonies of the planet, such as: communications with the System Sovereign or with the Most Highs, special visualization ceremonies designed to reveal the personality presence of spirit beings, and silent cosmic contemplation. The schools of cosmic philosophy here conduct their graduation exercises, and here also do the mortals of the realm receive planetary recognition for achievements of high social service and for other outstanding attainments." P. 622.

4. Translations take place in the temple.

"Such a morontia temple also serves as the place of assembly for witnessing the translation of living mortals to the morontia existence. It is because the translation temple is composed of morontia material that it is not destroyed by the blazing glory of the consuming fire which so completely obliterates the physical bodies of those mortals who therein experience final fusion with their divine Adjusters. On a large world these departure flares are almost continuous, and as the number of translations increases, subsidiary morontia life shrines are provided in different areas of the planet. Not long since I sojourned on a world in the far north whereon twenty-five morontia shrines were functioning." P. 622.

5. Death and translation.

"Natural, physical death is not a mortal inevitability. The majority of advanced evolutionary beings, citizens on worlds existing in the final era of light and life, do not die; they are translated directly from the life in the flesh to the morontia existence.

"This experience of translation from the material life to the morontia state—fusion of the immortal soul with the indwelling

Adjuster—increases in frequency commensurate with the evolutionary progress of the planet. At first only a few mortals in each age attain translation levels of spiritual progress, but with the onset of the successive ages of the Teacher Sons, more and more Adjuster fusions occur before the termination of the lengthening lives of these progressing mortals; and by the time of the terminal mission of the Teacher Sons, approximately one quarter of these superb mortals are exempt from natural death." P. 623.

III. THE MORONTIA SELF

1. **Progressive evolution of the morontia self.**

"Just as a butterfly emerges from the caterpillar stage, so will the true personalities of human beings emerge on the mansion worlds, for the first time revealed apart from their onetime enshroudment in the material flesh. The morontia career in the local universe has to do with the continued elevation of the personality mechanism from the beginning morontia level of soul existence up to the final morontia level of progressive spirituality." P. 1235.

2. **Morontia personality forms.**

"It is difficult to instruct you regarding your morontia personality forms for the local universe career. You will be endowed with morontia patterns of personality manifestability, and these are investments which, in the last analysis, are beyond your comprehension. Such forms, while entirely real, are not energy patterns of the material order which you now understand. They do, however, serve the same purpose on the local universe worlds as do your material bodies on the planets of human nativity." P. 1235-6.

3. **The morontia mind.**

"In the morontia estate the ascending mortal is endowed with the Nebadon modification of the cosmic-mind endowment of the Master Spirit of Orvonton. The mortal intellect, as such, has perished, has ceased to exist as a focalized universe entity apart from the undifferentiated mind circuits of the Creative Spirit. But the meanings and values of the mortal mind have not perished. Certain phases of mind are continued in the surviving soul; certain experiential values of the former human mind are held by the Adjuster; and there persist in the local universe the records of the human life as it was lived in the flesh, together with certain living registrations in the numerous beings who are concerned with the final evaluation of the ascending mortal, beings extending in range from seraphim to Universal Censors and probably on beyond to the Supreme." P. 1236.

4. **Morontia memory.**

"The persistence of memory is proof of the retention of the identity of original selfhood; it is essential to complete self-consciousness of personality continuity and expansion. Those mortals who ascend without Adjusters are dependent on the instruction of seraphic associates for the reconstruction of human memory; otherwise the morontia souls of the Spirit-fused mortals are not limited. The pattern of memory persists in the soul, but this pattern requires the presence of the former Adjuster to become *immediately* self-realizable as continuing memory. Without the Adjuster, it requires considerable time for the mortal survivor to re-explore and relearn, to recapture, the memory consciousness of the meanings and values of a former existence." P. 1236-7.

IV. MORONTIA MOTA

1. **Mota is stereoscopic philosophy.**

"Mota is more than a superior philosophy; it is to philosophy as two eyes are to one; It has a stereoscopic effect on meanings and values. Material man sees the universe, as it were, with but one eye—flat. Mansion world students achieve cosmic perspective—depth—by superimposing the perceptions of the morontia life upon the perceptions of the physical life. And they are enabled to bring these material and morontial viewpoints into true focus largely through the untiring ministry of their seraphic counselors, who so patiently teach the mansion world students and the morontia progressors. Many of the teaching counselors of the supreme order of seraphim began their careers as advisers of the newly liberated souls of the mortals of time." P. 554.

2. **Mota as related to human philosophy.**

"The lower planes of morontia mota join directly with the higher levels of human philosophy. On the first mansion world it is the practice to teach the less advanced students by the parallel technique; that is, in one column are presented the more simple concepts of mota meanings, and in the opposite column citation is made of analogous statements of mortal philosophy.

"Not long since, while executing an assignment on the first mansion world of Satania, I had occasion to observe this method of teaching; and though I may not undertake to present the mota content of the lesson, I am permitted to record the twenty-eight statements of human philosophy which this morontia instructor was utilizing as illustrative material designed to assist these new mansion world sojourners in their early efforts to grasp the significance and meaning of mota. These illustrations of human philosophy were:

"1.   A display of specialized skill does not signify possession of spiritual capacity. Cleverness is not a substitute for true character.

"2.   Few persons live up to the faith which they really have. Unreasoned fear is a master intellectual fraud practiced upon the evolving mortal soul.

"3.   Inherent capacities cannot be exceeded; a pint can never hold a quart. The spirit concept cannot be mechanically forced into the material memory mold.

"4.   Few mortals ever dare to draw anything like the sum of personality credits established by the combined ministries of nature and grace. The majority of impoverished souls are truly rich, but they refuse to believe it.

"5.   Difficulties may challenge mediocrity and defeat the fearful, but they only stimulate the true children of the Most Highs.

"6.   To enjoy privilege without abuse, to have liberty without license, to possess power and steadfastly refuse to use it for self-aggrandizement—these are the marks of high civilization.

"7.   Blind and unforeseen accident do not occur in the cosmos. Neither do the celestial beings assist the lower being who refuses to act upon his light of truth.

"8.   Effort does not always produce joy, but there is no happiness without intelligent effort.

"9.   Action achieves strength; moderation eventuates in charm.

"10. Righteousness strikes the harmony chords of truth, and the melody vibrates throughout the cosmos, even to the recognition of the Infinite.

"11. The weak indulge in resolutions, but the strong act. Life is but a day's work—do it well. The act is ours; the consequences God's.

"12. The greatest affliction of the cosmos is never to have been afflicted. Mortals only learn wisdom by experiencing tribulation.

"13. Stars are best discerned from the lonely isolation of experiential depths, not from the illuminated and ecstatic mountain tops.

"14. Whet the appetites of your associates for truth; give advice only when it is asked for.

"15. Affectation is the ridiculous effort of the ignorant to appear wise, the attempt of the barren soul to appear rich.

"16. You cannot perceive spiritual truth until you feelingly experience it, and many truths are not really felt except in adversity.

"17. Ambition is dangerous until it is fully socialized. You have not truly acquired any virtue until your acts make you worthy of it.

"18. Impatience is a spirit poison; anger is like a stone hurled into a hornet's nest.

"19. Anxiety must be abandoned. The disappointments hardest to bear are those which never come.

"20. Only a poet can discern poetry in the commonplace prose of routine existence.

"21. The high mission of any art is, by its illusions, to forshadow a higher universe reality, to crystallize the emotions of time into the thought of eternity.

"22. The evolving soul is not made divine by what it does, but by what it strives to do.

23. Death added nothing to the intellectual possession or to the spiritual endowment, but it did add to the experiential status the consciousness of *survival*.

"24. The destiny of eternity is determined moment by moment by the achievements of the day by day living. The acts of today are the destiny of tomorrow.

"25. Greatness lies not so much in possessing strength as in making a wise and divine use of such strength.

"26. Knowledge is possessed only by sharing; it is safeguarded by wisdom and socialized by love.

"27. Progress demands development of individuality; mediocrity seeks perpetuation in standardization.

"28. The argumentative defense of any proposition is inversely proportional to the truth contained.

"Such is the work of the beginners of the first mansion world while the more advanced pupils on the later worlds are mastering the higher levels of cosmic insight and morontia mota." P. 556-7.

V. FUNCTIONS OF MORONTIA LIFE

1. **Morontia spans local universe career.**

"The Gods cannot—at least they do not—transform a creature of gross animal nature into a perfected spirit by some mysterious act of creative magic. When the Creators desire to produce perfect beings, they do so by direct and original creation, but they never undertake to convert animal-origin and material creatures into beings of perfection in a single step.

"The morontia life, extending as it does over the various stages of the local universe career, is the only possible approach whereby material mortals could attain the threshold of the spirit world. What magic could death, the natural dissolution of the material body, hold that such a simple step should instantly transform the mortal and material mind into an immortal and perfected spirit? Such beliefs are but ignorant superstitions and pleasing fables." P. 541.

2. Morontia intervenes between mortal and spirit status.

"Always this morontia transition intervenes between the mortal estate and the subsequent spirit status of surviving human beings. This intermediate state of universe progress differs markedly in the various local creations, but in intent and purpose they are all quite similar. The arrangement of the mansion and higher morontia worlds in Nebadon is fairly typical of the morontia transition regimes in this part of Orvonton." P. 541.

3. Constellation sojourn typical morontia life.

"This entire sojourn on the constellation training worlds, culminating in Edentia citizenship, is a period of true and heavenly bliss for the morontia progressors. Throughout your sojourn on the system worlds you were evolving from a near-animal to a morontia creature; you were more material than spiritual. On the Salvington spheres you will be evolving from a morontia being to the status of a true spirit; you will be more spiritual than material. But on Edentia, ascenders are midway between their former and their future estates, midway in their passage from evolutionary animal to ascending spirit. During your whole stay on Edentia and its worlds you are 'as the angels'; you are constantly progressing but all the while maintaining a general and a typical morontia status.

"This constellation sojourn of an ascending mortal is the most uniform and stabilized epoch in the entire career of morontia progression. This experience constitutes the prespirit socialization training of the ascenders. It is analogous to the prefinaliter spiritual experience of Havona and to the preabsonite training on Paradise." P. 495.

VI. MORONTIA WORK AND HABITS

1. Morontia worlds.

"The morontia spheres are the transition phases of mortal ascension through the progression worlds of the local universe. Only the seven worlds surrounding the finaliters' sphere of the local systems are called mansion worlds, but all fifty-six of the system transition abodes, in common with the higher spheres around the constellations and the universe headquarters, are called morontia worlds. These creations partake of the physical beauty and the morontia grandeur of the local universe headquarters spheres." P. 541.

2. Habits of morontia life.

"Though you have morontia bodies, you continue, through all seven of these worlds, to eat, drink, and rest. You partake of the morontia order of food, a kingdom of living energy unknown on the material worlds. Both food and water are fully utilized in the morontia body; there is no residual waste. Pause to consider: Mansonia number one is a very material sphere, presenting the early beginnings of the morontia regime. You are still a near human and not far removed from the limited viewpoints of mortal life, but each world discloses definite progress. From sphere to sphere you grow less material, more intellectual, and slightly more spiritual. The spiritual progress is greatest on the last three of these seven progressive worlds." P. 535.

3. Technique of morontia memory.

"Your Adjuster memory remains fully intact as you ascend the morontia life. Those mental associations that were purely animalistic and wholly material naturally perished with the physical brain, but everything in your mental life which was worthwhile, and which had survival value, was counterparted by the Adjuster and is retained as a part of personal memory all the way through the ascendant career. You will be conscious of all your worthwhile experiences as you advance from one mansion world to another and from one section of the universe to another—even to Paradise." P. 535.

4. Morontia training on World No. 4.

"It is during the period of training on world number four that the ascending mortals are really first introduced to the demands and

delights of the true social life of morontia creatures. And it is indeed a
new experience for evolutionary creatures to participate in social
activities which are predicated neither on personal aggrandizement
nor on self-seeking conquest. A new social order is being introduced,
one based on the understanding sympathy of mutual appreciation, the
unselfish love of mutual service, and the overmastering motivation of
the realization of a common and supreme destiny—the Paradise goal
of worshipful and divine perfection. Ascenders are all becoming self-
conscious of God-knowing, God- revealing, God-seeking, and God-
finding." P. 536.

VII. PLAY LIFE AND FELLOWSHIP

1. **Morontia Companions are play sponsors.**

"These children of the local universe Mother Spirits are the friends
and associates of all who live the ascending morontia life. They are
not indispensable to an ascender's real work of creature progression,
neither do they in any sense displace the work of the seraphic
guardians who often accompany their mortal associates on the
Paradise journey. The morontia Companions are simply gracious
hosts to those who are just beginning the long inward ascent. They
are also skillful play sponsors and are ably assisted in this work by
the reversion directors." P. 282.

2. **All the way to Paradise there is time for play.**

"Though you will have earnest and progressively difficult tasks to
perform on the morontia training worlds of Nebadon, you will always
be provided with regular seasons of rest and reversion. Throughout
the journey to Paradise there will always be time for rest and spirit
play; and in the career of light and life there is always time for
worship and new achievement." P. 282.

3. **Companionship provided for all the Paradise journey.**

"These Morontia Companions are such friendly associates that,
when you finally leave the last phase of the morontia experience, as
you prepare to embark upon the superuniverse spirit adventure,
you will truly regret that these companionable creatures cannot
accompany you, but they serve exclusively in the local universes.
At every stage of the ascending career all contactable personalities
will be friendly and companionable, but not until you meet the
Paradise Companions will you find another group so devoted to
friendship and companionship." P. 282.

4. Morontia life and the celestial artisans.

"Any morontia personality or spirit entity is eligible for admission to the corps of the celestial artisans; that is, any being below the rank of inherent divine sonship. Ascending sons of God from the evolutionary spheres may, after their arrival on the morontia worlds, apply for admission to the artisans corps and, if sufficiently gifted, may choose such a career for a longer or shorter period. But no one may enlist with the celestial artisans for less than one millennium, one thousand years of superuniverse time." P. 497.

VIII. TRAITS ERADICATED AND FRUSTRATED AMBITIONS

1. Traits eradicated by morontia life.

"One of the purposes of the morontia career is to effect the permanent eradication from the mortal survivors of such animal vestigial traits as procrastination, equivocation, insincerity, problem avoidance, unfairness, and ease seeking. The mansonia life early teaches the young morontia pupils that postponement is in no sense avoidance. After the life in the flesh, time is no longer available as a technique of dodging situations or of circumventing disagreeable obligations." P. 551.

2. Realization of frustrated ambitions.

"But every human being should remember: Many ambitions to excel which tantalize mortals in the flesh will not persist with these same mortals in the morontia and spirit careers. The ascending morontians learn to socialize their former purely selfish longings and egoistic ambitions. Nevertheless, those things which you so earnestly longed to do on earth and which circumstances so persistently denied you, if, after acquiring true mota insight in the morontia career, you still desire to do, then will you most certainly be granted every opportunity fully to satisfy your long-cherished desires." P. 508.

IX. SUNDRY FEATURES OF MORONTIA LIFE

1. Morontia and the survival experience.

"The morontia phase of revealed religion has to do with the *experience of survival*, and its great urge is the attainment of spirit perfection. There also is present the higher urge of worship, associated with an impelling call to increased ethical service. Morontia insight entails an ever-expanding consciousness of the Sevenfold, the Supreme, and even the Ultimate." P. 1111.

2. In morontia assurance of truth replaces assurance of faith.

"Increasingly throughout the morontia progression the assurance of truth replaces the assurance of faith. When you are finally mustered into the actual spirit world, then will the assurances of pure spirit insight operate in the place of faith and truth or, rather, in conjunction with, and superimposed upon, these former techniques of personality assurance." P. 1111.

3. **Adjusters and the morontia life.**

"The Thought Adjusters are the children of the universe career, and indeed the virgin Adjusters must gain experience while mortal creatures grow and develop. As the personality of the human child expands for the struggles of evolutionary existence, so does the Adjuster wax great in the rehearsals of the next stage of ascending life. As the child acquires adaptative versatility for his adult activities through the social and play life of early childhood, so does the indwelling Adjuster achieve skill for the next stage of cosmic life by virtue of the preliminary mortal planning and rehearsing of those activities which have to do with the morontia career. Human existence constitutes a period of practice which is effectively utilized by the Adjuster in preparing for the increased responsibilities and the greater opportunities of a future life. But the Adjuster's efforts, while living within you, are not so much concerned with the affairs of temporal life and planetary existence. Today, the Thought Adjusters are, as it were, rehearsing the realities of the universe career in the evolving minds of human beings." P. 1195.

4. **Revelation bridges the morontia gulf.**

"Revelation is evolutionary man's only hope of bridging the morontia gulf. Faith and reason, unaided by mota, cannot conceive and construct a logical universe. Without the insight of mota, mortal man cannot discern goodness, love, and truth in the phenomena of the material world." P. 1137.

5. **Master Spirit stamp continues in the morontia.**

"The physical stamp of a Master Spirit is a part of man's material origin. The entire morontia career is lived under the continuing influence of this same Master Spirit. It is hardly strange that the subsequent spirit career of such an ascending mortal never fully eradicates the characteristic stamp of this same supervising Spirit. The impress of a Master Spirit is basic to the very existence of every pre-Havona stage of mortal ascension." P. 191.

6. Paul knew about morontia worlds.

"Paul learned of the existence of the morontia worlds and of the reality of morontia materials, for he wrote, 'They have in heaven a better and more enduring substance.' And these morontia materials are real, literal, even as in 'the city which has foundations, whose builder and maker is God.' And each of these marvelous spheres is 'a better country, that is, a heavenly one.'" P. 542. Heb. 10:34; 11:10,16.

X. JESUS AND THE MORONTIA LIFE

"Now is the mortal transit of Jesus—the morontia resurrection of the Son of Man—completed. The transitory experience of the Master as a personality midway between the material and the spiritual has begun. And he has done all this through power inherent within himself; no personality has rendered him any assistance. He now lives as Jesus of morontia, and as he begins this morontia life, the material body of his flesh lies there undisturbed in the tomb. The soldiers are still on guard, and the seal of the governor about the rocks has not yet been broken." P. 2022.

MORONTIA IN THE BIBLE

1. Paul had some idea about morontia reality.

"Since you know that you yourselves had a better possession and an abiding one." **Heb. 10:34.** (The King James Version reads: "Ye have in heaven a better and an enduring substance.")

2. Jesus' morontia appearances.

a. *Human eyes had to be opened.*
    "And their eyes were opened and they recognized him; and he vanished out of their sight." **Luke 24:31.**

b. *The morontia form appears suddenly.*
    "Jesus himself stood among them. But they were startled and frightened, was supposed that they saw a spirit." **Luke 24:36,37.**

c. *Disappears instantly.*
    "While he blessed them, he parted from them." **Luke 24:51.**

d. *Morontia Jesus eats fish.*
    "He said to them, 'Have you anything to eat?' They gave him a piece of broiled fish, and he took it and ate before them." **Luke 24:41-43.**

e. *Jesus Mary not to touch him.*
"*Jesus said to her, 'Do not holize, for I have not yet ascended to the the Father.'*"**John 20:17.**

f. *Comes and goes without hindrance.*
"*The doors being shut...for fear of the Jews, Jesus came and stood Among them and said to them, 'Peace be with you.'*" **John 20:19.**
NOTE: Eight days later he repeated this. **See John 20:26.**

3. **Morontia may be our "treasure in heaven."**

"*But Lay up for yourselves treasures in heaven, where neither moth nor rust consumes and where thieves do not break in and steal.*"**Matt. 6:20.**

4. **Even spirit beings may real to human vision.**

"*Do not neglect to show hospitality to strangers, for thereby some have entertained angels unawares.*" **Heb. 13:2.**

EXAMPLES:

1. Three visitors to Abraham. **Gen. 18:1-8.** (One was Yahweh.)
2. Two angels visit Lot. **Gen. 19:1-3.**
3. To Moses at the burning bush. **Ex. 3:2.**
4. Angel of the Lord appears to Hagar. **Gen. 16:10.**
5. Angel calls to Hagar. **Gen. 21:17.**
6. Angel awakens Elijah. **1 Kings 19:5.**
7. An angel accosts Jacob. **Gen. 32:1.**
8. Elisha's servant's eyes opened. **2 Kings 6:17.**
9. Isaiah and the seraphim. **Isa. 6:6.**
10. Angel talks with Zechariah. **Zech. 1:9.**
11. Jacob wrestles with an angel. **Gen. 32:25-26.**
12. The angel stays Abraham's hand. **Gen. 22:10-11.**

5. The morontia (spiritual) body.

"*It is sown in weakness, it is raised in power. It is sown a physical body, it is raised as spiritual body.*"**I Cor. 15:43-44.**

MORONTIA PROGRESSION THROUGH THE LOCAL UNIVERSE

This is an attempt to trace the surviving mortal through the morontia life from the conception of his immortal soul on Urantia to the completion of his morontia progression on Salvington as he prepares to enter upon the first stage of his spirit status.

I. MORONTIA EXPERIENCE ON URANTIA

1. The human mind and the divine Adjuster unite to create the morontia soul.

2. This morontia soul experiences evolutionary growth throughout the lifetime of the Urantia mortal.

3. This soul is neither material nor spiritual—it is morontial.

4. This morontial soul is immortal, and becomes more and more permeated by truth, beauty, and goodness. P. 1218-19.

5. During the death transition, the morontia soul is in the custody of the guardian seraphim. P. 1230.

II. THE FIRST MANSION WORLD

1. You wake up with the resurrection hall.

2. You begin the morontia life just where the mortal life was terminated by death.

3. Consciousness of identity is restored by the meeting of the memory and personality factors in the keeping of the Adjuster with the identity soul factors in the custody of the seraphim.

4. From the resurrection hall you go to the Melchizedek center where you get your assignment to a permanent residence.

5. Next you are introduced to your educational program designed to make up your Urantia deficiencies—especially biologic deficiencies.

6. Parental deficiencies are ascertained and, when present, are made up by ministering to children on the nursery world and by subsequent service in the homes of the Material Sons on Jerusem.

7. After getting located, you have ten days in which to visit, explore, and look up fellow Urantians.

8. The Morontia Companions assist you in planning study and work, and accompany you on excursions, including Jerusem.

9. In the main, mansion world number one is a deficiency sphere, but much time is also devoted to mind and soul progress. P. 530-34.

III. THE SECOND MANSION WORLD

1. You learn to live with Spirit-fused ascenders.

2. Social organization and community life progresses.

3. You continue to eat, drink, and sleep. There is no residual waste to morontia food.

4. The chief business on this sphere is to get rid of intellectual conflicts and mental disharmony.

5. You begin to master morontia mota. P. 534-5.

6. You get the harps of God.

IV. THE THIRD MANSION WORLD

1. This is the headquarters of Mansion World Teachers—they go with you to the morontia finish.

2. On each mansion world you get permission to visit the corresponding satellite.

3. Visits to Jerusem continue.

4. More positive work begins. The first two worlds were largely negative— making up shortcomings.

5. If not attained before, the seven psychic circles are usually completed on this sphere.

6. Special work is done in the correalation of morontia mota and mortal logic.

7. One of the chief studies has to do with cosmic meanings and universe inter-relationships. P. 535-6.

V. THE FOURTH MANSION WORLD

1. You get acquainted with the Brilliant Evening Stars and other superangels.

2. On Jerusem visits you learn more about the Sons of God.

3. There are more group projects.

4. You learn more from the universe broadcasts.

5. You are introduced to the demands and delights of true morontia social life.

6. A new social culture is based not on personal aggrandizement, but on:

    a. *Understanding sympathy of mutual appreciation.*
    b. *Unselfish love of mutual service.*
    c. *Realization of supreme destiny.*

7. You become self-conscious of God-knowing, God-revealing, God-seeking, and God-finding.

8. Local universe language is mastered. P. 536.

VI. THE FIFTH MANSION WORLD

1. There is a great advance in spiritual culture—a foretaste of Jerusem life.

2. The Uversa tongue is mastered.

3. There is a foretaste of the constellation study worlds.

4. The real birth of cosmic consciousness occurs. Horizons are extended.

5. Real enthusiasm for the Havona ascent is born.

6. Study becomes voluntary.

7. Worship is spontaneous.

8. A real morontia character is budding. P. 537.

VII. THE SIXTH MANSION WO+RLD

1. First lessons in the forthcoming spirit career take place.

2. You are introduced to universe administration.

3. Normally the perfect fusion of human mind and the divine Adjuster occurs here—actual working identity. (Fusion may have occurred previously.)

4. The archangel pronounces: "This is a beloved son in whom I am well pleased."

5. Conferring of the ascender's new name is followed by the 40 days of spiritual retirement.

6. You are divested of the coarse vestiges of animal origin. P. 537-8.

VIII. THE SEVENTH MANSION WORLD

1. Preparation begins for residence on Jerusem.

2. The purpose of the early morontia training is to eradicate vestigial animal tendencies, such as:

    a. Procrastination.
    b. Equivocation.
    c. Insincerity.
    d. Problem avoidance.
    e. Unfairness.
    f. Ease seeking. P. 551.

3. Signs of differential origins are obliterated.

4. You are purged of all remnants of:

    a. Unfortunate heredity.
    b. Unwholesome environment.
    c. Unspiritual tendencies.

5. The "mark of the beast" is eradicated.

6. You visit the world of the Father and attain new levels of worship.

7. Classes form for graduation to Jerusem.

8. Graduating classes depart from the sea of glass, with residential status. P. 538-9.

IX. THE JERUSEM SOJOURN

1. All Jerusem welcomes these graduating classes, as they arrive on the sea of glass with the harps of God.

2. No more "resurrections"—this morontia body will go through to the end of the morontia career. P. 539-40.

3. This morontia form will undergo 570 changes before achieving first-stage spirit status. P. 542.

4. There is time for morontia play and the realization of frustrated ambitions.

5. Deficiencies, if any, in parental training, are made up by service in the homes of the Material Sons and Daughters.

6. The schools of Jerusem citizenship are conducted by the Material Sons and the Melchizedeks.

7. The morontians study and practice representative government.

8. The vote ranges in value from one to one thousand according to the mota achievement.

9. The over-all task of Jerusem training is the creation of a mota personality— morontia unification of personality. P. 518.

10. You learn to submit the self to the discipline of group require-ments. P. 494.

11. There is a unification of personality around a master motive, with an integration to secondary motivations.

12. Free time for visitation of other worlds is available.

X. THE CONSTELLATION TRAINING

1. The over-all purpose of the constellation sojourn is the perfected socialization of the morontia personality.

2. Progressively and in varied association you learn to live with the ten orders of univitatia—morontia-like natives of the constellation.

3. The major study is the mastery of group ethics—submission of the self to the discipline of testing group activities.

4. There are seven phases of interpersonal relationship embraced in the varied associations with univitatia and morontians. P. 494.

5. After graduation from World No. 70 you are granted Edentia citizenship and take up residence on the headquarters planet.

6. Edentia is the midpoint in the morontia life—you are about half material and half spiritual.

7. On Edentia you will have frequent contact with the celestial artisans and the reversion directors. P. 495.

8. You will meet people from other systems—foreigners.

9. You will enjoy receptions given by the Faithful of Days. P. 489.

10. You will meet many new personalities, such as:
    a. *Law forecasters.*
    b. *Social architects.*
    c. *Ethical sensitizers, etc. P. 432.*

XI. ON THE LOCAL UNIVERSE CAPITAL

There are 490 Salvington satellites—10 groups of 7 primary worlds, each with 6 subsatellites.

1. Here occurs progressive spiritual training—preparation for later graduation into the spirit world.

2. This is the beginning of the end of the morontia life.

3. First business is a complete review of the morontia career—from the world of origin.

4. Then comes the attempted correlation of all these experiences.

5. Study and work follow on the special Salvination world groups.
    a. **The Melchizidek worlds.** *The Michael bestowals.*
    b. **Vorondadek worlds.** *Co-ordination of universe legislation.*
    c. **Lanonandek worlds.** *Administration. Schools of applied knowledge.*
    d. **Life Carrier worlds.** *Life planning, conservation, and evolution.*
    e. **Finaliter worlds.** *Fraternize with midsoniters and beings from superuniverse and central universe.*
    f. **Evening Star worlds.** *Enter schools of the Teacher Sons and the Evening Stars.*
    g. **Archangel worlds.** *Study the ascending careers of mortals.*
    h. **Spirit-fused Mortal** *worlds. Visit on invitation—indefinite.*

    i.   **Seraphic worlds**. *Indefinite. Meet all orders of angels—and some unrevealed.*

    j.   *Nothing is said about this group of worlds.*

6.   Salvington.

    a.   *You enter morontia finishing schools.*

    b.   *Study begins in extension schools—conducted by teachers from Uminor the third.*

    c.   *You may visit Michael and the Creative Spirit and hear about Michael's bestowal on Urantia.*

    d.   *There is considerable leisure and you enjoy the sweetness of success.*

    e.   *Final examinations for Adjuster-fused mortals are passed.*

    f.   *You enter the first-stage spirit status.*

    g.   *You go before Michael and receive credentials for transit to the minor sector of the superuniverse of Orvonton.*

21. THE CORPS OF THE FINALITY

Heaven in the Bible

THE CORPS OF THE FINALITY

I. COMPOSITION OF THE MORTAL FINALITER CORPS

1. Composition of the Mortal Finaliter Corps.

"The Corps of Mortal Finaliters represents the present known destination of the ascending Adjuster-fused mortals of time. But there are other groups who are also assigned to this corps. The primary finaliter corps is composed of the following:

"1. Havona Natives.
"2. Gravity Messengers.
"3. Glorified Mortals.
"4. Adopted Seraphim.
"5. Glorified Material Sons.
"6. Glorified Midway Creatures.

"These six groups of glorified beings compose this unique body of eternal destiny. We think we know their future work, but we are not certain. While the Corps of the Mortal Finality is mobilizing on Paradise, and while they now so extensively minister to the universes of space and administer the worlds settled in light and life, their future destination must be the now-organizing universes of outer space. At least that is the conjecture of Uversa." P. 345.

2. The corps does not obliterate individuality.

"The corps is organized in accordance with the working associations of the worlds of space and in keeping with the associative experience acquired throughout the long and eventful ascendant career. All the ascendant creatures admitted to this corps are received in equality, but this exalted equality in no way abrogates individuality or destroys personal identity. We can immediately discern, in communicating with a finaliter, whether he is an ascendant mortal, Havona native, adopted seraphim, midway creature, or Material Son." P. 345.

3. Finaliters are always serving on Urantia.

"During the present universe age the finaliters return to serve in the universes of time. They are assigned to labor successively in the different superuniverses until after they have served in all the other six supercreations. Thus may they acquire the sevenfold concept of the Supreme Being.

"One or more companies of the mortal finaliters are constantly in service on Urantia. There is no domain of universe service to which they are not assigned; they function universally and with alternating and equal periods of assigned duty and free service." P. 345.

4. **Gravity Messengers and the primary Finality Corps.**

"Wherever and whenever Gravity Messengers are functioning, the finaliters are in command. All Gravity Messengers are under the exclusive jurisdiction of Grandfanda, and they are assigned only to the primary Corps of the Finality. They are invaluable to the finaliters even now, and they will be all-serviceable in the eternal future. No other group of intelligent creatures possesses such a personalized messenger corps able to transcend time and space. Similar types of messenger-recorders attached to other finaliter corps are not personalized; they are absonitized.

"Gravity Messengers may be attached to a finaliter company in unlimited numbers, but only one messenger, the chief of his fellows, is mustered into the Mortal Corps of the Finality. This chief however has assigned to him a permanent staff of 999 fellow messengers, and as occasion may require, he may call upon the reserves of the order for assistants in unlimited numbers.

"Gravity Messengers and glorified mortal finaliters achieve a touching and profound affection for one another; they have much in common: One is a direct personalization of a fragment of the Universal Father, the other a creature personality existent in the surviving immortal soul fused with a fragment of the same Universal Father, the spirit Thought Adjuster." P. 346-7.

5. **Seraphic members of the Finality Corps.**

"Many of the faithful seraphic guardians of mortals are permitted to go through the ascendant career with their human awards, and many of these guardian angels, after becoming Father fused, join their subjects in taking the finaliter oath of eternity and forever accept the destiny of their mortal associates. Angels who pass through the ascending experience of mortal beings may share the destiny of human nature; they may equally and eternally be mustered into this Corps. of the Finality. Large numbers of the adopted and glorified seraphim are attached to the various nonmortal finaliter corps." P. 348-9.

6. **Material Sons in the Finality Corps.**

"There is provision in the universes of time and space whereby the Adamic citizens of the local systems, when long delayed in receiving planetary assignment, may initiate a petition for release from permanent-citizenship status. And if granted, they join the ascending pilgrims on the universe capitals and thence proceed onward to Paradise and the Corps of the Finality." P. 349.

7. Midwayers and the Finality Corps.

"On many planets the midway creatures are produced in large numbers, but they seldom tarry on their native world subsequent to its being settled in light and life. Then, or soon thereafter, they are released from permanent-citizenship status and start on the ascension to Paradise. Passing through the morontia worlds, the superuniverse, and Havona in company with the mortals of time and space." P. 349.

8. Evangels of Light and the finaliters.

"At the present time every finaliter company numbers 999 personalities of oath status, permanent members. The vacant place is occupied by the chief of attached Evangels of Light assigned on any single mission. But these beings are only transient members of the corps." P. 349.

II. RESIDENTIAL PROVISIONS FOR THE FINALITY CORPS

1. The finaliter world in the local system.

"This is the headquarters of the finaliter corps of the local system and is surrounded by the receiving worlds, the seven mansion worlds, dedicated so fully to the scheme of mortal ascension. The finaliter world is accessible to the inhabitants of all seven mansion worlds. Transport seraphim carry ascending personalities back and forth on these pilgrimages, which are designed to cultivate their faith in the ultimate destiny of transition mortals. Although the finaliters and their structures are not ordinarily perceptible to morontia vision, you will be more than thrilled, from time to time, when the energy transformers and the Morontia Power Supervisors enable you momentarily to glimpse these high spirit personalities who have actually completed the Paradise ascension, and who have returned to the very worlds where you are beginning this long journey, as the pledge of assurance that you may and can complete the stupendous undertaking. All mansion world sojourners go to the finaliter sphere at least once a year for these assemblies of finaliter visualization." P. 509.

2. Residential provision for the corps in Havona.

"At present, although the spheres of the seven circuits are maintained in all their supernal glory, only about one percent of all planetary capacity is utilized in the work of furthering the Father's

universal plan of mortal ascension. About one tenth of one percent of
the area of these enormous worlds is dedicated to the life and
activities of the Corps of the Finality, beings eternally settled in light
and life who often sojourn and minister on the Havona worlds.
These exalted beings have their personal residences on Paradise." P.
156.

3. **Paradise the home and playground of finaliters.**

"Paradise is the home, and Havona the workshop and playground,
of the finaliters. And every God-knowing mortal craves to be a
finaliter.

"The central universe is not only man's established destiny, but it is
also the starting place of the eternal career of the finaliters as they
shall sometime be started out on the undisclosed and universal
adventure in the experience of exploring the infinity of the Universal Father." P. 163.

III. MASTER ARCHITECTS AND TRANSCENDENTALERS

1. **Master Architects and finaliters.**

"The senior Master Architect has the oversight of the seven Corps
of the Finality, and they are:

"1. The Corps of Mortal Finaliters.
"2. The Corps of Paradise Finaliters.
"3. The Corps of Trinitized Finaliters.
"4. The Corps of Conjoint Trinitized Finaliters.
"5. The Corps of Havona Finaliters.
"6. The Corps of Transcendental Finaliters.
"7. The Corps of Unrevealed Sons of Destiny.

"Each of these destiny corps has a presiding head, and the seven
constitute the Supreme Council of Destiny on Paradise; and during
the present universe age Grandfanda is the chief of this supreme body
of universe assignment for the children of ultimate destiny." P. 352-3.

2. **Significance of mobilization of all finaliters.**

"The gathering together of these seven finaliter corps signifies
reality mobilization of potentials, personalities, minds, spirits,
absonites, and experiential actualities that probably transcend even
the future master universe functions of the Supreme Being. These
seven finaliter corps probably signify the present activity of the
Ultimate Trinity engaged in mustering the forces of the finite and
the absonite in preparation for inconceivable developments in the

universes of outer space. Nothing like this mobilization has taken
place, since the near times of eternity when the Paradise Trinity
similarly mobilized the then existing personalities of Paradise and
Havona and commissioned them as administrators and rulers of the
projected seven superuniverses of time and space. The seven
finaliter corps represent the divinity response of the grand universe
to the future needs of the undeveloped potentials in the outer
universes of future-eternal activities." P. 353.

3. **The Trinity oath of the finaliters.**

"When mortal ascenders are admitted to the finaliter corps of
Paradise, they take an oath to the Paradise Trinity, and in taking this
oath of allegiance, they are thereby pledging eternal fidelity to God
the Supreme, who is the Trinity as comprehended by all finite
creature personalities. Subsequently, as the finaliter companies
function throughout the evolving universes, they are solely
amenable to the mandates of Paradise origin until the eventful times
of the settling of local universes in light and life. As the new
governmental organizations of these perfected creations begin to be
reflective of the emerging sovereignty of the Supreme, we observe
that the outlying finaliter companies then acknowledge the
jurisdictional authority of such new governments. It appears that
God the Supreme is evolving as the unifier of the evolutionary
Corps of the Finality, but it is highly probable that the eternal
destiny of these seven corps will be directed by the Supreme as a
member of the Ultimate Trinity." P. 1292.

4. **Transcendentalers and finaliters.**

"Part of the perfected mortal's experience on Paradise as a finaliter
consists in the effort to achieve comprehension of the nature and
function of more than one thousand groups of the transcendental
supercitizens of Paradise, eventuated beings of absonite attributes.
In their association with these superpersonalities, the ascendant
finaliters receive great assistance from the helpful guidance of
numerous orders of transcendental ministers who are assigned to
the task of introducing the evolved finaliters to their new Paradise
brothern. The entire order of the Transcendentalers live in the west
of Paradise in a vast area which they exclusively occupy." P. 350.

IV. ADJUSTERS AND GUARDIAN SERAPHIM

1. Adjuster-fused finaliters.

"*Fused Adjusters*—finaliters—those who have become one with the ascending creatures of the superuniverses, the eternity partners of the time ascenders of the Paradise Corps of the Finality. Thought Adjusters ordinarily become fused with the ascending mortals of time, and with such surviving mortals they are registered in and out of Ascendington; they follow the course of ascendant beings. Upon fashion with the ascending evolutionary soul, it appears that the Adjuster translates from the absolute existential level of the universe to the finite experiential level of functional association with an ascending personality. While retaining all of the character of the existential divine nature, a fused Adjuster becomes indissolubly linked with the ascending career of a surviving mortal." P. 1179.

2. Adjusters and finaliters.

"Upon the attainment of the finaliter levels of ascendant experience, these spirits of the sixth stage appear to transmute some mind factor representing a union of certain phases of the mortal and Adjuster minds which had previously functioned as liaison between the divine and human phases of such ascending personalities. This experiential mind quality probably 'supremacies' and subsequently augments the experiential endowment of evolutionary Deity—the Supreme Being." P. 1182.

3. Adjuster and mortal destiny.

"On the Adjuster-fusion worlds the destiny of the Mystery Monitor is identical with that of the ascending mortal—the Paradise Corps of the Finality. And neither Adjuster nor mortal can attain that unique goal without the full co-operation and faithful help of the other. This extraordinary partnership is one of the most engrossing and amazing of all the cosmic phenomena of this universe age." P. 1238.

4. Guardians and the Finality Corps.

"Only destiny guardians are mustered into the primary or mortal Corps of the Finality, and such pairs have engaged in the supreme adventure of identity at-oneness; the two beings have achieved spiritual bi-unification on Seraphington prior their reception into the finaliter corps. In this experience the two angelic natures, so complemental in all universe functions, achieve ultimate spirit two-in-oneness, repercussing in a new capacity for the reception of, and fusion with, a non-Adjuster fragment of the Paradise Father. And so do some of your loving seraphic associates in time also become our finaliter associates in eternity, children of the Supreme and perfected sons of the Paradise Father." P. 1249.

V. CENTRAL UNIVERSE AND THE FINALITY CORPS

1. Havoners seek to enter Mortal Finality Corps.

"Many of the Havona natives who serve as teachers in the pilgrim-training schools of the central universe become greatly attached to the ascending mortals and still more intrigued with the future work and destiny of the Corps of Mortal Finaliters. On Paradise there is maintained, at the administrative headquarters of the corps, a registry for Havona volunteers presided over by the associate of Grandfanda. Today, you will find millions upon millions of Havona natives upon this waiting list. These perfect beings of direct and divine creation are of great assistance to the Mortal Corps of Finality, and they will undoubtedly be of even greater service in the far-distant future. They provide the viewpoint of one born in perfection and divine repleteness. The finaliters thus embrace both phases of experiential existence—perfect and perfected." P. 346.

2. Conditions for entering the Mortal Finality Corps.

"Havona natives must achieve certain experiential developments in liaison with evolutionary beings which will create reception capacity for the bestowal of a fragment of the spirit of the Universal Father. The Mortal Finaliter Corps has as permanent members only such beings as have been fused with the spirit of the First Source and Center, or who, like the Gravity Messengers, innately embody this spirit of God the Father.

"The inhabitants of the central universe are received into the corps in the ratio of one in a thousand—a finaliter company. The corps is organized for temporary service in companies of one thousand, the ascendant creatures numbering 997 to one Havona native and one Gravity Messenger. Finaliters are thus mobilized in companies, but the finality oath is administered individually. It is an oath of sweeping implications and eternal import. The Havona native takes the same oath and becomes forever attached to the corps." P. 346.

3. Nativity fruits continue through eternity.

"The distinctive personality trends exhibited in the life experience of evolutionary mortals, which are characteristic in each superuniverse, and which are directly expressive of the nature of the dominating Master Spirit, are never fully effaced, not even after such ascenders are subjected to the long training and unifying discipline encountered on the one billion educational spheres of Havona. Even the subsequent intense Paradise culture does not suffice to eradicate the earmarks of superuniverse origin. Throughout all eternity an ascendant mortal will exhibit traits indicative of the presiding Spirit of his superuniverse of nativity. Even in the Corps of the Finality, when it is desired to arrive at or to portray a *complete* Trinity relationship to the evolutionary creation, always a group of seven finaliters is assembled, one from each superuniverse." P. 191.

VI. SUPREME BEING AND ETERNAL SON

1. The Supreme unifier.

"The Supreme Being has a threefold function in the experience of mortal man: First, he is the unifier of time-space divinity, God the Sevenfold; second, he is the maximum of Deity which finite creatures can actually comprehend; third, he is mortal man's only avenue of approach to the transcendental experience of consorting with absonite mind, eternal spirit, and Paradise personality.

"Ascendant finaliters, having been born in the local universes, nurtured in the superuniverses, and trained in the central universe, embrace in their personal experiences the full potential of the comprehension of the time-space divinity of God the Sevenfold unifying in the Supreme. Finaliters serve successively in superuniverses other than those of nativity, thereby superimposing experience upon experience until the fullness of the sevenfold diversity of possible creature experience has been encompassed. Through the ministry of the indwelling Adjusters the finaliters are enabled to *find* the Universal Father, but it is by these techniques of experience that such finaliters come really to *know* the Supreme Being, and they are destined to the service and the *revelation* of this Supreme Deity in and to the future universes of outer space." P. 643.

2. Spirit of Eternal Son and the finaliters.

"The evolving immortal soul of man, the joint creation of the material mind and the Adjuster, ascends as such to Paradise and subsequently, when mustered into the Corps of the Finality, becomes allied in some new way with the spirit-gravity circuit of the Eternal Son by a technique of experience known as *finaliter transcendation*. Such finaliters thus become acceptable candidates for experimental recognition as personalities of God the Supreme. And when these mortal intellects in the unrevealed future assignments of the Corps of the Finality attain the seventh stage of spirit existence, such dual minds will become triune. These two attuned minds, the human and the divine, will become glorified in union with the experiential mind of the then actualized Supreme Being." P. 1286.

VII. TRINITIZATION BY MORTAL FINALITERS

1. Trinitization by mortal finaliters.

"The ascendant Adjuster-fused mortal finaliters who have attained certain levels of Paradise culture and spiritual development are among those who can essay to trinitize a creature being. Mortal-finaliter companies, when stationed on Paradise, are granted a recess every millennium of Havona time. There are seven different ways such finaliters may elect to spend this duty-free period, and one of these is, in association with some fellow finaliter or some Paradise-Havona personality, to attempt the enactment of creature trinitization.

"If two mortal finaliters, on going before the Architects of the Master Universe, demonstrate that they have independently chosen an identical concept for trinitization, the Architects are empowered, on their own discretion, to promulgate mandates permitting these glorified mortal ascenders to extend their recess and to remove themselves for a time to the trinitizing sector of the Paradise Citizens. At the end of this assigned retreat, if they report that they have singly and jointly elected to make the paradisiacal effort to spiritualize, idealize, and actualize a selected and original concept which has not theretofore been trinitized, then does Master Spirit Number Seven issue orders authorizing such an extraordinary undertaking." P. 249.

2. Trinitization by finaliters and Paradise Citizens.

"When a finaliter and a Paradise Citizen co-operate in the trinitization of a 'child of time and eternity'—a transaction involving the unrevealed mind potentials of the Supreme-Ultimate—and when such an unclassified personality is dispatched to Vicegerington, a Solitary Messenger (a conjectured personality repercussion of the bestowal of such deity mind) is always assigned as guardian-companion to such a creature-trinitized son. This messenger accompanies the new son of destiny to the world of his assignment and nevermore leaves Vicegerington. When thus attached to the destinies of a child of time and eternity, a Solitary

Messenger is forever transferred to the sole supervision of the Architects of the Master Universe. What the future of such an extraordinary association may be, we do not know. For ages these partnerships of unique personalities have continued to forgather on Vicegerington, but not even a single pair has ever gone forth therefrom." P. 262.

VIII. DESTINY OF MORTAL FINALITERS

1. Eternal future of finaliters.

"As we view this triune development, embracing creatures, universes, and Deity, can we be criticized for anticipating that something new and unrevealed is approaching culmination in the master universe? Is it not natural that we should associate this agelong mobilization and organization of physical universes on such a hitherto unknown scale and the personality emergence of the Supreme Being with this stupendous scheme of upstepping the mortals of time to divine perfection and with their subsequent mobilization on Paradise in the Corps of the Finality—a designation and destiny enshrouded in universe mystery? It is increasingly the belief of all Uversa that the assembling Corps of the Finality are destined to some future service in the universes of outer space, where we already are able to identify the clustering of at least seventy thousand aggregations of matter, each of which is greater than any one of the present superuniverses." P. 354.

2. Outer space destiny of finaliters.

"In traversing the ascending scale of living existence from mortal man to the Deity embrace, you actually live the very life of every possible phase and stage of perfected creature existence within the limits of the present universe age. From mortal man to Paradise finaliter embraces all that now can be—encompasses everything presently possible to the living orders of intelligent, perfected finite creature beings. If the future destiny of the Paradise finaliters is service in new universes now in the making, it is assured that in this new and future creation there will be no created orders of experiential beings whose lives will be wholly different from those which mortal finaliters have lived on some world as a part of their ascending training, as one of the stages of their agelong progress from animal to angel and from angel to spirit and from spirit to God." P. 558.

3. Destiny of the Finality Corps.

"The present known destiny of surviving mortals is the Paradise Corps of the Finality; this is also the goal of destiny for all Thought Adjusters who become joined in eternal union with their mortal companions. At present the Paradise finaliters are working throughout the grand universe in many undertakings, but we all conjecture that they will have other and even more supernal tasks to perform in the distant future after the seven superuniverses have become settled in light and life, and when the finite God has finally emerged from the mystery which now surrounds this Supreme Deity.....

"We believe that the mortals of Adjuster fusion, together with their finaliter associates, are destined to function in some manner in the administration of the universes of the first outer space level. We have not the slightest doubt that in due time these enormous galaxies will become inhabited universes. And we are equally convinced that among the administrators thereof will be found the Paradise finaliters whose natures are the cosmic consequence of the blending of creature and Creator." P. 1239.

4. The superb mortal adventure.

"What an adventure! What a romance! A gigantic creation to be administered by the children of the Supreme, these personalized and humanized Adjusters, these Adjusterized and eternalized mortals, these mysterious combinations and eternal associations of the highest known manifestation of the essence of the First Source and Center and the lowest form of intelligent life capable of comprehending and attaining the Universal Father. We conceive that such amalgamated beings, such partnerships of Creator and creature, will become superb rulers, matchless administrators, and understanding and sympathetic directors of any and all forms of intelligent life which may come into existence throughout these future universes of the first outer space level.

"True it is, you mortals are of earthly, animal origin; your frame is indeed dust. But if you actually will, if you really desire, surely the heritage of the ages is yours, and you shall someday serve throughout the universes in your true characters—children of the Supreme God of experience and divine sons of the Paradise Father of all personalities." P. 1239-40.

5. Destiny of sublime service.

"Ascendant Adjuster-fused mortals compose the bulk of the primary Corps of the Finality. Together with the adopted and glorified seraphim they usually constitute 990 in each finaliter company. The proportion of mortals and angels in any one group varies, though the mortals far outnumber the seraphim. The Havona natives, glorified Material Sons, glorified midway creatures, the Gravity Messengers, and the unknown and missing member make up only one percent of the corps; each company of one thousand finaliters has places for just ten of these nonmortal and nonseraphic personalities.

"We of Uversa do not know the 'finality destiny' of the ascendant mortals of time. At present they reside on Paradise and temporarily serve in the Corps of Light and Life, but such a tremendous course of ascendant training and such lengthy universe discipline must be designed to qualify them for even greater tests of trust and more sublime services of responsibility." P. 347.

6. **Speculations regarding finaliter destiny.**

"Notwithstanding that these ascendant mortals have attained Paradise, have been mustered into the Corps of the Finality, and have been sent back in large numbers to participate in the conduct of local universes and to assist in the administration of superuniverse affairs—in the face of even this *apparent* destiny, there remains the significant fact that they are of record as only sixth-stage spirits. There undoubtedly remains one more step in the career of the Mortal Corps of the Finality. We do not know the nature of that step, but we have taken cognizance of, and here call attention to, three facts:

"1. We know from the records that mortals are the spirits of the first order during their sojourn in the minor sectors, and that they advance to the second order when translated to the major sectors, and to the third when they go forward to the central training worlds of the superuniverse. Mortals become quartan or graduate spirits after reaching the sixth circle of Havona and become spirits of the fifth order when they find the Universal Father. They subsequently attain the sixth stage of spirit existence upon taking the oath that musters them forever into the eternity assignment of the Corps of the Mortal Finality. "We observe that spirit classification, or designation, has been determined by actual advancement from one realm of universe service to another realm of universe service or from one universe to another universe; and we surmise that the bestowal of seventh-spirit classification upon the Mortal Corps of the

Finality will be simultaneous with their advancement to eternal assignment for service on hitherto unrecorded and unrevealed spheres and concomitant with their attainment of God the Supreme. But aside from these bold conjectures, we really know no more about all this than you do; our knowledge of the mortal career does not go beyond present Paradise destiny.

"2. The mortal finaliters have fully complied with the injunction of the ages, 'Be you perfect'; they have ascended the universal path of mortal attainment; they have found God, and they have been duly inducted into the Corps of the Finality. Such Beings have attained the present limit of spirit progression but not *finality of ultimate spirit status*. They have achieved the present limit of creature perfection but not *finality of creature service*. They have experienced the fullness of Deity worship but not *finality of experiential Deity attainment*.

"3. The glorified mortals of the Paradise Corps of Finality are ascendant beings in possession of experiential knowledge of every step of the actuality and philosophy of the fullest possible life of intelligent existence, while during the ages of this ascent from the lowest material worlds to the spiritual heights of Paradise, these surviving creatures have been trained to the limits of their capacity respecting every detail of every divine principle of the just and efficient, as well as merciful and patient, administration of all the universal creation of time and space." P. 347-8.

7. **Speculation regarding seventh group of mortal finaliters.**

"As the Mortal Corps of the Finality is at present constituted, there are just six classes of permanent members. The finaliters, as might be expected, engage in much speculation as to the identity of their future comrades, but there is little agreement among them.

"We of Uversa often conjecture respecting the identity of the seventh group of finaliters. We entertain many ideas, embracing possible assignment of some of the accumalating corps of the numerous trinitized groups on Paradise, Vicegerington, and the inner Havona circuit. It is even conjectured that the Corps of the Finality may be permitted to trinitize many of their assistants in the work of universe administration in the event they are destined to the service of universes now in the making.

"One of us holds the opinion that this vacant place in the corps will be filled by some type of being of origin in the new universe of their future service; the other inclines to the belief that this place will be occupied by some type of Paradise personality not yet created, eventuated, or trinitized. But we will most likely await the entrance of the finaliters upon their seventh stage of spirit attainment before we really know." P. 350.

8. **Finaliter destiny.**

"I once sojourned in a universe where a certain group of beings taught that the finaliters, in eternity, were eventually to become the children of the Deity Absolute. But I am unwilling to accept this solution of the mystery which enshrouds the future of the finaliters.

"The Corps of the Finality embrace, among others, those mortals of time and space who have attained perfection in all that pertains to the will of God. As creatures and within the limits of creature capacity they fully and truly know God. Having thus found God as the Father of all creatures, these finaliters must sometime begin the quest for the superfinite Father. But this quest involves a grasp of the absonite nature of the ultimate attributes and character of the Paradise Father. Eternity will disclose whether such an attainment is possible, but we are convinced, even if the finaliters do grasp this ultimate of divinity, they will probably be unable to attain the superultimate levels of absolute Deity.

"It may be possible that the finaliters will partially attain the Deity Absolute, but even if they should, still in the eternity of eternities the problem of the Universal Absolute will continue to intrigue, mystify, baffle, and challenge the ascending and progressing finaliters, for we perceive that the unfathomability of the cosmic relationships of the Universal Absolute will tend to grow in proportions as the material universes and their spiritual administration continue to expand.

"Only infinity can disclose the Father-Infinite." P. 116-7.

HEAVEN IN THE BIBLE

1. **Hebrew concept of heaven.**

The Hebrews had vague ideas of heaven. They thought the earth was flatsquare. Sheol (hell) was under the world and heaven above.

2. **Heaven rested on pillars.**

"The pillars of heaven trembled." **Job 26:11**.

3. Jews believed in seven heavens.

"To the Lord your God belong heaven and the heaven of heavens."
Deut. 10:14.

"The highest heaven cannot contain thee." **1 Kings 8:27.**

a. *God's throne was in the seventh heaven—Aravoth.*

b. *Paradise was the third heaven.* "I know a man…who…was caught up to the third heaven." *2 Cor. 12:2.*

c. *Jews thought the second heaven was the prison sphere for the hosts of sin and rebellion.* "…against the spiritual hosts of wickedness in the heavenly places." *Ex. 6:12.*

4. Old Testament references to heaven.

"God created the heavens and the earth." **Gen. 1:1.**

"I will rain bread from heaven for you." **Ex. 16:4.**

"I saw the Lord sitting on his throne, and all the host of heaven standing beside him." **1 Kings 22:19.**

"We are servants of the God of heaven and earth." **Ezra 5:11.**

"Is not God high in the heavens?" **Job 22:12.**

"The Lord is in the holy temple, the Lord's throne is in heaven." **Ps. 11:4.**

"Thus says the Lord: 'Heaven is my throne.'" **Isa. 66:1.**

"'Do I not fill heaven and earth?' says the Lord." **Jer. 23:24.**

5. New Testament references to heaven.

Heaven non-sensous. *"For when they rise from the dead, they neither marry nor are given in marriage."* **Mark 12:25.**

"Blessed are the poor in spirit, for theirs is the kingdom of heaven."
Matt. 5:3.

"To you it has been given to know the secrets of the kingdom of heaven."
Matt. 13:11.

"I will give you the keys of the kingdom of heaven." **Matt. 16:19.**

"I saw Satan fall like lightning from heaven." **Luke 10:18.**

"Truly, I say to you, today you will be with me in Paradise." **Luke 23:43.**

22. GOD'S ETERNAL PURPOSE

    I.   UNIVERSE MADE TO BE INHABITED.

    II. INFINITE PLANS OF THE ETERNAL PURPOSE.

    III. ALL THINGS UNFOLD ACCORDING TO THE ETERNAL PURPOSE.

    IV. THE ETERNAL PURPOSE WILL TRIUMPH.

Bible Teaching Regarding God's Purpose

    I.   THE ETERNAL PURPOSE.

    II. PREDESTINATION.

    III. ELECTION.

GOD'S ETERNAL PURPOSE

I. UNIVERSE WAS MADE TO BE INHABITED

1. Universes made to be inhabited.

"The myriads of planetary systems were all made to be eventually inhabited by many different types of intelligent creatures, beings who could know God, receive the divine affection, and love him in return. The universe of universes is the work of God. and the dwelling place of his diverse creatures. 'God created the heavens and formed the earth; he established the universe and created this world not in vain; he formed it to be inhabited.'" P. 21. Isa. 45:18.

2. Finites exist because of the eternal purpose.

"The realm of the finite exist by virtue of the eternal purpose of God. Finite creatures, high and low, may propound theories, and have done so, as to the necessity of the finite in the cosmic economy, but in the last analysis it exists because God so willed. The universe cannot be explained, neither can a finite creature offer a rational reason for his own individual existence without appealing to the prior acts and pre-existent volition of ancestral beings, Creators or procreators." P. 1260.

3. The eternal purpose is attainable by all.

"There is in the mind of God a plan which embraces every creature of all his vast domains, and this plan is an eternal purpose of boundless opportunity, unlimited progress, and endless life. And the infinite treasures of such a matchless career are yours for the striving!

"The goal of eternity is ahead! The adventure of divinity attainment lies before you! The race for perfection is on! Whosoever will may enter, and certain victory will crown the efforts of every human being who will run the race of faith and trust, depending every step of the way on the leading of the indwelling Adjuster and on the guidance of that good spirit of the Universe Son, which so freely has been poured out upon all flesh." P. 365.

II. INFINITE PLANS OF THE ETERNAL PURPOSE

1. Infinite plans of the eternal purpose.

"Because the First Father is infinite in his plans and eternal in his purposes, it is inherently impossible for any finite being ever to grasp or comprehend these divine plans and purposes in their fullness.

Mortal man can glimpse the Father's purposes only now and then, here and there, as they are revealed in relation to the outworking of the plan of creature ascension on its successive levels of universe progression. Though man cannot encompass the significance of infinity, the infinite Father does most certainly fully comprehend and lovingly embrace all the finity of all his children in all universes." P. 35.

2. **Vast scope of God's eternal purpose.**

"The Father constantly and unfailingly meets the need of the differential of demand for himself as it changes from time to time in various sections of his master universe. The great God knows and understands himself; he is infinitely self-conscious of all his primal attributes of perfection. God is not a cosmic accident; neither is he a universe experimenter. The Universe Sovereigns may engage in adventure; the Constellation Father may experiment; the system head may practice; but the Universal Father sees the end from the beginning, and his divine plan and eternal purpose actually embrace and comprehend all the experiments and all the adventures of all his subordinates in every world, system, and constellation in every universe of his vast domains." P. 34.

3. **All creation is a part of the divine plan.**

"There is a great and glorious purpose in the march of the universes through space. All of your mortal struggling is not in vain. We are all part of an immense plan, a gigantic enterprise, and it is the vastness of the undertaking that renders it impossible to see very much of it at any one time and during any one life. We are all a part of an eternal project which the Gods are supervising and outworking. The whole marvelous and universal mechanism moves on majestically through space to the music of the the meter of the infinite thought and the eternal purpose of the First Great Source and Center." P. 364.

4. **The glorious plan of the eternal purpose.**

"The eternal purpose of the eternal God is a high spiritual ideal. The events of time and the struggles of material existence are but the transient scaffolding which bridges over to the other side, to the promised land of spiritual reality and supernal existence. Of course, you mortals find it difficult to grasp the idea of an eternal purpose; you are virtually unable to comprehend the thought of eternity, something never beginning and never ending. Everything familiar to you has an end." P. 364.

III. ALL THINGS UNFOLD ACCORDING TO THE ETERNAL PURPOSE

1. **All things unfold according to the eternal purpose.**

    "Within the bounds of that which is consistent with the divine nature, it is literally true that 'with God all things are possible.' The long-drawn-out evolutionary processes of peoples, planets, and universes are under the perfect control of the universe creators and administrators and unfold in accordance with the eternal purpose of the Universal Father, proceeding in harmony and order and in keeping with the all-wise plan of God. There is only one lawgiver. He upholds the worlds in space and swings the universes around the endless circle of the eternal circuit." P. 46. Matt. 19:26.

2. **Differential execution of the eternal purpose.**

    "The reactions of a changeless God, in the execution of his eternal purpose, may seem to vary in accordance with the changing attitude and the shifting minds of his created intelligences; that is, they may apparently and superficially vary; but underneath the surface and beneath all outward manifestations, there is still present the changeless purpose, the everlasting plan, of the eternal God.

    "Out in the universes, perfection must necessarily be a relative term, but in the central universe and especially on Paradise, perfection is undiluted; in certain phases it is even absolute. Trinity manifestations vary the exhibition of the divine perfection but do not attenuate it." P. 36.

3. **Who really knows the eternal purpose?**

    "The Universal Father has an eternal purpose pertaining to the material, intellectual, and spiritual phenomena of the universe of universes, which he is executing throughout all time. God created the universes of his own free and sovereign will, and he created them in accordance with his all-wise and eternal purpose. It is doubtful whether anyone except the Paradise Deities and their highest associates really knows very much about the eternal purpose of God. Even the exalted citizens of Paradise hold very diverse opinions about the nature of the eternal purpose of the Deities." P. 54.

IV. THE ETERNAL PURPOSE WILL TRIUMPH

1.   The eternal purpose will triumph.

"In the affairs of men's hearts the Universal Father may not always have his way; but in the conduct and destiny of a planet the divine plan prevails; the eternal purpose of wisdom and love triumphs." P. 51.

2.   God pursues the realization of an eternal purpose.

"The infinite and eternal Ruler of the universe of universes is power, form, energy, process, pattern, principle, presence and idealized reality. But he is more; he is personal; he exercises a sovereign will, experiences self-consciousness of divinity, executes the mandates of a creative mind, pursues the satisfaction of the realization of an eternal purpose, and manifests a Father's love and affection for his universe children. And all these more personal traits of the Father can be better understood by observing them as they were revealed in the bestowal life of Michael, your Creator Son, while he was incarnated on Urantia." P. 53.

3.   Predestination and free will.

"You are all subjects of predestination, but it is not foreordained that you must accept this divine predestination; you are at full liberty to reject any part or all of the Thought Adjusters' program." P. 1204.

4.   Mission of adversity.

"The confusion and turmoil of Urantia do not signify that the Paradise Rulers lack either interest or ability to manage affairs differently. The Creators are possessed of full power to make Urantia a veritable paradise, but such an Eden would not contribute to the development of those strong, noble, and experienced characters which the Gods are so surely forging out on your world between the anvils of necessity and the hammers of anguish. Your anxieties and sorrows, your trials and disappointments, are just as much a part of the divine plan on your sphere as are the exquisite perfection and infinite adaptation of all things to their supreme purpose on the worlds of the central and perfect universe." P. 258.

BIBLE TEACHING REGARDING GOD'S PURPOSE
I. THE ETERNAL PURPOSE

"This was according to the eternal purpose which he has realized in Christ Jesus our Lord." **Eph. 3:11**.

"For the Lord of hosts has purposed, and who will annul it?" **Isa. 14:27**.

"As I have planned, so shall it be, and as I have purposed, so shall it stand." **Isa. 14:24.**

"This is the purpose that is purposed concerning the whole earth." **Isa. 14:26.**

"I have purposed, and I will do it." **Isa. 46:11.**

"My counsel shall stand, and I will accomplish all my purpose." **Isa. 46:10.**

"According to the purpose of him who accomplishes all things according to the counsel of his will." **Eph. 1:11.**

"I have purposed; I have not relented nor will I turn back." **Jer. 4:28.**

"He has made known to us in all wisdom and insight the mystery of his will, according to his purpose which he set forth in Christ." **Eph. 1:9.**

"We know that in everything God works for good with those who love him." **Rom. 8:28.**

II. PREDESTINATION

(In the Revised Version predestination is usually rendered "foreordained.")

"You meant evil against me; but God meant it for good." **Gen. 50:20.**

"And as many as were ordained to eternal life beleived." **Acts 13:48.**

"For those whom he foreknew he also predestined to be conformed to the image of his Son." **Rom. 8:29.**

"He destined us in love to be his sons through Jesus Christ, according to the purpose of his will." **Eph. 1:5.**

"Even as he chose us in him before the foundation of the world." **Eph. 1:4.**

"We impart a secret and hidden wisdom of God…decreed before the ages for our glorification." **1 Cor. 2:7.**

"Chosen and destined by God the Father and sanctified by the Spirit." **1 Peter 1:2.**

"They disobey the word, as they were destined to do." **1 Peter 2:8.**

"To do whatever thy hand and thy plan had predestined to take place." **Acts 4:28. Eph. 3:11.**

"But you are a chosen race, a royal priesthood, a holy nation, God's own people." **1 Peter 2:9.**

III. ELECTION

"Though they were not yet born and had done nothing either good or bad, in order that God's purpose of election might continue, not because of works, but because of his call." **Rom. 9:11.**

"Therefore, bretheren, be the more zealous to confirm your call and election." **2 Peter 1:10.**

"But for the sake of the elect those days will be shortened." **Matt. 24:22.**

"And will not God vindicate his elect, who cry to him day and night?" **Luke 18:7.**

"Who shall bring any charge against God's elect?" **Rom. 8:33.**

"Therefore I endure everything for the sake of the elect." **2 Tim. 2:10.**

"In the presence of God and of Christ Jesus and of the elect angels I charge you to keep these rules without favor." **1 Tim. 5:21.**

Notwithstanding all these teachings about predestination and election, Jesus unceasingly proclaimed: "Whosoever will may come."

Note concerning the Perfection Plan. Jesus' mandate—*"You therefore must be perfect, as your heavenly Father is perfect"* (**Matt. 5:48**)—was foreshadowed by the Old Testament injunction—*"For I am the Lord your God...be holy, for I am holy."* (**Lev. 11:44**).

THE SHORT COURSE IN DOCTRINE

A Summary of the Theology of
The Urantia Book

THE SHORT COURSE IN DOCTRINE

SUMMARY OF THE THEOLOGY
OF *THE URANTIA BOOK*

TABLE OF CONTENTS

THE SHORT COURSE IN DOCTRINE

SUMMARY OF THE THEOLOGY
OF *THE URANTIA BOOK*

SECTION ONE
THE DOCTRINE OF GOD

I. THE FIRST SOURCE AND CENTER

1. God, as the First Source and Center, is primal in relation to total reality—unqualifiedly; infinite as well as eternal and therefore limited or conditioned only by volition. P. 5.

2. The God of the First Source and Center exercises cosmic overcontrol by absolute Paradise gravity. P. 24.

3. The Universal Father is the personality of the First Source and Center. P. 5.

4. The First Source and Center is that infinity who unqualifiedly transcends all mind. all matter, and all spirit. P. 31.

5. Finite actualities are derived from the First Source and Center by means of self-existent free will. P. 1158.

II. THE I AM

1. The concept of the I AM is a philosophic concession which is made to the time-bound, space-fettered, finite mind of man, to the impossibility of creature comprehension of eternity existences, nonbeginning, nonending realities and relationships. P. 6.

2. The I AM achieves personality by becoming the Eternal Father of the Original Son and the Eternal Source of Paradise. P. 6.

3. Ab solute causation resides in the Universal Father functioning as the I AM. P. 1152.

4. The sevenfold nature of the I AM is suggested by the Seven Absolutes of Infinity:

    1. The Universal Father.
    2. The Universal Controller.
    3. The Universal Creator.
    4. The Infinite Upholder.
    5. The Infinite Potential.
    6. The Infinite Capacity.
    7. The Universal One of Infinity. P. 1154-5.

5. The I AM postulate of the infinite and the absolute transcenda all time-past. present and future. p. 1296.

BIBLE REFERENCE: Ex. 3.4.

III. GOD THE FATHER

1. THE DIVINE IDENTITY

1. The Universal Father is the God of all creation. P. 21.

2. First think of God as a creator, then as a controller, and lastly as an infinite upholder. P. 21.

3. In science God is a cause, in philosophy. a reality; in religion, a loving Father. P. 59.

4. God is spirit. P. 25.

5. God is a universal spirit—an infinite spirit person. P. 25.

6. The spiritual luminosity of the Father's personal presence is a light which no man can approach. P. 25.

BIBLE REFERENCES: Neh. 9:6. John 4:24. I Tim. 1:17. Ex. 33:20. I Tim. 6:16.

2. THE PERSONALITY OF GOD

1. God functions on three personality levels:
    1. Prepersonal—Thought Adjusters.
    2. Personal—as in evolutionary creatures.
    3. Superpersonal—absonite beings. P. 3.

2. God is personality. P. 28.

3. The concept of the personality of God is the measure of religious maturity. P. 28.

4. While God must be more than a personality, he cannot be anything less. P. 27.

5. The concept of the personality of Deity facilitates fellowship, favors intelligent worship, and promotes refreshing trustfulness. P. 31.

6. Only a person can love and be loved. P. 28.

7. God's conduct is personal—conscious and volitional. He is not a slave to his own perfection and infinity. P. 138.

8. God is a person who can know and be known. P. 28.

BIBLE REFERENCES: Ps. 94:9. Jas. 2:23.

3. THE NATURE OF GOD

1. God is not a synonym for nature, neither is he natural law personified. God is a transcendent reality, not mans traditional concept of supreme values. God is not a psychological focalization of spiritual meanings, neither is he "the noblest work of man." God may be any or all of these concepts, but he is more. He is a saving and loving Father. P. 23.

2. God is neither manlike nor machinelike. P. 23.

3. The nature of God can best be understood by the revelation of the Father which Michael unfolded in his manifold teachings and in his superb mortal life in the flesh. P. 33.

A. The Infinity of God

1. The Father is infinite and eternal. P. 59.
2. The unstinted bestowal of himself upon his universes does not diminish his potential of power, wisdom, and love. P. 49.
3. The infinity of God should be the supreme assurance that throughout all endless futurity an ascending personality will have before him the possibility of Deity association which even eternity will neither exhaust nor transcend. P. 1169.

BIBLE REFERENCES: Job 5:9; 36:26. Isa. 46:10.

B. The Justice of God

1. Willful sin and unmitigated iniquity are inherently and automatically suicidal. P. 37.
2. The final result of wholehearted sin is annihilation. P. 37.

BIBLE REFERENCES: Ps. 145:17; 103:6; 7:9. Il Chron. 19:7.

C. The Mercy of God

1. The creature's need is wholly sufficient to insure the full flow of the Father's tender mercies and his saving grace. P. 38.

2. Mercy is not a contravention of justice, but rather an understanding interpretation of the demands of supreme justice as it is fairly applied to material creatures. P. 38.

BIBLE REFERENCES: II Cor. 1:3.

D. **The Love of God**

1. God is love. P. 38.
2. The Father's love follows us now and throughout the endless circle of the eternal ages. P. 40.
3. Love identifies the volitional will of God. P. 42.
4. The face which the Infinite God turns toward all personalities is the face of a loving Father. P. 1153.
5. It is wrong to think that God loves us only because of the sacrifices of his Sons. P. 39.

BIBLE REFERENCES: John 3:1. Pe. 103:17. John 16:27.

E. *The Goodness of God*

1. God is related to the universe as the being of final goodness plus a free will of creative infinity. P. 58.
2. In bestowing himself upon the universes, God reserves only that which is required to insure the bestowal. P. 364.

BIBLE REFERENCES: Rom. 2:4. Ps. 68:20; 111:4; 34:8. I Peter 1:15.

4. THE ATTRIBUTES OF GOD

A God's Omnipresence

1. The omnipresence of God is in reality a part of his infinite nature; space constitutes no barrier to Deity. P. 45.
2. God alone can be in two places, in numberless places, at the same time. P. 44.
3. The Universall Controller is present in the gravity circuits of the universes. P. 45.

BIBLE REFERENCES: Ps. 139:7.

B. **God's Omnipotence**

1. God is omnipotent. P. 47.
2. The divine omnipotence is only limited by the love of God, the will of God, and the law of God. P. 48.
3. God is omnipotent, but not omnificent he does not do all that is done. P. 1299.
4. He upholds the worlds in apace and swings the universes around the endless circle of the eternal circuit. P. 46.
5. God is unlimited in power, divine in nature, final in will, infinite in attributes, eternal in wisdom, and absolute in reality. P. 48.

BIBLE REFERENCES: Matt. 19:26. Dan. 4:35. Job 42:2.

C. **God's Omniscience.**

1. God knows all things. The divine mind is conscious of all creation. P. 48.
2. The Father sees the end from the beginning. P. 34.
3. Only God actually knows the number of the stars. P. 49.
4. Omniscience does not imply the knowing of the unknowable. P. 49.

BIBLE REFERENCES: I John 3:20. Heb. 4:13.741 Job 37:16. Ps. 33:13; 147:4. Prov. 15:3. Matt. 6:8.

D. **The Primacy of God**

1. God is the universal unity of unqualified Reality. P. 645.
2. The Universal Father is still primal; his hand is on the mighty lever of the circumstances of the universal realms. P. 52.
3. The divine reach extends around the circle of eternity. P. 55.

BIBLE REFERENCES: Ps. 24:1. Col. 1:17.

5. GOD'S RELATION TO THE UNIVERSE

A. **God and Nature**

1. Nature is in a limited sense the physical habit of God. P. 56.

2. Nature is a combination of Paradise perfection and evolutionary im-perfection. P. 56.
3. Nature is not God. Nature is not an object of worship. P. 57.
BIBLE REFERENCES: Ps. 119:89; 104:30. Heb. 1:3.

B. **God's Changelessness**

1. God is the only stationary, self-contained, and changeless being in the whole universe. P. 58.
2. God and the universe are not identical—one is cause and the other effect. P. 1126.
3. There is a finality of completeness and a perfection of repleteness in the mandates of the Father. P. 35.
BIBLE REFERENCES: Mal. 3:6. Jas. 1:17. I Pet. 4:19. Deut. 32:4. Ps. 33:4. John 1:9. I Cor. 1:9. I John 1:9. Lam. 3:21. Ps. 33:4; 119:90.

C. **God's Eternal Purpose**

1. Do not get the idea that, since God delegates so much of himself and his power to others, he is a silent member of the Deity partnership. P. 362.
2. God never does that which others can do. P. 362.
3. The Father has an eternal purpose pertaining to the universe of universes. P. 54.
BIBLE REFERENCE: Eph. 3:11.

6. GOD'S RELATION TO THE INDIVIDUAL

A. **The Presence of God**

1. God is not in hiding; he craves to reveal himself. P. 62.
2. The Father dwells within us. P. 139.
3. God is in intimate touch with his evolutionary children. P. 139.
4. In him we live and move and have our being. P. 139.
5. The eternal God is incapable of wrath and anger. P. 57.
BIBLE REFERENCES: Deut. 33:27.

B. **God in Religion**

1. It is a great blunder to humanize God, but that is not so stupid as to mechanize him. P. 53.
2. Neither science nor logic can prove the existence of God; only human experience can validate his reality. P. 24.
3. The Urantia Benediction. P. 53.

C. **The God of Personality**

1. The Father is bestower and conservatior of every personality. P. 70.
2. Personality is an unsolved mystery. P. 70.
3. The personality circuit of all creation centers in the person of the Universal Father. P. 71.
4. And when all is said and done. there is nothing more helpful than to reiterate that God is our Father—we are all his planetary children. P. 72.

IV. GOD THE SON

1. IDENTITY OF THE SON

1. The Eternal Son is the original and only-begotten Son of God. P. 73.

2. The Eternal Son is the perfect and final expression of the first personal and absolute concept of the Universal Father. P. 73.

3. As the upholder of spiritual realities, the Second Source and Center is the eternal counterpoise of the Isle of Paradise, which so magnificently upholds all things material. P. 81.

4. The Son is the spiritual and personal nature of God made manifest to the universes. P. 79.

5. The Eternal Son is the eternal Word of God. P. 74.

6. The Eternal Son is the great mercy minister to all creation. P. 75.

2. THE ATTRIBUTES OF THE SON

1. The Son is the fullness of God's absoluteness in personality and spirit. P. 75.

2. Spiritually the Eternal Son is omnipresent. P. 76.

3. The Son knows all, he is never surprised. P. 76.

4. The Son is omnipotent only in the spiritual realn. P. 76.

5. The Eternal Son is an absolute personality. P. 79.

3. SPIRIT GRAVITY

1. The Eternal Son motivates the spirit level of cosmic reality. P. 76.

2. The pure and universal spirit gravity of all creation leads directly back to the person of the Son. Thus does the Son exercise absolute spiritual sovereignty. P. 81.

3. The gravity control of spiritual things operates independently of time and space. Spirit gravity never suffers time delays, nor does it undergo space diminution. P. 82.

4. There is a direct attractiveness of a spirit nature between spiritually minded persons of like tastes and longings. P. 82.

5. The spirit-gravity circuit is the basic channel for transmitting genuine prayers. P. 84.

6. Spirit gravity is absolute. P. 82.

7. The spiritual-gravity pull of the Eternal Son constitutes the inherent secret of the Paradise ascension of surviving mortals. P. 84.

4. THE SON'S RELATION TO INDIVIDUALS

1. The personal nature of the Eternal Son is incapable of fragmentation. P. 86.

2. But he does draw near to created personalities. He is able to stand in man's presence, and, at times, as man himself. P. 86.

3. The Eternal Son is the personal trustee, the divine custodian, of the Father's universal plan of creature ascension. P. 86.

4. The Eternal Son is the exclusive, universal, and final revelation of the spirit and the personality of the Universal Father. P. 88.

5. The sons of the Eternal Son can incarnate in the likeness of mortal flesh. P. 86.

V. GOD THE SPIRIT

1. THE GOD OF ACTION

1. The very instant that God the Father and God the Son conjointly conceive an identical and infinite action—the execution of an absolute thoughtplan—the Infinite Spirit springs full-fledgedly into existence. P. 90.

2. The God of Action functions and the dead vaults of space are astir. P. 91.

3. The Conjoint Creator is the manipulator of energy. P. 101.

4. As the divine Sons are the Word of God, the Infinite Spirit is the Act of God. P. 111.

5. The Infinite Spirit is the effective agent for the execution of the FatherSon plan of perfection attainment. P. 93.

2. THE SPIRIT OF DIVINE MINISTRY

1. God is love, the Son is mercy, the Spirit is ministry. P. 98.

2. The Infinite Spirit is the correlator of all actual reality. P. 99.

3. The Infinite Spirit is a personalized spiritualization of the Eternal Son and the Universal Father. P. 100.

4. On the anvils of justice the hammers of suffering are wielded by the children of mercy. P. 100.

3. PERSONALITY OF THE INFINITE SPIRIT

1. The Infinite Spirit is a complete and perfect personality and reacts to the universe as a person. P. 96.

2. The Infinite Spirit is a universe presence, an eternal action, a cosmic power, a holy influence, and a universal mind; but he is also a true and divine personality. P. 96.

3. All of the personal and nonpersonal doings of the Infinite Spirit are volitional acts. P. 101.

4. ATTRIBUTES OF THE INFINITE SPIRIT

1. The outstanding attribute of the Infinite Spirit is omnipresence. P. 95.

2. The Spirit inclines towards the mercy of the Eternal Son, thus becoming the mercy minister of the Paradise Deities. P. 92.

3. The Infinite Spirit possesses a unique and amazing power— antigravity. P. 101.

4. Paradise is the pattern of infinity; the God of Action is the activator of that pattern. P. 101.

5. THE MINISTER OF MIND

1. The absolute mind is the mind of the Third Person of Deity. P. 102.

2. Mind does not have to be added to pure spirit. Spirit is always minded in some way. P. 102.

3. The Conjoint Actor is absolute only in the domain of mind. P. 102.

4. Infinite mind ignores time, ultimate mind transcends time, cosmic mind is conditioned by time. P. 102.

5. All these activities of mind are grasped in the absolute mind-gravity circuit of the Third Source and Center. P. 103.

6. Mind alone can interassociate physical energies with spiritual powers. P. 136.

7. Universe reflectivity is that unique and inexplicable power to see, hear, sense, and know all things as they transpire throughout a superuniverse. P. 105.

8. The functional family of the Third Center falls into three groups: Supreme Spirits, Power Directors, and other personalities which include Ministering Spirits. P. 107.

9. God the Sevenfold functionally co-ordinates finite evolution. P. 1164.

VI. GOD THE SUPREME

1. THE FINITE GOD

1. God the Supreme is the actualizing or evolving God of time and space. P. 4.

2. The Supreme is the experiential God of evolutionary creatures. P. 4.

3. As the Trinity was the absolute inevitability, the Supreme is the evolutionary inevitability. P. 1266.

4. God the Supreme will not be discovered by one creature until all creatures find him. P. 1290.

5. The Supreme co-ordinates the unchanging overworld with the ever-changing underworld. P. 1297.

6. With God the Supreme, one must do something as well as be something. P. 1260.

7. The personality of the nonsurvivor is absorbed into the oversoul of creation—the Supreme. P. 1283.

8. The evolving mind of the Supreme is a relationship between finite and absolute mind. P. 105.

9. God the Supreme is the personalization of the totality of evolutionary universe experience. P. 1304.

10. The Supreme evolves as the personality synthesis of finite mind, matter, and spirit. P. 1304.

2. NATURE OF THE SUPREME

1. The Supreme Being is the unification of three phases of Deity reality: God the Supreme, the spiritual unification of certain finite aspects of the Paradise Trinity; the Almighty Supreme, the power unification of the grand universe Creators; and the Supreme Mind, the individual contribution of the Third Source and Center and his co-ordinates to the reality of the Supreme Being. P. 251.

2. This evolutionary Deity does appear to reflect the attitude of the Trinity of Supremacy. P. 115.

3. The Supreme Being is absolutely dependent on the existence and action of the Paradise Trinity. P. 1264.

4. God the Supreme is the personalization of all universe experience, the focalization of all finite evolution. P. 1304.

5. The Almighty Supreme is a living and evolving Deity of power and personality. P. 1268.

6. The Supreme is the beauty of physical harmony, the truth of intellectual meaning, and the goodness of spiritual value. P. 1278.

7. The Supreme knows you because he is creaturelike as well as creatorlike. P. 1288.

8. God the Supreme was a spiritual person in Havona before the creation of the grand universe. P. 641.

9. The Supreme embraces all of infinity that a finite creature can ever really comprehend. P. 1290.

3. THE ALMIGHTY SUPREME

1. God the Supreme is power-actualizing in the doings of the Creator Sons, the Ancients of Days, and the Master Spirits. P. 1269.

2. The Almighty Supreme is evolving as the overcontroller of the physical power of the grand universe. P. 1274.

3. The Infinite Spirit compensates for the incompleteness of the evolving Supreme. P. 1272.

4. SOURCE OF EVOLUTIONARY GROWTH

1. The Supreme grows as the Creators and creatures of the evolving universes attain to Godlikeness. P. 1265. The Supreme is the sum total of all finite growth. P. 1281.

2. The Supreme Being becomes the finite synthesis of the experience of the perfect-Creator cause and the perfecting-creature response. P. 1278.

3. As man attains human destiny, so does the Supreme achieve Deity destiny. P. 1285.

4. The Supreme is the catalyzer of all universe growth. P. 1283.

5. The experience of every evolving mortal is a part of the experience of the Almighty Supreme. P. 1268.

6. As God is our Father, the Supreme Being is our universe Mother. P. 1289.

7. The Adjuster, the Holy Spirit, and the Spirit of Truth are unified in human experience by the ministry of the Supreme. P. 1107.

8. God the Supreme is truth, beauty, and goodness—the finite maximum of ideational experience. P. 1279.

9. Rejection of ascension is cosmic suicide. The personality of a nonascender returns to the Supreme as a drop of water returns to the sea. P. 1283.

10. God the Father journeys through the cosmos with man, while the very way traversed is the presence of the Supreme. P. 1291.

5. REFLECTIVITY

1. Reflectivity is an association of energy, mind, and spirit under the overcontrol of the Supreme. P. 105.

2. The reflectivity of the Supreme explains the consciousness of the cosmos. P. 105.

6. THE FUTURE OF THE SUPREME

1. At the end of the present universe age the Supreme Being will function as an experiential sovereign of the grand universe. P. 1280.

2. In the eternal future, God the Supreme will be actualized in the spiritualized minds and the immortal souls of ascenders. P. 1286.

3. In the next universe age, outer-spacers will pass through the Supreme rule of the grand universe. P. 1280.

4. After attaining God the Supreme, the challenge will be to find God the Ultimate. P. 1293.

5. The Supreme may not be omnipresent, but he is ubiquitous. P. 1296.

VII. GOD THE ULTIMATE

1. GOD THE ULTIMATE

1. The Ultimate is the unification of the Paradise Trinity comprehended by absonite beings. P. 12.

2. God the Ultimate exists in transcendence of time and space, but is subabsolute. P. 1167.

3. The Ultimate is identified with transcendentals. P. 1160.

4. The Ultimate will eventually extend throughout the master universe. P. 137.

5. The Ultimate is apiritually present in Havona—and we know of the Qualified Vicegerents of the Ultimate. P. 1166.

2. THE TRANSCENDENTAL LEVEL

1. The Architects of the Master Universe are the governing corps of the Paradise Transcendentalers. P. 351.

2. On absonite levels things and beings are without beginnings and endings. Absoniters are not created—they are eventuated. P. 2.

3. The universe exists in three levels: finite, transcendental, and absolute. P. 1160.

VIII. GOD THE ABSOLUTE

1. God the Absolute would be the experientialization of divinity realities now existential as the Deity Absolute. P. 4.

2. God the Absolute is the attainment goal of all superabsonite beings. P. 13.

IX. DEITY

1. Deity may be existential, as in the Eternal Son; experiential, as in the Supreme Being; associative, as in God the Sevenfold; undivided, as in the Paradise Trinity. P. 3.

2. Deity is the source of all that which is divine, but all that which is divine is not necessarily Deity. P. 3.

3. Divinity is creature comprehensible as truth, beauty, and goodness; correlated in personality as love, mercy, and ministry; disclosed on impersonal levels as justice, power, and sovereignty. P. 3.

4. The equivalent of mind, the ability to know and be known, is indigenous to Deity. P. 78.

5. The ubiquity of Deity must not be confused with the ultimacy of the divine omnipresence. P. 1296.

6. Compossibility is innate in divine power. P. 1299.

7. Deity is personalizable as God and is characterized by unity—actual or potential. P. 2.

8. In contemplating Deity, the concept of personality must be divested of the idea of corporeality. P. 29.

THE PARADISE TRINITY

I. TRINITY UNION OF DEITY

1. God functions as absolute Deity only in the Paradise Trinity and in relation to universe totality. P. 112.

2. The Trinity is existential and was inevitable. P. 15.

3. The Trinity constitutes the only Deity reality embracing infinity. P. 15.

4. The Trinity facilitates the Father's escape from personality absolutism. P. 108.

5. The Trinity is an association of infinite persons as a corporate entity. P. 112.

II. FUNCTIONS OF THE TRINITY

1. The Trinity does not have attributes—it has functions, such as justice administration, totality attitudes, co-ordinate action, and cosmic overcontrol. P. 113.

2. Justice is one of the functions of the Trinity. P. 114.

3. The Paradise Trinity is concerned with totals. The Trinity is the totality of Deity. P. 115.

4. While the Supreme Being is not a personalization of the Trinity, he is the nearest approach comprehensible by finite creatures. P. 113.

III. SONS OF THE TRINITY

1. There are seven orders of Supreme Trinity Personalities:

    1. Trinitized Secrets of Supremacy.
    2. Eternals of Days.
    3. Ancients of Days.
    4. Perfections of Days.
    5. Recents of Days.
    6. Unions of Days.
    7. Faithfuls of Days. P. 207.

2. There are seven orders of Co-ordinate Trinity-origin Beings:

   1. Trinity Teacher Sons.
   2. Perfectors of Wisdom.
   3. Divine Counselors.
   4. Universal Censors.
   5. Inspired Trinity Spirits.
   6. Havona Natives.
   7. Paradise Citizens. P. 214.

IV. TRINITARIAN CONCEPTS

1. The Trinity is an absolute entity—supersummative Deity. P. 1145.

2. The absolute attitude of the Trinity concerns absolute existences and the action of total Deity. P. 113.

3. A triunity is not an organic entity—it is functional. P. 1147.

4. The Ultimate Trinity, now evolving, will consist of the Supreme Being, Supreme Creator Personalities, and the Architects of the Master Universe. P. 16.

5. The Absolute Trinity will consist of God the Supreme, God the Ultimate, and the Consummator of Universe Destiny. P. 16.

THE ABSOLUTES

1. Total infinity exists as seven Absolutes:

    1. The Universal Father.
    2. The Eternal Son.
    3. The Infinite Spirit.
    4. The Isle of Paradise.
    5. The Deity Absolute.
    6. The Universal Absolute.
    7. The Unqualified Absolute. P. 1146.

2. *The Deity Absolute* is the all-powerful activator. P. 14.

3. *The Unqualified Absolute* is nonpersonal, extradivine, and undeified. P. 14. It dominates nether Paradise and upholds the physical universe. P. 120, 637.

4. *The Universal Absolute* equalizes tensions between: finite and infinite; potantials and actuals; Paradise and space; time and eternity; man and God. P. 15.

5. The First Source and Center is the Volitional Absolute; the Second Source and Center, the Personality Absolute. P. 74.

6. The First Source and Center is the absolute reality which embraced all potentials and gave origin to all actuals. P. 1262.

7. The Absolutes of potentiality operate upon the eternal level of the cosmos. On subabsolute levels the Supreme and the Ultimate function. P. 1262.

Section Four
PARADISE

I. THE NATURE OF PARADISE

1. The Universal Father revealed the infinity potential of his nonpersonal self as Paradise. P. 127.

2. Paradise is not spherical—it is ellipsoid. P. 119.

3. Time and space are nonexistent on Paradise. P. 2.

4. Paradise is the center of the universe of universes. P. 118.

5. Paradise is the geographic center of infinity. P. 126.

6. Paradise is motionless—it is the Absolute of material-gravity control. P. 7.

7. Paradise is composed of absolutum. P. 120.

8. Paradise is the absolute of patterns. P. 127.

9. Paradise is divided into three domains:

    1. Upper Paradise.
    2. Peripheral Paradise.
    3. Nether Paradise. P. 119.

10. Paradise is not a creator—it is a unique controller. P. 7.

11. Paradise is not Deity—it is not conscious. P. 127.

II. THE DIVINE RESIDENCE

1. Paradise is the dwelling place of the eternal God. P. 1.

2. The Universal Father is cosmically focalized, spiritually personalized, and geographically resident on Paradise. P. 118.

III. UPPER PARADISE

1. Upper Paradise consists of three spheres:

    1. Deity presence.
    2. Most Holy Sphere.
    3. Holy Area. P. 120.

2. Each of numerous residential units lodges one billion working groups. P. 121.

3. Worship is the highest joy of Paradise residents. P. 304.

4. Paradise is the destiny of all ascendant mortals. P. 126.

IV. PERIPHERAL PARADISE

1. On peripheral Paradise are the landing and dispatching fields; also the force-focal headquarters of the Seven Master Spirits. P. 121.

2. Here are the historic and prophetic exhibit areas. P. 121.

V. NETHER PARADISE

1. On nether Paradise, all physical-energy circuits have their origin. P. 122.

2. Here is the space presence of the Unqualified Absolute. P. 123.

3. On nether Paradise is found the center for space respiration. P. 122.

4. Paradise exists without time and has no location in space. P. 120.

5. Space is a bestowal of Paradise. P. 124.

THE PARDISE HAVONA SYSTEM

I. GEOGRAPHY

1. Havona consists of one billion perfect worlds revolving around Paradise in seven concentric circuits. P. 152.

2. Between Havona and Paradise are the three seven-world circuits of the Father, the Son, and the Spirit. P. 143.

3. The dark islands of space lie between Havona and the seven superuniverses. P. 153.

4. The Paradise-Havona system is a unit of creative perfection. P. 155.

II. THE HAVONA WORLDS

1. The Havona worlds consist of one thousand elements and seven forms of energy. P. 154. Each world is unique. P. 159.

2. Havona natives are the children of the Trinity. P. 157.

3. There is no government on the Havona worlds. P. 155.

4. The standard time of the grand universe is the Paradise-Havona day- a little over seven minutes less than one thousand years of Urantia time. P. 153.

III. LIFE IN HAVONA

1. There are seven forms of life in Havona. P. 156.

2. Sin has never appeared in Havona. P. 155.

3. The Deities derive varied satisfactions from the perfect Havona universe. P. 162.

IV. THE SACRED SPHERES OF PARADISE

1. Each of the twenty-one worlds of the Deities is highly specialized. P. 143.

2. The worlds of the Father are directed by the Trinitized Secrets of Supremacy. P. 144.

3. The worlds of the Father are:
   1. Divinington.
   2. Sonarington.
   3. Spiritington.
   4. Vicegerington.
   5. Solitarington.
   6. Seraphington.
   7. Ascendington. P. 144-7.

4. The seven worlds of the Son are the home of the seven phases of purespirit existence. P. 149.

5. The seven worlds of the Spirit are the headquarters of the Seven Master Spirits. From these worlds the cosmic-mind circuits to the grand universe are equalized and stabilized. P. 150.

SECTION SIX
COSMOLOGY

I. THE COSMIC CENTER

1. Paradise is the absolute source and the eternal focal point of all energy-matter in the universe of universes. P. 126.

2. We are not sure about the relation of the Unqualified Absolute to space motion. We think the Conjoint Actor initiates motion in space. P. 133.

3. The Unqualified Absolute pervades all space. P. 137.

4. The diverse levels of creation are unified by a divine plan and eternal purpose. P. 637.

II. PARADISE GRAVITY

1. The Universal Father is infinite and acts over all four absolute gravity circuits. P. 131.

2. Gravity is the omnipotent strand on which are strung the gleaming stars, blazing suns, and whirling spheres which constitute the universal physical adornment of the eternal God. P. 125.

3. The center and focal point of absolute material gravity is the Isle of Paradise. P. 125.

4. Every form of known reality has the bend of the ages, the trend of the circle, the swing of the great ellipse. P. 125.

5. The Unqualified Absolute is the revealer, regulator, and repository of all that which has origin in Paradise. P. 126.

III. SPACE

1. All space alternately contracts and expands. P. 123.

2. Pervaded space is now nearing the mid-point of the expansion phase. P. 124.

3. Space is real—it contains and conditions motion. P. 133.

4. Space comes the nearest of all nonabsolute things to being absolute. P. 1297.

5. We do not know if an idea occupies space. We are sure that an idea pattern does not contain space. P. 1297.

6. Man's mind is less time-bound than space-bound. P. 135.

7. Time and space are a conjoined mechanism of the master universe. P. 2303.

8. The apparent velocity of the supposedly "exploding" universe is not real. P. 134.

9. All cosmic space levels are separated by relative quiescent space zones. P. 125.

IV. UNIVERSE OVERCONTROL

1. Universe stability is the result of balanced energies; co-operative minds, co-ordinated morontias, spirit overcontrol, and personality unification. P. 135.

2. The master universe is fostered by the Paradise Trinity. P. 136.

3. The universes are unified. God is one in power and personality. P. 646.

4. The absonite architects eventuate a universe plan. The Supreme Creators materialize it, the Supreme Being will consummate it. P. 1165.

V. THE SUPERUNIVERSES

1. The grand universe is the present organized and inhabited creation. P. 129.

2. Orvonton, the seventh superuniverse, is the Milky Way. P. 167.

3. The rotational center of our minor sector is Sagittarius. P. 168.

4. Uversa, the capital of Orvonton, is the administrative headquarters for one trillion inhabited worlds. P. 175.

5. It is on such worlds as Uversa that the beings representative of the autocracy of perfection and the democracy of evolution meet face to face. P. 179.

6. A superuniverse government is directed by one of the Seven Master Spirits, through one of the Seven Supreme Executives. P. 178.

VI. ASTRONOMY

1. Of the ten major divisions of Orvonton, eight have been roughly identified by Urantia astronomers. P. 167.

2. The Universe Power Directors have ability to condense and contain, or to expand and liberate, varying quantities of energy. P. 175.

3. The universes are engaged in an orderly and perfectly controlled procession, swinging in majestic grandeur around the First Great Source and Center. P. 164.

4. Paradise Force Organizers are nebulae originators. P. 169.

5. The superuniverse of Orvonton is illuminated and warned by more than ten trillion blazing suns. P. 172.

6. Only those suns which function in the direct channels of the main streams of universe energy can shine on forever. P. 464.

7. One half million light-years beyond the grand universe, in the first outer space level, unbelievable action is taking place—extending for twentyfive million light-years. P. 130.

8. The alternate clockwise and counterclockwise movement of the galaxies is a factor of gravity control and acts as a brake on dangerous velocities. P. 125.

9. There is mystery associated with the force-charge of space. It does not respond to gravity, but it ever swings around Paradise. P. 169.

10. The mysterious stretches of outer space exhibit the amazing evolution of the plans of the Architects of the Master Universe. P. 130.

11. Some suns are solitary; some are double stars. There are also suns that shine without heat. P. 172.

12. Light is real. Sunlight would be economical at a million dollars a pound. P. 460.

THE LOCAL UNIVERSE

1. Urantia belongs to a system which is well out towards the borderland of your local universe. P. 165.

2. Local evolutionary universes are the handiwork of the Paradise Creator Sons. P. 357.3.

3. The Universe Mother Spirit is co-creator in the local universe. P. 162.

4. The identification of Urantia up through the grand universe is given on P. 182.

5. The density of our sun is about one and one-half that of water. P. 459.

6. Architectural worlds enjoy ten forms of material life—three vegetable and three animal—with four difficult of comprehension. P. 492.

SECTION EIGHT
EVOLUTION

I. GENERAL CONSIDERATIONS

1. While reason demands monotheistic unity, experience requires diversity of Absolutes—even differentials, variables, modifiers, and qualifiers. P. 1146.

2. The analysis of dead protoplasm does not disclose the true nature of living protoplasm. P.737.

3. Pulsating stars give origin to solar systems. P. 465.

4. Both mental and spiritual transformations may occur suddenly. P. 740.

5. In the evolutionary universes energy-matter is dominant, except in personality, where spirit, through the mediation of mind, is struggling for the mastery. P. 1275.

6. Land is the stage of society; men are the actors. P. 768.

II. MIND SYSTEMS

1. The potential to learn from experience marks the functioning of the adjutant spirits. P. 739.

2. The universe is mind planned, mind made, and mind administered. P. 481.

3. Mind levels:

    Preadjutant spirit minds.
    Adjutant spirit minds.
    Morontia minds.
    Cosmic mind. P. 480-1.

4. Physics and chemistry alone cannot explain how a human being evolves out of primeval protoplasm. P. 738.

III. UNIVERSE MECHANISMS

1. The evolution of universe mechanisms indicates the presence and dominance of creative mind. P. 483.

2. The higher the mind associated with a universe phenomenon, the more difficult is its detection. P. 482.

3. The controlling mind of the universe is infinite and therefore beyond the full discernment of the finite mind. P. 482.

IV. LIFE CARRIERS

1. Life Carriers are the living catalyzers who initiate material life; they are the instigators of the energy circuits. P. 560.

2. The Universe Mother Spirit actually vitalizes the lifeless patterns. P. 404.

3. In the human blood stream there exists the possiblity of upward of 15,000,000 chemical reactions. P. 737.

V. THE URANTIA ADVENTURE

1. The midwayers have assembled over 50,000 facts of physics and chemistry which are incompatible with the theory of chance in human evolution. P. 665.

2. Evolution can be delayed but it cannot be stopped. P. 900.

3. The frog finally culminated in man himself. p. 732.

4. The human race has no surviving ancestry between the frog and the Eskimo. P. 732.

5. Remember that Urantia was a life-experiment world. P. 734.

6. More than a hundred thousand facts prove the presence of mind in the planning of the cosmos. P. 665.

7. Many bacteria and fungi represent retrograde movement in evolution and explain disease-causing proclivities. P. 732.

8. There were two unique features in the Urantia experiment:
   1. The Andonic race appearing before the colored races.
   2. The simultaneous appearance of the six Sangik colored races. P. 735.

9. Failure to obtain more of the Adamic life plasm predisposed the human race to many diseases. P. 736.

10. From A.D. 1934 the birth of the first two human beings occurred 993,419 years ago. P. 707.

11. The color of the amalgamated human race is an alive shade of violet-the racial "white." P. 593.

12. Man's ascent from seaweed to lordship of the earth is a romance of biologic survival. P. 731.

13. Evolutionary creature life is beset by certain inevitabilities:

> 1. Courage.
> 2. Altruism.
> 3. Hope.
> 4. Faith.
> 5. Love of truth.
> 6. Idealism.
> 7. Loyalty.
> 8. Unselfishness.
> 9. Pleasure. P. 51.

VI. SOCIAL AND CULTURAL EVOLUTION

1. The two great influences contributing to early associations were hunger and sex love. P. 765.

2. Primitive man only thought when he was hungry. P. 765.

3. Man transcends animals in his ability to appreciate humor, art, and religion. P. 772.

4. Society rose through the stages of collection, hunting, pastoral, and agriculture. P. 768-9.

5. It is not altruism to bestow sympathy upon degenerate human beings. P. 592.

6. Modern man suffers from the overgrowth of supposed needs, desires, and longings. P. 765.

7. Evolution may be slow, but it is effective. P. 900.

VII. CIVILIZATION

1. The Jews taught: He who does not work shall not eat. P. 773.

2. There were no distrinct periods, such as Stone, Bronze, and Iron Ages. P. 903.

3. Modern writing originated in the early trade records. P. 775.

4. Fire building forever separated man from the animal world. P. 777.

5. The dog was the first animal to be domesticated. P. 773.

6. Civilization is a racial acquirement; it is not biologically inherent. P. 763.

7. Society is concerned with self-perpetuation, self-maintenance, and self-gratification. P. 764.

8. Hunger and love drove men together; vanity and ghost fear held them together. P. 766.

VIII. OVERCONTROL OF EVOLUTION

1. Evolution is always purposeful and never accidental. P. 730.

2. All mortal-inhabited worlds are evolutionary in origin and nature. P. 559.

3. Life is both mechanistic and vitalistic—material and spiritual. P. 403.

4. Since mind co-ordinates the universe, fixity of mechanisms is nonexistent. P. 482.

5. Never will scientists be able to produce living organisms; life is not inherent in matter. P. 403.

THE SUPREME SPIRITS
AND OTHER PERSONALITIES OF THE INFINITE SPIRIT

I. THE MASTER SPIRITS

1. The seven Supreme Spirit groups are:
   1. The Seven Master Spirits.
   2. The Seven Supreme Executives.
   3. The Reflective Spirits.
   4. Reflective Image Aids.
   5. Seven Spirit of the Circuits.
   6. Local Universe Creative Spirits.
   7. Adjustant Mind-Spirits. P. 197.

2. The Master Spirits maintain force-focal stations on the Paradise periphery. P. 184.

3. The executive headquarters of the Master Spirits are on the seven Paradise worlds of the Infinite Spirit. P. 198.

4. When assembled about the Conjoint Actor, the Master Spirits represent the power, wisdom, and authority of the Trinity. P. 185.

II. ATTRIBUTES AND FUNCTIONS
OF THE MASTER SPIRITS

1. Master Spirit Number Seven is nonfunctional with regard to the Trinity, and that is why he can function *personally* for the Supreme Being. P. 185.

2. Outside of Paradise and Havona the Infinite Spirit speaks only by the Seven Master Spirits. P. 186.

3. The Seven Master Spirits are the creators of the Universe Power Directors and their associates. P. 189.

4. The distinctive personality trends characteristic of each superuniverse are expressive of the nature of the Master Spirits and are never fully effaced. P. 191.

III. THE COSMIC MIND

1. The Master Spirits are the sevenfold source of the cosmic mind. P. 191.

2. There is in the cosmic mind a quality which might be called the "reality response." P. 191.

3. The cosmic mind responds to three levels of reality:

    1. Causation.
    2. Duty.
    3. Worship. P. 192.

4. Man is able to exercise scientific, moral, and spiritual insight prior to exploration. P. 193.

5. The inalienables of human nature are:

    1. Moral intuition.
    2. Scientific curiosity.
    3. Spiritual insight. P. 192.

6. The purpose of education is to develop and sharpen these innate endowments. P. 192.

7. Only a personality can know what it is doing before it does it. P. 193.

8. Personality can look before it leaps; therefore it can learn from looking as well as from leaping. P. 193.

IV. MAJESTON—REFLECTIVITY

1. Majeston is a true person, the infallible center of reflectivity in the grand universe. P. 200.

2. Majeston was the first creative act of the Supreme Being in association with the Deity Absolute. P. 200.

3. The Reflective Spirits are of Trinity origin. P. 199.

4. The Reflective Spirits are not only transmitting agents; they are also retentive personalities. P. 201.

V. SOLITARY MESSENGERS

1. Solitary Messengers are the personal and universal corps of the Conjoint Creator. P. 256.

2. There is a technical reason why these Solitary Messengers must travel and work alone. P. 257.

3. Solitary Messengers are able to function as emergency lines of communication. P. 261.

4. These messenger-explorers patrol the master universe. P. 260.

5. It is difficult to explain how a Solitary Messenger can be a real person and yet traverse space at such tremendous velocities. P. 261.

VI. HIGHER PERSONALITIES OF THE INFINITE SPIRIT

1. The Higher Personalities of the Infinite Spirit are:
    1. Solitary Messengers.
    2. Universe Circuit Supervisors.
    3. Census Directors.
    4. Personal Aids of the Infinite Spirit.
    5. Associate Inspectors.
    6. Assigned Sentinels.
    7. Graduate Guides. P. 264-72.

VII. MESSENGER HOSTS OF SPACE

1. There are seven groups of the Messenger Hosts of Space:
    1. Havona Servitals.
    2. Universal Conciliators.
    3. Technical Advisers.
    4. Custodians of Records on Paradise.
    5. Celestial Recorders.
    6. Morontia Companions.
    7. Paradise Companions. P. 273-34.

SECTION TEN

THE PARADISE SONS

The Creator, Magisterial. and Trinity Teacher Sons are the gifts of the eternal Deities to the children of men. P. 232.

I. CREATOR SONS

Considered elsewhere

II. MAGISTERIAL SONS

1. Much as the Creator Sons are personalized by the Father and the Son, the Magisterial Sons are personalized by the Son and the Spirit. P. 88.

2. Every time an original and absolute concept of being formulated by the Eternal Son unites with a new and divine ideal of loving service conceived by the Infinite Spirit, a new and original Magisterial Son is produced. P. 224.

3. These Avonal Sons have three functions:
    1. Judicial.
    2. Magisterial.
    3. Bestowal. P. 225.

4. Urantia may yet be visited by an Avonal Son to incarnate on a magisterial mission. P. 227.

5. The method of these incarnations is a universal mystery. P. 228.

6. Incarnated Paradise Sons have experienced Adjusters. P. 227.

7. When incarnated Sons enter the portal of death, they reappear on the third day. P. 229.

8. The attribute of bestowal is inherent in the Paradise Sons. P. 1308.

9. Avonals are the planetary ministers and judges and number about one billion. P. 225.

10. The mission of a Magisterial Son is just as effective as that of a Creator Son. P. 225.

11. The bestowal of Paradise Sons is not to placate the Heavenly Father. It is part of the experiential training of these Sons. P. 227.

III. TRINITY TEACHER SONS

1. Trinity Teacher Sons are the universal educators, being dedicated to the spiritual awakening and moral guidance of the realms. P. 230.

2. When an evolutionary world indicates that the time is ripe for a spiritual age, the Teacher Sons always volunteer for service. P. 231.

3. Trinity Teacher Sons usually remain on their visitation planets for one thousand years. P. 232.

4. There are more than twenty-one billion Teacher Sons in service in the grand universe. P. 230.

5. Trinity Teacher Sons will function on Urantia after its inhabitants are delivered from the shackles of animalism and the fetters of materialism. P.231.

IV. TRINITY-EMBRACED SONS

For this age, Trinity-embraced Sons are assigned to the service of the superuniverses. P. 244.

1. *Mighty Messengers* are rebellion-tested mortals. P. 245.

2. *Those High in Authority* are ascendant mortals of high administrative ability. P. 246.

3. *Those without Name and Number* are ascenders with unusual skill in worship. P. 246.

4. *Trinitized Custodians* are ascendant seraphim and midwayers. P. 248.

5. *Trinitized Ambassadors* are Spirit-fused and Son-fused mortals. P. 248.

6. *Celestial Guardians* are creature-trinitized sons embraced by the Trinity. P. 252.

7. *High Son Assistants* are a superior group of retrinitized trinitized sons of ascendant mortals. P. 253.

V. TECHNIQUE OF TRINITIZATION

1. These techniques are the secrets of Vicegerington and Solitarington. P. 249.

2. The Seven Master Spirits may authorize the trinitizing union of finaliters and paradise-Havona personalities. P. 250.

3. Trinitized sons are the very idea which achieved their trinitization. P. 253.

4. There are three groups of creature-trinitized sons:

   1. Ascender-trinitized Sons.
   2. Paradise-Havona-trinitized Sons.
   3. Trinitized Sons of Destiny. P. 251

SECTION ELEVEN
ANGELS

I. MINISTERING SPIRITS

1. The ministering spirits of the grand universe are:

    1. Supernaphim.
    2. Seconaphim.
    3. Tertiaphim.
    4. Omniaphim.
    5. Seraphim.
    6. Cherubim and Sanobim.
    7. Midwayers. P. 285.

2. Tertiaphim are created by the Infinite Spirit for the Creator Sons. P. 306. Omniaphim are the exclusive servants of the Supreme Executives. P. 307.

3. The angelic hosts are sustained by spiritual energy. P. 286.

II.THE SUPERNAPHIM

1. The primary supernaphim are:

    1. Conductors of Worship.
    2. Masters of Philosophy.
    3. Custodians of Knowledge.
    4. Directors of Conduct.
    5. Interpreters of Ethics.
    6. Chiefs of Assignment.
    7. Instigators of Rest. P. 298.

2. The secondary supernaphim are:

    1. Pilgrim Helpers.
    2. Superemacy Guides.
    3. Trinity Guides.
    4. Son Finders.
    5. Father Guides.
    6. Counselors and Advisers.
    7. Complements of Rest. P. 289.

3. The tertiary supernaphim are:

    1. Harmony Supervisors.
    2. Chief Recorders.

3. Broadcasters.
4. Messengers.
5. Intelligence Co-ordinators.
6. Transporters.
7. Reserve Corps. P. 288-9.

III. THE SECONAPHIM

1. The primary seconaphim are:

    1. Voice of the Conjoint Actor.
    2. Voice of the Seven Master Spirits.
    3. Voice of the Creator Sons.
    4. Voice of the Angelic Hosts.
    5. Broadcast Receivers.
    6. Transporters.
    7. Reserve Corps. P. 308-10.

2. The secondary seconaphim are:

    1. Voice of Wisdom.
    2. Soul of Philosophy.
    3. Union of Souls.
    4. Heart of Counsel.
    5. Joy of Existence.
    6. Satisfaction of Service.
    7. Discerner of Spirits. P. 310-13.

3. The tertiary seconaphim are:

    1. Significance of Origins.
    2. Memory of Mercy.
    3. Import of Time.
    4. Solemnity of Trust.
    5. Sanctity of Service.
    6. and 7. Secret of Greatness and the Soul of Goodness. P. 314-17.

IV. SERAPHIM

1. Angels possess automatic powers of knowing things. P. 419.

2. Angels are the offspring of the local Universe Mother Spirits. P. 420.

3.   The seraphim are:

    1.   Supreme Seraphim.

    2.   Superior Seraphim.

    3.   Supervisor Seraphim.

    4.   Administrator Seraphim.

    5.   Planetary Helpers.

    6.   Transition Ministers.

    7.   Seraphim of the Future. P. 426.

V. GUARDIAN ANGELS

1.   Guardian angels are assigned in three divisions:

    1.   Subnormal minds.

    2.   Average—normal minds.

    3.   Supernormal minds. P. 1241.

2.   Upon the attainment of the third psychic circle, mortals are assigned personal guardians for life. P. 1242.

3.   Guardian angels correlate the influences of:

    1.   Infinite Spirit.

    2.   Physical Controllers.

    3.   Adjutant Mind-spirits.

    4.   Holy Spirit.

    5.   Thought Adjusters. P. 1244.

4.   Guardians and Thought Adjusters work in perfect harmony. P. 1245.

5.   At death the guardians are the custodians of:

    1.   Mind patterns.

    2.   Memory formulas.

    3.   Soul realities. P. 1244.

6.   Some guardians go on to the Corps of the Finality with their subjects. P. 1248.

VI. SERAPHIM OF PLANETARY GOVERNMENT

The angels of planetary government have much to do with the kingdoms of men.

They are:

    1.   Epochal angels.

2. Progress angels.
3. Religions guardians.
4. Angels of nation life.
5. Angels of the races.
6. Angels of the future.
7. Angels of enlightement.
8. Angels of health.
9. Home seraphim.
10. Angels of industry.
11. Angels of diversion.
12. Angels of superhuman ministry. P. 1255-56.

BIBLE REFERENCES: Matt. 26:53. John 1:51. Heb. 1:14. Ps. 91:11.

THE CREATOR SONS

I. ORIGIN AND NATURE

1. Sometimes the sovereign of Nebadon is referred to as Christ Michael. P. 234.

2. Our Creator Son is the personification of the 611,121st infinite concept of the Father and the Son. P. 366.

3. Each Creator Son is the unique, unqualified, and final expression of the infinite concept of his origin. P. 235.

4. When the concept of absolute ideation in the Eternal Son encounters an absolute personality concept in the Universal Father—there flashes into existence an original Creator Son. P. 234-5.

5. Each Creator Son is endowed with spiritual drawing power in his own realm. P. 224.

6. A Creator Son is limited by space, but not by time. P. 377.

7. There are more than seven hundred thousand Creator Sons in existence. P. 235.

II. CREATORS OF LOCAL UNIVERSES

1. The Creator Sons are preceded in universe organization by the power directors and other Third Source beings. P. 358.

2. From the energies of space, thus previously organized, our Creator Son established the inhabited worlds of Nebadon. P. 358.

3. Each Creator Son is accompanied by a Creative Daughter of the Infinite Spirit—the local universe Mother Spirit. P. 236.

4. The first creative act of the Creator Son and the Creative Mother Spirit produces the chief executive—Gabriel. P. 359.

5. The Creator Sons earn their sovereignty by bestowing themselves in the likeness of their own creatures. P. 1323.

6. The Michaels are the most versatile and powerful of all divine beings in the local universes. P. 366.

7. The local universe of Nebadon has 3,840,101 inhabited worlds. The local system of Satania has 619. P. 359.

8. In accepting vicegerent sovereignty, a Creator Son takes an oath not to assume complete sovereignty until he completes his seven bestowal experiences. P. 238.

III. THE MICHAEL BESTOWALS

1. In each bestowal experience the Creator Son adds to his nature that of the creature. P. 240.

2. Jesus of Nazareth was on his seventh bestowal when he sojourned on Urantia. P. 240.

3. The Creator Son is truly "the way, the truth, and the life." P. 242.

4. The Michael bestowals were:
    1. First—a Melchizedek.
    2. Second—Lanonandek Son.
    3. Third—Material Son.
    4. Fourth—Seraphim.
    5. Fifth—Spirit ascender.
    6. Sixth—Morontia mortal.
    7. Seventh—Urantia mortal. P. 1309-19.

IV. LOCAL UNIVERSE ORGANIZATION

1. To a local universe, to all practical purposes, a Michael Son is God. P. 66.

2. The entire judicial mechanism of Nebadon is under the supervision of Gabriel. P. 372.

LOCAL UNIVERSE CREATIVE SPIRIT

I. NATURE OF THE DIVINE MINISTER

1. Concomitant with the creation of a Creator Son, the Infinite Spirit individualizes a new and unique representation of himself to become the companion of this Creator Son. P. 374.

2. The Universe Creative Spirit of Nebadon is No. 611,121. P. 368.

3. The Universe Mother Spirit possesses all of the physical-control attributes of the Infinite Spirit including antigravity and, later, mind gravity. P. 375.

4. The Creative Spirit is co-responsible with the Creator Son for the creation and fostering of their universe. P. 376.

II. THE SON AND THE CREATIVE SPIRIT

1. Both the Son and the Spirit react to both physical and spiritual realities. P. 374.

2. While the Mother Spirit acknowledges the Son as sovereign, the Son accords the Spirit co-ordinate position and equality of authority. P. 368.

3. The Creative Spirit is limited by time, the Creator Son is not. Working together, they function independently of both time and space. P. 376-7.

4. The Mother Spirit never leaves the universe headquarters. P. 378.

III. MINISTRY OF THE SPIRIT

1. Being independent of space, the Creative Spirit is equally and diffusely present throughout the local universe. P. 376.

2. The Creative Spirit functions with the Creator Son to produce a vast array of personalities. P. 376.

3. In the evolution of mortal creatures the Life Carriers provide physical bodies while the Creative Spirit contributes the "breath of life." P. 376.

4. It is the purpose of Spirit ministry to provide strength for the "inner man." P. 381.

5. The presence of the divine Spirit is the "water of life." P. 381.

6. The Spirit never drives—only leads. P. 381.

7. The Spirit domination yields the "fruits of the spirit." P. 381.

8. Love, joy, peace, long-suffering, gentleness, goodness, faith, meekness, and temperance are the fruits of the Spirit. P. 381.

9. The spirit of the Divine Minister and the Spirit of Truth work with man as one spirit. P. 379.

IV. SEVEN STAGES OF DEVELOPMENT

There are seven stages in the development of a local universe Mother Spirit:

1. Initial Paradise Differentiation.
2. Preliminary Creatorship Training.
3. Stage of Physical Creation.
4. Life-Creation Era.
5. Postbestowal Ages.
6. Ages of Light and Life.
7. Unrevealed Career. P. 203-4.

V. THE ADJUTANT MIND-SPIRITS

These spirits function in the human mind in accordance with its capacity of receptivity.

1. Spirit of Intuition.
2. Spirit of Understanding.
3. Spirit of Courage.
4. Spirit of Knowledge.
5. Spirit of Counsel.
6. Spirit of Worship.
7. Spirit of Wisdom. P. 401.

THE POWER DIRECTORS

I. THE SUPREME POWER DIRECTORS

1. The Supreme Power Directors create seven groups of associates— they are the physical energy directors of the grand universe. P. 320.

2. These seven groups are:

    1. Supreme Center Supervisors.
    2. Havona Centers.
    3. Superuniverse Centers.
    4. Local Universe Centers.
    5. Constellation Centers.
    6. System Centers.
    7. Unclassified Centers. P. 320.

3. The Supreme Power Directors operate from the periphery of Paradise. P. 320.

4. Power Directors are energy catalyzers—they cause energy to organize and assemble in unit formation by their presence. P. 471.

5. In the evolutionary cosmos energy-matter is dominant except in personality, where spirit, through the mediation of mind, is striving for the mastery. P. 140.

6. Mortal mind can grasp only three of the seven levels of reality. P. 140.

7. Chemical elements exhibit a sevenfold recurrence of similar properties. P. 480.

II. POWER CENTERS AND CONTROLLERS

1. Power centers and controllers exert perfect control over seven of the ten forms of energy. P. 324.

2. The higher power creatures are intelligent and volitional. P. 321.

3. Physical controllers traverse space at velocities near those of Solitary Messengers. P. 324.

4. Lower types of mind can think even when deprived of the power of choice. P. 325.

5. Power centers and physical controllers never play. They are always on duty. P. 323.

6. There are seven grand divisions of the Master Physical Controllers:
    1. Associate Power Directors.
    2. Mechanical Controllers.
    3. Energy Transformers.
    4. Energy Transmitters.
    5. Primary Associators.
    6. Secondary Dissociators.
    7. Frandalanks and Chronoldeks. P. 324.

III. MASTER FORCE ORGANIZERS

1. Three groups of beings have to do with force control and energy regulation:
    1. Primary Eventuated Master Force Organizers.
    2. Associate Transcendental Master Force Organizers.
    3. Universe Power Directors. P. 319.

2. Paradise Force Organizers function throughout the master universe under the supervision of the Master Architects. P. 329.

3. Cosmic force comes from paradise and circulates throughout the master universe as the force-charge of pervaded space. P. 139.

4. Cosmic force swings on forever around the eternal space paths. P. 139.

5. There are seven divisions of universal energy:
    1. Space potency—Absoluta.
    2. Primordial force—Segregata.
    3. Emergent energy:
             a. Puissant energy
             b. Gravity energy—Ultimata.
    4. Universe power—Gravita.
    5. Havona energy—Triata.
    6. Transcendental energy—Tranosta.
    7. Monota. P. 469-71.

IV. NONSPIRITUAL ENERGY SYSTEMS

1. Pattern may be material, mindal, or spiritual. P. 10.

2. Cosmic matter becomes a philosophic shadow cast by mind in the presence of spirit luminosity. P. 140.

3. Matter is classified in ten divisions:

    1. Ultimatonic matter.
    2. Subelectronic matter.
    3. Electronic matter.
    4. Subatomic matter.
    5. Shattered atoms.
    6. Ionized matter.
    7. Atomic matter.
    8. Molecular stage of matter.
    9. Radioactive matter.
    10. Collapsed matter. P. 472.

V. ENERGY AND MATTER

1. Plus energy produces power disturbances; minus energy favors aggregation of matter. P. 176.

2. The creation of energy and the bestowal of life are Deity prerogatives. P.468.

3. There are ten types of wave energy:

    1. Infraultimatonic rays.
    2. Ultimatonic rays.
    3. Short space rays.
    4. The electronic stage.
    5. Gamma rays.
    6. The X-ray group.
    7. Ultraviolet rays.
    8. White light.
    9. Infrared rays.
    10. Hertzian waves. P. 474-5.

4. The ultimaton has three varieties of motion. P. 476.

5. Scientists will never create either matter or life. P. 468.

6. Typical electrons contain 100 ultimatons. P. 476.

7. Interelectronic space is not empty. P. 478.

8. Interelectronic space is activated by wavelike manifestations. P. 478.

9. If an electron should be magnified to equal one tenth of an ounce, the volume of such an electron would be as large as the earth. P. 477.

LOCAL UNIVERSE SONS

Immanuel, the Union of Days, No. 611,121 of the Supreme Trinity Personalities, is the personal representative of the Universal Father and the ambassador of the Paradise Trinity to the universe of Nebadon. P. 370.

I. GABRIEL

1. Gabriel is the personalization of the first concept of identity and ideal of personality conceived by the Creator Son and the Creative Spirit. P. 369.

2. Gabriel is the chief executive of the universe of Nebadon. P. 370.

II. THE MELCHIZEDEKS

1. The Father Melchizedek was created by the Creator Son and the Creative Spirit. P. 384-5.

2. Melchizedeks are created by the Creator Son, Creative Spirit, and the original Father Melchizedek. P. 385.

3. There are over ten million Melchizedeks in Nebadon. P. 387.

4. They are called emergency Sons. Wherever special help is needed, there you will find them. P. 389.

5. Melchizedeks patrol the entire local universe. P. 386.

III. THE VORONDADEKS

1. They are the Constellation Fathers—the Most Highs. P. 389.

2. There are one million Vorondadeks in Nebadon. P. 389.

3. One hundred of these Sons make up the supreme cabinet of the Creator Son. P. 390.

IV. THE LANONANDEKS

1. They perform many tasks, but are best known as System Sovereigns and Planetary Princes. P. 392.

2. Nebadon started with twelve million Lanonandeks—in three groups:
   1. Primary. 709,841.
   2. Secondary. 10,234,601.
   3. Tertiary. 1,055,558. P. 392.

3. Over seven hundred of these Sons have been lost in rebellion. P. 393.

V. THE LIFE CARRIERS

1. Life Carriers initiate life on the evolutionary worlds. P. 399. There are one hundred million in Nebadon. P. 396.

2. They catalyze the lifeless material. P. 399.

3. The essentials of life come from the Universe Mother Spirit. P. 399.

4. Each local system has a midsonite world on which a Melchizedek has functioned as a Life Carrier. P. 400.

VI. THE BRILLIANT EVENING STARS

1. There are two orders of Evening Stars—created and ascendant. They are special assistants to Gabriel. P. 407.

2. There are 4,832 created and 8,809 ascendant Evening Stars. P. 407.

VII. ARCHANGELS

1. Archangels are largely dedicated to creature survival. P. 408.

2. In recent times, a division of archangels was established on Urantia. P. 408.

VIII. THE MATERIAL SONS

1. These are the sex Sons and Daughters created by the Creator Son and stationed on the headquarters worlds of the local systems. P. 580.

2. They are the permanent citizens of the local systems. P. 581.

IX. OTHER SONS

1. *Most High Assistants*—volunteers from outside the local universe. P. 409.

2. *High Commissioners*—Spirit-fused mortals. P. 410.

3. *Celestial Overseers*—a recruited teaching corps. P. 412.

4. *Mansion World Teachers*—glorified cherubim. P. 413.

5. *Spironga*—spirit helpers of the local universe. P. 416.

SECTION SIXTEEN

PERMANENT CITIZENS

1. *Inhabited Planets.* Midwayers are the permanent citizens of the inhabited worlds. P. 415.

2. *Local Systems.* The Material Sons and Daughters. P. 515.

3. *Constellations.* The Univitatia. P. 493.

4. *Local Universe.*

    1. The Susatia. P. 414.
    2. Spirit-fused mortals. P. 451.

5. *Superuniverse.*

    1. Abandonters. P. 416.
    2. Son-fused mortals. P. 450

6. *Havona.* The Havona Natives. P. 221.

7. *Paradise.*

    1. Paradise Citizens. 222.
    2. Ascendant probation nursery children. P. 532.

8. *Worlds of the Father's and the Spirit's circuits.* Each world has a distinct type of permanent citizenship. P. 143.

SECTION SEVENTEEN
MAN

I. ANDON AND FONTA

1. Andon and fonta were the first human beings. P. 711.

2. Mortal man is not an evolutionary accident. P. 560.

3. Andon and Fonta discovered how to make fire. P. 712.

4. They developed language. P. 714.

5. They are now on the first mansion world, where they welcome Urantia pilgrims. P. 717.

6. The evolutionary worlds harbor seven physical varieties of mortals.

    1. Atmospheric types.
    2. Elemental types.
    3. Gravity types.
    4. Temperature types.
    5. Electric types.
    6. Energizing types.
    7. Unnamed types. P. 560-1.

II. THE COLORED RACES

1. The Sangik family gave origin to the six colored races. P. 722.

2. There were three primary and three secondary colored races. P. 564.

3. The primary races were the red. yellow, and blue; the secondary were the orange, green, and indigo. P. 564.

III. ADAM AND EVE

1. Adam and Eve, the biologic uplifters, were agriculturists and horticulturists. P. 575.

2. The second garden was the center of civilization for thirty thousand years. P. 868.

3. By 19,000 B.C. the Adamites numbered 4,500,000. P. 870.

4. The Aryan races sprang from the Adamites—also the Sumerians. P. 875.

5. The Andites were a blend of violet, Nodite, and Sangik peoples. P. 871.

6. There were seven major invasions of Europe by the Andites. P. 892.

7. The last exodus of the Andites from Turkestan was the Aryan invasion of India. P. 882.

IV. RACIAL TYPES

1. The early five types resulted in three modern groups:
    1. Caucasoid.
    2. Mongoloid.
    3. Negroid. P. 905.

2. There came to be three white races:
    1. Nordic.
    2. Mediterranean.
    3. Alpine. P. 897-8.

3. The blue men were the founders of an aggressive civilization. P. 889.

4. The modern white races were derived largely from the blue man and the later Adamic stock. P. 889.

5. Early Europeans were a blend of the art and vigor of the blue man and the creative imagination of the Adamites—the Cro-Magnons. P. 891.

6. The yellow men were the first to achieve social solidarity. P. 885.

7. The red men came from Asia to North America 85,000 years ago. p. 884.

8. For three thousand years the military headquarters of the Andites was in Denmark. P. 893.

V. CIVILIZATION

1. There are three classes of human institutions.
    1. Self-maintenance.
    2. Self-perpetuation.
    3. Self-gratification. P. 772.

2. Andites (blended with Vanite-Nodites) settled in Crete in 12,000 B.C. P. 895.

3. Sato, a direct descendant of Adamson, led 375 Adamsonites to Greece. P. 895.

4. Civilization was predicated on fifteen factors:

   1. Natural circumstances.
   2. Capital goods.
   3. Scientific knowledge.
   4. Human resources.
   5. Effectiveness of material resources.
   6. Effectiveness of language.
   7. Effectiveness of mechanical devices.
   8. Character of torch bearers.
   9. Racial ideals.
   10. Co-ordination of specialists.
   11. Place-finding devices.
   12. Willingness to co-operate.
   13. Effective and wise leadership.
   14. Social changes.
   15. Prevention of transitional breakdown. P. 906-11.

5. The economics of a world settled in light and life:

   1. Of the tithe tax three per cent is spent on education—truth.
   2. Three per cent on recreation—beauty.
   3. Three percent on social welfare and religion—goodness.
   4. One per cent on insurance against age, sickness, and accidents. P. 625.

VI. THE DIVINE MONITOR

1. In the choice of eternal survival, the human will is absolutely sovereign. P.71.

2. Man, by the aid of his Monitor, can transcend nature. P. 1221.

3. In spiritual endowment, all men are unique and equal. P. 63.

4. Man has an eternal spirit nucleus. P. 142.

5. The Monitor will always recall all personal relationships in the eternal future. P. 1235.

6. Adjuster-indwelt minds possess innate realization of cosmic reality—the fact, law, and love of God—science, duty, and religion. P. 195-6.

VII. PERSONALITY

1. Mind is fully stabilized only on both extremes—wholly mechanized and entirely spiritualized. P. 1217.

2. We know much about personality, but we have no definition. P. 1225-6.

3. Personality is not mind, body, soul, or spirit. P. 9.

4. Personality is changeless and unifies all factors of individuality. P. 9.

5. Personality is the gift of God. P. 1226.

6. Personality of nonsurvivors lodges in the Supreme Being. P. 1232.

7. The bestowal of personality is antecedent to the bestowal of Thought Adjusters. P. 194.

8. Personality confers cosmic citizenship. P. 195.

VIII. SEVEN STAGES OF LIGHT AND LIFE

1. The era of light and life is inaugurated by the Trinity Teacher Sons. P. 621.

2. The Planetary Prince becomes the Planetary Sovereign. P. 622.

3. In light and life the chief pursuit of mortals is truth, beauty, and goodness philosophy, cosmology, and divinity. P. 646.

4. Mortals have one philosophy, one language, and one religion. P. 626.

5. During these times many translations occur. P. 622.

6. Impending translation is often known in advance. P. 623.

IX. SURVIVAL

1. Mortal choosing determines survival. P. 69.

2. Mind is mortal, but the surviving soul is immortal. P. 565.

3. At death, the unconscious soul goes into the custody of the guardian seraphim. P. 1234.

4. Resurrection is the reassembly of the Adjuster, soul, and personality—with the morontia mind and body. P. 1234-5.

5. Every person has one chance to choose survival. P. 1233.

6. Survival of the God-choosing soul cannot be prevented by any and all of the limitations of human nature. P. 69.

7. Evolutionary mortals ascend to Paradise to await mustering into the Corps of Finality. P. 354.

8. Special resurrections are conducted from time to time and always every one thousand years. P. 568.

9. Children dying before getting Thought Adjusters are repersonalized on the finaliter worlds concomitant with the arrival of either parent on the mansion worlds. P. 579.

10. When mortal man fails to survive, spiritual values of human experience survive in the Thought Adjuster—personality values persist in the Supreme Being. P. 195.

Section Eighteen
EDUCATION

1. Ideal education provides for association of instruction and work. P. 412.

2. The purpose of education:

    1. Acquirement of skill.
    2. Pursuit of wisdom.
    3. Realization of selfhood.
    4. Attainment of spiritual values. P. 806.

3. The goals of education are:

    1. Insight into human relations.
    2. Meanings of reality.
    3. Nobility of values.
    4. Goals of living.
    5. Cosmic destiny. P. 806.

4. Ideas originate in external stimuli; ideals are born in the inner life. P. 1220.

5. Civilizations are unstable because they are not cosmic. They must be nurtured by the constitutive factors of science, morality, and religion. P. 196.

MARRIAGE AND THE HOME

I. THE MATING INSTINCT

1. The sex urge is sufficient to bring men and women together for reproduction. P. 913.

2. Marriage is the ancestor of civilization's most sublime institution—the home. P. 931.

3. The purpose of marriage is to insure racial survival—not just personal happiness. P. 765.

4. The evolution of marriage is the story of sex control by social, civil, and religious restrictions. P. 914.

5. Women's low status during Old Testament times reflects the mores of the herdsmen. P. 934.

6. In primitive times marriage was the price of social distinction—a wife enhanced social standing. P. 915.

II. MARRIAGE—A SOCIAL INSTITUTION

1. Man's great danger is the unrestricted multiplication of inferior racial strains. P. 921.

2. The family is the master civilizer. P. 913.

3. Marriages are not made in heaven. P. 922.

4. Marriage is a social instiution embracing self-maintenance, self-perpetuation, and self-gratification. P. 931.

5. It was the factory, not religion, that emancipated woman. P. 937.

6. Woman has always been the standard-bearer—the spiritual leader. P. 938.

7. Marriage has always been closely linked with both property and religion. P. 917.

8. Marriage is a social program of antagonistic co-operation. P. 938.

III.TRUE MONOGAMY

1.   There were four sorts of wives under polygamy:

    1.   Legal wives.
    2.   Wives of affection.
    3.   Concubines.
    4.   Slave wives. P. 926

2.   Monogamy has always been the idealistic goal of marriage, and it is the yardstick measuring the advance of civilization. P. 927.

3.   Early woman was not a friend and lover—rather a servant and childbearer. P. 935.

4.   It was a great advance when the wife could own property. P. 936.

5.   But primitive women did not pity themselves. P. 936.

IV. FAMILY LIFE

1.   Man did not intentionally seize woman's rights—it was all an unconscious process. P. 937.

2.   Will modern woman be worthy of her newly won dignity and equality? P. 937.

3.   Divorce will persist as long as young people are not properly prepared for marriage. P. 929.

4.   The family-council of the Andites would be helpful today. P. 941.

5.   The differences between men and women persist throughout the ascendant career—even in the Corps of Finality. P. 939.

THE STATE

I. WAR

1. Violence is the law of nature. Peace is the yardstick measuring the advance of civilization. P. 783.

2. Primitive man enjoyed fighting. P. 784.

3. Wars were caused by hunger, women, slaves, revenge, vanity, monotony, and religion. P. 784.

4. Some wars had social value. P. 785.

5. Ancient wars destroyed inferior peoples; modern ware destroy the best stocks. P. 786.

6. Sometimes early man would stake all on a duel—like David and Goliath. P. 785.

II. EARLY HUMAN ASSOCIATIONS

1. Personal inequalities caused groupings in primitive society. P. 792.

2. Secret societies were the first political parties. P. 792.

3. Ten groups occur in primitive society:
     1. Natural.
     2. Personal.
     3. Chance.
     4. Economic.
     5. Geographic.
     6. Social.
     7. Vocational.
     8. Religious.
     9. Racial.
     10. Age. P. 792-3.

III. HUMAN RIGHTS

1. Kings were chosen for special abilities—heroes. P. 789.

2. The great myth was absoluteness of the state. P. 800.

3. Nature confers no rights on man—not even the right to live. P. 793.

4. Security is the gift of society to man. P. 793.

5. Equality is the child of civilization—it is not found in nature. P. 794.

IV. EVOLUTION OF JUSTICE

1. Government evolved by trial and error. P. 783.

2. Natural justice is a man-made theory—fiction. P. 794.

3. Law is a record of human experience—public opinion crystallized and legalized. P. 797.

4. Public opinion delays society, but preserves civilization. P. 802.

5. Democracy is ideal, but it is beset by certain dangers:

    1. Glorification of mediocrity.
    2. Choice of base and ignorant rulers.
    3. Failure to recognize social evolution.
    4. Dangers of universal suffrage.
    5. Slavery to public opinion. P. 801.

V. IDEALS OF STATEHOOD

1. The safeguards of statehood are :

    1. Prevention of usurpation of power by the state.
    2. Control of ignorant agitators.
    3. Maintenance of scientific progress.
    4. Prevention of dominanance of mediocrity.
    5. Control of vicious minorities.
    6. Control of clever dictators.
    7. Prevention of panics.
    8. Avoidance of exploitation by the unscrupulous.
    9. Avoidance of salavery by taxation.
    10. Maintenance of social and economic fairness.
    11. Prevention of union of churchand state.
    12. Preservation of personal liberty. P. 798.

2. Only love can prevent the strong from oppressing the weak. P. 805.

3. Statehood evolves slowly through a dozen levels.

    1. Threefold government—executive, legislative, and judicial.
    2. Freedom of social, political, and religious activities.
    3. Abolition of slavery and bondage.
    4. Control of taxation.
    5. Universal education.
    6. Adjustment of local and national governments.
    7. Fostering of science and conquest of disease.
    8. Sex equality.
    9. Liberation of machines and their mastery.
    10. Conquest of dialects.
    11. Ending of war.
    12. Universal pursuit of wisdom. P. 806-7.

4. The great problem of statehood is to prevent the state from becoming parasitical or tyrannical. P. 805.

VI. PROGRESSIVE CIVILIZATION

1. Civilization embraces:

    1. Preservation of liberties.
    2. Protection of the home.
    3. Economic security.
    4. Prevention of disease.
    5. Compulsory education.
    6. Compulsory employment.
    7. Profitable leisure.
    8. Care of unfortunates.
    9. Race improvement.
    10. Promotion of science and art.
    11. Promotion of philosophy.
    12. Cosmic insight. P. 804.

2. Society has not progressed very far when it permits idleness and tolerates poverty. P. 803.

3. Profit motivation should prevail until a better motivation is provided. P. 805.

4. Industry demands law and private property. P. 783.

5. Communism failed because it fostered idleness and because it ran counter to family, religion, liberty, and security. P. 780.

6. Make changes only when they are for the better. P. 782.

7. Slavery was indispensable in the development of civilization. It compelled lazy people to work and thus provided wealth and leisure for the advancement of superior peoples. P. 779.

VII. SUPERHUMAN GOVERNMENT

1. The Most Highs rule in the kingdoms of men. P. 1253.

2. The reserve corps of destiny may assist. P. 1257.

3. The angels of planetary supervision are:

   1. Epochal angels.
   2. Progress angels.
   3. Religious guardians.
   4. Nation life.
   5. The races.
   6. Angels of the future.
   7. Enlightenment.
   8. Health.
   9. Home.
   10. Industry.
   11. Diversion.
   12. Superhuman ministry. P. 1255-6.

ASCENDING SONS OF GOD

There are seven classes of the Ascending Sons of God. P. 443.

I. ASCENDING MORTALS—FATHER-FUSED

1. Mortal curiosity, adventure, and exploration will be gloriously gratified during the long ages to come. P. 160.

2. Mortals are the lowest group of beings called the Sons of God. P. 445.

3. Grandfanda was the first mortal to attain Paradise. P. 270.

4. When fused with an Adjuster, a mortal becomes in fact a son of God. P. 449.

5. At death, two factors survive: The Thought Adjuster and the morontia soul. P. 1230.

II. SON-FUSED MORTALS

When mortals fail of Adjuster fusion, through no fault of their own, they become Son fused. P. 449.

III. SPIRIT-FUSED MORTALS

1. Mortals incapable of Adjuster fusion are fused with the spirit of the Divine Minister. P. 450.

2. In general, Spirit-fused mortals are confined to the local universe. P. 452.

IV. EVOLUTIONARY SERAPHIM

All guardian angels attain Paradise and many become finaliters. P. 443.

V. MATERIAL SONS

Many Material Sons attain the Corps of the Finality. P. 444.

VI. TRANSLATED MIDWAYERS

Midwayers also ascend to Paradise and the Finality Corps. P. 444.

VII. PERSONALIZED ADJUSTERS

They are the highest order of ascending Sons, P. 445.

(In the ascending scheme, MIDSONITERS are a mystery. P. 401.)

VII. THE PATH OF ASCENSION

1.   Ascenders first traverse the mansion worlds and Jerusem. P. 532-40.

2.   They then go through the constellation training spheres. P. 493-5.

3.   After traversing the local universe and superuniverse they go through Havona. P. 290.

4.   Finally they attain Paradise. P. 294-299.

SECTION TWENTY-TWO

THE MORONTIA LIFE

I. THE MORONTIA

1. The morontia is the beginning of a gigantic universe school of experiential training. P. 558.

2. Seven worlds of corrective training and cultural education introduce the transition which intervenes between material existence and spirit attainment. P. 540.

3. Resurrected mortals have the same type of body that Jesus had when he arose from the tomb. P. 2029.

II. MORONTIA WORLD PERSONALITIES

1. Morontia Companions. P. 545-7.

2. Reversion Directors. P. 547-50.

3. Mansion World Teachers. P. 550-1.

4. Morontia World Seraphim. P. 551-5.

5. Celestial Artisans. P. 497-508.

6. Morontia Power Supervisors. P. 542-5.

III. MORONTIA MOTA

1. Mota is more than a superior philosophy. It is to philosophy as two eyes are to one. Material man sees with one eye—morontians with two. P. 554.

2. Without mota man cannot discern truth and goodness in the material world. P. 1137.

3. Mota does what metaphysics fails to do. P. 1136.

4. Revelation is man's only substitute for mota. P. 1137.

IV. THE MORONTIA SELF

1. Morontians are endowed with the local universe modification of the cosmic mind. Certain phases of mortal mind persist in the surviving soul. P. 1236.

2. Paul spoke of morontia as the "better and more enduring substance."
    P. 542.

3. Upon Adjuster fusion the "new name" is conferred. P. 538.

V. THE PROBATION NURSERY

There is a probationary nursery for children dying without Adjusters or
before making a survival choice. P. 531-2.

VI. SPORNAGIA

Spornagia do not have survival souls. They do not have Adjusters. They do
not have personality. They are the only beings in the universe to experience
reincarnation. P. 528.

THE CORPS OF THE FINALITY

I. FINALITERS

1. The seven Finaliter Corps are controlled by the senior Master Architect.

    1. Corps of Mortal Finaliters.
    2. Corps of Paradise Finaliters.
    3. Corps of Trinitized Finaliters.
    4. Corps of Conjoint Trinitized Finaliters.
    5. Corps of Havona Finaliters.
    6. Corps of Transcendental Finaliters.
    7. Corps of Unrevealed Sons of Destiny. P. 352.

2. Finaliters are destined to serve in the universes of outer space. P. 131.

II. CORPS OF MORTAL FINALITERS

1. Havona Natives. P. 346.
2. Gravity Messengers. P. 346-7.
3. Glorified Mortals. P. 347-8.
4. Adopted Seraphim. P. 348-9.
5. Glorified Material Sons. P. 349.
6. Glorified Midway Creatures. P. 349.

III. EVANGELS OF LIGHT

Evangels of Light are the transient seventh members of the Mortal Finality Corps. P. 349-50.

YAHWEH

I. DEITY AMONG THE SEMITES

1. The evolution of Hebrew theology embraced five concepts of Deity:

   1. Yahweh.
   2. El Elyon.
   3. El Shaddai.
   4. El.
   5. Elohim. P. 1053.

2. The Hebrews deanthropomorphized God without making him an abstraction of philosophy. P. 1062.

3. The Kenites held many of the concepts of Melchizedek respecting Deity. P. 1052.

4. There was a continuous evolution of Deity concept from the primitive Yahweh to the high level of the Isaiahs. P. 1057.

II. TIMES OF MOSES

1. Moses taught that Yahweh was a jealous God. He was building a national conscience—he awed the people with the justice of God. P. 1057-8.

2. The Hebrew belief in Yahweh explains why they tarried so long about Mt. Sinai. P. 1056.

3. Joshua tried to maintain Moses' teachings. P. 1059.

III. SAMUEL AND ELIJAH

1. Samuel proclaimed the changelessness of God—a sincere and covenant-keeping God—a God of great mercy. P. 1063.

2. Elijah continued Samuel's work, but paid more attention to the land problems of the Baalites. P. 1064-5.

IV. AMOS AND HOSEA

1. Amos proclaimed that God would punish his own people because of their sins—justice. P. 1065.

2. Hosea presented a God of forgiveness—he rejected all sacrifices. P. 1066.

V. JEREMIAH

Jeremiah proclaimed the internationalization of Yahweh. P. 1067.

VI. THE ISAIAHS

1. The first Isaiah taught punishment for both personal and national sins. P. 1066.

2. The second Isaiah proclaimed the universal Creator, the forgiving God, and the heavenly Father. P. 1069.

SIN

I. THE CONCEPT OF SIN

1. God loves the sinner, but hates the sin. P. 41.

2. The love of God saves the sinner; the law of God destroys the sin. P. 41.

3. Sin is potential when imperfect beings are endowed with free will. p. 613.

4. Sin is the attitude of a person who is knowingly resisting cosmic reality. P. 754.

5. Iniquity is open defiance of reality and leads to cosmic insanity. P. 754.

6. Violation of taboo becomes a vice. Law makes vice a crime. Religion makes it a sin. P. 976.

7. Violation of the mores—feelings of guilt—are not necessarily sin. P. 984.

8. The power of Jesus' love breaks the hold of sin. P. 2018.

9. The deliberate choice of evil is sin. P. 613.

II. THE LUCIFER REBELLION

1. Lucifer, a brilliant administrator, through evil and error, embraced sin. He surrendered to the urge of self and the sophistry of personal liberty. P. 601.

2. Self-contemplation is disastrous—pride, fatal. P. 601.

3. Lucifer became insincere—evil evolved into willful sin. P. 603.

4. Lucifer's threefold declaration of liberty:

    1. Rejection of the Universal Father.
    2. Defiance of Michael.
    3. Attack on plan of mortal ascension. P. 603-4.

5. Self-assertion was the battle cry of the rebellion—"the brotherhood of intelligence." P. 604.

6. Lucifer's folly was the attempt to do the nondoable—short-circuit time. P. 614.

7. The bestowal of Michael terminated the Lucifer rebellion in Satania. P. 609.

8. The case of Gabriel vs. Lucifer is pending in the courts of Uversa. P. 611.

9. Liberty is self-destroying when uncontrolled. True liberty is regardful of:

    1. Social equity.
    2. Cosmic fairness.
    3. Universe fraternity.
    4. Divine obligations. P. 613.

10. True liberty is the associate of self-respect; false liberty, the consort of self-admiration. P. 614.

11. Man should learn to enjoy liberty without license and pleasure without debauchery. P. 977.

12. In applying justice mercy provides the interval between seedtime and harvest. P. 616.

13. After the Caligastia rebellion, human society quickly reverted to its old biologic level. P. 759.

14. Rebellion time-penalizes all Urantians, but no person suffers in his personal religious experience. P. 761.

15. Not a single a scender on Jerusem participated in the Lucifer rebellion. P. 608.

16. Amadon was the outstanding hero of the Lucifer rebellion. P. 757, 762.

17. Ever since the rebellion the Edentia Fathers have exercised a special care over the isolated worlds. P. 491.

III. FORGIVENESS OF SIN

1. The concept of "original sin" started every person out in debt to the gods. P. 978.

2. Man acquired the moral dignity to bargain with the gods—make a covenant. P. 983.

3. Forgiveness does not have to be sought—only received. P. 985.

4. Animal natures may be hereditary—but sin is not. Sin is a conscious rebellion against the Father's will. P. 2016.

IV. THE PENALTY FOR SIN

1. Wholehearted indentification with sin is the equivalent of nonexist-
    ence—annihilation. P. 615.

2. The system circuits will not be restored as long as Lucifer lives. P.
    611.

THE PLAN OF SALVATION

I. THE LOVE OF GOD

1. God uniquely individualizes his love for every person. P. 138.

2. Love, not pressure, stimulates growth. P. 1135.

   BIBLE REFERENCES: Acts 10:34, 35. II Cor. 3:17. I John 4:8.

II. THE PERFECTION PLAN

1. God's will may not prevail in the part, but it always does with the whole. P. 137.

2. We are all a part of a vast and eternal purpose. P. 364.

3. Victory is assured for all who enter the race for eternal perfection. P. 365.

4. The plan of perfection attainment is one of the chief concerns of the superuniverses. P. 54.

5. The Father's plan of evolutionary mortal ascension was concurred in by the Eternal Son. P. 85.

   BIBLE REFERENCES: Eph. 3:11. Rom. 8:28. Gen. 1:26. Matt. 5:48.

III. THE BESTOWAL PLAN

The incarnate bestowal of the Paradise Sons upon the mortal races is a project of the Eternal Son. P. 85.

BIBLE REFERENCES: Luke 19:10.

IV. THE MERCY MINISTRY PLAN

1. When the perfection and bestowal plans were proclaimed, the Infinite Spirit promulgated his plan of mercy ministry. P. 85.

2. The Infinite Spirit ministers for the Father and the Son and also in his own behalf. P. 95.

BIBLE REFERENCES: Rom. 8:26.

V. THE SALVAGE PLAN

1. In case of sin or delay, the Paradise Sons act as retrievers. P. 85.

2. The Creators are the first to attempt to save man from the results of transgression. P. 39.

BIBLE REFERENCES: Isa. 63:9. Heb. 12:10. I Pet. 1:5.

VI. THE FAITH SONS OF GOD

1. Sonship with God is inherent in divine love; it is not dependent on the bestowals of the Paradise Sons. P. 2002.

2. Providence is the function of the Trinity motivating the cosmic march through time toward the goals of eternity. P. 1307.

3. God loves the individual; providence functions with regard to the whole. P. 1304.

4. God may at any time interpose a Fatherly hand in the stream of cosmic events. P. 1305.

BIBLE REFERENCES: Rom. 8:14. John 3:3. II Cor. 5:17. I John 5:4.

VII. JESUS' LIFE ON EARTH

1. Jesus wants you to believe *with* him—rather than *in* him. P. 2089.

2. The atonement idea is a philosophical assault upon both the unity and volition of God. P. 41.

3. God is not a divided personality—one of justice and one of mercy. P. 41.

4. God as a Father transcends God as a judge. P. 41.

5. Jesus did not die as a sacrifice for sin—to atone for the inborn guilt of the race. P. 2003.

6. Christ is not engaged in the ignoble task of persuading his Father to love his lowly creatures. P. 75.

BIBLE REFERENCES: II Cor. 5:19.

VIII. THE RELIGION OF SURVIVAL

1. Having embarked on the way of life everlasting, do not fear the limitations of human nature. At every crossroad, the Spirit of Truth will speak—"This is the way." P. 383.

2. We have begun an endless unfolding of an almost infinite panorama of everwidening opportunity for matchless adventure and boundless attainment. P. 1194.

3. When the clouds gather overhead, by faith we should look beyond the mists of mortal uncertainty into the clear shining of the sun of eternal righteousness on the beckoning heights of the mansion worlds of Satania. P. 1194.

4. The present destiny of surviving mortals is the Paradise Corps of the Finality. P. 1239.

BIBLE REFERENCES: I John 5:4.

SECTION TWENTY-SEVEN

ADAM AND EVE

I. ARRIVAL OF ADAM AND EVE

1. The Adams and Eves are biologic uplifters. P. 580.

2. Van had long proclaimed the arrival of a Son of God. P. 822.

3. The secondary midwayers are indigenous to the Adamic missions. P. 583.

4. Adam and Eve arrived on Urantia, from A.D. 1934, 37,848 years ago. P. 828.

5. The bodies of Adam and Eve gave forth a shimmering light. P. 834.

6. Van proclaimed Adam and Eve rulers of Urantia. P. 830.

7. Their arrival brought the end of a dispensation with resurrection of sleeping survivors. P. 830.

8. Adam was confronted with confusion, degeneracy, and isolation— he had no one to advise him. P. 839.

II. THE GARDEN OF EDEN

1. The Garden provided homes and land for one million. P. 824.

2. The Father's Temple was at the center of the Garden. P. 824.

3. The law of the Garden consisted of seven commandments:
    1. Health and sanitation.
    2. Social regulations.
    3. Trade and commerce.
    4. Fair play and competition.
    5. Home life.
    6. Golden rule.
    7. The seven moral rules. P. 836.
4.. The tree of life was real. P. 825.

III. DEFAULT OF ADAM AND EVE

1. Through flattery and persuasion Eve was led to compromise the divine plan. P. 842.

2. The default consisted in the practice of good and evil. P. 842.

3. Solonia informed the pair of their default. P. 842.

4. Adam deliberately defaulted. He did not want to be separated from Eve. P. 843.

5. Nothing is ever gained by attempting circumventing short cuts of the divine plan. P. 846.

IV. THE SECOND GARDEN

1. Adam and twelve hundred followers went forth to the second garden. P. 844.

2. The pair learned that they were adjudged in default and had become human beings. P. 845.

3. The default of Adam was not the "fall of man." P. 845.

4. Adam found the site of the second garden between the rivers vacated when he arrived. P. 847.

V. CAIN AND ABEL

1. Cain and Sansa were born enroute to the second garden. Laotta died. Eve adopted Sansa. P. 847.

2. Abel became a herder; Cain a farmer. P. 848.

3. Abel mad animal of ferings; Cain, the fruits of the field. P. 848.

4. At ages eighteen and twenty, the brothers' hatred reached the point where Cain killed Abel. P. 848.

5. Cain fled to the land of Nod and married Remona. P. 849.

VI. THE VIOLET RACE

1. Adam and Eve were the founders of the violet race—the ninth human race. P850.

2. Adam's progeny were more resisant to disease than the other Urantian races. P. 851.

3. The Adamites excelled in culture and produced the third alphabet. P. 850.

4. Adam and Eve had 105 children, many of whom contributed to the Andite race. P. 834.

5. Adam left 1,570 offspring of superior evolutionary races who also contributed to the founding of the mighty Andite race. P. 351.

VII. DEATH AND SURVIVAL OF ADAM AND EVE

1. Adam lived 530 years. Eve died nineteen years before Adam. P. 852.

2. The third day after death, Adam and Eve were repersonalized with 1,316 of their associates, in special resurrection No. 26. P. 853.

3. The Adamic acceleration of civilization was soon submerged. P. 854.

4. It is the people who make a civilization; civilization does not make the people. P. 854.0

MACHIVENTA MELCHIZEDEK

I. THE MACHIVENTA INCARNATION

1. Machiventa incarnated on Urantia 1,973 years ago. P. 1015.

2. Machiventa spoke several languages and wore a breastplate of three concentric circles. P. 1015.

3. He had a special body and never married. P. 1015.

4. His Thought Adjuster subsequently indwelt Jesus. P. 1016.

II. MELCHIZEDEK'S TEACHINGS

1. The three circles represented the Trinity. P. 1016.

2. Machiventa taught that God accepted man on terms of personal faith. P. 1017.

3. The Salem cult had three simple beliefs:
    1. I believe in El Elyon, the Universal Father and Creator.
    2. I accept the Melchizedek covenant—the favor of God by faith, not by sacrifices.
    3. I promise to obey the seven commandments. P. 1017.

4. The seven commandments were:
    1. You shall not serve any God but the Most High Creator of heaven and earth.
    2. You shall not doubt that faith is the only requirement for eternal salvation.
    3. You shall not bear false witness.
    4. You shall not kill.
    5. You shall not steal.
    6. You shall not commit adultery.
    7. You shall not show disrespect for your parents and elders. P. 1017-18.

5. Melchizedek tried to substitute the sacrament of bread and wine for animal sacrifices. P. 1018.

III. THE COVENANT WITH ABRAHAM

1. It may be wrong to speak of a "chosen people," but Abraham was a "chosen individual." P. 1018.

2. Abraham became head of the eleven tithe-paying tribes. P. 1020.

3. Melchizedek made a formal covenant with Abraham. P. 1020.

4. The Abraham covenant provided that God did everything—faith alone gained God's favor. P. 1020.

5. Abraham became civil and military leader of the Salem colony. P. 1021.

IV. DEPARTURE OF MELCHIZEDEK

1. Machiventa retired one night and departed before morning. P. 1022.

2. He became one of the 24 directors on Jerusem—and later Vicegerent Planetary Prince of Urantia. P. 1025.

V. SPREAD OF MELCHIZEDEK'S TEACHINGS

1. Moses got much of Machiventa's teachings through the Katro family. P. 1016.

2. His teachings were preserved by the Kenites. P. 1052.

3. Melchizedek's trained natives carried the gospel over the entire Eastern Hemisphere. P. 1027.

4. His teachings largely failed among the Greeks but survived among the Roman Cynics. P. 1077.

5. His teachings were carried all over Europe and Asia—even to Africa. P. 1077.

SECTION TWENTY-NINE

CHRISTOLOGY

I. BESTOWALS OF MICHAEL

1. The technique of the bestowals is a universal mystery. P. 1315.

2. The bestowals covered a billion years. P. 1318.

3. Michael was born a creator, trained an administrator, but was required to earn his sovereignty. P. 1318.

4. He not only revealed the Father but also achieved the sevenfold will of the Supreme. P. 1324.

5. Jesus' mission was to:

    1. Acquire creature experience.
    2. Reveal the Father.
    3. Terminate Lucifer rebellion.
    4. Acquire sovereignty. P. 1417.

6. He lived his life *on* Urantia but *for* his entire universe. P. 1424.

II. JOSEPH AND MARY

1. Gabriel selected Joseph and Mary to be the parents of Jesus. P. 1344.

2. Mary came from a long line of illustrious ancestors, but she was hardly a Jewess. P. 1345.

3. Joseph was a mild-mannered introvert—subject to mild mood swings. P. 1348.

4. Mary was an even-tempered extrovert. P. 1345.

5. Jesus derived his gentleness from his father—his teaching ability from his mother. P. 1348.

6. It was a trying experience to rear Jesus. His parents never dreamed he was the Creator incarnate. P. 1372.

III. THE BIRTH OF JESUS

1. Joseph and Mary were married in March 8 B.C. P. 1350.

2. Jesus was born at noon, Aug. 21, 7 B.C. P. 1351.

3. Jesus was born just as all babies before that day and since that day. P. 1351.

4. The wise men saw no star. This myth was based on a subsequent astronomical occurrence. P. 1352.

5. On October 6 B.C. Herod ordered the massacre of 16 Bethlehem babies. P. 1354.

IV. ALEXANDRIA AND NAZARETH

1. Jesus spent two years in Alexandria, leaving in August 4 B.C. P. 1355-6.

2. Jesus was a little over three years old when they returned to Nazareth. P. 1356.

3. During his fourth year he developed his friendship for the neighbor boy Jacob. P. 1357.

4. Jesus' Thought Adjuster arrived February 11, 2 B.C. P. 1357.

5. John the Baptist visited Jesus during the summer of 1 B.C. P. 1359.

V. THE EDUCATION OF JESUS

1. From five years of age until ten, Jesus was one continuous question mark. P. 1358.

2. At seven Jesus entered school, speaking two languages. P. 1362.

3. Jesus got his moral training and spiritual culture at home; his practical education mingling with his fellow men. P. 1363.

4. Jesus belonged to the upper third of his class, was therefore excused from attendance one week each month. P. 1364.

5. Jesus made serious trouble for his parents by drawing a picture of his teacher on the schoolroom floor. P. 1366.

6. Jesus graduated March 20, A.D. 7. P. 1373.

VI. JESUS' EARLY CHILDHOOD

1. When six years old, Jesus was disconcerted to learn that his supposedly all-wise father did not know the cause of earthquakes. P. 1359.

2. On a visit to Scythopolis Jesus was enthused over the Greek games, but was rebuked by his father. P. 1370-1.

3. Never could Jesus escape the conflict between personal convictions and demands of loyalty to the family usages. P. 1372.

4. They had trouble with Jesus regarding his prayers—he wanted to have just a little talk with his Father in heaven. P. 1360.

5. Jesus was subject to ordinary accidents and illness. P. 1361.

6. Jesus refused to believe that his human father was kinder than his heavenly Father. P. 1378.

VII. GROWTH OF DIVINITY CONSCIOUSNESS

1. When ten years old, Jesus first talked to his parents about his mission. P. 1368.

2. At Jerusalem, when thirteen, a messenger appeared, saying: "It is time that you began to be about your Father's business." P. 1376.

3. It was the Book of Enoch that suggested he adopt the title "Son of Man." P. 1390.

4. His spiritual experience well-nigh reached the apex during his twenty-ninth year. P. 1425.

5. The attainment of totality of divinity was marked by seven events:
    1. Arrival of the Thought Adjuster.
    2. Messenger at Jerusalem.
    3. Manifestations at baptism.
    4. Experiences on the mount of transfiguration.
    5. The morontia resurrection.
    6. The spirit ascension.
    7. Bestowal of sovereignty. P. 2091.

    BIBLE REFERENCES: Luke 6:12. Mark 1:35. Matt. 14:23; 26:36. Luke 22:44. Heb. 5:7.

VIII. GOD AND MAN

1. Jesus was God and man—but he was not a double personality. P. 1331.

2. Of his human nature he was never in doubt, but of his divine nature there could be doubt—from the Jerusalem experience to his baptism. P. 1408.

3. He began life as God appearing as man, and finished as man appearing as God. P. 1484.

4. Such a transcendental bestowal of man-saving and God-revealing should restrain theologians from making creedal bondage out of his teachings. P. 2084.

    BIBLE REFERENCES: John 14:28; 8:29; 14:10. I Cor. 15:27. John 5:30.

IX. THE TEMPLE DISCUSSIONS

1. Jesus goes to Jerusalem to celebrate his first Passover. P. 1374.

2. The Nazareth family meets Simon and his Bethany family. P. 1375.

3. Jesus was sickened by the sights and sounds of animal slaughter. P. 1378.

4. In the temple discussions, Jesus was confronted with difficulties because of his youth and Nazareth nativity. P. 1382.

5. Jesus focused the attention of the temple discussions upon numerous pointed questions. P. 1382.

6. He did not seem to comprehend that his parents would be worried about his having been left behind. P. 1383.

7. When his parents found him in the temple it was a tense moment. Joseph was speechless, but Mary gave vent to her anxiety. P. 1384.

8. Jesus' reply to his mother was both considerate and wise. P. 1384.

X. JESUS' ADOLESCENCE

1. Jesus studied the flowers by day and the stars by night. P. 1360.

2. Jesus' unwillingness to fight for his rights occasioned little trouble because his chum Jacob was an ever-ready defender. P. 1368.

3. He was an alert pupil, well socialized, a director of play, and a born teacher. P. 1369.

4. His knowledge of international affairs was gained from the travelers met at the caravan repair shop. P. 1370.

5. Joseph and Mary were frustrated about Jesus because nothing miraculous ever happened. P. 1387.

6. At Joseph's death, Jesus accepted the responsibilities so suddenly thrust upon him. P. 1388.

7. Jesus employed the *positive* method of child-culture. P. 1401.

XI. EARLY MANHOOD

1. The "Lord's Prayer" was an evolution of the Nazareth family altar. P. 1389.

2. Jesus was frequently thwarted and frustrated, but never discouraged. P. 1393.

3. He passed through all the conflicts and confusions of the average youth. P. 1393.

4. Even though his mother favored it, Jesus refused to join the Zealots. P.1396-7.

5. Jesus and John the Baptist had a visit. P. 1400.

6. By his conduct at the death of Amos, Jesus became the real head of the family. P. 1400.

7. Rebecca fell in love with Jesus. P. 1402.

8. Broken-hearted Rebecca followed him through his life and was present at the crucifixion. P. 1403.

9. Jesus celebrated the bloodless Passover with the Bethany youngsters. P. 1404.

10. Jesus lived the full human life in the flesh. P. 1405.

11. He gained wisdom by experience and before his baptism he utilized no superhuman power. P. 1407-8.

12. One of the touching episodes of the trip to Rome was Ganid's proposal that they make a new religion. P. 1467.

XII. ON MOUNT HERMON

1. The isolation on Mount Hermon marked the end of Jesus' purely human career. P. 1492.

2. Jesus dismissed his guardian seraphim and entered the great test with only his Adjuster to guide him. P. 1493.

3. On Mount Hermon, Jesus completed the mastery of mind and attained the goal of human achievement. P. 1493.

4. The great achievement—the universe trial—occurred on Mount Hermon. P. 1493.

5. On a summer's day, amid the silence of nature, Michael won the unquestioned sovereignty of his universe. P. 1494.

XIII. THE BAPTISM

1. John baptized Jesus and his brothers and heard the voice: "This is my beloved Son in whom I am well pleased." P. 1504.

2. Jesus stood in the Jordan a perfected mortal of the evolutionary worlds. P. 1511.

3. Ordinarily, when man and his Adjuster are synchronized, fusion takes place. Jesus' Adjuster was personalized. P. 1511.

4. The forty days were the period of his great decisions. P. 1515.

5. The Personalized Adjuster reminded Jesus of his inability to limit his life as regards time. P. 1516.

    BIBLE REFERENCES: Matt. 3:13-17. Mark. 1:9-11. Luke 3:21-23. Matt. 4:1-11. Mark 1:12,13. Luke 4:1-13.

XIV. MIRACLES

1. Jesus refused to be a wonder-worker. P. 1520.

2. Out of tender feelings for his mother, Jesus was led, unwittingly, to turn the water into wine. P. 1529.

3. Curing the withered hand was a miracle wrought in reponse to a challenge by his enemies. P. 1665.

4. Many unexplained miracles occurred throughout his ministry. P. 1669.

5. Feeding the five thousand was the only nature miracle Jesus performed as a result of conscious preplanning. P. 1701-2.

XV. PETER'S CONFESSION

1. Peter proclaims: "You are the Deliverer, the Son of the living God." P. 1746.

2. Jesus declared he could build the Father's kingdom upon this rock of spiritual reality. P. 1747.

3. Jesus delivered the keys of the kingdom—authority over things temporal—to his associates. P. 1747.

4. For years Jesus had proclaimed himself the "Son of Man"—now he reveals that he is the Son of God. P. 1748.

5. Jesus now enters upon the fourth and last stage of his bestowal. P. 1749.

6. Jesus rebuked Peter's well-meant affection because it was against the Father's will. P. 1760.

   BIBLE REFERENCES: Matt. 16:13-20. Mark 8:27-30. Luke 9:18-21.

XVI. THE TRANSFIGURATION

1. Jesus began the final phase of his bestowal on the mount of transfiguration. P. 1751.

2. The three frightened apostles heard a voice say: "This is my beloved Son; give heed to him." P. 1753-4.

3. The revelation of God to the world, through Jesus, shall not fail. P. 2097.

   BIBLE REFERENCES: Matt. 17:1-13. Mark 9:2-13. Luke 9:28-36. John 14:31. John 15:9. Luke 19:10. John 11:36. Mark 6:34.

XVII. JESUS' HUMAN NATURE

1. Jesus was emotionally well-balanced. He was so well-poised because he was so perfectly unified. P. 1102.

2. He was a cheerful person. He trusted God and was so touchingly considerate of men. P. 1102.

3. He was not a man of sorrows, he was the soul of gladness. P. 1103.

4. His courage was always linked with discretion and controlled by reason. His watchword was "Fear not." P. 1103.

5. Jesus had great capacity for humor and play. P. 1361.

6. In every respect he was made like his brethren that he might become a merciful and understanding sovereign. P. 1408.

7. He lived the mortal life from the bottom to the top; from the beginning to the end. P. 1425.

8. Before he was thirty years old, he became the fullness of man awaiting to become manifest to God. P. 1426.

9. His humiliation and death were the great proofs of his humanity. P. 1968.

10. By prayer, his humanity laid firmer faith-hold upon his divinity. P. 1969.

11. Jesus may be regarded as a valiant and courageous hero. P. 1013.

12. The human Jesus must not be taken away from men. P. 2090.

    BIBLE REFERENCES: John 1:14. Gal. 4:4. John 4:6. Matt. 3:24. John 19:28. Luke 22:44. Luke 2:52. Phil. 2:7. Heb. 4:15. Matt. 11:29.

XVIII. JESUS' DIVINE NATURE

1. The babe, the lad, the youth, the man of Nazareth, was the incarnated Creator of a universe. P. 1408.

2. Even as he wrestled with poverty, there was a growing awareness that he was a Son of God. P. 1409.

3. Nalda talked of the Deliverer, and Jesus said: "I who speak to you am he." P. 1614.

4. The Master was known by sixteen names, all indicative of his divinity:

    1. I am the bread of life.
    2. I am the living water.
    3. I am the light of the world.
    4. I am the desire of all ages.
    5. I am the open door to eternal salvation.
    6. I am the reality of endless life.

7. I am the good shepherd.
8. I am the pathway of infinite perfection.
9. I am the resurrection and the life.
10. I am the secret of eternal survival.
11. I am the way, the truth, and the life.
12. I am the infinite Father of my finite children.
13. I am the true vine; you are the branches.
14. I am the hope of all who know the living truth.
15. I am the living bridge from one world to another.
16. I am the living link between time and eternity. P. 1965.
    BIBLE REFERENCES: Luke 22:70. Phil. 2:11; 2:6. John
    5:25; 6:64. Col. 1:17. Heb. 13:8; 1:3. Luke 7:48. Phil.
    3:21.

XIX. THE LAST SUPPER

1. The old "cup of blessing," Jesus renamed the "cup of remembrance." P. 1941.

2. The "bread of remembrance" is the symbol of the united life of the Father and the Son. P. 1942.

3. But believers failed to follow his leading. Of all Jesus' teachings none has become more standarized. P. 1942.

BIBLE REFERENCES: Matt. 26:17-30. Mark 14:12-26. Luke 22:7-30. John 13:1-30.

XX. THE CRUCIFIXION

1. It was man, not God, who planned and executed the death of Jesus on the cross. P. 2002.

2. Of his own free will Jesus submitted to mortal death on the cross. P. 2004.

3. Jesus did not die as the atonement for man's supposed racial guilt. P. 2016.

4. Death is a part of the full mortal life which Jesus desired to live. P. 2016.

5. Jesus lived and died for a whole universe—illuminating the way of salvation for all. P. 2017.

6. The cross was a supreme expression of love—a completed revelation of mercy. P. 2018.

7. The cross portrays the supreme devotion of the true shepherd for even the unworthy members of his flock. P. 2017.

8. Love does not condone hate—it destroys it. Salvation is redemption if you mean eternal rehabilitation. P. 2018.

   BIBLE REFERENCES: Matt. 27:32-56. Mark 15:21-41. Luke 23:26-49. John 19:16-37.

XXI. THE RESURRECTION

1. After the morontia resurrection of Jesus, his physical body was still in the tomb. P. 2021.

2. Jesus came forth from the tomb with a morontia body. P. 2021.

3. The chief of archangels was given permission to proceed with the immediate dissolution of the physical body of Jesus. P. 2022-3.

4. The midwayers rolled away the entrance stone, dispersing the guards. P. 2023.

5. Belief in the resurrection based on the empty tomb is a fact—but not the truth. P. 2023.

6. Notwithstanding the doubting apostles, David sent forth his messengers as heralds of the resurrection. P. 2030.

7. Jesus said to Mary: Touch me not, but go and tell my apostles and Peter—that I have risen. P. 2027.

8. His seventh appearance was to the two brothers on the way to Emmaus. P. 2034.

9. He appeared to the eleven and prayed with them on their mount of consecration. P. 2050.

   BIBLE REFERENCES: Matt. 28:1-10. Mark 16:1-11. Luke 23:56; 24:12. John 20:1-18.

XXII. SOVEREIGNTY

1. The bestowal of Michael on Urantia was necessary to his earning the experiential sovereignty of his universe. P. 60.

2. The sovereignty bestowals of Michael covered a billion years of Urantia time. P. 1309.

3. Michael's sovereignty is supreme because:

   1. It embodies the sevenfold attitudes of Paradise Deity.

2. It embodies the creature viewpoint of time and space. P. 1324.

XXIII. THE SECOND ADVENT

1. Urantia is the sentimental shrine of all Nebadon—and Jesus has promised to come again. P. 1319.

2. The times of the reappearing of the Son of Man are known only in the councils of Paradise. P. 1915.

3. You would do well to disassociate the Master's return from all set events or settled epochs. P. 1919.

4. It is of no serious concern whether we go to him or whether he should first come to us. P. 1919.

   BIBLE REFERENCES: Matt. 24. Mark 13. Luke 21. John 14:3. Matt. 16:27. I John 3:2. Acts 1:11. Rev. 1:7. II Tim. 4:1. Phil. 3:20.

XXIV. THE FAITH OF JESUS

1. Jesus experienced the tranquillity of unquestioned trust in God and felt the tremendous thrill of living in the very presence of the heavenly Father. P. 2087.

2. In Jesus' life all worlds discover a new religion based on personal spiritual relations with the Universal Father. P. 2087.

3. Theology may fix dogmatic faith, but Jesus had a personal and original faith that securely held him. P. 2087.

4. He devoted himself to doing the will of God with amazing and unbounded enthusiasm, but throughout all his extraordinary life there never appeared the fury of the fanatic nor the superficial frothiness of the religious egotist. P. 2088.

XXV. THE ASCENSION

1. Jesus gathered the eleven apostles on Mount Olivet, and after speaking farewell words to them, he vanished. P. 2057.

   BIBLE REFERENCES: Mark 16:19, 20. Luke 24:44-53.

SECTION THIRTY

THE KINGDOM OF HEAVEN

I. CONCEPTS OF THE KINGDOM

1. The Jewish religion embraced many and confusing concepts of the kingdom of Heaven. P. 1858.

2. Though Jesus presented varying aspects of the kingdom, his last word always was: "The kingdom is within you." P. 1859.

3. Jesus presented five cardinal features of the gospel of the kingdom.

    1. Pre-eminence of the individual.
    2. Will as determining factor.
    3. Sonship with God the Father.
    4. The loving service of men.
    5. Transcendency of the spiritual over the material. P. 1863.

4. The gospel of the kingdom is the Fatherhood of God and the brotherhood of man. P. 2052.

II. THE BROTHERHOOD OF MAN

1. Brotherhood means that the part profits or suffers in measure with the whole. P. 138.

2. Always must God first find man that man may later find God. P. 1299.

3. Said Jesus: "I send you forth, not to love the souls of men, but rather to love men." P. 2043.

3. The Jews exalted goodness, the Greeks beauty, the Hindus devotion. The ascetics taught reverence, the Romans demanded loyalty. But Jesus required life—loving service for our brothers in the flesh. P. 2043.

III. THE KEYS OF THE KINGDOM

1. The keys of the kingdom are sincerity—and more sincerity. P. 435.

2. Jesus taught two essentials for entering the kingdom—sincere faith and truth hunger. P. 1861.

    BIBLE REFERENCES: Heb. 11:1. John 14:1. John 1:12. Heb. 12:2.

IV. THE NEW AND LIVING WAY

1. Jesus established the new and living way—he was the truth that makes men free. P. 596.

2. This new way means that mortals may again proceed directly to the mansion worlds after death. P. 596.

3. There are two ways of choosing the Father's will:
    1. Negative—not my will but yours.
    2. Positive—I will that yours be done. P. 1221.

V. THE RELIGION OF JESUS

1. The religion of Jesus provides final salvation—the seven essentials:
    1. Salvation from material bondage.
    2. Salvation from mind bondage.
    3. Salvation from spiritual blindness.
    4. Salvation from incompleteness of self.
    5. Salvation even from self.
    6. Salvation from time.
    7. Salvation from the finite. P. 1112-3.

2. Jesus warned his followers about the danger of changing the gospel into a religion *about* him. P. 1543.

3. Jesus' new commandment was: Love one another as I have loved you. P. 1944.

VI. SIX PHASES OF THE KINGDOM

1. Personal experience. The kingdom of heaven is within you. Luke 17:21.

2. Social aspects of the kingdom. Preach, saying: The kingdom of heaven is at hand. Matt. 10:17.

3. The superhuman brotherhood. I will not drink of the cup until I drink it new with you in my Father's kingdom. Matt. 26:29.

4. The next age of man. It is your Father's good pleasure to give you the kingdom. Luke 12:32.

5. The age of light and life. Your kingdom come, your will be done. Luke 11:2.

6. Sovereignty of Michael. Remember me when you come into your kingdom. Luke 23:42

THOUGHT ADJUSTER

I. NATURE OF THOUGHT ADJUSTERS

1. Thought Adjusters come direct from the Universal Father—they are fragmented entities of the infinite God. P. 1177.

2. Descending from God, the Adjuster embraces the mortal soul and ascends to God. P. 380.

3. The transit time of an Adjuster from Divinington to Urantia is less than 118 hours. P. 1186.

4. Seven grand divisions of Adjusters are recognized.
    1. Virgin Adjusters.
    2. Advanced Adjusters.
    3. Supreme Adjusters.
    4. Vanished Adjusters.
    5. Liberated Adjusters.
    6. Fused Adjusters.
    7. Personalized Adjusters. P. 1178-9.

5. Adjusters are the divine presence—they are true realities. P. 1183.

6. While Adjusters utilize gravity, they are not subject thereto. P. 1183.

7. Adjusters are not personalities, but they have prerogatives of will, choice, and love. P. 1183.

II. MYSTERY MONITORS

1. This divine presence in the minds of men is the mystery of mysteries. P. 26.

2. The Mystery Monitors are the Father's love incarnate in human souls. P. 1176.

3. Nonpersonalized and nonfused Adjusters are visible only to Personalized Adjusters. P. 1180.

4. Adjusters are identified by the "pilot light"—spirit luminosity. P. 1181.

5. Adjusters are pure spirit and pure energy and possess mindedness—premind. P. 1182.

6. Adjuster mindedness is like the mindedness of the Universal Father and the Eternal Son. P. 1181.

7. Adjusters have a form of premind; they know as they are known. P. 78.

III. ASSIGNMENT OF THOUGHT ADJUSTERS

1. Adjusters and all other prepersonal entities live on Divinington. P. 1179.

2. Adjusters are bestowed in accordance with some wise policy of eternal fitness. P. 1185.

3. Volunteer Adjusters are in possession of the seraphic drafts of the life plans of their subjects. P. 1185.

4. The first moral decision of a child brings the Adjuster—the average on Urantia being on the 2,134th day. P. 1186.

5. Prior to the bestowal of the Spirit of Truth, numerous influences determine the gift of Adjusters. P. 1187.

6. Adjusters communicate directly with God as well as over the spirit-gravity circuit of the Eternal Son. P. 65.

IV. PREREQUISITES OF ADJUSTER INDWELLING

1. The prospective Adjuster is interested in three qualifications of the human candidate:

    1. Intellectual capacity.
    2. Spiritual perception.
    3. Combined mental and spiritual powers. P. 1186.

2. It is the Adjuster who creates within man the longing to be Godlike. P. 1176.

3. The Adjuster's mission is to be God to mortal creatures. P. 1185.

4. The Adjuster is an infallible cosmic compass which unerringly points the soul Godward. P. 1177.

5. The Adjuster is the potential of the new and next order of existence. P. 1191.

6. The love of an Adjuster is the most truly divine affection in all existence. P. 1203.

V. GOD IN MAN

1. The Adjusters are a reflection of the image of God abroad in the universe. P. 1193.

2. The Adjuster is God's manifest presence to the creature. P. 363.

3. Unity of religious experience in a group derives from the identical nature of their indwelling Adjusters. P. 1129.

VI. SELF-ACTING ADJUSTERS

1. Just like all beings, Adjusters must secure experience by actual living. P. 1195.

2. Self-acting Adjusters can leave the human body to perform special tasks. P. 1197.

3. Self-acting Adjusters have had numerous special experiences. P. 1196.

4. The experienced Adjuster may become a potent force on the planet. P. 1198.

5. Animal natures, shifting attitudes, settled opinions, and prejudices may thwart the Adjuster's work. P. 1199.

VII. PERSONALIZED ADJUSTERS

1. Adjusters of special distinction, who are not fused, are many times personalized. P. 1179.

2. Personalized Adjusters combine Creator and creature experience. They are conjoint time and eternity beings. P. 1201.

3. Personalized Adjusters are the all-wise and powerful executives of the Architects of the Master Universe. P. 1201.

VIII. ADJUSTERS AND THE WILL

1. Avoid confusing Adjuster activity with dreams and conscience. P. 1208.

2. The Adjuster communicates with the superconscious. P. 1203.

3. The will of personality transcends the volition of the prepersonal Adjuster. P. 1183.

4. Adjusters manipulate but never dominate man's mind against his will. P. 1217.

5. Mind is the ship, the Adjuster is the pilot, but human will is captain. P. 1217.

IX. ADJUSTER COMMUNION

1. Adjuster communication involves moral, mental, and spiritual status. P. 65.

2. The Monitor urges altruism but a misguided conscience may cause much unhappiness. P. 1132.

3. Deliverance from fear supplies a fulcrum for the Adjuster's uplifting spiritual lever. P. 1192.

4. Sometimes it is possible for the illuminated mind to hear the divine voice. P. 1199.

5. Adjuster communication is difficult—too often the message is aborted, perverted, or garbled. P. 1207.

6. Rarely do we hear the Adjuster's voice—except:
    1. In moments of supreme desire.
    2. In a supreme situation.
    3. After a supreme decision. P. 1213.

7. The inner voice is distinct from conscience. P. 1104.

8. Conscience is not the voice of God to the soul. P. 1207.

X. THE SEVEN PSYCHIC CIRCLES

1. Personality realization ascends through seven levels of conquest. P. 1209.

2. The psychic circles are concerned with personality status, mind attainment, soul growth, and Adjuster attunement. P. 1209.

3. Conquest of the psychic levels is reflected in three ways:
    1. Adjuster attunement.
    2. Soul evolution.
    3. Personality reality. P. 1210.

4. Circle progression has more to do with supreme relationship than with God-consciousness. P. 1211.

XI. THE EVOLUTION OF THE SOUL

1. The Adjuster is the will of God abroad in the universe. P. 25.

2. Man's soul is an experiential acquirement. P. 8.

3. By moral choice man facilitates the divine invasion of his soul. P. 2095.

4. On the mind loom the Adjuster threads the spirit pattern of a potential finaliter. P. 1217.

5. Material mind and divine spirit are the factors in the evolution of the soul. P. 1218.

6. In survival without delay, the Adjuster joins the soul in the new morontia form. P. 1232.

7. There is nothing which can prevent a divinely motivated soul from ascending to the portals of Paradise. P. 63.

8. Mind knows quantity—quality is felt. The spirit reality-izes. P. 1219.

9. Temporal identity of mind and eternal identity of Adjuster produce the surviving identity of the soul. P. 71.

XII. ADJUSTER FUSION

1. The Adjuster, subjective Deity, is carrying on an endless revelation of God—objective Deity. P. 1181.

2. Upon fusion, the Adjuster translates from the absolute existential level to the finite experiential level. P. 1179.

3. After Adjuster fusion you receive your new name. P. 1188.

4. When evolving soul and divine Adjuster are fused, each gains the experiencible qualities of the other. P. 1212.

5. Adjuster fusion can occur anywhere from the nativity world to the universe headquarters. P. 1237.

6. Adjuster fusion ends all danger to the eternal career. P. 1237.

7. The Adjuster-mortal partnership is the amazing phenomenon of this universe age. P. 1238.

XIII. THE ADJUSTERS AFTER DEATH

1. Monitors leave their subjects upon physical, intellectual, or spiritual death. P. 1231.

2. In failure of survival, the Adjuster carries all values over into some future service. P. 1200.

3. What the Adjuster cannot do for you in this life, he will do for you in the next. P. 1191.

   BIBLE REFERENCES: Job 32:8. Prov. 20:27. Eccl. 12:7. Ezek. 36:27. Rom. 8:16. I Cor. 2:11; 3:16. I John 3:24.

SECTION THIRTY-TWO
PRAYER AND WORSHIP

I. NATURE WORSHIP

1. Early worship was suggested by nature objects close at hand. P. 944.

2. Man has worshipped everything on the face of the earth—including himself. P. 944.

3. The first object of worship was a stone. P. 944.

4. Hills and mountains were early worshipped; gods lived on mountains, demons in caves. P. 945.

5. The cults of tree worship are among the oldest religions. P. 945.

6. Clouds, hail, windstorms, thunder and lightning overawed early man. P. 947.

7. Nature worship led to the deification of sun, moon, and stars. P. 947.

8. Fire was long worshipped. P. 947.

9. Man's early fear became religious as nature became personalized, spiritized, and eventually deified. P. 950.

II. CHANCE AND LUCK

1. Early man lived in fear of chance—existence was a gamble. P. 950.

2. Even the wise man said: "The race is not to the swift, nor the battle to the strong." P. 951.

3. The savage personalized everything—both nature and chance. P. 951.

4. Presently, good luck was associated with good spirits—bad luck with bad spirits. P. 955.

5. The savage willingly paid the premiums of fear and priest gifts toward his magic insurance against bad luck. P. 956.

6. Modern man has removed the insurance business from the realm of priests to the domain of economics. P. 956.

III. THE GHOST CULT

1. Ghost fear was the fountainhead of world religion. P. 961.

2. Men viewed ghosts as having unlimited rights but no duties. P. 962.

3. Self-deprecation was an effort to avoid ghost jealousy. All this led to civilized modesty and restraint. P. 963.

4. The effort to placate ghosts and bribe spirits led to a world philosophy. P. 963.

5. The ghost cult rendered ancestor worship inevitable. P. 960.

6. Evolutionary religion was born of man's fear of the unknown, the inexplicable, and the incomprehensible. P. 986.

IV. DEATH FEAR

1. To primitive man, death was a shocking combination of chance and mystery. P. 952.

2. Dreams gave origin to the belief in a future life. P. 953.

3. The ghost cult led to the belief in recurring incarnations. P. 953.

4. Death was feared, because it released another ghost to be contended with. P. 958.

5. The funeral service was an effort to get rid of the ghost. P. 959.

6. Man inherited a natural environment, acquired a social environment, and imagined a ghost environment. The state is man's reaction to natural environment, the home to his social environment, the church to his illusory ghost environment. P. 955.

V. FETISHES, MAGIC, AND CHARMS

1. For ages the "breath of life" was a fetish. P. 955.

2. The doctrine of spirit possession is fetishism. P. 967.

3. Belief in relics is an outgrowth of the fetish cult. P. 968.

4. Magic developed science; astrology led to astronomy; magic numbers to mathematics. P. 972.

5. Magic still lingers—many fossil words afford evidence—spell-bound, entrancing, and astonished. P. 972-3.

6. Ancient magic was the cocoon of modern science. P. 973.

VI. SACRAMENTS AND RITUALS

1. Salvation depended on vows, oaths, pledges, fasting, and prayer. Then came self-denial, suffering, and deprivation. P. 965.

2. The cult of sacrifice evolved into the cult of sacrament. P. 984.

3. Religious observances evolved through placation, avoidance, exorcism, coercion, conciliation, and propitiation to sacrifice, atonement, and redemption. P. 986.

4. Ritual sanctifies custom and perpetuates myths. P. 992.

5. Mysticism often leads to social isolation and religious fanaticism. P. 1000.

6. The common people craved consolation and promises of salvation. P. 1081.

VII. EVOLVING PRAYER

1. The first prayers were not addressed to God—they were like saying: "Wish me luck." P. 994.

2. With the coming of God-consciousness, these petitions attained the level of prayer. P. 994.

3. Man prayed before he knew God—when in need or when jubilant. P. 1001.

4. Primitive prayer was bargaining, argument, with the gods. P. 983.

5. Early prayer was hardly worship. It sought health, wealth, and life. P. 983.

6. Prayer may be an angry cry for vengeance or the joy of a liberated son of God. P. 1001.

VIII. PROVINCE OF PRAYER

1. Prayer is communion between man and his Maker. P. 996.

2. It is impossible to separate the psychological and spiritual aspects of prayer. P. 997.

3. Prayer can never be ethical when the petitioner seeks selfish advantage over his fellows. P. 997.

4. Prayer must not be so prostituted as to become a substitute for action. P. 997.

5. Prayer does not change God, but it may effect great changes in the one who prays. P. 998.

6. Prayer is a sure cure for the habit of criticizing others. P. 998.

7. We should be tolerant of those who pray in primitive fashion. P. 999.

8. Prayer is not the cure for organic diseases. P. 999.

9. Prayer enriches the life; worship illuminates destiny. P. 1123.

10. Jesus taught sixteen conditions for effective prayer. P. 1638-41.

IX. TRUE WORSHIP

1. In the highest sense, we worship only the Universal Father. P. 65.

2. Worship is dispatched over the Father's personality circuit. P. 65.

3. Worship asks nothing for the worshiper. P. 65.

4. From the standpoint of worship, God is one—a unified and personal Deity. P. 640.

5. Worship is the highest joy of Paradise existence. P. 304.

X. REAL RELIGION

1. The early Christian cult was most effective, but is today devitalized by the loss of fundamental ideas. P. 965.

2. No cult will survive unless it embodies some masterful mystery. P. 966.

3. Doctrines may differ, but in worship unity can be realized. P. 1012.

4. Religion is the foundation and guiding star of enduring civilization. P. 1013.

5. Jesus enlarged the neighbor concept to embrace the whole of humanity. P. 1133-4.

6. The great need of both science and religion is fearless self-criticism. P. 1138.

7. The religion of the Hebrews exalted morals, the Greeks beauty. Paul preached faith, hope, and charity. Jesus revealed a religion of love, security, and service. P. 2095.

8. To Jesus, prayer was "doing the Father's will"—a way of religious living. P. 2088-9.

XI. RELIGION AND CIVILIZATION

1. The power of an idea lies not in its truth, but in its vividness of appeal. P. 1005.

2. Religion handicaps social development, but without it, there would be no morals or ethics. P. 1006.

3. Evolutionary religion is man's most expensive but effective institution. P. 1006.

4. Religion is the efficient scourge which drives indolent mankind from inertia forward to levels of reason and wisdom. P. 1006.

5. The church, in fostering racial degeneracy, has retarded civilization. P. 1088.

6. In these unsettled times, as never before, man needs the stabilization of sound religion. P. 1090.

7. The cosmology of the Urantia revelation is not inspired. P. 1109.

8. Every new revelation gives rise to a new cult—with new and appropriate symbolism. P. 966.

9. There have been five epochal revelations on Urantia:

   1. The Dalamatian teachings.
   2. The Edenic teachings.
   3. Melchizedek of Salem.
   4. Jesus of Nazareth.
   5. The Urantia Papers. P. 1007-8.

BIBLE REFERENCES: Ps. 66:18. Prov. 21:13. I John 5:14, 15. Ps. 34:17. Prov. 15:8. John 15:7. Ps. 37:4. James 1:5. Luke 18:1. Mark 14:38. Phil. 4:6, 19. Jer. 29:12, 13. Ps. 92:1. Col. 4:2. IThese. 5:18.

RELIGIOUS EXPERIENCE

I. GOD-CONSCIOUSNESS

1. God-consciousness progresses from the idea of God to the ideal of God and ends with the spirit reality of God. P. 69.

2. God-consciousness leads to increased social service. P. 1121.

3. Finding God is consciousness of identity with reality. P. 2094.

II. TRUTH, BEAUTY, AND GOODNESS

1. The goodness of God is found only in personal religious experience. P. 40.

2. Jesus revealed a God of love—all-embracing of truth, beauty, and goodness. P. 67.

3. Truth relates to science, beauty to art, goodness embraces ethics, morality, and religion. P. 647.

4. Truth, beauty, and goodness represent man's approach to mind, matter, and spirit. P. 647.

5. Spirituality enhances the ability to discover beauty in things, truth in meanings, and goodness in values. P. 1096.

III. RELIGION AND SOCIAL INSTITUTIONS

1. Religion is not directly concerned with creating new social orders or with preserving old ones. P. 1086.

2. The primary mission of religion is the stabilization of ideals. P. 1086.

3. Religion is the cosmic salt which prevents the destruction of the cultural savor of civilization. P. 1087.

4. Religionists function in human affairs as individuals—not as religious groups. P. 1087.

5. The kingdom of heaven is neither social nor economic—it is a brotherhood. P. 1088.

6.   Sectarianism is a disease of institutional religion. P. 1092.

7.   Religion is always dynamic. P. 1121.

8.   Religion leads to service and revelation to the eternal adventure. P. 1122.

IV. TRUE RELIGION

1.   The chief inhibitors of spiritual growth are prejudice and ignorance. P. 1094.

2.   Growth is indicated not by products but by progress. P. 1094.

3.   Progress is meaningful, but growth is not mere progress. P. 1097.

4.   Religion takes nothing away from life—but it does add new meanings to all of it. P. 1100-1.

5.   Evolutionary religion drives men, revelation allures them. P. 66.

6.   It requires faith and revelation to transform the First Cause of science into a God of salvation. P. 1106.

7.   The first promptings of a child's moral nature have to do with justice, fairness, and kindness. P. 1131.

V. MARKS OF RELIGIOUS LIVING

1.   The religionist is conscious of universe citizenship and aware of contact with the supernatural. P. 1100.

2.   The most amazing earmarks of religion are dynamic peace and cosmic poise. P. 1101.

3.   Genuine religious experience is evidenced by twelve characteristics.

> 1.   Causes ethics and morals to progress despite inherent animalistic tendencies.
>
> 2.   Produces sublime trust in the goodness of God in the face of bitter disappointment and crushing defeat.
>
> 3.   Generates profound courage and confidence despite natural adversity and physical calamity.

4. Exhibits inexplicable poise and sustaining tranquillity notwithstanding baffling diseases and acute physical suffering.

5. Maintains a mysterious composure of personality in the face of maltreatment and the rankest injustice.

6. Maintains a divine trust in ultimate victory in spite of the cruelties of seemingly blind fate and the apparent utter indifference of natural forces to human welfare.

7. Persists in the unswerving belief in God despite all contrary demonstrations of logic and successfully withstands all other intellectual sophistries.

8. Exhibits undaunted faith in the soul's survival regardless of the deceptive teachings of false science and the persuasive delusions of unsound philosophy.

9. Lives and triumphs irrespective of the crushing overload of the complex and partial civilizations of modern times.

10. Contributes to the survival of altruism in spite of human selfishness, social antagonisms, industrial greeds, and political maladjustments.

11. Steadfastly adheres to a sublime belief in universe unity and divine guidance regardless of the perplexing presence of evil and sin.

12. Goes right on worshipping God in spite of anything and everything. Declares: "Even though he slay me, yet will I serve him." P. 1108.

VI. FAITH AND BELIEF

1. Our senses tell us of things, mind discovers meanings, but spiritual experience reveals true values. P. 1098.

2. You must have faith as well as feeling. P. 1099.

3. In the morontia, the assurance of truth replaces the assurance of faith. P. 1111.

4. Belief has become faith when it motivates life. Belief fixates, faith liberates. P. 1114.

5. Faith is the bridge between moral consciouseness and spiritual reality. P. 1116.

6. There is a great difference between the will-to-believe and the will that believes. P. 1122.

7. Faith transforms a God of probability into a God of certainty. P. 1124.

8. The individual becomes God-knowing only by faith. P. 1124.

9. Man is educated by fact, ennobled by wisdom, and saved by faith. P. 2094.

VII. RELIGIOUS INSIGHT

1. Religion persists in the absence of learning. P. 1107.

2. Religion may be the feeling of experience, but it is not the experience of feeling. P. 1110.

3. The liberated religious soul begins to feel at home in the universe. P. 1117.

4. Contrast spiritual liberation with the despair of materialism. P. 1118.

VIII. FACT OF RELIGIOUS EXPERIENCE

1. Religious experience can never be fully understood by the material mind. P. 69.

2. Religious experience ranges from the primitive to the superb consciousness of sonship with God. P. 1104.

3. Avoid allowing your religious experience to become egocentric. P. 1130.

4. Spiritual birth may be either complacent or "stormy." P. 1130.

5. The experiencing of God may be valid, even when its theology is fallacious. P. 1140.

6. The reality of religious experience transcends reason, science, philosophy, and wisdom. P. 1142.

7. Personal religious experience is an efficient solvent for most mortal difficulties. P. 2093.

8. Religious experience knows God as a Father, and man as a brother. P. 1090.

9. Dynamic religion transforms the mediocre individual into a person of idealistic power. P. 1094.

10. Religion is the experience of experiencing the reality of believing in God as the reality of such a purely personal experience. P. 1105.

11. Reason and logic can never validate the values of religious experience. P. 1116.

12. In the triumphant struggle of the faith son, "Even time itself becomes but the shadow of eternity cast by Paradise realities upon the moving panoply of space." P. 117.

13. Religionists live as if already in the presence of the Eternal. P. 1119.

IX. SCIENCE AND RELIGION

1. Neither science nor philosophy can validate the personality of God, only the personal experience of faith sons. P. 31.

2. However men view God, the religionist believes in a God who fosters survival. P. 68.

3. Nature does not afford ground for believing in human survival. P. 1106.

4. To science and philosophy God may be possible and probable, but to religion he is a certainty. P. 1125.

X. PHILOSOPHY AND RELIGION

1. Religion becomes the unification of all that is good, true, and beautiful in human experience. P. 67.

2. Religion becomes real as it emerges from the slavery of fear and the bondage of superstition. P. 141.

3. Philosophy transforms primitive religion into ascending values of reality. P. 1114.

4. Mortals can experience spiritual unity, but not philosophical uniformity. P. 1129.

5. When thelogy masters religion, religion dies. Reason, wisdom, and faith introduce man to facts, truth, and religion. P. 1141.

6. The religious soul of spiritual illumination knows and knows now. P. 1120.

7. It is the mission of religion to prepare man for bravely and heroically facing the vicissitudes of life. P. 1121.

SECTION THIRTY-FOUR
THE SPIRIT OF TRUTH

1. Jesus said that it was better that he leave his followers in the flesh, that he might more fully be with them in spirit. P. 1948.

2. This new teacher is the living conviction of truth. P. 1949.

3. It is the work of the spirit to personalize truth and destroy all feelings of orphanhood. P. 2060-1.

4. Bestowal of the Son's spirit prepares normal minds for the reception of Adjusters. P. 2061.

5. The spirit leads into all truth and enhances the realities of Jesus' teachings. P. 2061.

6. The Spirit of Truth completes the sevenfold spirit bestowal.
    1. Spirit of the Universal Father—Thought Adjusters.
    2. Spirit of the Eternal Son—spirit gravity circuit.
    3. Spirit of the Infinite Spirit—the universal mind.
    4. Spirit of the Father and Son—the Spirit of Truth.
    5. Spirit of the Infinite Spirit and the Universe Mother Spirit—the Holy Spirit.
    6. The Mind-spirit of the Undverse Mother Spirit—the adjutant mind-spirits.
    7. The spirit of the Father, Sons, and Spirits—the new-name spirit bestowed at fusion with the Adjuster. P. 2062.

7. Pentecost signifies that the Jesus of history has become the divine Son of living experience. P. 2065.

8. Influence of the Spirit of Truth continues beyond the local universe. P. 1286.

CHRISTIANITY

I. BEGINNINGS OF THE CHRISTIAN CHURCH

1. The gospel is: the fact of the fatherhood of God, coupled with the truth of the sonship-brotherhood of men. P. 2059.

2. Unintentionally, some facts associated with the gospel were substituted for the gospel message. P. 2059.

3. Only baptism was required for admission to the Jesus brotherhood. P. 2067.

4. The Lord's Supper was celebrated at the end of a fellowship meal. P. 2067.

5. At Pentecost, Peter really founded the Christian church. P. 2069.

6. Paul's adaptations of Jesus' gospel were superior to all other religions. P. 1337.

7. Philo's teachings had considerable influence on Paul. P. 1339.

8. It was the second century before Greco-Roman culture turned to Christianity. P. 2069.

9. The Christians made shrewd bargains with the pagans, but did not do so well with the Mithraics. P. 2070.

10. The early plan of Christian worship followed the synagogue and Mithraic rituals. P. 2074.

II. CONTENT OF THE CHRISTIAN MESSAGE

1. The Christian concept of God combines three ideas.
    1. Hebrew concept—God a vindicator of moral values—a righteous God.
    2. Greek concept—God as a unifier—a God of wisdom.
    3. Jesus' concept—God as a living friend, a loving Father. P. 67-8.

2. Christianity is a religion about Jesus, modified by much theology. P. 1011.

3. Early Christianity and Mithraism had many things in common. P. 1083.

4. Paul's theology was based on Jesus' life, but was also influenced by the Greeks and the Stoics. P. 1340.

5. Christ becomes the creed of the new fellowship. P. 2066-7.

6. Abner's more authentic version of the gospel made little progress. P. 2072.

III. INFLUENCE OF THE GREEKS AND ROMANS

1. The Greek Stephen's death led to the organization of the first church at Jerusalem. P. 2068.

2. Greek culture was quick to embrace Christianity as a new and better religion. P. 2071.

3. Christians accepted the Roman Empire; the empire adopted Christianity. P. 2073.

4. Conditions at Rome were favorable for the adoption of a new religion. P. 2073.

5. The church, becoming an adjunct of society and an ally of politics, was doomed to suffer during the "dark ages." P. 2074.

IV. THE MODERN PROBLEM

1. Viewing what Christianity has endured indicates great inherent vitality. P. 2075.

2. Christianity now faces the gigantic struggle between the secular and the spiritual. P. 2075.

3. Religion needs new leaders—men who will depend solely on the incomparable teachings of Jesus. P. 2082.

4. The hour is striking for the rediscovery of the original foundations of Christianity. P. 2083.

5. Christianity has become a social and cultural movement as well as a religion. P. 2083.

6. Christianity is handicapped because it sponsors a society which staggers under a tremendous overload of materialism. P. 2086.

7. Christianity is threatened by the doom of one of its own slogans: "A house divided against itself cannot stand." P. 2085.

8. But Christianity contains enough of the teachings of Jesus to immortalize it. P. 2086.

9. The hope of Christianity is that it shall learn anew the greatest of all truths—the fatherhood of God and the brotherhood of man. P. 2086.

V. MATERIALISM

1. If man were only a machine, he could not formulate his materialistic concepts. P. 2078.

2. Machines do not struggle to find God nor strive to be like him. P. 2079.

3. Man exhibits the control attributes of mind and the creative qualities of spirit. P. 2079.

4. Religion is not so much concerned with science, morality, and philosophy—as it is with the scientist, the moralist, and the philosopher. P. 2080.

VI. SECULAR TOTALITARIANISM

1. Secularism broke the bonds of church control, and now threatens to establish a new and godless control of men. P. 2081.

2. World wars are the result of overdoing the secularistic revolt. P. 2081.

3. Secularism discards ethics and religion for politics and power. P. 2082.

4. Materialism denies God, secularism simply ignores him. P. 2081.

5. The majority of Christians are unwittingly secularists. P. 2081.

VII. THE RELIGION OF JESUS

1. Jesus is the new and living way whereby man comes into his divine inheritance. P. 1113.

2. Men evade the religion of Jesus for fear of what it will do to them and with them. P. 2083.

3. The apostles were demoralized by the Master's death. P. 2066.

4. Comes the resurrection—God is no longer a doctrine in their minds; he has become a living presence in their souls. P. 2066.

5. Paul's Christianity made sure of the divine Christ, but almost wholly lost sight of the human Jesus. P. 2092

6. Jesus founded a religion of personal experience in doing the will of God; Paul founded a religion for the worship of the glorified and risen Christ. P. 2092.

7. Jesus did not found the Christian church, but he has fostered it. P. 2085.

8. The Oriental peoples do not know that there is a religion *of* Jesus as well as a religion *about* Jesus. P. 2086.

9. The time is ripe for the figurative resurrection of the human Jesus from the burial tomb of theologic traditions and religious dogmas. P. 2090.

10. You can preach a religion about Jesus, but you must *live* the religion of Jesus. P. 2091.

11. The New Testament is a superb Christian document, but it is only meagerly Jesusonian. P. 2091.

NOTES